THE INN AND THE TRAVELLER
DIGRESSIVE TOPOGRAPHIES IN THE
EARLY MODERN EUROPEAN NOVEL

CW01020011

THE EUROPEAN HUMANITIES RESEARCH CENTRE

UNIVERSITY OF OXFORD

Director
Professor Martin McLaughlin, Magdalen College

The European Humanities Research Centre of the University of Oxford organizes a range of academic activities, including conferences and workshops, and publishes scholarly works under its own imprint, LEGENDA. Within Oxford, the EHRC bridges, at the research level, the main humanities faculties: Modern Languages, English, Modern History, Classics and Philosophy, Music and Theology. The Centre stimulates interdisciplinary research collaboration throughout these subject areas and provides an Oxford base for advanced researchers in the humanities.

The Centre's publications programme focuses on making available the results of advanced research in medieval and modern languages and related interdisciplinary areas. An Editorial Board, whose members are drawn from across the British university system, covers the principal European languages. Titles currently include works on Arabic, Catalan, Chinese, English, French, German, Italian, Portuguese, Russian, Spanish and Yiddish literature, and linguistics. In addition, the EHRC co-publishes with the Society for French Studies, the Modern Humanities Research Association and the British Comparative Literature Association. The Centre also publishes a Special Lecture Series under the LEGENDA imprint, and a journal, *Oxford German Studies.*

Enquiries about the Centre's publishing activities should be addressed to:
Professor Ritchie Robertson, Co-Director (Publications)

Further information:
Kareni Bannister, Senior Publications Officer
European Humanities Research Centre
University of Oxford
76 Woodstock Road, Oxford OX2 6HP
enquiries@ehrc.ox.ac.uk
www.ehrc.ox.ac.uk

LEGENDA

European Humanities Research Centre

University of Oxford

The Inn and the Traveller

Digressive Topographies in the Early Modern European Novel

❖

WILL MCMORRAN

LEGENDA

European Humanities Research Centre
University of Oxford
2002

Published by the
European Humanities Research Centre
of the University of Oxford
47 Wellington Square
Oxford OX1 2JF

LEGENDA is the publications imprint of the
European Humanities Research Centre

ISBN 1 900755 64 5

First published 2002

British Library Cataloguing in Publication Data
A CIP catalogue record for this book is available from the British Library

LEGENDA series designed by Cox Design Partnership, Witney, Oxon
Printed in Great Britain by
Information Press
Eynsham
Oxford OX8 1JJ

Copy-Editor: Hilary Walford

CONTENTS

ACKNOWLEDGEMENTS

My first and greatest debt is to Tony Nuttall, the general supervisor of this book in its prior incarnation as a D.Phil. thesis in Oxford. Without his encyclopedic knowledge and inspirational spirit of adventure, this book could never have been written. He has my heartiest thanks. I would also like to express my gratitude to Nicholas Cronk, who read my chapters on Scarron and Diderot, and to Richard Parish, who kindly allowed me to consult the manuscript of his then forthcoming book on the *Roman comique*. For his unerring judgement and generous support in overseeing the transformation of my manuscript from a thesis into a 'real' book, I owe another great debt to Terence Cave.

On a familial note, I would like to take this opportunity to thank Sarah McMorran for putting up with a distracted boyfriend and then husband during the years it took to write this book, and Louis McMorran for providing me with delicious distractions ever since. For introducing me to Tristram at the age of 17, my mother has a lot to answer for; this book is dedicated to her.

Finally, many thanks to everyone at Legenda for all their cheerful assistance and hard work.

ABBREVIATIONS

A. Garci Rodríguez de Montalvo, *Amadís de Gaula*, ed. Juan Manuel Cacho Blecua, 2 vols. (Madrid: Cátedra, 1987). References are to volume and page. Translations are from *Amadís of Gaul*, trans. E. B. Place and H. C. Behm, 2 vols. (Lexington, KY: Kentucky University Press, 1974–5)

DQ Miguel de Cervantes, *El ingenioso hidalgo don Quijote de la Mancha*, ed. Luis Andrés Murillo, 2 vols. (Madrid: Castalia, 1978). References are to part and chapter. Translations are from *Don Quixote*, trans. Charles Jarvis, ed. E. C. Riley (Oxford: Oxford University Press, 1992)

G. Mateo Alemán, *Aventuras y vida de Guzmán de Alfarache*, ed. Benito Brancaforte, 2 vols. (Madrid: Cátedra, 1979). References are to part, book and chapter. Translations are from *The Rogue or the Life of Guzman de Alfarache*, trans. James Mabbe, ed. Charles Whibley, 4 vols. (London: Constable & Co., 1924)

GA Apuleius, *Metamorphoses*, ed. and trans. J. Arthur Hanson, 2 vols., Loeb Classical Library (Cambridge, MA: Harvard University Press, 1989). References are to book and chapter. Translations are from the above edition

HTJ *Histoire de Tom Jones, ou l'enfant trouvé*, trans. Pierre-Antoine de La Place, 4 vols. (London: Nourse, 1750). References are to book and chapter

JA Henry Fielding, *Joseph Andrews*, ed. Martin C. Battestin (Middletown, CT: Wesleyan University Press, 1967). References are to book and chapter

JF Denis Diderot, *Jaques le Fataliste et son maitre*, ed. Simone Lecointre and Jean Le Galliot (Paris: Droz, 1976). References are to page only

JWN Henry Fielding, *A Journey from this World to the Next*, in *Miscellanies*, vol. ii, ed. Hugh Amory and Bertrand A. Goldgar

	(Oxford: Wesleyan University Press, 1993). References are to book and chapter
O.	*The Odyssey*, trans. A. T. Murray, rev. George Dimock, 2 vols., Loeb Classical Library (Cambridge, MA: Harvard University Press, 1998). References are to book and line. Translations are from the above edition
OF	Lodovico Ariosto, *Orlando furioso*, ed. Lanfranco Caretti, 2 vols. (Turin: Einaudi, 1992). References are to canto, stanza and line. Translations are from *Orlando furioso*, trans. Guido Waldman (Oxford: Oxford University Press, 1974)
RC	Paul Scarron, *Le Romant comique*, published in *Romanciers du XVIIᵉ siècle*, ed. Antoine Adam (Paris: Gallimard, 1958), 531–797. References are to part and chapter
SJ	Laurence Sterne, *A Sentimental Journey through France and Italy*, ed. Tom Keymer, The Everyman Library (London: J. M. Dent, 1994). References are to volume and page
TJ	Henry Fielding, *Tom Jones*, ed. Martin C. Battestin and Fredson Bowers, 2 vols. (Oxford: Wesleyan University Press, 1975). References are to book and chapter
TS	Laurence Sterne, *The Life and Opinions of Tristram Shandy, Gentleman*, ed. Melvyn and Joan New, 3 vols. (Gainesville, FL: University of Florida Press, 1978–84). References are to volume and chapter

Periodicals

CAIEF	*Cahiers de l'Association internationale des études françaises*
ELH	*English Literary History*
MLN	*Modern Language Notes*
PMLA	*Proceedings of the Modern Languages Association of America*
SVEC	*Studies on Voltaire and the Eighteenth Century*

POUR MAMOUSHKA

INTRODUCTION

This book explores the fictional topographies generated by digressive strategies in a selection of early modern comic fictions. Just as in the 'adventure novel of everyday life', as Bakhtin terms Apuleius' *The Golden Ass* and Petronius' *Satyricon*, each of the texts examined here generates narrative through the mobility of its central character, recording his progress in a varied series of travelogues. Even when the physical errancy of the protagonist is invaded by the intellectual errancy of the narrator, a phenomenon of which *Tristram Shandy* is only the most extreme example, the same collection of topological and topographical markers persist. Bakhtin identifies such fiction as being based upon a chronotope of the road, in which the course of an individual's life is fused with his actual spatial path.[1] While he alludes to a number of other chronotopes, from the castle of Gothic fiction to the *salon* of the great realist French novels, the nearest he comes to mentioning the inn is a fleeting reference to 'the edge of the road'.[2] The inn, however, constitutes a highly magnetic chronotope in its own right; perfectly placed as a setting for chance encounters and thus for internal storytelling between characters, it plays a pivotal role in the structuring of digressive fiction in the seventeenth and eighteenth centuries. The relationship of the road to the inn provides a paradigmatic expression of the tension between progression and digression in the early modern novel, as leaving the road repeatedly implies leaving the main plot behind.

The focus here will indeed be on narrative. While this study brings together works from different literatures, these are texts that exploit the same narrative syntax of road and inn, and feature many of the same *topoi*—in these respects, they speak the same language. This common ground has been the main consideration in the selection of sources, but there is a secondary and related factor. The placing of *Joseph Andrews*, *Tom Jones* and *Tristram Shandy* alongside the *Quijote*, the *Roman comique* and *Jacques le Fataliste et son maître* reflects an attempt to situate the novels of Fielding and Sterne within a European tradition of self-conscious and digressive comic fiction. Although the question of influence is not central to this examination of narrative topographies, it has thus been a determining factor in the selection of materials chosen for examination. Debts and borrowings are noted where they are deemed pertinent; on the whole, however, the novels have been left to speak for themselves in this regard—and speak they most certainly do. If every reader or critic, as well as every author, creates his own tradition, the one created below at least has the merit of being suggested by the authors themselves. Fielding's explicit description of his work as being written 'in Imitation of The *Manner* of CERVANTES'[3] on the title page of *Joseph Andrews* is typical of the process by which each of Cervantes's successors self-consciously attaches a highly visible 'Cervantick' label to his works.[4] Ironically, Fielding himself constitutes an exception to the rule that sources are proudly paraded: it is difficult to imagine Sterne managing to avoid contact with Fielding's fiction, but no such familiarity is made explicit in any of his writings. As his contemporary, we may presume Fielding lacked the cachet of more distant and eminent precedents; as Ferriar demonstrated in his *Illustrations of Sterne*,[5] even the most allusive of authors chooses to conceal some of his sources and influences.

When Lennard Davis states entirely reasonably of Sterne that 'his consciousness is pure eighteenth-century', it is in order to emphasize that he was 'no modern critic or nascent James Joyce', and to warn against the dangers of anachronistic reading.[6] 'Pure' eighteenth-century consciousness must, however, be understood in a rather loose sense: while every work is to some degree a product of its own time and place, it is demonstrably also the product of other times and places. By stepping back from the local and the immediate in order to embrace a broader perspective and timescale, certain details inevitably disappear; to borrow Tristram Shandy's phrase, however, fresh 'views and prospects' (*TS* I. 14)[7] emerge that more than compensate for this loss. Rather than arguing against the importance of contemporary or localized influences upon each of the texts examined below, this book aims to complement the existing studies of these by bringing into play materials commonly regarded as foreign or remote. The enduring popularity of the *Quijote* in England and France in the eighteenth century perfectly illustrates the extent to which a work from one period and literature may form part of the contemporary world of other periods and other literatures.[8] While the following chapters are not intended as a study of the *Nachleben* of Cervantes's text, the history of digressive comic fiction in the seventeenth and eighteenth centuries is to a considerable degree a record of its influence in this period.[9]

While critics of French literature have long recognized the impact of the English novel in France in the mid-eighteenth century, a significant number of their English counterparts have been reluctant to recognize the influence of continental fiction in England. Davis, following the example of Ian Watt,[10] briefly discusses the *Quijote* and heroic romance only to dismiss them, as this allows him to treat 'the development of the novel in England in relative isolation from continental developments'.[11] He defends this choice on the grounds that 'in the middle of the eighteenth century it seems quite likely that the English novel came to be a model for the French novel far more than the French novel did for the English'.[12] This is a dangerous simplification of eighteenth-century Anglo-French literary relations and interactions, however, as William Warner observes: 'The consensus within contemporary British literary studies that the first real novels appeared in English is a post-Romantic idea. By contrast, eighteenth-century cultural critics often gave France precedence over England in the invention of several different species of romances and novels.'[13] Maximilian Novak justifiably remarks that 'the kind of nationalism we carry into the study of literature has little place between 1660 and 1730',[14] while Georges May affirms that this is equally true of the mid-eighteenth century: 'nowhere else is a comparative approach more legitimate, indeed more necessary [...] the Channel was no one-way street and [...] the French and British Novel never stopped cross-fertilizing each other throughout the eighteenth century ... and ever after'.[15]

Fielding provides a particularly illuminating example of the cross-channel traffic of novelistic discourse in the eighteenth century. While the remarkable success of *Tom Jones* in its French incarnation reveals one side of the story,[16] the wealth of intertextual allusions displayed in Fielding's comic fiction reveals another. With rare exceptions, however, few have taken Fielding's attempts to relate his work to earlier and existing fictional forms seriously—J. Paul Hunter, for example, refers rather disparagingly to Fielding's 'muddy quest for formal lineage'.[17] Fielding's bold proclamation that he is founding a 'new Province of Writing' (*TJ* II. 1)[18] has tended to deflect attention away from his continual alignment of his works with the continental tradition of comic fiction. While he unquestionably seeks to distance his own writings from 'foolish Novels, and monstrous Romances' (*TJ* IX. 1) in *Tom Jones*, he describes *Joseph Andrews* as a 'comic Romance' (*JA*, preface), thereby echoing the French *roman comique* in general (and Scarron's novel in particular).[19] Of the numerous authors mentioned in the introductory chapter to book III of *Joseph Andrews*, the English are conspicuous by their virtual absence: the only English writer to whom Fielding alludes—with some venom—is Mrs Manley. He presents himself as an original only within an English context, and is keen to emphasize the European tradition from which he draws his inspiration: he includes among 'us Biographers' Cervantes, Scarron, the author of the *Arabian Nights* (which arrived in England via the French translation of Galland), Lesage and Marivaux.[20] He, moreover, describes his preface to *Joseph Andrews* as 'a few Words concerning this kind of Writing, which I do not remember to have seen hitherto attempted in *our* Language' (*JA*, preface; emphasis added). The significance of the possessive pronoun is crucial here, as Fielding implies once again that his precedents are foreign rather than English.

If the English novel has too often been separated from its European roots, this must be understood within the context of the ongoing debate over the novel's origins. In 1990, Hunter accurately warned that, 'in comparative studies on the one hand and in cultural ones on the other, some deep disagreements and mighty conflicts are sure to spring', and rather provocatively divided critics of the novel into two camps: 'Those who seek to study novelistic origins in the habits, popular outlets, and consciousness of a single culture—people like Watt, Spacks, McKeon, and myself—will have to fight it out with those who see form beyond culture and ultimately beyond history— for example, Robert, ter Horst, Doody, and Reed.'[21] The question of origins is inextricably linked to the vexed question of genre. It is, therefore, no coincidence that the critics who believe firmly in the English eighteenth-century origins of the novel are often those most adamant in their insistence upon the separation of novel and romance. One might indeed mischievously suggest that they believe in these origins in order to cement the distinction, and vice versa. The drawing of any line between novel and romance, however, is inevitably both subjective and arbitrary. Warner alludes to the normative 'gatekeeping fiction' of the term 'novel' according to which 'it has filtered out noncanonical novels',[22] while Brown observes that 'Watt's and McKeon's institutions of the novel seem set to allow them to use a sort of generic cleansing to exclude it from any contamination by the dreaded term romance'.[23] When Hunter refers above to those critics who study the novel 'beyond' culture and history, he really means beyond English culture, and beyond the eighteenth century (rather as Watt's seminal study, despite being exclusively confined to English fiction, was called *The Rise of the Novel*, not *The Rise of the English Novel*). Each of the critics Hunter mentions has in fact simply taken a broader view, seeing culture in European terms and over a greater period of time. And the broader the temporal or cultural perspective, the weaker the case for differentiating between novel and romance generally appears. The panoramic sweep of Doody's recent study of origins thus leads her to the conclusion, 'Romance and the Novel are one. The separation between them is part of a problem, not part of a solution.'[24] Warner's response to the same problem is to use the term 'novel' in 'an inclusive fashion to designate both the books early modern readers call novels and the elevated novels of Defoe, Richardson, and Fielding'.[25] There are, moreover, good grounds for regarding the transition from romance to novel as a terminological rather than a generic phenomenon, a view corroborated by the fact that this shift is largely confined to critics of literature in English, the only language to distinguish between 'novel' and 'romance'.

While this study makes no generic distinction between novel and romance, the issue of terminology remains a delicate one. Doody, because of the negative associations of 'romance', labels all prose fiction of a certain length a 'novel', 'the term we feel most positively about [...] an encouraging word'.[26] There is, however, an uncomfortable sense of anachronism in the description of, for example, the *Aethiopica* or the *Amadís* as novels. At the same time, it is clear that we are too used to calling prose fictions of the eighteenth century and after 'novels' to abandon the term in favour of the generally unfashionable 'romance'. The appellation 'romance' is, therefore, retained below for those works (such as classical, chivalric and pastoral prose fictions) that have traditionally been described in this manner; the novel is distinguished from romance only on broad chronological grounds to apply to the majority of prose fiction from the early nineteenth century onwards—the period in which, according to Brown's persuasive argument, it displaces 'romance' as the dominant term for prose fiction.[27] For the fiction of the early modern period that falls into neither of these categories, I have followed the example of Fielding in treating 'romance' and novel' as synonyms.[28] No evaluative or normative distinction between the two is intended, and 'novel' should be read below simply as a variant spelling of 'romance'. Those who would continue to separate novel and romance would do well to follow Benedetto Croce's advice regarding genre in his *Estetica*, where he argues that, although there is nothing 'scientificamente erroneo' [scientifically incorrect] in referring to tragedies, comedies, dramas or romances if one desires to draw attention to certain groups of works in general or approximate terms, 'egli adopera vocaboli e frasi, non stabilisce definizioni e leggi. L'errore si ha solamente quando al vocabolo si dia peso di distinzione scientifica' [to employ words and phrases is not to establish laws and definitions. The mistake only arises when the weight of a scientific definition is given to a word].[29]

The opening chapter of this book sets the scene with snapshots of three early illustrations of the link between hospitality and storytelling: the uncommercial and therefore inn-less world of the *Odyssey*, in which acts of narration repeatedly impede the progress of both Odysseus and Telemachus; the fleeting visit to an inn in *The Golden Ass*; and the remarkable appearance of an *albergo* in the chivalric world of Ariosto's *Orlando furioso*. Using these narratives as examples, a distinction is then made between two contrasting methods of interpolation, the 'connective' and the 'disconnective'. Although the inn plays the occasional cameo role prior to the early modern period, most famously perhaps as the Tabard inn in Chaucer's *Canterbury Tales*, the *Quijote* is the first work of European literature to exploit the full potential of the inn as a vehicle for both internal narrations and (burlesque) episodes. Chapter 2 studies the diversifying effects of Palomeque's inn upon the first part of the *Quijote*, before contrasting these with the impact made by the ducal castle upon the structure of the second part. In both cases, the topographical design of the narrative plays a crucial part in the parodic process, as Cervantes subverts the castle *topos* of chivalric romance externally, introducing the inn as its anti-type, then internally, in the degraded form of the ducal *castello*. Chapter 3 examines the central role in the *Roman comique* played by the *Tripot de la Biche*, which follows the Cervantine model in providing the setting for the novel's defining confrontation between the *romanesque* and the burlesque. The *Biche* is instrumental to the introduction of both the actors' personal histories and the Spanish *nouvelles*, and the relationship between inn and interpolation thus holds the key to a true understanding of a digressive but classically structured narrative. The inn's internal geography, and its setting within the novel's external geography, are both revealed to reflect spatially the tension between the different registers of Scarron's work.

The two chapters that follow examine two related aspects of Fielding's *Joseph Andrews* and *Tom Jones*. Chapter 4 concentrates upon the topographical spaces through which the two heroes pass, from the domestic sphere that frames each of their journeys to the open roads and wayside inns around which their journeys are structured. Chapter 5 explores the degree to which travel invades the rhetoric of Fielding's fiction as well as the narrative itself, with the inn and the stagecoach in particular providing prominent metaphors for the reading process. While the rhetoric of travel sits comfortably alongside the hero's fictionalized travels in *Tom Jones*, *Tristram Shandy*, the subject of Chapter 6, goes a step further, the journey as metaphor almost entirely displacing the journey as subject: the horse is largely succeeded by the hobby-horse, while Don Quijote's sallies on Rocinante give way to Walter's verbal sallies. The world of physical travel, however, strikingly reasserts itself in volume VII with Tristram's tour through France; in miniaturized form it moreover informs both the movements of the Shandy household, and the introduction of digressions and interpolations—shrinking Europe to the size of a bowling green, and the chronotopes of road and inn to the scale of a staircase and landing.

The final chapter of this book finds objective and subjective errancy coexisting uneasily once again, as the travels of Jacques and his master fall prey to both direct and indirect narratorial interference. Diderot follows Sterne in depicting narrative as a form of travelogue, but complements this by conversely presenting his travelogue as an inherently narrative process, subject to the will of a particularly capricious authorial persona. In its adoption of the familiar narrative syntax of road and inn, the topography of *Jacques* is more overtly Cervantine than that of *Tristram Shandy*. Diderot, however, does not parody novels or romances only: his so-called *antiroman* is equally, as one critic describes it, an '*anti-voyage*'.[30] Nevertheless, while he variously subverts the reader's expectations, Diderot in fact conforms to many of the conventions of narrative he appears to undermine. As unlikely as it may seem, *Jacques*—like the *Roman comique*—is structured according to a classical model; in contrast to Scarron, moreover, Diderot sees his narrative through to a logical resolution.

The emphasis throughout is upon the fictional rather than the

historical. It would nevertheless be foolish not to recognize the manner
in which fictional topographies are influenced by the world outside the
author's window. The development of commercial infrastructures across
Europe in the seventeenth and eighteenth centuries is evidently
reflected in both the frequent appearance of inns in picaresque and
Quixotic literature, and the seemingly continuous traffic of carriers that
passes through them. In concentrating upon the fictionalities over the
actualities of travel, however, this book once again follows the example
set by the majority of its sources. Tristram's discussion of the problems
of travelling by post-chaise (*TS* VII) aside, only the journeys described
in Fielding's novels, with their allusions to actual inns and innkeepers
and their evocation of the politics of the stagecoach, are visibly rooted
in contemporary reality and convey any striking impression of the
experience of travel in the period in which they are set. While the
decor of *Tom Jones* and *Joseph Andrews* features coaching inns instead of
castles, and stagecoaches instead of ships, the structuring role of the
journey remains paramount: from Joseph's *nostos* or journey home to
Tom's errant progress through the English countryside, earlier forms of
fiction continue to provide the archetypes for the hero's travels. As if
to confirm the predominance of the fictional over the actual journey
as a narrative model, none of the novelists below sees fit to provide
physical descriptions of any of the inns appearing in his work. The
narratological function repeatedly assigned to the inn—the accommodation of foreign, generally interpolated material—produces a
virtually featureless if internally complex space. Herein perhaps resides
the secret of the inn's great versatility: it is defined as a *topos* by those
who occupy it, and characters ranging from bourgeois society to the
criminal underclass may therefore all find room there.

Notes to the Introduction

1. In his essay 'Forms of Time and of the Chronotope in the Novel', Bakhtin
examines what he terms the 'chronotopes' of Greek romance; this term alludes
to the manner in which time and space are conceived and represented together
in literary narrative; in *The Dialogic Imagination: Four Essays*, trans. Caryl
Emerson and Michael Holquist, ed. Michael Holquist (Austin, TX: University
of Texas Press, 1981), 84–5. The connection Bakhtin makes between an
individual's life and his spatial progress brings to mind Tristram's evasion of death
by taking to the road on his journey to France (see below, Ch. 6, 'The Travel of
Language').
2. Ibid. 120.

3. Quotations are taken from Henry Fielding, *Joseph Andrews*, ed. Martin C. Battestin (Middletown, CT: Wesleyan University Press, 1967).
4. Sterne refers to his own work as a 'Cervantick satyr' in a letter to Jane Fenton, in *Letters of Laurence Sterne*, ed. Lewis P. Curtis (Oxford: Clarendon Press, 1935), 120 (letter 66). Arthur Cash includes, among the 'great writers he usually named or alluded to in some way, probably because he wanted his reader to associate *Tristram Shandy* with them—Cervantes, Montaigne, Locke and usually Rabelais' (*Laurence Sterne: The Later Years* (London: Methuen, 1986), 76).
5. John Ferriar, *Illustrations of Sterne With Other Essays and Verses* (London: Cadell & Davies, 1798).
6. Lennard Davis, *Resisting Novels: Ideology and Fiction* (New York: Methuen, 1987), 151.
7. Quotations are taken from Laurence Sterne, *The Life and Opinions of Tristram Shandy, Gentleman*, ed. Melvyn and Joan New, 3 vols. (Gainesville, FL: University of Florida Press, 1978–84). References are to volume and chapter.
8. As Ronald Paulson also illustrates in his *Don Quixote in England: The Aesthetics of Laughter* (Baltimore: Johns Hopkins University Press, 1998).
9. The impact of Cervantes's novel outside Spain is corroborated by the thirty-five editions of the *Quijote* in French between 1614 and 1713, and the eighteen English translations of the first half of the eighteenth century (eight of which were published in the 1740s).
10. Ian Watt, *The Rise of the Novel: Studies in Defoe, Richardson and Fielding* (London: Chatto & Windus, 1957).
11. Lennard Davis, *Factual Fictions: The Origins of the English Novel* (New York: Columbia University Press, 1983), 43.
12. Ibid. 44.
13. William B. Warner, *Licensing Entertainment: The Elevation of Novel Reading in Britain, 1684–1750* (Berkeley and Los Angeles: University of California Press, 1998), 20.
14. Maximilian Novak, 'Some Notes toward a History of Fictional Forms', *Novel*, 6 (1973), 120–33 (123). Novak's dates seem a rather peculiar choice, particularly given the popularity of the works of Fielding and Richardson in France in the 1740s and 1750s, and, indeed, the international impact of, for example, Greek romance and the Spanish picaresque in the seventeenth century.
15. Georges May, 'The Influence of English Fiction on the French Mid-Eighteenth-Century Novel', in Earl R. Wasserman (ed.), *Aspects of the Eighteenth Century* (Baltimore: Johns Hopkins University Press, 1965), 265–81 (266).
16. See below, Ch. 5, 'The Introductory Chapters: The Case of La Place'.
17. J. Paul Hunter, 'The Novel and the Contexts of Discourse', in Richard B. Schwartz (ed.), *Theory and Tradition in Eighteenth-Century Studies* (Carbondale, IL: Southern Illinois University Press, 1990), 118–40 (126). Among the 'rare exceptions', three studies in particular deserve a mention: Henry K. Miller, *Henry Fielding's 'Tom Jones' and the Romance Tradition*, English Literary Studies Monograph Series, 6 (Victoria, BC: University of Victoria Press, 1976); James J. Lynch, *Henry Fielding and the Heliodoran Novel: Romance, Epic, and Fielding's New Province of Writing* (London: Associated University Presses, 1986) and Nancy A. Mace, *Henry Fielding's Novels and the Classical Tradition* (Newark, DE: University of Delaware Press, 1996).

18. Quotations are taken from Henry Fielding, *Tom Jones*, ed. Martin C. Battestin and Fredson Bowers, 2 vols. (Oxford: Wesleyan University Press, 1975). References are to book and chapter.

19. Cf. Charles Sorel's allusion to this tradition in his *Bibliothèque françoise*: 'Les bons Romans Comiques & Satyriques semblent plûtost estre des images de l'Histoire que tous les autres; Les actions communes de la Vie estans leur objet, il est plus facile d'y rencontrer de la Verité' (2nd edn. (Paris: Compagnie des librairies du Palais, 1667), 188).

20. Homer Goldberg thus justifiably includes extracts from Cervantes, Scarron, Lesage and Marivaux in the 'Backgrounds and Sources' section of his edition of *Joseph Andrews* (New York: Norton, 1987).

21. Hunter, 'The Novel and the Contexts of Discourse', 137–8.

22. Warner, *Licensing Entertainment*, p. xii.

23. Homer Obed Brown, *Institutions of the English Novel: From Defoe to Scott* (Philadelphia: University of Pennsylvania Press, 1997), p. xii. The same clearly also applies to Davis and Hunter.

24. Margaret Anne Doody, *The True Story of the Novel* (New Brunswick, NJ: Rutgers University Press, 1996), 15. Brown's account of Scott's understanding of the novel is fascinating in this respect; the views of Scott and his contemporaries in fact bear a striking resemblance to those of Doody: 'it is possible to say that by 1814, Scott shared several assumptions about the novel with a number of other critics and historians: It [*sic*] had existed in one form or another at all times and all places. If there were a distinction to be made between the romance and the novel it was not so much a generic as a "generational" difference—in Scott's words, "in its first appearance, the novel was the legitimate child of romance"' (Brown, *Institutions*, 10).

25. Warner, *Licensing Entertainment*, p. xii. Warner, in differentiating between 'novel' and 'elevated novel', arguably preserves the romance/novel distinction in a more discreet form.

26. Doody, *True Story*, 16.

27. Those that draw most strongly from the traditions of romance in this age of the novel, such as the works of Walter Scott, are generally called 'romance novels', a term that encapsulates both the debt to romance and the acknowledgement of the change in terminology in the early nineteenth century (in which Scott indeed plays an important part).

28. It may be pertinent to note in this context that the entry for 'novel' in the Chambers dictionary of 1728 reads simply 'see ROMANCE', under which it observes ''tis certain an Epic Poem, and a *Romance* are almost the same thing' (*Chambers Dictionary*, 2 vols. (London, 1728)). The distinction between 'novel' and 'romance' offered by Johnson's dictionary seems more French than English: a novel is defined as 'a small tale, generally of love' and thus resembles the French 'nouvelle', while a romance is described as 'a military fable of the middle ages; a tale of wild adventures in war and love' (Samuel Johnson, *Johnson's Dictionary: A Modern Selection*, ed. E. L. McAdam Jr. and George Milne (London: Victor Gollancz, 1963)).

29. Benedetto Croce, *Estetica come scienza dell'espressione e linguistica generale* (Bari: Gius. Laterza & Figli, 1912), 45–6. The translation given is from *Aesthetic as*

Science of Expresssion and General Linguistic, trans. Douglas Ainslie (London: Vision Press, 1967), 38.

30. Roger Kempf, *Diderot et le roman, ou le démon de la présence* (Paris: Seuil, 1964), 186.

CHAPTER 1

Before Palomeque:
Hospitality and Storytelling

With few exceptions, the inn does not feature conspicuously in classical or medieval literature. Given that it owes its existence to basic human necessities, it is perhaps inevitable that it should be almost entirely excluded from the idealized topographies generated by epic poetry or classical and chivalric romances. The Quixotically deluded hero of Bougeant's eighteenth-century *Voyage merveilleux*, Fan-Férédin, recognizes that such mundane considerations as food and lodging are largely alien to the world inhabited by the heroes and heroines of romance; upon his arrival in the mythical land of 'Romancie',[1] he discovers the answer to a perplexing question: 'Je n'avais jamais compris dans la lecture des romans, comment les princes et princesses, les héros et leurs héroïnes, leurs domestiques mêmes et toute leur suite passaient toute leur vie, sans jamais parler de boire ni de manger.' The explanation, he discovers, is in the air of *Romancie*: 'cet air a surtout une propriété singulière, c'est de tenir lieu de nourriture à tous ceux qui le respirent.'[2]

Bougeant's criticism of the omission of the daily needs of human existence from all works of fiction (his *Romancie* does not distinguish between epic and romance[3]) fails to recognize the discreet and ritualized manner according to which such needs are satisfied. If Odysseus and Amadís are not prone to the pangs of hunger that afflict, for example, a picaro such as Lázaro, it is because their journeys are punctuated by a series of willing hosts offering both food and lodging. As Marie-Luce Chênerie remarks, 'les conventions du roman courtois et encore plus celles du roman arthurien font que le chevalier en déplacement ne s'arrête que chez des hôtes nobles'.[4] In this respect, the hero of romance generally resembles his epic counterpart and ancestor in his dependence on the hospitality of those he encounters on his travels. It is indeed a condition of *xenia*, the 'guest-friendship' that features so prominently in the *Odyssey*, that host and guest be of equal social status.[5] The closed social circle within which Homeric scenes of hospitality generally operate evidently contrasts with the broad social spectrum the inn will increasingly come to represent from the *Quijote* onwards. Nevertheless, in its scenes of hospitality as in so many other aspects, the influence of the *Odyssey* upon the fictions of the road that form the basis of this study is inescapable. Before turning to two striking early appearances of the inn in narrative fiction, a brief foray into epic conventions of hospitality and storytelling in the absence of inns may therefore be pertinent.

The Odyssey

It would have been more accurate of Bougeant to complain of a surfeit rather than a shortage of eating and drinking in *Romancie*, particularly given the experiences of both Odysseus and Telemachus during the course of their wanderings. As Steve Reece notes, 'By far the most pervasive type-scene in the *Odyssey* is the hospitality scene— the description of events that take place between the time of a visitor's arrival and his departure. Such hospitality scenes make up a large part of the narrative of the *Odyssey*.'[6] The reception accorded to Odysseus by a succession of hosts, however, reveals the ambivalence at the root of hospitality—its power to impede as well as assist the traveller on his homeward journey.[7] Aside from the unambiguous hostility of the Cyclops, who has guests for dinner in a less than hospitable sense, a series of hosts, from Calypso and Circe at one extreme to the Pylians, Spartans and the Phaeacians at another, variously impede the *nostoi* of Odysseus and Telemachus by an apparent excess of hospitality, which, Reece observes, 'often borders dangerously on forced detention'.[8] While the cases of Calypso and Circe require little elaboration, with each attempting to erase her guest's memory of his homeland in order to keep him as a husband, Odysseus' time with the Phaeacians and the manner of Telemachus' reception by Nestor and Menelaus merit further consideration.

In Telemachus' visits to Pylos and Sparta, the link between storytelling and hospitality is firmly established. On both occasions he is warmly welcomed by his hosts, who, according to custom, allow him to eat in peace before enquiring into his identity and the purpose of his journey. As his mission is to seek information regarding his father, Telemachus takes on a passive listening role, while both Nestor and Menelaus clearly relish the storytelling role they are consequently invited to assume—indeed, they appear to enjoy their part a little too much. When Nestor is asked for news of Odysseus, he initially evades the question to dwell instead on his own experiences at Troy. As if to make his guest aware that he could continue in this vein *ad infinitum*, he reflects, 'many other ills we suffered besides these; who of mortal men could tell them all? No, even if for five years' space or six years' space you were to abide here, and ask of all the woes which the noble Achaeans endured there, you would grow weary before the end and get yourself back to your native land' (*O*. III. 113–17).[9] Telemachus' wait for a more direct response to his question is further protracted as Nestor proceeds to relate his own journey home from Troy, before finally admitting he has no knowledge of Odysseus' fate.

Telemachus' apparently childlike desire to hear more of Nestor's stories is characteristic of the subordinate role to which he is confined both in his dialogue with Nestor and in the *Odyssey* as a whole. As he invites his host to tell the circumstances of Agamemnon's death, he is very much the schoolboy; in awe of his father's generation—and indeed of Nestor, on whom he looks as 'like an Immortal' (*O*. III. 246)—he appears at this moment oddly detached from them and the recent history they represent, as if his own growth into adulthood reflected the rise of a modern world removed from its epic past. As a listener in the text, Telemachus here seems to belong to the poem itself rather than the story the poem relates, as if he were a member of Homer's—rather than Nestor's—audience. Hospitality here not only embraces storytelling but serves as a metaphor for the storytelling contract between the poet and his audience and, ultimately, the novelist and his reader. The story Nestor tells at this point moreover prepares for the transition from Pylos to Sparta, as Menelaus is introduced first within an internal narration and then into the main narrative. Although Nestor expresses his eagerness for Telemachus to embark on his visit to Menelaus immediately, the theme of detention is subtly introduced to be further developed on Telemachus' homeward visit to Pylos, upon which he enlists Pisistratus' help in forgoing another encounter with the latter's father.[10]

While Nestor's hospitality merely threatens to delay Telemachus, Menelaus' comportment provides a more concrete obstacle to his guest's journey home. The Spartan episode resembles a magnified version of its precedent in Pylos, as the relative grandeur and opulence of Menelaus' palace reflects; the same pattern is followed but takes far longer to complete—it is not until the next day, for example, that any enquiry into the purpose behind Telemachus' journey is made. Both Menelaus and Helen employ a variety of means to distract Telemachus from his present troubles: as a complement to the drug that Helen uses to dispel 'all pain and strife' and 'bring forgetfulness of every ill' from her guests (O. IV. 221),[11] both she and Menelaus exploit the similarly lotus-like potential of storytelling to retain their guests. Telemachus acknowledges that Menelaus in particular is a consummate storyteller, while hinting at the danger of such irresistible entertainment: 'Son of Atreus, keep me no long time here, for truly for a year would I be content to sit in your house, nor would desire for home or parents come upon me; for wondrous is the pleasure I take in listening to your tales and your speech. But even now my comrades are chafing in sacred Pylos, and you are keeping me long here' (O. IV. 593–9). The one story Telemachus desires to hear, that of his father's homecoming, is the one story his hosts cannot tell. Menelaus seeks to fill the void left by this absent narrative with an apparently inexhaustible supply of substitute narratives: when asked for details concerning Odysseus' *nostos*, he follows (at even greater length) the digressive example of Nestor in responding with reminiscences of Troy and with the stories of other homecomings, including his own. The physical errancy that had brought Telemachus to Sparta is succeeded by the verbal errancy of his talkative host, whose narratives of *nostoi* defer the actual *nostos* of Telemachus until Pallas Athene intervenes 'to remind the glorious son of great-hearted Odysseus of his return, and to hasten his coming' (O. XV. 2–3).

Within the parallel situations of Telemachus in Sparta and Odysseus in Scheria, the contrasting roles of father and son are reflected in their distinctive contributions to the hospitality type-scenes in which they both participate. While Telemachus is twice the passive recipient of hospitality, Odysseus is comparatively active: aside from taking part in the Phaeacians' games, he reciprocates the entertainments offered with the extended narration of his recent adventures. The theme of detention resurfaces as Odysseus' narrative so enthrals his audience that he is not allowed to break it off in order to sleep, but is obliged to continue well into the night until it has finally reached its logical conclusion. The act of storytelling again defers the physical progress of the traveller, as action and narrated action cannot coincide but are obliged to alternate. The domestic environment of Alcinous' palace (and, subsequently, Eumaeus' house) follows the precedent of the homes of Nestor and Menelaus in providing a sanctuary in which the narrative act is protected from interruption. Although no fresh adventures intrude upon Odysseus' narration, Alcinous' hospitality is compromised by his failure wholly to protect his guest from further unwelcome trials in the form of the Phaeacian games (and, potentially, his proposal of his daughter's hand in marriage). In this respect, Alcinous' palace may be distinguished from its counterparts in the Telemachy; the sporting competition that takes place there may moreover be seen to anticipate the more serious contest facing Odysseus on his return to Ithaca—where the domestic world and the external world of adventure finally and violently clash with the slaughter of Penelope's suitors.[12]

Transformed into a public space by the absence of its proprietor, with Penelope reluctantly playing the part of hostess to the suitors she attends, Odysseus' home resembles in many respects a prototype inn, catering for a local community. Whereas the rituals of hospitality place the other hosts of the *Odyssey* in a position of authority over those they receive, Penelope is forced by her uninvited guests to assume a subordinate role, according to which she serves them without any expectation of the reciprocity implicit in *xenia*. Odysseus' disguise, moreover, reduces his status from that of the master of the house to that of a supplicant, as he begs from his own guests. The theme of detention is similarly inverted in the Ithacan sequence, as Penelope is presented as the hostage of her suitors pending the liberating return of her husband. Ironically, the conventions of hospitality are most strikingly observed in Odysseus' palace between husband and wife, as Penelope asks that Odysseus reveal his identity and history in return for her hospitality. Odysseus is not the first beggar to have participated in this form of exchange with his wife: as Eumaeus reveals, 'wanderers in need of sustenance tell lies at random, and have no desire to speak the truth. Whoever in his wanderings comes to the land of Ithaca goes to my mistress and tells a deceitful tale. And she, receiving him kindly, gives him entertainment, and questions him of all things' (XIV. 124–7). Here, as in Eumaeus' hut and his father's garden, Odysseus and his respective hosts exchange woeful histories— as a beggar this is the only way in which he may reciprocate. For him, as for Nestor and Menelaus, Troy provides a treasure trove of stories to be plundered. There is even, as Nietzsche observes, the suggestion within the poem that this was the very purpose of the Trojan war:

Is there anything more audacious, uncanny or unbelievable shining down on the destiny of man like a winter sun than the idea that we find in Homer:

> Then did the gods make resolve and ordain unto men
> *Destruction, that in after times too there might be matter for song.*

Thus we suffer and perish so that the poets shall not lack *material*—and this according to the decree of the gods of Homer, who seem to be very much concerned about the pleasures of coming generations but very indifferent to us, the men of the present.[13]

As Steven Hutchinson, in reference to the same passage, notes succinctly, 'Tellable experience appears to be made for the telling.'[14] Although the heroic past thus repeatedly enters the present in narrated and therefore mediated form, in his imaginative construction of fake histories for himself Odysseus distinguishes himself from his storytelling peers.[15] Just as his son, in listening to Nestor and Menelaus, resembles one of Homer's audience, so Odysseus, in telling tales for the entertainment of his audience, invites comparison with the poet(s) who immortalized him, and cements the link between storytelling and hospitality.

The Golden Ass

While the inn is manifestly alien to the topography of epic poetry, it appears compatible with the fictionalized worlds of such Latin novels as the *Satyricon* and *The Golden Ass* (also known as *Metamorphoses*). In the fragments of the *Satyricon* that have survived, the function of the inn is limited to the provision of accommodation for Encolpius, Ascyltus and Giton on their travels; in *The Golden Ass*, the role of the inn is again limited. Nevertheless, even at this early stage in the history of the fictionalized inn, there are signs of its literary potential as a meeting place and consequently as a *locus* for storytelling. The opening story of *The Golden Ass* is not about Lucius but is an account of witchcraft related to him on the road to Thessaly. His chance encounter with Aristomenes, the narrator of the story, is succeeded within the latter's narration by the encounter between Aristomenes and his friend, Socrates. This second meeting takes place neither on the road nor in an inn, but at the public baths of Hypata—the town in which Lucius himself is later transformed. Once again a meeting prompts an embedded narration, as Socrates, in the comfort of Aristomenes' inn, tells of his earlier encounter with Meroe, an innkeeper and witch. These two sides to Meroe epitomize the combination of the fantastic and the earthily realistic in *The Golden*

Ass as a whole (a mixture that, as we shall see below, prefigures the *Furioso*); at this stage, the inn is thus no guarantor of verisimilitude— Meroe, for example, is reported to turn a rival innkeeper into a frog.

The narrative frame for the interpolations of *The Golden Ass*, like those of the fictions examined in the following chapters, is provided by the hero's journey. The path of Lucius' travels is the path of his narrative: he relates all that happens to him, including all he hears. His primary role upon being transformed is that of listener; as Bakhtin notes, both *The Golden Ass* and the picaresque genre with which it is often associated have heroes who, as servants, are in an ideal position for spying and eavesdropping on private life.[16] Lucius himself remarks, 'quod auribus grandissimis praeditus cuncta longule etiam dissita facillime sentiebam' [with my enormous ears I could hear everything very easily, even at a considerable distance] (*GA* IX. 15).[17] Thus, when his own adventures reach a hiatus, the ensuing blank in the narrative is filled with the stories of various peripheral characters. This process essentially reflects the narrative as a whole: Lucius' adventures begin with his transformation into an ass and end when he is returned to his human form. They are crucially prolonged when he fails to eat any roses, the cure for his affliction, before the season changes and there are none left to be eaten. His adventures fill the time (and narrative space) until spring returns, and returns *him* to his former self. The various internal narrations inserted into his narrative are set in a variety of locations: the opening tale is told on the road to pass the time; another interpolation, the fable of Cupid and Psyche, is told in a cave. The inn provides the setting for only one interpolation on Lucius' journey, while he is travelling with the homosexual priests: upon their arrival at a small village, 'hospitio proximi stabuli recepti, cognoscimus lepidam de adulterio cuiusdam pauperis fabulam, quam vos etiam cognoscatis volo' [We obtained lodgings at the nearest inn, and there we heard an amusing story about the cuckolding of a certain poor workman, which I want you to hear too] (*GA* IX. 4).

At this early stage in its literary career, the inn is evidently far from being the only place for internal storytelling; even at this point, however, it possesses certain distinguishing qualities. The storytelling at the inn is an inherently social process: a local community gathers there to exchange stories and gossip, and the guests at the inn form an audience who seek entertainment as well as accommodation. Such a setting evidently contrasts with the isolated cave in which the story of Cupid and Psyche is told. The inn is not simply an empty topographical space—or cave—temporarily inhabited by the main narrative; it represents a community with a life of its own, which in turn generates the bawdy tale of a local cuckold. As a place dealing with basic physical needs, it seems appropriate that the inn produces a story whose emphasis is equally physical, thereby reminding the reader, as well as the traveller, of his own basic needs and desires. Whereas the inn in *The Golden Ass* provides a story that conforms to the tone of the rest of the narrative, the cave allows a radical shift in tone: isolating those inside from the rest of human society, the cave consequently provides an appropriate setting for a relatively elevated fable or myth.

Orlando furioso

Despite the experience of Fan-Férédin in *Romancie*, it is not quite the case that the inn, and the concession to a more everyday view of reality it represents, is entirely incompatible with the idealizing tendencies of classical and chivalric romance. While we shall concentrate here on Ariosto's *Orlando furioso*, a work that provides spectacular evidence to the contrary, the example of twelfth-century French romance also reveals the dangers of such generalizations. Although a knight errant in this form of fiction will usually find accommodation in the appropriately aristocratic setting of a castle, when none is available, 'A tent can then substitute or, if even that fails, a clearing in the forest'.[18] An early form of inn is, however, available to the travelling knight in the form of the *hostel* within the castle walls of a court, where a knight might find accommodation during a tournament. Matilda Brückner draws attention to the distinction between courtly and bourgeois hospitality in this type of romance, and notes the striking case of *Floire et Blancheflor*.

Commercial Hospitality is available on a 'cash and carry' basis, offered by a bourgeois host, most often a merchant, to any guest who can afford to pay or repay the expenditure made in his behalf. *Floire et Blancheflor* uses this category exclusively, developing it as a prototype inn where the customer/guest buys his own provisions (ll. 1046–50, 1245–48) and must pay extra if he spills his wine (ll. 1115–20).[19]

This abandonment of courtly hospitality offers a valuable insight into the topological connotations of the inn, the inappropriateness of which provides the very motivation for its inclusion: the hero hides his identity by disguising himself as a merchant, for whom only commercial hospitality would be available, a pretence that is, 'on the literal level, a necessary precaution for his pursuit; on the figurative, a debasement out of tune with Floire's nobility, yet in harmony with the fate of poor Blancheflor sold into slavery'.[20] The inn represents a social milieu normally excluded from the courtly world to which Floire belongs, and its inclusion thus represents topographically the degradation forced on the hero.

The topography of Ariosto's *Orlando furioso* is, as one might expect of a chivalric romance, dominated by forests and castles (the reader notably spends relatively little time in either the Christian or the Saracen camps). The poem nevertheless escapes the constraints of romance topology and topography with the dramatic introduction of apparently foreign motifs and locations. Thomas Hart remarks, 'Ariosto repeatedly juxtaposes the real and the fantastic, a practice that no doubt owes something to Dante's introduction of realistic details drawn from everyday life into the terrifying visions of his *Inferno*.'[21] One might with equal force suggest a debt to Apuleius, particularly as Ariosto also uses the *topos* of the inn to create his own juxtaposition of magic and realism: when Ruggiero flies across the globe on his hippogriff, the narrator adds the pseudo-authenticating detail,

> Non crediate, Signor, che però stia
> per sí lungo camin sempre su l'ale:
> ogni sera all'albergo se ne gía,
> schivando a suo poter d'allogiar male.
> (*OF* X. 1–4)[22]

[You must not imagine, my Lord, that he was constantly on the wing; every evening he put up at some hostelry, avoiding poor accommodation as best he could.]

Within the context of the poem, the reference to the mundane ironically appears more fantastic than the fantastic itself: the inn, not the hippogriff, takes the reader by surprise by its subversion of the *romanesque* illusion.[23] Ariosto thereby achieves a distancing effect, as he does with his continual self-referential intrusions into his narrative. Elsewhere in the poem, however, the juxtaposition of the ordinary and the fantastic may seem more ambiguous. This is not the only occasion on which the *topoi* of hippogriff and inn are brought together: the first appearance of both occurs almost simultaneously as Bradamante is on her way to Atlante's castle to rescue Ruggiero. Shortly after her arrival at an inn, she hears 'un gran rumor' (*OF* IV. 3. 5):

E vede l'oste e tutta la famiglia,
e chi a finestre e chi fuor ne la via,
tener levati al ciel gli occhi e le ciglia,
come l'ecclisse o la cometa sia.
Vede la donna un'altra maraviglia,
che di leggier creduta non saria:
vede passar un gran destriero alato,
che porta in aria un cavalliero armato.
(*OF* IV. 4. 1–8)

[Here she found the innkeeper with all his family and many others at their windows and yet more in the street, all looking up at the sky as if there were a comet or eclipse. She witnessed a prodigious sight, one which would not be readily believed: a great winged horse was passing through the sky, with an armed man mounted upon him.]

The hippogriff, the most fantastic of Ariosto's creations, is thus introduced with a little more detail into the most unchivalresque of settings.[24] The presence of the innkeeper and his family hardly supplies a large enough dose of realism to authenticate the 'maraviglia'. It may seem here that the hippogriff manages to undermine the reader's idea of the inn as a realistic *topos*, rather than be undermined by it. This is certainly true of one famous reader of the *Furioso*, the admittedly less than reliable Don Quijote: Cervantes's hero has far more difficulty believing in the reality of an inn than that of a flying horse, and one may consequently assume that the presence of the former in this episode failed at least in his case to exert any distancing effect that may have been intended.

To translate the inn as it is represented here exclusively as a neutrally realistic setting is, however, to risk oversimplification. The contrast between inn and hippogriff is particularly accentuated by the brutal, and even criminal reality with which the inn is associated and which it thereby comes to represent. Bradamante does not stop at an inn because she requires lodging but because the sorceress Melissa has advised her that there she will meet Brunello, who in turn will guide her to Atlante's castle. The introduction of the inn is thus simultaneous with the appearance of a thief, a man 'di sí ignobil sorte' (*OF* IV. 14. 2); although the inns of the *Furioso* accommodate a higher class of crook than their equivalents in picaresque fiction—Brunello is one of Agramante's barons—they maintain an association with the felonious and disreputable. This is confirmed later in the poem when Grifon stays at an inn outside Damascus with his former lover, Orrigille, and the knight, Martano, whom the narrator describes as 'perfido l'uno e l'altro e traditore' (*OF* XVI. 6. 6). Their perfidy is indeed demonstrated as they steal Grifon's armour and horse, the inn hence providing the opportunity for a highly unchivalresque plot. Like Meroe's inn in *The Golden Ass*, and those we shall be visiting in the following chapters, Ariosto's inn here is not a safe place to rest. Just as the knights of chivalric romance are more likely to encounter new adventures than rest when they arrive at a castle,[25] so Martano's theft from Grifon demonstrates that the inn may be subject to the same unpredictable laws as the castle, even if the episode it generates is appropriately less than illustrious.

The disreputable associations of the inn that these early appearances in the poem imply are, it must be admitted, subtle rather than striking. Indeed, were it not for Rodomonte's experience of a French inn later in the poem, the role of the inn in the *Furioso* might scarcely seem worthy of notice. Rodomonte, having been betrayed by his betrothed Doralice, leaves the Saracen camp in humiliation. While Angelica's perceived infidelity to Orlando provokes both intellectual and physical errancy in the latter, Rodomonte's response to Doralice's betrayal is primarily verbal. Rodomonte's lament[26] has a rippling, even snow-balling effect on the poem, as the infidelity motif is explored on one narrative level after another; it immediately provokes a narratorial intervention—a 'defence' of womankind that is even more damning than Rodomonte's complaint:

> e certo da ragion si dipartiva;
> che per una o per due che trovi ree,
> che cento buone sien creder si dee.
>   Se ben di quante io n'abbia fin qui amate,
> non n'abbia mai trovata una fedele,
> perfide tutte io non vo' dir né ingrate,
> ma darne colpa al mio destin crudele.
> Molte or ne sono, e più già ne son state,
> che non dan causa ad uom che si querele;
> ma mia fortuna vuol che s'una ria
> ne sia tra cento, io di lei preda sia.
>   (*OF* XXVII. 122. 6–123. 8)

[Of course he was not being reasonable: for every one or two women to be held at fault we must believe that a hundred are to be accounted virtuous./ Even though among all the women I have ever loved I have yet to find a single constant one, I would not say that they are all faithless and thankless— I'd merely blame my own cruel fate. There are many women, and there have

been many more, who have not given men grounds for complaint; but if
there is only one bad woman in a hundred, it has always been my fate to fall
prey to her.]

Ariosto shifts the reader's attention from the main narrative to its
frame (or, to use Genette's useful if unwieldy terminology, from the
diegetic to the extradiegetic level of the narrative[27]).

The infidelity motif immediately exerts a formative impact on the
poem, determining the path that Rodomonte, and thus the narrative,
must take. When darkness falls, Rodomonte decides to accept the
invitation of a local innkeeper ('un ostier paesan' (*OF* XXVII. 130.
3)), who provides a rich and varied meal ('di varii cibi' (*OF* XXVII.
130. 6)) for his distinguished guest. This varied dinner echoes the
narrator's earlier culinary metaphor for his poem:

> Come raccende il gusto il mutar esca,
> cosí mi par che la mia istoria, quanto
> or qua or là piú varïata sia,
> meno a chi l'udirà noiosa fia.
> (*OF* XIII. 80. 5–8)

[As varying the dishes quickens the appetite, so it is with my story: the more
varied it is, the less likely it is to bore my listeners.]

The implicit bond between hospitality and storytelling is rendered explicitly by the choice of metaphor: the poet, like the host, must ensure
that his guests' appetites are continually stimulated but never sated. In
so doing, Ariosto anticipates Fielding's reference in *Tom Jones* to his
story as a meal served at an Ordinary, and Sterne's comparable
metaphor of a dinner party in *Tristram Shandy* (in which Tristram has
left 'half a dozen places purposely open' for 'the criticks', (*TS* II. 2)).
In each of these cases, the authorial persona resembles a convivial host
careful to keep his guests/readers entertained—indeed, the conviv-
iality of each often appears to provide the source of their digressiveness. These self-conscious fictions, in which the author addresses his
readership directly, seem designed to evoke the former communality
of storytelling. The congenial setting that such digressive authorial
personae seek to recreate in their dialogue with the reader may indeed
be found in Ariosto's evocation of Rodomonte's stay with the *ostier*.
The transition from one register to another, and from one mode of
fiction to another, is signalled by the narrator's sly remark that the
knight's drinking habits were more French than Moorish:

che 'l Saracin nel resto alla moresca,
ma vòlse far nel bere alla francesca.
(*OF* XXVII. 130. 7–8)

[Rodomont was Moorish in all things else, but his drinking habits were French.]

Rodomonte, still smarting from his humiliation at the hands of Doralice, is not, however, an easy guest to entertain. His eyes lowered, he eats his meal in silence; when he does speak, it is to ask those around him whether they believe their wives to be faithful. All of them answer in the affirmative except the innkeeper himself, who then offers as evidence a story told him by a former guest, a Venetian gentleman named Gian Francesco Valerio.[28] Valerio, it appears, could provide a veritable compendium[29] of tales of female infidelity:

Le fraudi che le mogli e che l'amiche
sogliano usar, sapea tutte per conto:
e sopra ciò moderne istorie e antiche,
e proprie esperïenze avea sí in pronto,
che mi mostrò che mai donne pudiche
non si trovaro, o povere o di conto;
e s'una casta piú de l'altre parse,
veniá, perché piú accorta era a celarse.
    E fra l'altre (che tante me ne disse,
che non ne posso il terzo ricordarmi),
sí nel capo una istoria mi si scrisse,
che non si scrisse mai piú saldo in marmi [...]
(*OF* XXVII. 138.1–139.4)

[He was familiar in every detail with the tricks normally practised by wives and mistresses; on this score he could reel off stories of today and long ago and experiences of his own to show me that the chaste woman, whether poor or well-to-do, never did exist—and if one appeared more chaste than the rest, she was simply more adept at concealment./ He told me so many stories that I cannot remember a third of them. But one of them so etched itself on my mind that never was anything more firmly inscribed on marble.]

The anachronistic allusion to this priest and friend of Ariosto reasserts the juxtaposition between the chivalric past and the (cynical) reality of the present. This confrontation is reflected in the physical position-ing of speaker and listener: Rodomonte asks the innkeeper to seat himself opposite him so that he can see his face.[30]

As C. P. Brand notes, 'whereas the love stories in the first half of the poem are largely concerned with bachelor knights and unwedded maidens, the later cantos present us with a succession of married women and especially men, no longer concerned to win their lovers but preoccupied with keeping those incipient horns from their worried heads'.[31] The innkeeper's tale is the first and bawdiest of these tales of infidelity: the scene of its telling, and the identity of its narrator, appear to provide the poet with the latitude he requires in order to incorporate such an unromanesque narrative. Ariosto breaks away from his chivalric precedents by forging a different kind of inner space in which to insert an internal narration. The inn and its keeper provide a doorway into a different genre from which the poet is keen to distance himself and for the inclusion of which he apologizes. Before the host is allowed to tell his story, the narrator invites all ladies and their admirers to disregard the disparaging tale, and the 'lingua sí vile' (OF XXVIII. 1. 6) of the innkeeper.[32] This act of dissociation is compounded by the narrator's assertion of the gratuitousness of the following interpolation:

> Lasciate questo canto, che senza esso
> può star l'istoria, e non sarà men chiara.
> Mettendolo Turpino, anch'io l'ho messo [...]
> (OF XXVIII. 2. 1–3)[33]

[Skip this canto: it is not essential—my story is no less clear without it. As Turpin included it, so have I.]

The narrator's attempt to hide behind his alleged source constitutes the first of two disclaimers; the second is an ironic warning to those who choose to read the tale to do so as a legend or fable rather than a true story.[34] The poet masterfully executes his double bluff: the ostensible implication is evidently that the narrator concedes the interpolation to be untrue for purely diplomatic reasons; however, a second, disguised implication that the tale is incredible but true belies the obvious fact that it is pure fiction. The ambivalence resides in the blurred and ironized space between the author and his narratorial persona.

Lennard Davis argues that the authorial assertion of a fiction's veracity is a procedure that broadly distinguishes novels from romances.[35] Were this the case, it would appear that Ariosto's assertion of the fictionality of the innkeeper's tale were a parody of a convention that has not yet come into existence. Davis ignores the widespread claims to veracity of a variety of narrative fiction before the eighteenth century, including chivalric romance:[36] Montalvo, for example, goes to considerable lengths to assert the authenticity of the fifth volume of the *Amadís*.[37] Ariosto's ironic questioning of the plausibility of the innkeeper's tale not only parodies the claims of romancers such as Montalvo: the absence of any such discussion regarding the narrative that encapsulates this interpolation playfully implies the veracity of the rest of the *Furioso*. The story of Astolfo and Iocondo thus ironically guarantees the framing reality of the diegesis or main narrative. This technique becomes a common feature of prose fiction from *Guzmán de Alfarache* and the *Quijote* onwards; with the more pervasive realism introduced by picaresque and Quixotic fictions, the intercalation of autonomous internal narrations is exploited more seriously as a means of preserving the realistic aspirations of the main narrative. In other words, the disruption of formal integrity serves to affirm the realistic integrity of the main body of the narrative. By this method the author may accommodate different registers of narration, particularly those with romance undertones, within a clearly defined and enclosed inner space. Among the most obvious examples of this procedure are the interpolated romance narrations of the *Guzmán*.[38]

With the introduction of the innkeeper's tale, Ariosto thus creates an inner or hypodiegetic space in which a different order of representation may be accommodated.[39] The change in register marked by the innkeeper's tale in the *Furioso* is perhaps not as dramatic as it is, for example, in the romanesque interludes of the *Guzmán*; nevertheless, it constitutes a radical departure from both the chivalric romances that precede it and the chivalric romance that incorporates it in the *Furioso*. The story begins in a royal palace, in which Astolfo, king of the Lombards, is said to spend much of his time admiring his own beauty. While this courtly setting evidently conforms to the romanesque topography of the surrounding poem, its role here is to accommodate a fairy-tale-like opening. The idyllic tone of the story continues as far as the introduction of the equally handsome Iocondo, whose marriage is described in similarly flawless terms. The idealized opening is steadily eroded, with the once beautiful Iocondo transformed by grief to 'il piú brutto' (*OF* XXVIII. 28. 6), when he discovers his wife's infidelity. The fairy tale is then combined with bawdy farce, with the parallel discovery of the adultery of Astolfo's queen; this odd hybrid of genres is symbolically and graphically represented by the grotesque coupling of the queen and the dwarf:

Quindi mirando vide in strana lutta
ch'un nano aviticchiato era con quella:
et era quel piccin stato sí dotto,
che la regina avea messa di sotto.
(*OF* XXVIII. 34. 5–8)[40]

[What he [Iocondo] saw here was the queen and a dwarf entwined together in a sort of wrestling match; the little man was so expert at this that he had thrust the queen beneath him.]

While the surrounding narrative never presents infidelity as a physical act but as a spiritual betrayal, the bodily aspect is repeatedly (and grotesquely) emphasized in the innkeeper's tale. In contrast to Angelica, who spends much of the poem evading the sexual advances of those she encounters, the women described by the innkeeper compulsively pursue rather than avoid every possibility of a sexual encounter.

The revelations of their wives' infidelities are seen to cure Iocondo and Astolfo of their romantic delusions. They consequently leave behind the court, with all its now discredited fairy-tale associations, and vow not to return until they have despoiled a thousand men's wives. Astolfo and Iocondo thus transform themselves from king and knight respectively into sexual picaros, and traverse Italy, France, Flanders and England. Eventually wearying of their numerous sexual exploits, they decide to settle down and share one woman between them, thereby ensuring that her appetites as well as theirs are satisfied. It seems fitting, given the anticipatory hints of picaresque literature in the tale, that the two adventurers find what they are looking for in Spain, and even more appropriate that it should be at an inn. Despite some common ground with picaresque fiction, the innkeeper's tale may not, however, itself be considered a picaresque text. It comprises not a *vida*, but an exemplary, burlesque representation of a single (female) vice; picaresque fiction is, moreover, generally uninterested in sex, as the picaro is entirely preoccupied with the basic physical necessities of his own survival. Thus, having begun in a royal court, the innkeeper's narrative finally unfolds in a location that belongs to a 'lower' (less idealized) mode of representation. The progression of the interpolation thus parallels that of the knight whose journey frames it: Rodomonte, like Astolfo, leaves his own castle and kingdom and finds himself at an inn in a foreign country; the chivalric adventures of the former are thus reflected (and subverted) by the sexual escapades of the latter.

The denouement of the interpolation finally occurs when Astolfo and Iocondo descend beneath their social ranks, as their wives have done, to share between them Fiammetta, the daughter of the poor innkeeper. From the inn owned by Fiammetta's father, Astolfo and Iocondo travel with their new partner to another inn, at Zattiva. Here, despite her two 'husbands' sleeping either side of her in bed, Fiammetta manages to satisfy her passion for a servant from the inn, who crawls into her arms having entered from the foot of the bed:

> Cavalcò forte, e non andò a staffetta;
> che mai bestia mutar non gli convenne:
> che queste pare a lui che sí ben trotte,
> che scender non ne vuol per tutta notte.
> (OF XXVIII. 64. 5–8)[41]

[He straddled her till daybreak: indeed he rode her hard, without once changing horses, for he found no need to—this one he thought, trotted so nicely that he did not want to dismount her once all night.]

Astolfo and Iocondo each initially presumes that the other is responsible for the jolting of the bed, but when they discover the truth their reaction is one of laughter rather than rage. The 'moral' of this tale—that all women are sexually incontinent—is then delivered by the two cuckolds, who subsequently return home to their wives to live happily ever after, freed from the delusion that a woman could ever be faithful.

The innkeeper's tale is immediately followed by a discussion among the listeners. Whereas, prior to its narration, no one at the inn dared speak in the presence of Rodomonte ('de' quai non era alcun di parlar oso' (OF XXVII. 132. 7)), the storytelling process creates a bond between the listeners, which sees monologue turn into dialogue. The inn, through the medium of storytelling, characteristically creates a community of its own from guests of diverse social and cultural backgrounds: this potential is exploited in each of the works to be examined below, from Palomeque's inn in the Quijote to the Grand Cerf in Jacques. Whereas Ariosto's albergo here accommodates a single guest only, the versatility of the inn as a literary location is already suggested. The manner in which the tale of Astolfo and Iocondo is introduced into the Furioso thus becomes clear: the inn provides a solution to the problem posed by Ariosto's inheritance of a structure that naturally embraces multiplicity rather than diversity. Despite being able to incorporate an infinite number of new characters and episodes within the architecture of his poem through the *topos* of encounter,[42] he is constrained by the terms that govern such meetings. As suggested earlier, the errant knight of pre-Ariostan chivalric romance will generally pause overnight in the appropriately noble setting of a castle; on the rare occasions he is obliged to spend the night in, for example, a clearing in a forest, the latter, like the castle, serves exclusively as the domain of knights and knightly adventures: Marie-Luce Chênerie notes of Arthurian romance, 'la forêt arthurienne [...] est essentiellement aristocratique'.[43] Thus, despite the expansiveness of such romances as the *Amadís*, the tone of such works varies little: a knight seeking adventures will generally meet only either another knight or a (royal) damsel in distress. These constraints create a subgenre of romance in which the cast of characters varies little even in comparison with such idealized forms as epic poetry or classical romance—in the *Odyssey*, for example, a swineherd does battle alongside his royal master, while the hero and heroine of Heliodorus' *Aethiopica* encounter bandits, merchants and slaves as well as kings, queens and soldiers. It should be added, however, that this diversity of characters does not translate to the heterogeneity of register—the 'social diversity of speech types' or *heteroglossia*—which Bakhtin identifies as inherently novelistic.[44] R. Bracht Banham thus observes, 'There is, of course, linguistic characterization of individual voices in epic; the speeches of Achilles, for example, exhibit distinctive types of imagery, but such distinctions can only be registered against the monumental consistency of Homeric style, a kind of consistency entailed by the nature of oral traditions.' Consequently, 'The swineherd Eumaios's speech is stylistically contiguous with that of the gods and heroes,'[45] and the same principle of linguistic homogeneity may be observed in the *Aethiopica*.

In the *Furioso*, Ariosto counters in a variety of ways the uniformity of tone that seems endemic to chivalric romance: the remarkable versatility of his *ottava rima* is vital in this respect; as Italo Calvino notes, 'The secret of the *ottava* in Ariosto's hands lies in the way he follows the varied rhythms of the spoken language [...] But colloquialism is only one of his registers, which extend from the lyrical to the tragic to the aphoristic, and can occur together in the same stanza.'[46] Ariosto may thus vary the register of his poetry, but cannot diversify the narrative matter itself without transgressing the boundaries of chivalric romance. The innkeeper's tale is simultaneously digressive and transgressive: by his topographical deviation from romance with the introduction of the *albergo*, Ariosto thus creates a hypodiegetic space that is not subject to the laws of chivalric romance. Designed as a narratological shelter from the romance narrative that encompasses it, the inn becomes a location wherein the outside world exists only through the filtering medium of a human voice.

Connective and Disconnective Interpolations

The innkeeper's tale is unique among the many interpolations embraced by the *Furioso*'s expansive structure. The other interpolations generally may be said to provide the narrative 'glue' that bonds each new episode to the main action of the poem; these interpolations, which will henceforth be referred to as *connective*, are symptomatic of the basic technique by which the main action of classical and chivalric romances is formally expanded and integrated: A meets a stranger B, B tells A his (unhappy) history, and A then provides a happy resolution to B's history. Todorov remarks of this method, 'Tout nouveau personnage signifie une nouvelle intrigue. Nous sommes dans le royaume des hommes-récits.'[47] As Ruth El Saffar notes in reference to the internal narrators of the *Quijote*, 'Just as Ginés de Pasamonte's life story cannot end until his life does, so the life stories of the narrators do not end with the end of their narrations.'[48] These connective interpolations are generally autodiegetic[49] and always explanatory, with the narrator providing the listener with an account of the events leading up to their present encounter. The innkeeper's tale, however, is neither autodiegetic nor explanatory: in contrast to the other interpolations in the *Furioso*, it seeks no more than a thematic connection to the main action or diegesis of the poem. It is what might be termed *disconnective*, introducing new material into the poem without seeking formally to integrate it: A meets B, B tells a story about C, A says goodbye to B. This type of interpolation insists upon its formal distinctness and autonomy: in the context of narrative fiction, it is an unequivocal form of digression, and consequently that which is most likely to attract critical censure.[50]

The difference between connective and disconnective types of interpolation is at times reducible to a simple question of presentation. While one kind of interpolation seeks to erase the border that separates it from the rest of the narrative, the other self-consciously draws attention to its own separateness. Even the most expansive of (non-parodic) chivalric romances generally insists upon the interconnectedness of its episodes and hence introduces only connective interpolations; in other genres, as we have already seen, disconnective interpolations may feature alongside their connective counterparts. This, for example, is the case in *The Golden Ass*, and in all of the source texts discussed below; there are, moreover, many works that consist almost entirely of disconnective interpolations. The fictions examined below may be seen in this respect to fall between two extremes: the first of these comprises a formally unified narrative with no disconnective hypodiegetic narrative whatsoever; the second comprises a basic narrative frame in which the disconnective hypodiegetic narrative provides the *raison d'être* of the work in question. Celebrated examples of the latter include the *Decamerone*, *The Canterbury Tales* and *The Arabian Nights*.[51]

The relationship between a narrative frame and its interpolations is suggestive of a parasitic host–guest relationship. In the case of connective interpolations, one may say that the guest is entirely dependent on its host, and cannot easily survive without the contextual habitat it provides. In the case of disconnective interpolations, however, the very identification of host and guest is more complex: while the innkeeper's tale, within the context of the *Furioso*, depends for its insertion on the contextual frame the poem provides, it could easily be extracted from this narrative and embedded in another. Similarly, Boccaccio may adopt tales from Apuleius' narrative frame and place them in his own, while Chaucer may do the same to Boccaccio. In such cases, where the hypodiegetic narrative outweighs the narrative that frames it, the relationship of host and guest is altered: the host/frame becomes dependent on its guests/interpolations for its existence—this is quite obviously the case, for example, in *The Canterbury Tales* or the *Decamerone*. Even if the situation of these works does not quite constitute a complete inversion of the host–guest relationship, one may at least describe the relationship between frame and interpolation as symbiotic rather than parasitic. In this sense, the relationship between embedding and embedded narratives comes to resemble that of a different kind of host and guest—namely, those who respectively manage and visit the inns that feature in the very same works.

While disconnective interpolations consistently spill over locally into their frames with the subsequent discussions of its fictive audience, the interpolations themselves remain entirely self-contained. There is furthermore in such works a marked antithesis between the clear linear progression and conclusive closure of the embedded narration and the narrative that frames it. The journey-based structure of the majority of interpolating fictions creates the potential for almost infinite expansion between beginning and end: Lucius' conversion at the end of *The Golden Ass* is not the inevitable final stage of the hero's evolution, but an ending that could be attached at any point; similarly, Don Quijote's deathbed enlightenment is not an inevitable culmination of a character's psychological development but a flash of recognition that signals the end of his travels (and his life). Bakhtin's discussion of the transformation of Lucius into an ass and then back into a man in fact applies equally well to Don Quijote: 'there is no evolution in the strict sense of the word; what we get, rather, is crisis and rebirth.'[52] Alonso Quijano's transformation into Don Quijote—a metaphorical rather than literal ass—is ultimately followed by his sudden return to his former identity immediately prior to his death: 'fui don Quijote de la Mancha, y soy agora, como he dicho, Alonso Quijano el Bueno' [I was Don Quijote de la Mancha; I am now, as I have said, the good Alonso Quixano] (*DQ* II. 74).[53] These sudden transitions belie the fact that the episodic construction of both *The Golden Ass* and the *Quijote* contributes to an impression of psychological inertia that undermines the significance of any physical progress the hero may make on his journey.

The subjective stasis of the hero may indeed seem to be reflected in the restrictions imposed upon his objective mobility: this is partly because the journey must not pass too smoothly or without distractions for the narrative to progress. Fictions tied to the linear progress of the road are in fact extremely dependent on deviations from the straight line—this is evidently why the inn becomes an extremely useful and popular means of diversifying a narrative. This is true of a wide variety of fictionalized journeys: in her discussion of Arthurian romance, Marie-Luce Chênerie follows Propp's view of the structure of fairy tales when she observes, 'On a dit que tout le développement du conte merveilleux marchait avec les arrêts',[54] and adds, 'il est difficile de voir une progression "rituelle" dans l'immense variété des scènes d'étape'.[55] The journey provides a frame in which interpolated episodes may naturalistically accumulate in between the adventures encountered by the hero. As the interpolated tales of *The Golden Ass* demonstrate, the internal logic of interpolating fiction generally represents a disconnective narration as the means by which uneventful periods in the main storyline are made entertaining. When the diegetic level reaches an apparently natural hiatus (such as nightfall, for example), the hypodiegetic level may take over to provide an entertaining interlude. Hypodiegetic spaces are thus created so that they may be filled with diversifying material.

The autonomy of disconnective interpolations is reflected in the manner in which they are introduced: in each of the works treated below, inserted narrations are often presented as if they belonged in the public domain, remaining independent of any single agent. This constitutes an essential difference from the connective interpolation, such as a particular character's personal history, which is by contrast exclusively tied to the voice that tells it. Neither the disconnective tale of Cupid and Psyche in *The Golden Ass* nor that of Astolfo and Iocondo in the *Furioso* is told by its ostensibly original narrators: the transformed Lucius is obviously in no position simply to transcribe the former of these narrations—as he is careful to point out to the reader, he had no writing tablets to set down the story when he originally heard it (nor, indeed, a hand with which to grip a stylus). The story as we read it is consequently a different rendering from the narration related in the cave by the drunken old woman. The mythological and allegorical elements of the tale further elevate it beyond the level of ordinary human experience.[56] The fairy-tale component of the story of Astolfo and Iocondo similarly has the effect of distancing it from any single human agent; this impression is compounded by the fact that it arrives on the page via at least three intermediaries: Valerio, the innkeeper, and the narrator of the *Furioso*. As the following chapters illustrate, this multiple retelling is typical of the disconnective interpolations that feature in comic fiction from Cervantes to Diderot, from the *novela* read by the curate in the *Quijote* to the story of Mme de la Pommeraye in *Jacques*. These inserted narratives are often presented as second-hand, and equally often seem to pre-exist the frame in which they are inserted; as Richard Lanham in fact notes in his guide to rhetoric, digressions were commonly 'prepared in advance on a commonplace subject'.[57] The exemplary character of the innkeeper's tale is moreover representative of a significant trend in interpolating fiction, with each of the works examined below incorporating exemplary tales of various kinds.

The rise to literary prominence of the inn as a shelter for both guests and interpolated stories is not quite as inevitable a phenomenon as one might assume. Although a work such as *The Canterbury Tales* hints at the potential of the inn as a plausible location for bringing together a broad cross-section of society, the road is the setting Chaucer chooses for his characters' narrations. In other interpolating fictions, a variety of sites, from private houses to caves, provide ample opportunity for storytelling.[58] Nor does the emergence of picaresque fiction in the latter half of the sixteenth century immediately herald the pre-eminence of the inn as a location for meeting and storytelling. *Lazarillo de Tormes*, the first of the Spanish picaresque fictions, contains only the most fleeting visit to an inn, perhaps because Lázaro is able to meet a cross section of society without paying one a visit; the virtual absence there moreover notably coincides with the absence of any interpolated stories, for the narrator digresses for no more than a single paragraph in the whole work. It is only with the roughly contemporaneous *Guzmán* and *Quijote* that both inn and interpolation come to the fore of the emerging forms of comic and picaresque prose fiction.

Notes to Chapter 1

1. Translated as 'Arcadia' in the English translation of 1789, translator unknown (Dublin: Zachariah Jackson).
2. Guillaume-Hyacinthe Bougeant, *Le Voyage merveilleux du Prince Fan-Férédin dans la Romancie, Contenant plusieurs observations historiques, géographiques, physiques, critiques et morales*, ed. Jean Sgard and Geraldine Sheridan (Saint-Étienne: Université de Saint-Étienne, 1992), 46.
3. Bougeant moreover refers to both the *Iliad* and the *Odyssey* in the course of his assault on literary fiction (ibid. 40, 45).
4. Marie-Luce Chênerie, *Le Chevalier errant dans les romans arthuriens en vers des XIIᵉ et XIIIᵉ siècles* (Geneva: Droz, 1986), 504–5.
5. For this reason, although the welcome offered by Eumaeus the Swineherd to Odysseus is undeniably a scene of hospitality, it is not strictly speaking a scene of *xenia*.
6. Steve Reece, *The Stranger's Welcome: Oral Theory and the Aesthetics of the Homeric Hospitality Scene* (Ann Arbor: University of Michigan Press, 1993), 190–1.
7. Chênerie also refers to the ambivalence of hospitality when she notes that the hero of Arthurian romance can never be confident of finding 'la seule détente, le repos banalement honorifique; sa qualité d'étranger, son statut de combattant pourront à chaque instant faire surgir ce vieux fond d'hostilité lié à l'hospitalité' (*Le Chevalier errant*, 514). Although one might expect the theme of detention to dwindle in the transition in representation from private to commercial hospitality in the novel—that paying for accommodation might release the traveller from some of the unexpected and unwelcome impositions of an either overzealous or hostile host—this proves to be far from the case.
8. Reece, *The Stranger's Welcome*, 34.
9. Quotations are from *The Odyssey*, trans. A. T. Murray , rev. George Dimock, 2 vols., Loeb Classical Library (Cambridge, MA: Harvard University Press, 1998). References are to book and line.

10. Pisistratus notes, 'well I know this in mind and heart, so overpowering is his spirit he will not let you go [...]' (*O.* XV. 212–13). Reece explores this matter in greater detail (*The Stranger's Welcome*, 67–9).
11. A scene with obvious and unsettling parallels with the lotus eating of Odysseus' crew and their subsequent drugging at the hands of Circe—and, of course, the Sirens' song.
12. Penelope's suitors, it is pertinent to note, entertain themselves with sporting contests of their own (*O.* XVII. 166–9).
13. Friedrich Nietzsche, *Human All Too Human: A Book for Free Spirits*, trans. R. J. Hollingdale (Cambridge: Cambridge University Press, 1986), 260. The reference is to *O.* VIII. 577–8).
14. Steven Hutchinson, *Cervantine Journeys* (Madison: University of Wisconsin Press, 1992), 206.
15. With the possible exception of Helen, the veracity of whose account of her meeting with Odysseus in Troy is questioned by her husband (*O.* IV. 274–84).
16. Bakhtin, *The Dialogic Imagination*, 124–5.
17. Both the original Latin and the English translations are taken from Apuleius, *Metamorphoses*, ed. and trans. J. Arthur Hanson, 2 vols., Loeb Classical Library (Cambridge, MA: Harvard University Press, 1989). References are to book and chapter.
18. Matilda Tomaryn Brückner, *Narrative Invention in Twelfth-Century French Romance: The Convention of Hospitality (1160–1200)* (Lexington, KY: French Forum, 1980), 15–16.
19. Ibid. 118.
20. Ibid. 118–19.
21. Thomas Hart, *Cervantes and Ariosto: Renewing Fiction* (Princeton: Princeton University Press, 1989), 33.
22. Quotations are from Lodovico Ariosto, *Orlando furioso*, ed. Lanfranco Caretti, 2 vols. (Turin: Einaudi, 1992). References are to canto, stanza and line. All English translations are taken from Guido Waldman's translation (Oxford: Oxford University Press, 1974). The debt to Apuleius would appear to be confirmed by Orlando's discovery of Isabel (and an old woman), held prisoner in a cave by a gang of brigands (*OF* XII. 89 ff.).
23. Unless stated otherwise, I use the word *romanesque* as it is used in French, to describe the *roman*, a term that covers both of the English categories 'romance' and 'novel'; Félix Martínez-Bonati, faced with the same difficulty, uses the term *romancesque* 'to avoid the ambiguity of "romantic", which, although it is used to denote "idealistic" works of imagination, is applied especially to a historical current of the nineteenth century' (*'Don Quixote' and the Poetics of the Novel*, trans. Dian Fox (Ithaca, NY: Cornell University Press, 1992), 252).
24. In order to distinguish between chivalry and chivalric romance, *chivalric* and *chivalresque* respectively are used as their adjectival forms.
25. On this theme, see Charles Ross, *The Custom of the Castle: From Malory to 'Macbeth'* (Berkeley and Los Angeles: University of California Press, 1997).
26. Which begins '—Oh feminile ingegno (egli dicea), | come ti volgi e muti facilmente' [O feminine mind, he said, how easily you turn and change] (*OF* XXVII. 117. 5–6).

27. See Gérard Genette, *Figures III* (Paris: Seuil, 1972), ch. 5.

28. The story of Iocondo and Astolfo is retold in abbreviated form by Fielding in *The Covent-Garden Journal and A Plan of the Universal Register-Office*, ed. B. A. Goldgar (Oxford: Clarendon Press, 1988), 22: 145.

29. The compendium or treasury of tales is a motif common to the *Quijote* (the library at Palomeque's inn), the *Roman comique* (the *novelas* written by Inezilla's husband and La Garouffière's *portefeuille* of poems and stories) and *Tristram Shandy* (Walter's library, which contains Slawkenbergius's 'decads').

30. 'Perch'io possa udir meglio, e tu narrarmi, | siedemi incontra, ch'io ti vegga in faccia' (*OF* XXVII. 140. 5–6).

31. C. P. Brand, *Ariosto: A Preface to the 'Orlando furioso'* (Edinburgh: Edinburgh University Press, 1974), 78.

32. The poet adds 'che 'l volgare ignorante ognun riprenda, | e parli più di quel che meno intenda' [The ignorant herd will always carp at everything; the deeper their ignorance, the more they will talk] (*OF* XXVIII. 1. 7–8), as if in anticipation of the verbal incontinence of Sancho Panza in the *Quijote*.

33. Cf. *Tom Jones*, in which the narrator invites his readers to skip the prologues (see below, Ch. 5, 'The Introductory Chapters: The Case of La Place'.

34. 'gli dia quella medesima credenza | che si suol dare a finzïoni e a fole' [those who prefer to read them must regard the story in the same light as legends and fables] (*OF* XXVIII. 3. 3–4).

35. e.g. 'Romances make clear they are mixing fact and fiction to create an essentially fictional plot; novels tend to deny that they are fictional' (Davis, *Factual Fictions*, 40).

36. Michael McKeon also notes this in *The Origins of the English Novel 1600–1740* (Baltimore: Johns Hopkins University Press, 1987), 52 ff.

37. Montalvo concocts, without any hint of irony, an account of the finding of this fifth book: 'que hasta aquí no es en memoria de ninguno ser visto, que por gran dicha parescío en una tumba de piedra, que debaxo de la tierra en una hermita, cerca de Constantinopla fue hallada, y traído por un úngaro mercadero' [which up to now within no-one's memory has been seen, for very fortunately it came to light in a stone tomb discovered underground below a hermitage near Constantinople and was brought to this part of Spain by a Hungarian merchant] (*A., Prologo*, I. 224). (Quotations are from Garci Rodríguez de Montalvo, *Amadís de Gaula*, ed. Juan Manuel Cacho Blecua, 2 vols. (Madrid: Cátedra, 1987). References are to volume and page. Translations are taken from *Amadís of Gaul*, trans. E. B. Place and H. C. Behm, 2 vols. (Lexington, KY: Kentucky University Press, 1974–5).) This passage provided the target for Cervantes's well-known parodic finding of Cide Hamet's lost manuscript in the *Quijote*. Montalvo even criticizes certain Roman writers 'de más baxa suerte' or 'of lower quality' for the 'historias fengidas en que se hallan las cosas admirables fuera de la orden de natura, que más por nombre de patrañas que de crónicas con mucha rázzon deven ser tenidas y llamadas' [feigned histories in which marvelously unnatural things are to be found, which very rightly ought to be deemed fakes] (*A*. I. 223).

38. Namely the story of Dorido and Clorinia, narrated by an ambassador (*G*. I. III. 10), and that of Ozmín and Daraja (*G*. I. I. 8); the latter of these lasts for over seventy pages and is by far the longest interpolated narration in Guzmán's narrative. (Quotations are from Mateo Alemán, *Aventuras y vida de Guzmán de*

Alfarache, ed. Benito Brancaforte, 2 vols. (Madrid: Cátedra, 1979). References are to part, book and chapter. Translations are from James Mabbe's colourful translation, *The Rogue or the Life of Guzman de Alfarache*, trans. James Mabbe, ed. Charles Whibley, 4 vols. (London: Constable & Co., 1924).)

39. I have followed the example of Shlomith Rimmon-Kenan in adopting Mieke Bal's term 'hypodiegetic' to describe the level of narrative embedded within the diegesis in preference to Genette's term 'metadiegetic', which, as Rimmon-Kenan remarks, 'is confusing in view of the opposed meaning of "meta" in logic and linguistics (a level above, not below)' (*Narrative Fiction: Contemporary Poetics* (London: Methuen, 1983), 140). See Mieke Bal, *Narratologie: Essais sur la signification narrative dans quatre romans modernes* (Paris: Klincksieck, 1977), 59–85.

40. Cf. the wrestling of Lucius and Fotis in *The Golden Ass*, and also the eavesdropping view onto private life that is characteristic of Apuleius' work.

41. Cf. the earlier sexual encounter between the queen and the dwarf, 'che la giumenta altrui sotto si tiene, | tocca di sproni e fa giuocar di schene' [he was mounted on another's filly, spurring her as his back jerked up and down] (*OF* XXVIII. 43. 7–8). The equine sexual metaphor becomes a staple of Sterne's *Tristram Shandy*, particularly with the various connotations of the hobby horse (see below, Ch. 6, 'The Travel of Language'). Of course, *The Golden Ass* transposes this metaphor into actuality with the scene of bestial sex between the transformed Lucius and the matron.

42. Which, as Bakhtin notes in *The Dialogic Imagination*, 'is one of the most ancient devices for structuring a plot in the epic (and even more in the novel)' (p. 98).

43. Chênerie, *Le Chevalier errant*, 149.

44. Bakhtin, *The Dialogic Imagination*, 263.

45. R. Bracht Banham, 'Inventing the Novel', in Amy Mandelker (ed.), *Bakhtin in Contexts: Across the Disciplines* (Evanston, IL: Northwestern University Press, 1995), 79–87 (82).

46. Italo Calvino, 'The Structure of *Orlando furioso*', in *The Uses of Literature*, trans. Patrick Creagh (London: Harvest, 1986), 168.

47. Tzvetan Todorov, *Poétique de la prose* (Paris: Seuil, 1971), 82.

48. Ruth El Saffar, *Distance and Control in 'Don Quixote': A Study in Narrative Technique*, North Carolina Studies in the Romance Languages and Literatures (Chapel Hill, NC: University of North Carolina Press, 1975), 28.

49. Genette's term for narrators who tell their own story (Genette, *Figures III*, 255).

50. See e.g. the hostile critical response to the *novela* inserted in the *Quijote*, and to the *nouvelles* in the *Roman comique*, below, Ch. 2, and Ch. 3, 'The Reader and the *Roman comique*'.

51. See Victor Shklovsky's examination of framing narratives in his *Theory of Prose*, trans. Benjamin Sher (Elmwood Park, IL: Dalkey Archive Press, 1990), 65–7. Shklovsky refers to four distinctive types of framing relationship, concisely summarized by Peter Dunn as: 'tales told in order to retard the main action (*Arabian Nights*); a "debate of stories", where stories are used as a form of argument; telling stories "for the sake of storytelling itself"(*Decameron*); stories interwoven into a frame so as to create a complex structure' ('Framing the Story, Framing the Reader: Two Spanish Masters', *Modern Language Review*, 91 (1996), 94–106 (95)).

52. Bakhtin, *The Dialogic Imagination*, 115.

53. Quotations are from Miguel de Cervantes, *El ingenioso hidalgo don Quijote de la Mancha*, ed. Luis Andrés Murillo, 2 vols. (Madrid: Castalia, 1978). References are to part and chapter. Translations are from *Don Quixote*, trans. Charles Jarvis, ed. E. C. Riley (Oxford: Oxford University Press, 1992).

54. Cf. the cinematic equivalent to the picaresque, the road movie, in which most of the action takes place when the protagonists pause on their journey, and the road often provides little more than a scenic interlude between episodes (see, for example, *Bonnie and Clyde*). This relegation is not absolute, however: in the exemplary road movie *Easy Rider*, for example, the deaths of the two 'heroes' occurs literally *en route*, as they are shot from their motorbikes.

55. Chênerie, *Le Chevalier errant*, 503–4. See also Vladimir Propp, *Le radici storiche dei racconti di fate* (Turin: Einaudi, 1949), 76.

56. Even Aristomenes' tale, a connective eyewitness account, is no longer entirely his own: he tells the reader that the events he is about to recount have become common knowledge in Thessaly ('ibidem passim per ora populi sermo iactetur quae palam gesta sunt' (*GA* I. 5)). There is furthermore a certain ambiguity about who exactly is telling this story in its definitive form: although the direct speech in which the tale is related would seem to indicate Aristomenes as the speaker, direct speech is also used for the tale of Cupid and Psyche. Lucius furthermore asserts only a few pages earlier that he alone is responsible for the composition of these 'metamorphoses', and that he is the narrator skipping from one story to another like a circus rider leaping from horse to horse ('Iam haec equidem ipsa vocis immutatio desultoriae scientiae stilo quem accesimus respondet' (*GA* I. 1)). The implication may well be that Lucius metamorphoses not only into an ass but also from one narratorial voice into another, his true identity hidden by an unfamiliar form.

57. Richard Lanham, *A Handlist of Rhetorical Terms*, 2nd edn. (Berkeley and Los Angeles: University of California Press, 1991), 54.

58. In Greek romance, shelter is often provided by the house of a particular character, such as Nausikles' house or the bandits' hut in which Kalasiris and Knemon respectively tell their stories in the *Aethiopica*. In *The Golden Ass*, shelter for the most extensive interpolation, the story of Cupid and Psyche, is, as we have already seen, provided by the brigands' cave.

CHAPTER 2

Don Quijote
The Inn and the Castle

As Steven Hutchinson notes in his important study, *Cervantine Journeys*, 'Seldom in Cervantine criticism has there been any reflective acknowledgement or discussion of a quite extraordinary aspect of Cervantes's novelistic writings: the tendency of the narrative and its traveling protagonists to be drawn into world-like vortices.'[1] Hutchinson goes on to name a number of such worlds, from the cave of Montesinos and the Insula Barataria, which form the basis of his study of 'Quixotic Worlds',[2] to the islands of the *Persiles* and the community of rogues depicted in *Rinconete y Cortadillo*. To Hutchinson's list of such worlds might be added those with which this chapter is chiefly concerned: Palomeque's inn and the ducal castle.[3]

Part I: Palomeque's Inn

Cervantes's reading of Ariosto is regularly displayed in the *Quijote*, particularly in Part I, from the 'escrutinio' of I. 6 and the conversation between Vivaldo and Don Quijote (I. 13), to the latter's imitation of Orlando's madness (I. 25).[4] The situation of the *Furioso*, in which the inn seems alien to the world of knights errant, is reversed in the *Quijote*, where the knight errant, not the inn, now appears out of place (and time). The landscape painted by Cervantes, to be painted over by Don Quijote in accordance with his chivalric vision, clearly has much in common with picaresque fiction; Walter Reed speaks for many critics when he observes, 'Don Quixote is a reader of *Amadis of Gaul* and *Palmerin of England*, but the world he inhabits is the world of *Lazarillo de Tormes* and *Guzmán de Alfarache*.'[5] When the young picaro leaves home to take to the road, the inn generally provides a revealing setting for his first encounter with the world outside. The inn therefore typically performs the opposite function to the enchanted palace or castle of chivalric romance (such as Atlante's *palazzo* in the *Furioso*), where those who enter become the victim of illusions. The picaro's first encounter with an inn usually leaves him a contrastingly disillusioned figure, as he is taught a lesson in the brutal realities of the 'real world'.[6] Although Don Quijote is neither young nor a picaro, his first sally follows the same model, leading him directly from the realm of chivalric romance contained in his own library to the contrasting world represented by the wayside inn; unlike the picaro, of course, he spectacularly refuses to learn his lesson. The inevitable failure of his chivalric mission is signalled almost immediately by the uneventful course that leads him there, for he arrives at the inn having sought in vain all day an appropriate adventure ('Casi todo aquel día caminó sin acontecerle cosa que de contar fuese, de lo cual se desesperaba' [He travelled almost that whole day without meeting anything worth relating, which disheartened him very much] (I. 2)). This is not for want of trying, for he has precisely followed the example of the knights errant of innumerable chivalric romances: 'y prosiguió su camino, sin llevar otro que aquel que su caballo quería, creyendo que en aquello consistía la fuerza de las aventuras' [he went on his way, following no other road than what his horse pleased to take, believing that therein consisted the life and spirit of adventures] (I. 2). Rocinante, however, proves to be no instrument of Fate—when Don Quijote arrives soon after at a crossroads, 'soltó la rienda a Rocinante, dejando a la voluntad del rocín la suya, el cual siguió su primer intento, que fue el irse camino de su caballeriza' [he let go the reins, submitting his own will to be guided by that of his horse, who following his first motion, took the direct road toward his stable] (I. 4); once again, a familiar *topos* of chivalric romance—the arrival at the crossroads—is invoked only to be parodically deflated.

As everyone knows, when Don Quijote approaches an inn for the first time, as the day closes in, he famously mistakes it for a castle.[7] (If he does not make such an error in the second part, it may be because he no longer needs to invent castles by this point as, with the ducal *castello*, his author has already done so for him.) This first, unnamed inn functions as what can only be described as an 'anti-castle', the exact antithesis of what Don Quijote perceives, as if its comic potential were presumed to increase in proportion to its divergence from the castle model of chivalric romance. The inn thus ostentatiously flaunts its inability to provide the opulence or hospitality a knight would expect from a castle: there are no beds available, nor is there anything to eat 'sino unas raciones de un pescado' [excepting a parcel of dried fish]

(I. 2). The kind of hospitality the inn does offer—such as the prostitutes Don Quijote mistakes for ladies of quality—moreover only serves to emphasize the anti-idealism of Cervantes's alternative to chivalric romance. As at several other points in the *Quijote*, the parody here is executed within the fiction by an 'authorial surrogate' or 'stage-manager':[8] the innkeeper becomes the first of these, channelling Don Quijote's delusions for the entertainment of the whole inn, and assuming the role of governor of the castle so that his guest may be dubbed a knight. At this first inn, Don Quijote's role as the inadvertent entertainer of a fictive audience is thus firmly established.

On his second sally, and now accompanied by Sancho Panza, Don Quijote arrives at Palomeque's inn for the first time immediately after his violent encounter with the Yanguesian carriers. To Sancho's surprise, his master appears keen to find some shelter for the night; when Sancho reminds him that 'es muy de caballeros andantes el dormir en los páramos y desiertos lo más del año' [it is usual for knights errant to sleep on heaths and deserts most part of the year] (I. 15), Don Quijote responds that such knights expose themelves to the elements only when they have no choice or when they are in love. Once again the inn is presented in terms that underline the extent of the knight's distorted vision of reality. Maritornes, the servant of the inn, is introduced as a particularly grotesque figure, the antithesis of the beautiful princess into which Don Quijote's imagination soon transforms her: 'una moza asturiana, ancha de cara, llana de cogote, de nariz roma, del un ojo tuerta y del otro no muy sana [...] no tenía siete palmos de los pies a la cabeza, y las espaldas, que algún tanto le cargaban, la hacían mirar al suelo más de lo que ella quisiera' [an Asturian wench, broad-faced, flat-headed, and saddle-nosed, with one eye squinting, and the other not much better [...] She was not seven hands high from her feet to her head; and her shoulders, which burdened her a little too much, made her look down more than she cared to do] (I. 16). Furthermore, although only one other guest, a carrier, is initially mentioned,[9] the accommodation offered the new arrivals is in a garret (or 'camaranchón') 'que, en otros tiempos, daba manifiestos indicios que había servido de pajar muchos años' [which gave evident tokens of having formerly served many years as a horse-loft] (I. 16). It therefore appears that the accommodation provided for each guest is determined by his host's initial impression of his social rank.[10] Don Quijote arrives at Palomeque's inn laid across Sancho's ass, and is hence deemed to be on an equal footing with the carrier

with whom he shares the garret. Indeed, despite Sancho's assertion
that his master is a knight and he a squire, he too sleeps in the same
garret as his master, as if the innkeeper had rejected this attempt to
impose such obsolete social categories. Cervantes elaborates the
poverty of the accommodation with meticulous detail to invert
further its chivalresque model, the castle.[11]

Ian Watt justifiably argues that, 'if the novel were realistic merely
because it saw life from the seamy side, it would only be an inverted
romance',[12] explicitly dismissing picaresque fiction and (implicitly) the
Quijote on the grounds that the realism they exhibit is limited to the
inversion of romance. Watt's broadly Jamesian conception of realism
self-evidently derives from a very different corpus of texts from those
of sixteenth- and seventeenth-century Spain, and it is therefore
inevitable that the *Quijote* does not find a place in his conception of
the novel. The danger, however, whenever one discusses the extent to
which a work may be described as *realistic*, is that one confines the
discussion (as Watt must) to a single, and not necessarily appropriate,
conception of realism. There are clearly other forms of realism than
those exhibited by a particular tradition of nineteenth-century prose
fiction, and it is a mistake to regard all earlier works that exhibit realistic
tendencies as mere prototypes of the 'real thing'. As Anthony Close
affirms, from the curate's discourse on fiction at Palomeque's inn 'it is
evident that Cervantes's notions of verisimilitude are very different from
notions of realism based, say, on the nineteenth-century novel'.[13] Félix
Martínez-Bonati succinctly clarifies a complex issue when he observes,

> To satirize romancesque stylization (or any other style of imagination), the
> space in which the satirized form is introduced need not be realistic. It
> suffices that another law operates there, that the principle of stylization is
> different [...] the domestic world of Don Quixote and Sancho Panza—is
> doubtless much closer to the strictly realistic extreme than to the world of
> the books of chivalry. And that is what leads to the impression, strengthened
> by the contrast, that we are entirely in realistic terrain. That is not the case.[14]

As we shall see throughout the course of this chapter, the *Quijote*
embraces a multitude of registers and styles, from the pastoral (the
Grisóstomo and Marcela chapters) to the caricatural (the
aforementioned description of Maritornes). Among these is precisely
the form of realistic discourse upon which Watt bases his theory of the
novel, although in the *Quijote* it is certainly not the dominant style
that it is notably in nineteenth-century fiction. During Don Quijote's

first stay at Palomeque's inn, however, this form of discourse is sidelined by the picaresque or burlesque inversion of the romanesque. In fact, given the repeated *burlas* played on Don Quijote at the inn and elsewhere, the term 'burlesque' appears particularly appropriate when it comes to defining the kind of realism that dominates the *Quijote*.

At Palomeque's inn, the process of romance inversion reaches a dramatic climax during the first night, when Maritornes is intercepted by Don Quijote on her way to the carrier's bed. He predictably transforms the scene into its nearest chivalresque equivalent—a nocturnal encounter between a visiting knight and the daughter of the lord of the castle. The subsequent brawl, with all its picaresque brutality, is similarly transformed into an attack by wicked enchanters. While Don Quijote's consciousness is entirely immersed in chivalric romance, Sancho is lost somewhere between romance and his own reality: when he refers to the 'encantado moro que está en esta venta' [the enchanted Moor that is in this inn] (I. 17), he amalgamates two irreconcilable visions of the world. (Sancho's mixture of naivety and materialism is similarly displayed in his ambition to sell a magic healing balsam for more than two *reales* an ounce (I. 10)). While the 'encantado moro' is here emblematic of chivalric romance, he may also be seen as an image of authorship, and is thus clearly related to another Moor, Cide Hamete. This association between enchanters and authors is indeed confirmed in the second part, when Don Quijote tells Sancho, 'Yo te aseguro [...] que debe de ser algún sabio encantador el autor de nuestra historia' [Depend upon it [...] that the author of this history must be some stage enchanter] (II. 2), and Sancho reveals that this author is in fact Moorish.

Don Quijote soon recognizes that Palomeque's inn/castle is incompatible with the knightly adventures he is seeking: he 'quiso partirse luego a buscar aventuras, pareciéndole que todo el tiempo que allí se tardaba era quitársele al mundo y a los en él menesterosos de su favor y amparo' [would needs depart immediately in quest of adventures, believing that all the time he loitered away there was depriving the world, and the distressed in it, of his aid and protection] (I. 17). He thus leaves the inn in search of romance—which he finds, but not before an encounter with the picaresque, a genre personified by Ginés de Pasamonte. The intrusion of this picaro, evidently modelled on Guzmán de Alfarache, indeed provokes a dramatic change of scenery, which in turn signals an imminent transition in register—and one with considerable impact upon the rest of the first part of the *Quijote*. Stephen

Gilman also observes a shift in the structure of the narrative at this juncture: 'Dialogue and memory aside, prior to chapter twenty-two the *Quijote*'s narrative form had been essentially that of *Amadís*; in Sierra Morena it is that of *Orlando Furioso*.'[15] Although the introduction of Cardenio seems to derail the narrative from its ostensible subject, the adventures of a would-be knight errant, this transition continues to be accommodated within the cyclical structure shared by the *Quijote* and the *Amadís*.[16]

Martínez-Bonati has recently referred to 'the natural and seemingly stylistically neutral environment of the hills and forest'[17] of Cervantes's Sierra Morena. The Sierra, however, is a far from neutral space: when Don Quijote and Sancho enter there, they enter a world far more amenable to romance than the roads they had previously travelled. This is despite the fact that their motive for seeking 'aquellas asperezas' [those craggy rocks] (I. 23) is scarcely appropriate for a supposedly fearless knight errant and his squire: they are, in effect, on the run from the 'Santa Hermandad' or 'Holy Brotherhood', and are looking for a hiding place. They are simultaneously, of course, fleeing the picaresque world that has treated them so roughly. Don Quijote's delight at his new surroundings indicates his own ultimately justified anticipation of intriguing adventures: 'Así como don Quijote entró por aquellas montañas, se le alegró el corazón, pareciéndole aquellos lugares acomodados para las aventuras que buscaba. Reducíansele a la memoria los maravillosos acaecimientos que en semejantes soledades y asperezas habían sucedido a caballeros andantes' [Don Quixote's heart leaped for joy at entering into the mountains, such kind of places seeming to him the most likely to furnish him with those adventures he was in quest of. They recalled to his memory the marvellous events which had befallen knights-errant in such solitudes and deserts] (I. 23). Immediately afterwards, Don Quijote and Sancho stumble across a mysterious bundle on the ground, and the story of Cardenio is thereby introduced. Once again, our knight decides to give Rocinante the reins, 'siempre con imaginación que no podía faltar por aquellas malezas alguna estraña aventura' [still possessed with the imagination that he could not fail of meeting with some strange adventures among those briars and herbs] (I. 23), and this time his romanesque expectations prove well founded. In contrast to his earlier invocation of the familiar chivalresque *topos* of the crossroads, Cervantes here does not use the topography of romance to play tricks on his hero: the Sierra Morena is not presented in parodic terms, but serves instead as a magnet for romanesque, and ostensibly chivalresque, characters and events. Cardenio is introduced to the reader as '*el Roto de la mala Figura*' [the Ragged Knight of the Sorry Figure (or face)] (I. 23), and first appears as a man leaping 'de risco en risco y de mata en mata, con estraña ligereza' [from crag to crag, and from bush to bush, with extraordinary agility] (I. 23).[18] The sight of this latter-day Orlando in the Sierra, and the fact that 'estos lugares son tan acomodados para semejantes efectos' [this place is so well adapted for the purpose] (I. 25), together inspire Don Quijote himself to emulate the madness of Ariosto's hero.

The Sierra Morena, with its steep wooded slopes and narrow valleys, evidently evokes in the reader's imagination the forests of chivalric romance.[19] As the priest and the barber soon discover, there is more than one mystery waiting to be discovered through the trees. While they are resting in a traditionally conceived *locus amoenus*—'por donde corría un pequeño y manso arroyo, a quien hacían sombra agradable y fresca otras peñas y algunos árboles que por allí estaban'— they chance upon Cardenio: 'Estando, pues, los dos allí sosegados y a la sombra, llegó a sus oídos una voz que, sin acompañarla son de algún otro instrumento, dulce y regaladamente sonaba' [through which there ran a little smooth stream, cool, and pleasantly shaded by some rocks and neighbouring trees [...] While they reposed themselves in the shade, a voice reached their ears, which, though unaccompanied by any instrument, sounded sweetly and delightfully] (I. 27).[20] Just as Cardenio's narration has come to an end, a second lament is heard through the trees, and Dorotea is thus introduced into the narrative in highly idealized terms (Cardenio, upon seeing her, tells the curate: 'Ésta, ya que no es Luscinda, no es persona humana, sino divina' [Since this is not Lucinda, it can be no human, but must be a divine creature] (I. 28)). The rules of everyday life do not apply in the Sierra Morena, perhaps because everyday life (other than that of the goatherds who work there) has no business there: Sancho is not the only one to notice that there is no 'senda ni camino' [path or road] (I. 25) in these mountains.[21] As Ruth El Saffar observes in her discussion of the internal narrators of the first part of the *Quijote*—among whom both Cardenio and Dorotea feature—'all such narrators are suffering an unnatural suspension from their daily lives which gives them perspective. Their very presence in the mountains or in a roadside inn implies a distance from their normal center of activities.'[22] The Sierra nevertheless allows for more diversity of characters than the forests of chivalric romance, as the presence of the priest and the barber, and indeed Don Quijote and Sancho, illustrates. The Sierra provides the setting for comedy as well as romance as the narrative returns to Don Quijote, and the other visitors to the mountains contrive to take him home. After the apparently genuine romanesque encounter with Dorotea, a parodic version follows as Dorotea plays the role of the Princess Micomicona and enlists the enthusiastic support of the knight errant, Don Quijote.

The disparate company that gathers in the Sierra Morena travels together to Palomeque's inn. The arrival there of Cardenio and Dorotea suggests a romanesque invasion of a location that has hitherto appeared, within the context of the preceding narrative, burlesque in character; this shift succeeds and complements the burlesque invasion of a romanesque landscape constituted by Don Quijote's entrance into the Sierra Morena. Up to this point, the inns visited by Don Quijote had provided the backdrop to a series of burlesque episodes. The presence of Cardenio and Dorotea, and the impending arrival of a variety of other guests, illustrate the potential flexibility of the inn as a fictional location. In contrast to the castles and forests of chivalric romance, Palomeque's inn is able to embrace an almost infinite variety of characters. The inn is indeed largely defined by the guests it accommodates, and may therefore shelter a uniquely broad cross-section of society: everyone, regardless of his social status or background, must after all stop at an inn if he is on the road when night comes. As this is the world of 'hommes-récits',[23] in which each new character has a story to tell, the diversity of guests in the inn inevitably generates diversity in the stories that may be told there. 'After the initial clash of the picaresque and chivalresque,' Gilman notes, 'the pastoral skein functioned as a shock absorber and prepared the way [...] for the introduction of recognizable patterns taken from the theater, from Ariosto, from comic interludes (Cervantes's most successful and appealing plays), and, at the end of the Second Sally, from the Byzantine tale.'[24]

When the romanesque (in the form of Cardenio and Dorotea) and the burlesque (in the form of Don Quijote and Sancho) arrive together at Palomeque's inn, the former gains the upper hand. Don Quijote is immediately sent to the garret he had previously slept in, while the rest of the company remain together. Inevitably the strangers to the inn attract the most attention: 'Espantáronse todos los de la venta de la hermosura de Dorotea, y aun del buen talle del zagal Cardenio' [all the folks of the inn were surprised, both at the beauty of Dorotea, and the comely personage of the shepherd Cardenio] (I. 32). While Don Quijote sleeps, the staff of the inn and their new guests enjoy their supper together;[25] the atmosphere is convivial and relaxed, in marked contrast to the tense melodrama of the Sierra Morena, as the conversation flows naturally from the madness of Don Quijote to its cause, his books of chivalry. One type of romance thus entertains characters from other, less fantastic forms of romance. In the *Quijote*, the role of the inn is not simply to provide shelter but to entertain: as we have already seen, Don Quijote's madness is used by the innkeeper of the first inn of Part I to amuse his guests, while in Palomeque's inn the unfortunate knight again seems less a guest than part of the entertainment on offer to the other guests (as he will also in the Duke's castle in Part II). Other more conventional forms of entertainment are also on offer, however, such as the aforementioned prostitutes, for example, or the puppet show put on by Ginés de Pasamonte in an inn of Part II (II. 25).

Palomeque's inn also contains a small library, which provides a public service, offering communal entertainment for both the local population and those guests arriving from further afield.[26] This is clearly in marked contrast to Don Quijote's own library, which has disastrously isolated its naive, solitary reader from the world outside. The *Quijote* might in fact be seen as an early meditation on the psychopathology of private reading, despite the fact that the innkeeper is shown to be infected with a degree of Don Quijote's madness: it seems that Palomeque is protected from entirely losing his grip on reality by the communality of life at the inn, which evidently embraces the shared experience of the literary text. The innkeeper tells his guests he has among some other manuscripts 'dos o tres' chivalric romances: 'Porque cuando es tiempo de la siega, se recogen aquí, las fiestas, muchos segadores, y siempre hay algunos que saben leer, el cual coge uno destos libros en las manos, y rodeámonos dél más de treinta, y estámosle escuchando con tanto gusto, que nos quita mil canas' [For, in the harvest time, many of the reapers come hither every day for shelter, during the noonday heat; and there is always one or other among them that can read, who takes one of these books in hand, and about thirty of us place ourselves around him, and listen to him with so much pleasure that it prevents a thousand hoary hairs] (I. 32). For the more discerning guests at present at the inn, the inn-keeper's library provides the 'Novela del Curioso impertinente' or

'Novel of the Curious Impertinent', which is quite literally a traveller's tale, left behind by a former guest with some other books and papers (including two more chivalric romances and Cervantes's own *Rinconete y Cortadillo*).[27] It later transpires that the traveller in question is in fact Cervantes himself; the inclusion of chivalric romances in the satchel left by the author of the *Quijote* thus takes on new significance and, as Martínez-Bonati suggests, raises the possibility that this apparent anti-romance embraces the genre it has been presumed to attack.[28] Alternatively, and particularly in the light of the curate's damning criticism of these works (I. 32), one could playfully justify their presence among Cervantes's belongings as necessary research material for the writing of the *Quijote*.

The *novela* read by the curate is the only interpolation not to be brought into the inn by one of the characters: in this sense it is the inn's contribution to the entertainment. It is apt that the inn, which features prominently in the picaresque fiction of Cervantes's contemporaries, is the venue for a very modern introduction of a disconnective interpolation. Cervantes's insertion of a narrative that asserts its textuality provides an innovative equivalent to Ariosto's introduction of the story of Astolfo and Iocondo in the *Furioso*. The difference between this insertion and its non-textual precedents is essentially that between the implicitly unprepared and spontaneous and the explicitly manufactured and designed respectively.

Cervantes creates and clearly delineates an explicitly fictional space by his introduction of a distinction between books and oral narrations. The written word in the *Quijote* is associated exclusively with fiction, and is consequently presented as dangerous and unreliable, as its ability to turn the heads of Don Quijote and Palomeque testifies. The spoken word, invested with the authority of the speaker, is, by contrast, a medium for explanation and revelation, rather than artistic deception; it allows the speaker to identify himself and relate the events and adventures he has encountered. The author of the *Quijote* repeatedly implies that only a fool would believe a volume of romance to be true; the curate, after reading the *novela*, thus questions its veracity, and criticizes its lack of verisimilitude: 'si es fingido, fingió mal el autor, porque no se puede imaginar que haya marido tan necio, que quiera hacer tan costosa experiencia como Anselmo' [the author has erred against probability: for it cannot be imagined, there can be any husband so senseless, as to desire to make so dangerous an experiment, as Anselmo did] (I. 35). Its role is to entertain, and one must note that, despite the emphasis placed on its textuality, it is delivered orally by the curate, and thereby retains the communal aspect inherent to oral storytelling. Although he possibly underestimates the importance of the distinction between orality and textuality in the *Quijote*, Gilman is broadly justified in his observation that 'From the point of view of narrativity, the most significant thing about these interpolations is that they are ostensibly oral, presented as tales either told directly or read aloud. As a result, they are premised on a built-in antipathy to interruption; and if they are interrupted, violence is either a cause or an effect.'[29] This antipathy to interruption is built into each of the fictions examined below; Tristram Shandy speaks not just for himself but for all internal narrators when he remarks, 'there is nothing in this world I abominate worse, than to be interrupted in a story' (*TS* VII. 1). It is, of course, this hostility to interruption, on the part of the reader as well as the narrator, that prompts the authors of these works to exploit to varying degrees the interruptive potential offered by internalized oral narrations.

More than one critic has pointed out that Don Quijote covers remarkably little ground in comparison with his knight-errant role models. Cervantes's strategy of interpolation in Part I, however, allows the narrative to escape the constraints of a single location. In the case of 'El Curioso impertinente', for example, the audience is transported from La Mancha to Florence, while the Captive's tale takes its listeners across the Mediterranean to Algiers. When the narration is briefly interrupted (by Don Quijote's battle of the wineskins[30]), the extent to which the narrative has shifted away from the eponymous hero becomes clear. Don Quijote's latest misadventure, by its positioning within the telling of the *novela*, appears in the role of a digression upon a digression. Don Quijote is sidelined for the greater part of the time he spends at the inn; when he does emerge from his garret, it is generally to provide a subordinate, burlesque interlude to the romanesque story that has appropriated so much of the narrative. Don Quijote is no longer the principle of unity around which all else revolves; he is succeeded in this respect not, as one might expect, by Cardenio but by the inn that accommodates them both. In contrast to the first inn of the *Quijote* (and to the inns of *The Golden Ass* and the *Furioso*), where the inn is the setting for a single episode (actual or interpolated), Palomeque's inn is transformed by Cervantes into something less transitory. It is in this sense that one may say it has outgrown its conventional function: once the characters arrive there, they do not appear to have any inclination to leave.

The unity offered by the hero would thus seem at first to give way to unity of place. In fact, the inn does not offer the unity of one place but the diversity of many places. As we have already seen, the storytelling of the guests provides an escape from the stasis that restricts the narrative to the inn, transporting both fictive and actual audiences to more exotic locations. The inn is moreover an internally complex space: whereas the 'storytelling inns'[31] of Apuleius and Ariosto are single, featureless locations, memorable only for the stories that are told there, in the *Quijote* the storytelling inn has for the first time its own internal geography of various rooms. This is perhaps because, for the first time, the inn provides entertainment through both action and interpolation. In contrast to its literary precedents, Palomeque's inn is not just a frame in which a story is told for a traveller passing through. Although it retains its traditional role as a place of entertainment and distraction, it has also taken on a new function as a setting in which many of its guests may find the resolution of their own adventures. Steven Hutchinson notes that, in Cervantes's fiction, the inn is 'a place where the designs of novelistic necessity appear in the guise of chance, a place where many dramas resolve themselves, and where narrative thickens into a node of multiple strands'.[32] It is no doubt this aspect of the inn that leads Close to suggest that 'Juan Palomeque's inn serves both as a degraded mock-castle and as a substitute for the enchanted castles of pastoral romance where love's maladies are cured'.[33] This is confirmed by the arrival of Fernando and Luscinda, the other two sides of the Cardenio–Dorotea 'love square' (as opposed to 'love triangle') at the inn: 'habían llegado a aquella venta, que para él era haber llegado al cielo, donde se rematan y tienan fin todas las desventuras de la tierra' [they arrived at that inn, which to him [Fernando] was arriving at heaven, where all misfortunes have an end] (I. 36); this indeed proves to be the case— but not, of course, for the reasons Fernando supposes.

In order to fulfil its new function as the site for narrative resolution (as opposed to its earlier function—the deferment of narrative resolution), the inn is an even stronger people-magnet than the Sierra Morena. In contrast to the aforementioned inn of the *Furioso*, which has only one guest to cater for (the knight Rodomonte), Palomeque's inn is characterized by the numbers it is obliged to contain. Cervantes takes full advantage of the compartmentalized spaces afforded by the inn by filling it almost to bursting point. It is furthermore repeatedly made clear that Palomeque's inn does not normally enjoy such extraordinary powers of attraction. When the Captive and Zoraida arrive there, they are told no rooms are left; in the benevolent atmosphere of the inn, however, there are always solutions: Zoraida is thus invited by Dorotea and Luscinda to share their bedroom. Characters who have barely met are obliged to share rooms; on this occasion, however, as opposed to Don Quijote's first visit to the same inn, the sharing of rooms is not exploited to comic effect.[34] This demonstrates the extent to which the inn may change character from the burlesque to the romanesque under the elevating influence of its guests from the city. As Nabokov remarked, 'the inn becomes as crowded as a certain ship cabin in a certain old Marx Brothers movie'.[35] After the Captive and Zoraida, yet more guests arrive: 'En esto llegaba ya la noche, y al cerrar della, llegó a la venta un coche, con algunos hombres de a caballo. Pidieron posada; a quien la ventera respondío que no había en toda la venta un palmo desocupado' [By this time night was come on; and, about dusk, a coach arrived at the inn, with some men on horseback. They asked for a lodging. The hostess answered, there was not an inch of room in the whole inn, but what was taken up] (I. 42). In order to accommodate the judge and his daughter, Palomeque and his wife are obliged to give up their own bedroom.

The romanesque atmosphere generated by these guests runs counter to the tone of Don Quijote's prior adventures. Close remarks that Palomeque's inn has a 'picaresque genealogy';[36] it outgrows this genealogy, however, to become a *topos* that combines and alternates romance and comedy. At certain points it leaves its picaresque roots so far behind that Don Quijote's apparently deluded vision of it as enchanted begins to seem less absurd. Perhaps the most obvious illustration of this is provided by the presence of Don Luis at the inn. Luis, a young gentleman, has fallen in love with Clara and has followed her to the inn disguised as a muleteer.[37] The muleteer, one of the staple *dramatis personae* of picaresque fiction,[38] makes an early appearance in the *Quijote* at the first inn visited by the hero.[39] By transforming a muleteer into a nobleman in disguise, Cervantes arguably subverts the conventions of picaresque as well as romanesque fiction. Furthermore, when muleteers turn out to be nobles in disguise, Don Quijote's own 'romance transformations'[40]—of prostitutes into princesses, for example—begin to appear less absurd than before. In fact, this is not the first time the narrative confirms Don Quijote's belief that appearances are often deceptive: when

Dorotea first appears in the *Quijote*, she too is in disguise: 'el que parecía labrador era mujer, y delicada' [the person who seemed to be a peasant was, in reality, a woman, and a delicate one] (I. 28).[41] The narrative thus repeatedly performs similar transformations to those that render its hero ridiculous.[42]

Although Palomeque's inn is clearly inundated by characters and situations from romance fiction, it remains an essentially comic *topos*. Indeed, one might deduce from the fact that all the stories told there are to varying degrees romanesque that the function of the inn is to provide a burlesque counterpoint. No comic tales are told there because there is no need for them: as Cervantes's use of interpolation was intended to diversify his fiction, it is logical that he should have looked to forms that contrast with the tone of the rest of the narrative. It is precisely this strategy of narrative variation that led to criticisms of disunity when Part I of the *Quijote* was originally published, and has continued to attract critical attention ever since. Cervantes in fact incorporates this contentious issue within his narrative when Sansón Carrasco, in conversation with Don Quijote and Sancho at the beginning of Part II, notes that 'Una de las tachas que ponen a la tal historia [...] es que su autor puso en ella una novela intitulada «El curioso impertinente»: no por mala ni por mal razonada, sino por no ser de aquel lugar, ni tiene que ver con la historia de su merced del señor don Quijote' [One of the faults people charge upon that history [...] is, that the author has inserted in it a novel, entitled the *Curious Impertinent*; not that it is bad in itself, or ill-written; but for having no relation to that place, nor anything to do with the story of his worship Señor Don Quixote] (II. 3). This assertion of the importance of preserving unity is supported by the rather vain Don Quijote, who responds:

y no sé yo qué le movió al autor a valerse de novelas y cuentos ajenos, habiendo tanto que escribir en los míos: sin duda se debió de atener al refrán: «De paja y de heno ...», etcétera. Pues en verdad que en solo manifestar mis pensamientos, mis sospiros, mis lágrimas, mis buenos deseos y mis acometimientos pudiera hacer un volumen mayor, o tan grande, que el que pueden hacer todas las obras del Tostado. (II. 3)

[I cannot imagine what moved the author to introduce novels, or foreign relations, my own story affording matter enough: but without doubt we may apply the proverb, With hay or with straw, &c., for verily, had he confined himself to the publishing my thoughts, my sighs, my tears, my good wishes, and my achievements alone, he might have compiled a volume as big or bigger than all the works of Tostatus]

The same question has perplexed many modern critics of the *Quijote* just as it here perplexes the knight himself. He inadvertently reveals, however, the reason for the 'cuentos ajenos' when he argues that the narrator should have concentrated exclusively on him. One is left to infer that the author was keen to diversify his narrative in order to sustain the reader's interest; Part I of the *Quijote* implies a reader who demands variety rather than unity. One is also, however, reminded here of the narrator's teasing insistence in the *Furioso* that the abrupt shifts from one storyline to another (a technique that Cervantes adopts in his interweaving between the castle and Barataria in Part II) are designed to avert the tedium of a single subject.

Cide Hamete undertakes to include no such 'novelas sueltas ni pegadizas' [loose nor unconnected novels][43] in the second part of the *Quijote*, and to introduce only 'algunos episodios que lo pareciesen, nacidos de los mesmos sucesos que la verdad ofrece' [some episodes, resembling them, and such as flow naturally from such events as the truth offers] (II. 44). He makes it clear, however, that he does not enjoy these new constraints, and tells the reader that he regrets having undertaken

una historia tan seca y tan limitada como esta de don Quijote, por parecerle que siempre había de hablar dél y de Sancho, sin osar estenderse a otras digresiones y episodios más graves y más entretenidos; y decía que el ir siempre atenido el entendimiento, la mano y la pluma a escribir de un solo sujeto y hablar por las bocas de pocas personas era un trabajo incomportable, cuyo fruto no redundaba en el de su autor [...] (II. 44)

[a history so dry, and so confined as that of Don Quixote, thinking he must always be talking of him and Sancho, without daring to launch into digressions and episodes of more weight and entertainment. And he said, that to have his invention, his hand, and his pen, always tied down to write upon one subject only, and to speak by the mouths of so few characters, was an insupportable toil, and of no advantage to the author.]

Where the second part appears to practise an aesthetic of unity based around its hero, the first practises an aesthetic of diversity to which the inn is instrumental. As we have already seen, the inn is the site of both adventures and the narration of adventures: once the story of Cardenio and his peers has been happily resolved, the company at the inn settle down to listen to 'El Curioso impertinente', which Cide Hamete freely admits in Part II is, along with the Captive's story, 'como separadas de la historia' [in a manner detached from the history] (II. 44).

While Cervantes clearly made no attempt to integrate the *novela* formally with the surrounding narrative, a number of twentieth-century critics have sought to rectify this omission. Edward Dudley speaks for many when he writes:

> The irreducible critical problem is to discover the underlying concept of narrative unity between the tales and the hero. The stories must be understood as essential to the novel's *narrative* structure, not merely as interesting accretions. Don Quijote, as hero of the novel, must become the particular protagonist he does because of the tales, not in spite of them. Either Don Quijote and the interpolated tales form a symbiosis, a sort of meta-Quijote organized on a larger molecular basis, or the novel must be recognized once and for all as a brilliant but divided masterpiece.[44]

Given that Don Quijote is not even in the room when one such interpolation is told, it seems strange to suggest that it could have a formative effect on him. He is, in any case, someone who cannot learn in a gradual, progressive manner: as suggested above, his revocation of romance is not the final stage of an evolutionary process but a sudden flash of recognition—he is not the hero of a *Bildungsroman*.[45]

Dudley's assertion that there 'must' be underlying narrative unity between the interpolations and the hero in the *Quijote*, and that these interpolations must also be essential to its narrative structure, is revealing. The use of the imperative implies both the duty of the author to create a unified work and the duty of the critic to discern it. Each of the works examined below (and interpolating narratives generally) has suffered in varying degrees similarly normative readings. Dudley talks of a brilliant *but* divided masterpiece, and the inference is clearly that a divided masterpiece is a lesser masterpiece. While one group of critics condemns any interpolation or digression as a violation of structural unity, another defends them by arguing for an underlying thematic unity; both camps are nevertheless united in their (neoclassical) belief in the necessity of unity to the literary project. Martínez-Bonati notes that 'a thematic justification for the inclusion of this novel in the *Quixote* has been much sought after', and offers his own explanation for the inclusion of 'El Curioso impertinente':

> I believe that the reason for its presence there stems less from vague similarities of content than from the nature of its form, from the function of architectonic counterbalance that it fulfills in the Cervantine edifice of literary regions [...] Here Cervantes executes with perfect mastery the ideal of the severest neo-Aristotelian classicists of his time, and in doing so exposes by contrast the formal corruption of his various other configurations.[46]

Martínez-Bonati, however, arguably makes too much of the *novela*'s conformity to neoclassical values; as we have already seen in the *Furioso*, the use of disconnective interpolations often comprehends the insertion of unified, 'neo-Aristotelian' narrations within non-classical structures. This is true of narratives as varied as *The Canterbury Tales* and *Tristram Shandy*. When, by contrast, a neoclassical narration is introduced into a neoclassical plot structure (as, for example, when the story of the Man of the Hill is inserted into the narrative of *Tom Jones*), the neoclassical aesthetic that informs each thus becomes its own worst enemy, undermining the unity of the work into which it is introduced.

I suggested earlier that Palomeque's inn is, despite its accommodation of romance, an essentially comic or burlesque edifice; the relationship between comedy and romance should not, however, be regarded purely in antithetical terms. While the inn is clearly, in one context, the 'degraded mock-castle' seen by Close, it may also be held to resemble the stage of comic theatre; in fact, these two perceptions of the inn are quite compatible, for the comedic stage may be said to fulfil a role similar to the enchanted castle of romance, providing a place where 'love's maladies' may be cured. As Murillo remarks, 'the dramatic coincidences that bring about the resolution of the subordinate plots provide an analogy to stage comedy (where the conventional ending is the marriage of reunited couples) and convert the inn into a theatrical stage'.[47] Stage comedy (particularly Shakespearean comedy) often borrowed from romance—perhaps most notably in *A Midsummer Night's Dream*, in which the quartet of young nobles (rather like Cardenio and his peers) leave the city to find the solution to all their problems in the magical forest outside Athens. Indeed the mixture of 'low' and 'high' comedy in the *Dream* bears some affinity with the roughly contemporaneous *Quijote*. There has long been, in fact, a popular theory that Shakespeare turned the story of Cardenio and his peers into a play of his own that was subsequently lost, and that exists in revised form in Lewis Theobald's *Double Falsehood* of 1727.[48]

Don Quijote's burlesque misadventures at the inn serve as a kind of subplot to the genuine romanesque adventures of the other guests. The denouement of the narrative of the Cardenio quartet and the Captive is quintessentially dramatic, with scenes of shock recognition entailing reunion and resolution (although even the reunion of the Captive and his brother is in some respect stage-managed by the curate, while the Captive waits in the wings). Don Quijote's exploits by contrast ironically lack this quality because they are so conspicuously stage-managed. Furthermore, as his adventures are episodic in nature, one is never given any sense in Part I of a progression towards a dramatic resolution. As Don Quijote's role in Palomeque's inn (and indeed the rest of the *Quijote*) is largely to entertain others, these make little attempt to bring his madness to an end—indeed they seek to perpetuate it instead. One might in fact describe many of the Don Quijote episodes at the inn as *intraplots* rather than subplots, for they are largely the invention of the various staff and guests at the inn.

Almost everyone at the inn participates in the scripting and directing of Don Quijote's misadventures—the most notable exception to this being Palomeque himself, who, in contrast to the keeper of the first inn of the *Quijote* (who dubs Don Quijote a knight), is rendered unfit for this role by his own Quixotic tendencies. In fact, it is only when Don Quijote is outdoors, either on the open road or in the Sierra Morena, that his adventures are no longer stage-managed by one of many surrogate authors. Even in the Sierra, however, Don Quijote is not left alone, as the curate, arguably the most important surrogate author of Part I, scripts his own chivalresque episode in order to lead his deluded friend out of the mountains and into the inn. Don Quijote thus sallies forth according to a script of his own writing (albeit sourced in the corpus of chivalric romance contained in his library) but returns as an actor in someone else's play. While he plays no part in the adventures of Cardenio and his peers, they by contrast participate actively in his story. Dorotea in particular is instrumental in bringing him out of the Sierra and into the inn in her new role as the Princess Micomicona, while Cardenio and Fernando side with the knight in the dispute over Mambrino's helmet. Although the young nobles are happy to act their parts, it is generally left to others to direct the action. The barber, for example, 'como tenía tan bien conocido el humor de don Quijote, quiso esforzar su desatino y llevar adelante la burla para que todos riesen' [well acquainted with Don Quixote's humour, had a mind to work up his madness, and carry on the jest, to make the company laugh] (I. 45). He is unable to maintain control over his *burla*, however, which ends violently with a fight between, on the one side, Don Quijote, Sancho, Cardenio and Fernando, and, on the other, the recently arrived second barber and the officers of the 'Santa Hermandad': 'toda la venta era llantos, voces, gritos, confusiones, temores, sobresaltos, desgracias, cuchilladas, mojicones, palos, coces y efusión de sangre'

[Thus the whole inn was nothing but weepings, cries, shrieks, confusions, fears, fights, mischances, cuffs, cudgellings, kicks, and effusion of blood] (I. 45). Don Quijote imaginatively transforms this picaresque brawl into a chivalresque battle, imagining himself in Agramante's camp.

This is not the first time a burlesque episode interrupts a romanesque plot line, and on each occasion Don Quijote is responsible for what might snobbishly be described as lowering the tone. His fundamental incompatibility with romance is constantly underlined in Part I by his inability to contribute anything other than picaresque or burlesque diversions from romance. He thus ensures that the inn does not deviate entirely from its 'picaresque genealogy', and, as Sancho remarks, that 'no es posible vivir una hora con quietud en él!' [it is impossible to live an hour quietly in it] (I. 45). When, for example, the other guests have fallen asleep, Maritornes and the innkeeper's daughter emerge as surrogate authors to add brutally to the knight's catalogue of humiliations (I. 43–4). When a natural lull in the romanesque adventures unfolding at the inn arises, Don Quijote thus provides both a comic interlude for the reader and free entertainment for the guests and staff of Palomeque's inn. On the rare occasions that Don Quijote is able to escape the burlesque quality that plagues his experience at the inn, he remains the entertainer: although he does not tell a story of his own at the inn, he contributes to the proliferation of literary styles that it invites with his learned discourse on arms and learning (I. 38–9).

Part II: The Ducal Castle

As we have already seen, the hero's progress in the *Quijote* is, like that of his predecessor in the *Amadís*, cyclical; as with the *Amadís*, these cycles moreover encompass a successively wider field with the ever-increasing circles of Don Quijote's sallies: whereas his first sally is completed in five chapters, his third and final sally comprises the whole of the second part. Although he covers far more ground on his last sally, his progress nevertheless appears far more halting in Part II—despite the fact that he has, for the first time, a specific destination (Saragossa) in mind. While he never stops in the first part for longer than the two days he spends at Palomeque's inn, the second sees him spend very little time on the road and a great deal more as the guest of a succession of willing hosts. Since the publication of the first part, Don Quijote has apparently become an extremely desirable guest, and invitation follows invitation on the road from Camacho's wedding to Barcelona. He is thus rarely short of places to stay in Part II, and, while his third sally does feature the occasional tavern or inn, none occupies a central position equivalent to that owned by Palomeque in Part I. The obvious counterpart to Palomeque's *venta* is in fact not another inn but the comparatively grand setting of the summer palace or castle (*castillo*) of a duke and duchess, which similarly offers Don Quijote a home from home, and his extended stay there prompts a sequence of episodes that parallel his experiences in Palomeque's *venta*.

The abundance of hospitality enjoyed by Don Quijote and Sancho in Part II leads to an impression of relative immobility that is evidently incongruous with the hero's chivalric mission, and this sense of stasis is compounded by the relatively uneventful road travelled by Don Quijote and his squire in Part II. The two characters travel nowhere in Part I for longer than a day without meeting with some form of adventure, and this, paradoxically, creates an impression of greater movement and dynamism in the narrative. In the sequel, however, there is often an extended 'blank' between episodes: 'en más de seis días no le sucedió cosa digna de ponerse en escritura, al cabo de los cuales, yendo fuera de camino, le tomó la noche entre unas espesas encinas o alcornoques' [in above six days, nothing fell out worth setting down in writing: at the end of which, going out of the road, night overtook them among some shady oaks or trees] (II. 60). It is when they leave the road that a chance encounter takes place (with Roque the bandit); as with the Sierra Morena episodes of Part I, leaving the road in Part II constitutes an invitation to romance: when they enter 'una selva que fuera del camino estaba' [a wood, not far out of the road] (II. 58), Don Quijote and Sancho enter the pseudo-romance of the 'nueva y pastoril Arcadia' [a new pastoral Arcadia]. The fakeness of this pastoral setting is, one might infer, implied by its proximity to the road.

Don Quijote is repeatedly reported to be unhappy at the amount of time he spends away from the conventional habitat of knights errant: having spent four days at the house of Don Diego de Miranda, he decides to leave, as 'no parecer bien que los caballeros andantes se den muchas horas a ocio y al regalo' [it did not look well for knights-errant to give themselves up to idleness and indulgence too long] (II. 18). He similarly becomes an increasingly restless guest of the duke and duchess: 'Cuenta Cide Hamete que estando ya don Quijote sano de sus aruños, le pareció que la vida que en aquel castillo tenía era contra toda la orden de caballería que profesaba, y así, determino de pedir licencia a los duques para partirse a Zaragoza' [Cide Hamete relates, that Don Quixote, being now healed of his scratches, began to think the life he led in that castle was against all the rules of knight-errantry which he professed; and therefore he resolved to depart for Saragossa] (II. 52);[49] he does not, however, leave for some time after having arrived at this resolution, despite his increasing sense of guilt at his own inactivity.[50]

Don Quijote makes it clear early on in Part II, during a conversation with Don Diego, that he identifies himself with knights errant rather than knight courtiers: 'sobre todos éstos parece mejor un caballero andante, que por los desiertos, por las soledades, por las encrucijadas, por las selvas y por los montes anda buscando peligrosas aventuras [...] Mejor parece, digo, un caballero andante socorriendo a una viuda en algún despoblado que un cortesano caballero requebrando a una doncella en las ciudades' [a much finer appearance makes the knight-errant, who, through deserts and solitudes, through crossways, through woods, and over mountains, goes in quest of perilous adventures [...] A knight-errant, I say, makes a finer appearance in the act of succouring some widow in a desert place, than a knight-courtier in addressing some damsel in a city] (II. 17). However, whereas the furthest point of his second sally does indeed lead him into the suitable 'desiertos' and 'soledades' of the Sierra Morena, the destination of his third sally is the highly unchivalresque setting of a modern city, Barcelona. Don Quijote's unhappiness at the duke's castle further reflects the change in his role; notwithstanding his unimpeached fidelity to his Dulcinea, he has become more knight courtier than knight errant. The majority of Part II unfolds in surroundings traditionally alien to adventuring knights, confining Don Quijote to the domestic sphere of his various hosts. This domestic context is even further removed than the inn from the world of chivalric romance: while the inn is a public space, and may therefore provide unexpected encounters, the house of each host is essentially private, and therefore insulated from the possibility of genuine adventures. The chance meetings that occur in Part II conse-quently still take place in the same type of setting as those of Part I, from the inn in which Don Quijote encounters Ginés de Pasamonte for a second time, to the road upon which he meets Don Diego.

Don Quijote continues in the second part to provide entertainment for the other characters; as Ruth El Saffar notes, he is no longer the anonymous figure of Part I but a celebrity: 'The result is that rather than being unaware, or taken by surprise by Don Quixote's madness, the characters whom Don Quixote meets in Part II tend to anticipate and exploit for their own entertainment his credulity.'[51] This leads to a dramatic shift in the narrative, for the 'major fictional authors of Part II have Don Quixote, rather than their own life-stories as their subject'.[52] Whereas the first part was governed by no single, overriding principle of unity—the hero's adventures being supplanted by the events unfolding at Palomeque's inn—the second looks to its eponymous hero to provide structural unity. As mentioned previously, Don Quijote's third sally is the first to have a specific destination established at an early stage: the tournament at Saragossa. There would thus appear to be 'one great end' to which all the episodes of Part II tend. Don Quijote, however, decides *en route* to go to Barcelona instead, in order to distinguish himself from the hero of Avalleneda's spurious sequel. It is conceivable that this spontaneous refusal by Don Quijote to continue along the path to Saragossa implies a rejection of the unity reluctantly promised by Cide Hamete.[53] Even if this is not the case, the hero's remarkably sluggish progress towards a destination that is abandoned on the way suggests that the episodic and tonal diversity of the first part has not been entirely abandoned in the second. Although Don Quijote occupies a more central role in Part II, this should not be mistaken for a demonstration of strict neoclassicism on Cervantes's part—'unity of hero' does not, after all, equate to unity of action, and, although Part II deviates relatively little from its eponymous hero, it remains just as episodic in construction as Part I.[54]

The number of stage managers at work in Part II of the *Quijote* substantially diminishes the role of chance in the creation of adventures. El Saffar notes a 'major shift in Don Quixote's role in the novel from "author" to "character"',[55] and, by displacing the authorial role from the extradiegetic to the diegetic level, Cervantes executes a manœuvre reminiscent of some of Shakespeare's later plays. However, whereas stage managers such as the duke in *Measure for Measure* or Prospero in *The Tempest* appear to have near-absolute control over the development of the action, and its eventual happy resolution, those of the *Quijote* have less absolute powers, and things can and do go wrong. Gilman notes that Cervantes uses 'the previous two sallies themselves as a source of *topika*, thereby freeing Don

Quijote and Sancho from servitude to their creator-enchanter';[56] one should add, however, that, rather than liberating the knight and his squire, this merely changes the ostensible identity of their manipulators as they become the playthings of a series of surrogate authors. Don Quijote's progress to Barcelona is largely, if not entirely, stage-managed: his arrival there, for example, follows an epistle sent by Roque to his friend, Don Antonio Moreno,

dándole aviso cómo estaba consigo el famoso don Quijote de la Mancha, aquel caballero andante de quien tantas cosas se decían, y que le hacía saber que era el más gracioso y el más entendido hombre del mundo, y que de allí a cuatro días, que era el de San Juan Bautista, se le pondría en mitad de la playa de la ciudad (II. 60)

[acquainting him that the famous Don Quixote de la Mancha, that knight-errant of whom so many things were reported, was in his company; giving him to understand that he was the pleasantest and most ingenious person in the world; and that, four days after, on the feast of St. John the Baptist, he would appear on the strand of the city.]

Don Antonio is consequently able to make all the necessary preparations for his approaching guest, whom he consequently greets on his arrival as 'el espejo, el farol, la estrella y el norte de toda la caballería andante' [the mirror, the beacon, and polar star of knight errantry in its greatest extent] (II. 61). Don Quijote's new host is invested with all the attributes required of a surrogate author; he is described as a 'caballero rico y discreto, y amigo de holgarse a lo honesto y afable' [a rich and discreet gentleman, and a lover of mirth in a decent and civil way] (II. 62) and is hence qualified to manipulate Don Quijote's madness for the entertainment of both fictive and actual audiences. Although Don Quijote becomes a guest in Don Antonio's own home, there is a communal spirit there that echoes both Palomeque's inn and the ducal castle. In contrast to the inn, however, Don Quijote's hosts may choose their company, and both Don Antonio and his wife hence invite their respective friends to be entertained by their new visitor (II. 62). Don Antonio's doors moreover appear always to be open to deserving causes—he also welcomes the Moriscan Christian, Ana Félix, into his home (II. 65).

Don Antonio's attempts to stage-manage Don Quijote's adventures are only partially successful; as we shall also see when we come to the duke's castle, the surrogate authors of both parts of the *Quijote* have trouble maintaining control over their fictions. The unruliness of the burlesque is indeed suggested by the tendency of these jests to slip out of control, and the *burlador burlado*, or tricked trickster, consequently becomes a prominent figure in the second part of the *Quijote*. The difficulties of authorship encountered by certain characters in Cervantes's work are illustrated with particular clarity when, in the first part, the barber's perpetuation of Don Quijote's delusions regarding the basin/helmet culminates in a brawl. At other points, the surrogate authors' attempts to direct Don Quijote along a different path simply fail: the most notable of these being Sansón Carrasco's first duel with Don Quijote. In Barcelona, Don Antonio is able to control his fiction completely only when he confines Don Quijote to the insulated security of his own home. When Don Quijote leaves the house, an element of chance is again brought into play, and the unforeseen maritime adventure of the galleys, which leads to the death of two soldiers, and the 'nueva aventura de la hermosa morisca' [strange adventure of the beautiful Morisco] (II. 63), are thus allowed to unfold. A further element of play is introduced in Barcelona as, for only the second time in the narrative (the first being the joust organized by the duke), two surrogate authors clash in their attempts to impose their fictions on Don Quijote—a contest that parallels the battle between Cervantes and Avalleneda over the second part of the *Quijote*. The jousting tournament, organized by Don Antonio and the other 'caballeros de la ciudad' [gentlemen of the town] (II. 62), is aborted by Sansón Carrasco's victory (at the second attempt) over Don Quijote in a separate joust. The tournament, Don Quijote's only reason for travelling to either Saragossa or Barcelona, is aborted, further undermining any sense of the narrative tending towards 'one great end'.

The evident foreignness of the modern city to the traditional landscape of chivalric romance renders it a deeply ironic choice as the setting for a joust. The irony is doubled by the failure of the more conventionally chivalresque setting of the duke's castle to provide Don Quijote with such an opportunity to chance his arm. This failure reflects the considerable distance between the duke's castle and the castles of chivalric romance; Cervantes's variation on this archetypal *topos* is resolutely modern, and the duke's castle proves to be as alien to romance as the inn and the city. Having presented the reader with a parodic alternative to the castle in Part I, Cervantes now parodies the castle from within by adopting and adapting it. The modernization and subversion of the castle *topos* begin with the very admittance of Don Quijote and, just as importantly, Sancho, who continually embarrasses his master in the presence of the duke and duchess because he does not belong in this setting. The roles of Part I are thus reversed: while the knight appeared to be out of place in the inn, now the squire seems (to his master) to be out of place in the castle. Whereas Don Quijote failed in his attempt to impose chivalric romance on the inn, however, Sancho succeeds entirely in his burlesque appropriation of the castle—as, inadvertently, does his master. While Don Quijote quietly acquiesces in the parodic subversion of the rituals of hospitality, allowing his face and beard to be washed at the dining table, Sancho is treated more roughly, and consequently reacts more violently: 'A este punto llegaban de su coloquio el duque, la duquesa y don Quijote, cuando oyeron muchas voces y gran rumor de gente en el palacio, y a deshora entró Sancho en la sala, todo asustado, con un cernadero por babador, y tras él muchos mozos, o, por mejor decir, pícaros de coçina y otra gente menuda' [Thus far had the duke, the duchess, and Don Quixote proceeded in their discourse, when they heard several voices and a great noise in the palace, and presently Sancho came into the hall all in a chafe, with a dish-clout for a slabbering bib; and after him a parcel of kitchen-boys, and other lower servants] (II. 32). The rowdiness that had earlier characterized the inn now invades the castle, although this scene demonstrates one of the most notable differences between the two: while the former acts as a (temporary) social leveller, seating peasants alongside noblemen at the dining table, the latter operates according to a relatively strict social hierarchy. Sancho's place in this hierarchy, as this episode demonstrates, is among the 'gente menuda' or 'lower servants'. Despite his position as the favourite of the duchess, and his master's similarly privileged status, neither evades the hierarchy of the court: both are instead accommodated within it as fools or jesters. Don Quijote thus continues to play his designated role of entertainer.

It is perhaps more accurate to say that Sancho and his master expose elements of burlesque already present in the duke's castle rather than simply importing them there. Martínez-Bonati notes that 'the splendour of the ducal court (costumes, adornments, and settings) and its rejoicing are undermined by a great number of fleeting hints of mundane misery'.[57] Furthermore the duke, Javier Salazar Rincón notes, actually adds to the misery of his court, as Doña Rodríguez's grievance makes clear: 'El Duque vive ocupado en fiestas, cacerías y burlas de dudoso gusto, y provoqua con su desidia el malestar y las

quejas de sus súbditos: «... porque pensar que el Duque mi señor me
ha de hacer justicia [comenta doña Rodríguez] es pedir peras al olmo
...» (II. 52)' [The duke lives engaged in festivities, hunting, and jests
of dubious taste and by his apathy causes the discomfort and
complaints of his subjects: 'for, to think to meet with justice from my
lord duke [remarked doña Rodríguez], is to look for pears upon an
elm-tree'].[58] The chivalresque veneer of life at the ducal castle points
towards an escapist *fiesta* rather than a way of life, and functions as a
burla masking a far less enchanting reality; as Don Quijote's nocturnal
conversation with the duenna, Doña Rodríguez, reveals, the duchess
is no idealized heroine of romance:

¿Vee vuesa merced, señor don Quijote, la hermosura de mi señora la
duquesa, aquella tez de rostro, que no parece sino de una espada acicalada y
tersa, aquellas dos mejillas de leche y de carmín, que en la una tiene el sol y
en la otra la luna, y aquella gallardía con que va pisando y aun despreciando
el suelo, que no parece sino que va derramando salud donde pasa? Pues sepa
vuesa merced que lo puede agradecer, primero a Dios, y luego, a dos fuentes
que tiene en las dos piernas, por donde se desagua todo el mal humor de
quien dicen los médicos que está llena.
    —¡Santa María!—dijo don Quijote—. Y ¿es posible que mi señora la
duquesa tenga tales desaguaderos? (II. 48)

[Your worship, Señor Don Quixote, must have observed the beauty of my
lady duchess; that complexion like any bright and polished sword; those
cheeks of milk and crimson, with the sun in the one, and the moon in the
other; and that stateliness with which she treads, or rather disdains the very
ground she walks on, that one would think she went dispensing health
wherever she passes. Let me tell you, sir, she may thank God for it in the first
place, and next, two issues she has, one in each leg, which discharge all the
bad humours, of which the physicians say she is full.
    'Holy Mary!' quoth Don Quixote, is it possible my lady duchess has such
drains?]

Doña Rodríguez also reveals that Altisidora, one of the duchess's ladies,
'tiene más de presunción que de hermosura, y más de desenvuelta que
de recogida, además que no está muy sana: que tiene un cierto aliento
cansado, que no hay sufrir el estar junto a ella un momento' [has more
self-conceit than beauty, and more assurance than modesty: besides she
is none of the soundest; for her breath is so strong, there is no enduring
to be a moment near her] (II. 48). To complete the process of
'deromancification', the duchess and Altisidora, who have been
eavesdropping on this conversation, enter the bedroom and assault Don

Quijote and the duenna. This scene provides a parallel with the nocturnal brawl in the garret of Palomeque's inn, and brings the duke's castle closer to the inn than to its own chivalric model.

Although the duke is not reduced to such burlesque self-degradation, he is nevertheless seen to belong to the modern world rather than the old world of chivalry. The very fact that Doña Rodríguez is forced to seek the assistance of Don Quijote in the matter of her daughter reflects the duke's unchivalric values; once again she sheds light on the secret life of the castle:

y aunque el duque mi señor lo sabe, porque yo me he quejado a él, no una, sino muchas veces, y pedídole mande que el tal labrador se case con mi hija, hace orejas de mercader y apenas queire oírme; y es la causa que como el padre del burlador es tan rico y le presta dineros, y le sale por fiador de sus trampas por momentos [...] (II. 48)

[though my lord duke knows the affair, and I have complained again and again to him, and begged him to command this same young farmer to marry my daughter, yet he turns the deaf ear and will hardly vouchsafe to hear me; and the reason is, because the cozening knave's father is rich, and lends him money, and is bound for him on all occasions.]

As Rincón observes, Doña Rodríguez 'nos descubre, en la segunda parte de la novela, la penuria en que viven sus señores y la influencia que sobre ellos ejercen algunos de sus vasallos' [reveals to us, in the second part of the novel, the penury in which the duke and duchess live and the influence that some of their vassals exert over them].[59] The duke is shown to be bound by a commercial rather than a chivalric code, and his debt to the farmer demonstrates just how far removed his court is from the fiction constructed by Don Quijote's deluded imagination.

In contrast to Altisidora's self-conscious imitation of a romance *topos*, the plight of Doña Rodríguez's daughter is genuine. When she and her daughter appear covered 'de luto de los pies a la cabeza' [from head to foot with mourning weeds], the duke and duchess mistakenly presume this is 'alguna burla que sus criados querían hacer a don Quijote' [some jest their servants were putting upon Don Quixote] (II. 52). This turn of events reflects their failure to control the chivalresque fiction they seek to perpetuate at their court; as soon as they understand the situation, however, they take charge, and turn an authentic crisis into another source of entertainment. The joust organized by the duke to resolve the issue is a sham in every respect: Don Quijote's opponent is not the young man who dishonoured Doña Rodríguez's daughter, but 'un lacayo gascón, que se llamaba Tosilos' [a Gascon lackey called Tosilos] (II. 54), the real culprit having fled to Flanders. The duke furthermore instructs Tosilos to take care not to injure Don Quijote in any way, and orders the removal of the iron tips from the lances of each of the combatants (II. 58). When a chivalresque *topos* such as a joust is allowed into the castle, it is hence in a highly sanitized, deflated form. In fact, the anticipated episode is prepared but not executed, as Tosilos departs from the duke's script; the plight of Doña Rodríguez's daughter is thus ultimately resolved only by accident, and despite the intervention of the duke and duchess.

The other episodes set in the duke's castle are on the whole more successfully stage-managed. This is perhaps unsurprising given that the duke has at his disposal a 'mayordomo' or steward 'de muy burlesco y desenfadado *ingenio*' [of a very pleasant and facetious disposition] (II. 36; emphasis added), whose sole purpose is to stage entertainments for the court. The steward remains an essentially anonymous figure, confined to (and defined by) the role of an authorial surrogate. When he plays the part of Merlin (II. 34), the parallels between his role and that of the enchanters of chivalric romance becomes clear. At the castle, Don Quijote is rarely required to invent his own tormenting enchanters; as Murillo notes, 'Cervantes has imputed to the mayordomo the imaginative *ingenio* or wit which Quixote has shown in the more graphic or imaginative adventures.'[60] The steward's 'ingenio', in antithesis to that of Don Quijote, is neither spontaneous nor unwitting; each scenario he contrives requires careful preparation. More deliberately than Doña Rodríguez, he too initiates a parodic version of a chivalresque *topos* (which is arguably itself tinged with parody): Ariosto's hippogriff. Once again the chivalresque model is tamed and thereby subverted as Don Quijote and Sancho mount the wooden horse, Clavileño. Sancho's mock-flight on Clavileño at the castle provides a counterpoint to an earlier actual flight of sorts, when he is repeatedly tossed aloft in a blanket by some of the other guests staying at Palomeque's inn, and is therefore accurately given the name of 'el volador Sancho' or 'the flying Sancho' (I. 17). The Clavileño episode also recalls a prior debate over another chivalresque *topos*, that of Mambrino's helmet in Palomeque's inn; although it does not end as violently, it certainly ends explosively, with the firecrackers stuffed in Clavileño's tail.[61] In Palomeque's *venta* the violence erupts because the inn is an essentially open location: the new arrivals, who are not part of the conspiratorial fiction of Don Quijote's company, do not play along with but against the fiction of Mambrino's helmet. In the enclosed environment of the castle, such fictions may more easily be sustained, for almost everyone in the duke's court other than Don Quijote and Sancho is in on the act.

The story of the Countess Trifaldi, which culminates in the Clavileño episode, corresponds directly to another episode at Palomeque's inn: the story of the Princess Micomicona devised by the priest and Dorotea. In both cases a fiction is created in which Don Quijote is content to accept the role of hero; indeed, arguably the most striking feature of this role is the passiveness it requires of him; as Howard Mancing notes, 'while Don Quijote was with the duchess, he did not initiate anything but rather meekly accepted what was arranged for him'.[62] In Palomeque's inn Don Quijote is often inactive, but this is largely because the action no longer revolves around him. In the duke's castle his status as hero is undermined on the contrary by his sustained presence 'on stage', for he is reduced by the steward and his fellow conspirators to a puppet-like figure, the object rather than the subject of his own adventures. The greater the *burlador*'s preparation—and the preparation is indeed remarkably thorough in the castle—the lesser the role of the knight: when the duke hears that Don Quijote has been vanquished by Sansón Carrasco, he eliminates the element of chance by sending 'haciendo tomar los caminos cerca y lejos del castillo por todas las partes que imaginó que podría volver don Quijote, con muchos criados suyos de a pie y de a caballo, para que por fuerza o de grado le trujesen al castillo, si le hallasen' [a great many of his servants, on horseback, and on foot, to beset all the roads about the castle, everyway by which Don Quixote might possibly return, he ordered them, if they met with him, to bring him, with or without his goodwill, to the castle] (II. 70).[63]

The ducal castle and Palomeque's inn are the only two locations visited by Don Quijote and Sancho on both outward and homeward journeys (although they pass by the place where the new 'pastoral Arcadia' had been (II. 67)). Like the inn, the castle is seen to exert a magnetic pull. While the inn's powers of attraction are presented as the instrument of chance, the castle uses its considerable resources to eliminate chance from the equation. The duke, ensuring that every road that Don Quijote might take is covered by his men, subjugates an archetypal *topos* of accidental encounters to his own intent. The jurisdiction of the castle thus extends far beyond its walls to invade the surrounding landscape. Ruth El Saffar argues that the controlled environment of the castle allows the duke and duchess to be 'the most consummate of all the character-authors in the book and construct the most elaborate plays of all'.[64] Only those episodes directed by their steward, however, are executed entirely according to plan; he is therefore arguably the authorial surrogate endowed with the greatest *auctoritas* in the *Quijote*. When the duke and the duchess take it upon themselves to contrive adventures for their guest, they are comparatively unsuccessful: aside from the aborted joust alluded to above, the nocturnal episode they plan with Altisidora notably ends in a manner they had not anticipated. When Don Quijote is mauled by one of the cats they have dropped into his bedroom, they are forced to intervene; it is worth noting, however, that the duke and his court manage to do so without breaking the illusion they have sought to construct, as Altisidora improvises a speech in which she reiterates her love for the unfortunate knight. Nevertheless, by the time of the duke's rescue, Don Quijote is 'acribado el rostro y no muy sanas las narices' (or, as Jarvis neatly renders it, with a 'face like a sieve' and a 'nose not altogether whole') (II. 46): 'Los duques le dejaron sosegar, y se fueron, pesarosos del mal suceso de la burla; que no creyeron que tan pesada y costosa le saliera a don Quijote aquella aventura, que le costó cinco días de encerramiento y de cama' [The duke and duchess left him to his rest, and went away, not a little concerned at the ill success of their joke; for they did not think this adventure would have proved so heavy and so hard upon Don Quixote; for it cost him five days confinement to his bed] (II. 46). As this episode demonstrates, the castle repeatedly proves to be as inconducive to sleep for Don Quijote as the inn. Even when he is confined to his room, he cannot enjoy any rest (rather as Sancho is repeatedly deprived of any sustenance during his governorship of Barataria); his enforced passivity during his confinement thus obliges adventures to come to him as he receives the nocturnal visit of Doña Rodríguez.

When Don Quijote and Sancho leave the ducal castle, the latter warns his master, 'no siempre hemos de hallar castillos donde nos regalen: que tal vez toparemos con algunas ventas donde nos apaleen' [we shall not always find castles where we shall be made much of: now and then we must expect to meet with inns, where we may be soundly thrashed] (II. 58). For Sancho the castle has provided a welcome change from the often violent everyday reality of the inn. His less fortunate master, however, has been the victim of violence at both inn and castle. Although the castle clearly holds fewer dangers to the two travellers than the inn, an underlying threat of physical violence persists there too, particularly in the mock-chivalresque episodes designed by the steward—one of which concludes with the order that Sancho receive 3,300 lashes. It is nevertheless clear that Sancho relishes the relative luxury of the hospitality in Part II: when he arrives in Barcelona with his master, 'Sancho estaba contentísimo, por parecerle que se había hallado, sin saber cómo ni cómo no, otras bodas de Camacho, otra casa como la de don Diego de Miranda y otro castillo como el del duque' [Sancho was so highly delighted, thinking he had found, without knowing how or which way, another Camacho's wedding, another house like Don Diego de Miranda's, and another castle like the duke's] (II. 62).

Chance and contrivance evidently play a part in the events and episodes that unfold both at both Palomeque's inn and the duke's castle; the balance of the two, however, clearly changes from one location to the other. The ascendancy of chance over contrivance that operates in Palomeque's inn is reversed in the ducal castle. Indeed, the element of accident and coincidence is so strong in the inn that the author suggests divine intervention: 'no acaso, como parecía, sino con particular providencia del cielo, se habían todos juntado en lugar donde menos ninguno pensaba' [not by chance, as it seemed, but by the particular providence of heaven, they had all met in a place where one would have least imagined they should] (I. 36). Whether Fate or chance is responsible, the essential difference between the inn and the castle remains the same: while events at the inn are seen as the product of forces beyond human control, the adventures in the castle are presented as the invention of the characters themselves. The authorial contrivance that is disguised as Fate or chance in the inn is displaced in the castle, in which *auctoritas* is internalized to become part of the fiction. This variation may be said to reflect fundamental differences in the way the journey and narrative of each part is constructed. Perhaps because Don Quijote has no specific destination in mind on either his first or his second sally, the road of Part I always seems open to haphazard encounters and incidents. Palomeque's inn, which stands somewhere between the city and the Sierra Morena, is able to attract characters from either location and, of course, from the local area. With its ability to untie even the most entangled knots, and to resolve the most challenging narrative situations, the inn is closer to the Sierra than to the city topologically as well as geographically. Indeed, the magical atmosphere that follows the newly assembled company from the Sierra Morena to Palomeque's inn brings the latter closer than the duke's palace to the enchanted castles of chivalric romance.

The path to the ducal castle suggests at first an entrance into a (chivalric) romance landscape that could provide a counterpart to the Sierra Morena. Don Quijote and Sancho notably do not meet the duke and duchess on the road, as they had Don Diego, but in open country: 'Sucedío, pues, que otro día, al poner del sol y al salir de una selva, tendió don Quijote la vista por un verde prado, y en lo último dél vio gente' [It fell out then, that the next day, about sunset, and at going out of a wood, Don Quixote cast his eyes across a green meadow, and saw people at the farther side of it] (II. 30). Their return to the castle on their homeward journey also creates the expectation of a romanesque episode, as they are intercepted on their journey by 'diez hombres de a caballo y cuatro o cinco de a pie' [about half a score men on horseback, and four or five on foot]:

la gente que se les llegaba traía lanzas y adargas y venía muy a punto de guerra [...] arbolando las lanzas, sin hablar palabra alguna rodearon a don Quijote y se las pusieron a las espaldas y pechos, amenazándole de muerte. (II. 68)

[the men that were coming up carried spears and targets, and advanced in a very warlike manner [...] lifting up their lances, without speaking a word, they surrounded Don Quixote, and clapped their spears to his back and breast, threatening to kill him.]

Once again leaving the road implies leaving the everyday world behind for the world of adventures; the deceptive semblance of an authentic romanesque episode provides an example of Cervantes's frequently applied trick of delayed decoding. Throughout the *Quijote* he delights in presenting the reader with apparent mysteries or enigmas and temporarily withholding the explanation.[65]

The ducal castle bears little resemblance to its chivalresque original; although it resembles Palomeque's inn in certain respects, it ultimately has a deeper affinity with the inn Don Quijote visits on his first sally. The castle and the first inn of the *Quijote* can accommodate only episodes that may be broadly characterized as burlesque—romance can thus only be incorporated in parodic form. While Palomeque's inn also embraces parody, with the continuation of the mock-chivalresque tale of Micomicona, it also accommodates other forms of romance non-parodically, and thereby allows for a remarkable variety of register and form. This illustrates an important difference between Palomeque's inn and, on the one hand, the castle of chivalric romance, and, on the other, the ducal castle of Part II. What makes the inn a unique location in the *Quijote* is not the number but the variety of episodes and interpolations it can frame. The castle, in both its original and its parodic manifest-ations, remains strictly monotonous; the duke's castle, for example, inverts but retains the monotony of its chivalric model by the simple substitution of mock-chivalric burlesque for chivalric romance. The monotony of the castle is perhaps inevitable given that it is primarily a chivalresque *topos*: chivalric romances tend (in literal terms) towards relative monotony, and are designed to embrace multiplicity rather than diversity.[66] The criticism that Part I has consistently attracted since its first publication may largely be attributed to Cervantes's exploitation of the inn as a setting compatible with more than one type of literary discourse. With Cervantes the inn outgrows its genealogy to become a uniquely flexible setting in the literary landscape.

Cervantes's great innovation in Part I of the *Quijote* is to exploit the potential of the inn as a fictional setting more fully than any writer before him, including even his contemporary, Mateo Alemán. The *Quijote* invents the inn as a modern literary *topos*, transforming it into something far less transitory and fleeting than the overnight shelter it typically provides in earlier fiction to become somewhere characters may stay for more than one night and for more than one story. Put in linguistic terms, the inn as a literary signifier outgrows its signified to such a degree that it displaces Cervantes's knight as the organizational centre of the narrative in the first part: Don Quijote spends approxi-mately a third of Part I in Juan Palomeque's inn—and for much of that time is sidelined by a variety of episodes and encounters that might loosely be termed romanesque. As Victor Shklovsky observes of Palomeque's 'remarkable inn': 'Dozens of tales and recognitions cross paths within its confines. This place constitutes the geometric center of the individual crisscrossing lines of the novel.'[67]

Notes to Chapter 2

1. Hutchinson, *Cervantine Journeys*, 160.
2. Ibid. 189–97.
3. This chapter does not broach the subject, explored at some length by Hutchinson, of Cervantes's metaphorical and rhetorical use of journey; this aspect of the *Quijote* is examined in Chapter 4 below, within the revealing context of Fielding's own appropriation of the rhetoric of travel.

4. Quotations in Spanish are from *El ingenioso hidalgo don Quijote de la Mancha*, ed. Luis Andrés Murillo, 2 vols. (Madrid: Castalia, 1978). Quotations in English are from the translation by Charles Jarvis, ed. E. C. Riley (Oxford: Oxford University Press, 1992).

5. Walter L. Reed, *An Exemplary History of the Novel: The Quixotic versus the Picaresque* (Chicago: University of Chicago Press, 1981), 71.

6. As, for example, in Alemán's *Guzmán de Alfarache*, and, in the eighteenth century, Lesage's *Gil Blas*. In Cervantes's *Rinconete y Cortadillo*, the narrative opens at a wayside inn, where the two young rogues meet for the first time.

7. This good fortune—the appearance of an inn just as the day is ending—becomes the modern variant of the equally convenient introduction of castles at such points in chivalric romance; Scarron, Fielding and Diderot all follow Cervantes's example in this respect.

8. The term used by Luis Andrés Murillo in *A Critical Introduction to 'Don Quixote'* (New York: Peter Lang, 1988).

9. Later, when Don Quijote and Sancho leave, it transpires that there are about twenty people at the inn, including 'cuatro perailes de Segovia, tres agujeros del Potro de Córdoba y dos vecinos de la Heria de Sevilla' [four cloth-workers of Segovia, three needle-makers of the horse fountain of Córdova, and two butchers of Seville] (I. 17). The only other guest who comes into contact with the knight and his squire during this first stay is an officer of the 'Santa Hermandad' or 'Holy Brotherhood'.

10. This is even more evident in *Tom Jones*, in which the hero's treatment at each inn varies according to the first impression he makes on his hosts. Tom's indeterminate social standing—is he a gentleman or not?—becomes an important and contentious issue for the innkeepers of more than one inn (see below, Ch. 4, '*Joseph Andrews* and *Tom Jones*: The Topography of the Inn').

11. The reader is informed, for example, that the knight's bed 'sólo contenía cuatro mal lisas tablas, sobre dos no muy iguales bancos, y un colchón que en lo sutil parecía colcha, lleno de bodoques, que, a no mostrar que eran de lana por algunas roturas, al tiento, en la dureza, semejaban de guijarro, y dos sábanas hechas de cuero de adarga, y una frazada, cuyos hilos, si se quisieran contar, no se perdiera uno solo de la cuenta' [consisted of four not very smooth boards, upon two not very equal tressels, and a flock bed no thicker than a quilt, and full of knobs, which if one had not seen through the breaches that they were wool, by the hardness might have been taken for pebble-stones; with two sheets like the leather of an old target, and a rug, the threads of which, if you had a mind, you might number without losing a single one of the account] (I. 16).

12. Watt, *The Rise of the Novel*, 11. Ronald Paulson concurs, suggesting that burlesque or picaresque realism is as artificial as romance as it 'attacks idealization by means of a counter-reality based on exaggerated probability [...] thus the ugly and gross, the sensual and fecal, are real in contrast to the beautiful and harmonious' (*Satire and the Novel in Eighteenth-Century England* (New Haven: Yale University Press, 1967), 4).

13. Anthony J. Close, *Don Quixote* (Cambridge: Cambridge University Press, 1990), 5. See also E .C. Riley, *Cervantes's Theory of the Novel* (Oxford: Oxford University Press, 1962), ch. 5.

14. Martínez-Bonati, *'Don Quixote' and the Poetics of the Novel*, 41. Martínez-Bonati usefully derives from Aristotle's *Poetics* three defining features of realism: 'verisimilitude', 'familiarity' and 'objectivity' (pp. 9–12).

15. Stephen Gilman, *The Novel According to Cervantes* (Berkeley and Los Angeles: University of California Press, 1989), 157.

16. See also below, Ch. 3, 'Town and Country, Burlesque and Romanesque'.

17. Martínez-Bonati, *'Don Quixote' and the Poetics of the Novel*, 51.

18. Note the use of 'estraña' here, in the sentence immediately following that cited above in which Don Quijote is said to be anticipating 'alguna estraña aventura' [some strange adventure] (I. 23); the repetition provides further confirmation that he will not be disappointed in his romanesque expectations.

19. Javier Herrero suggests alternatively that the 'Sierra Morena is Cervantes's labyrinth', in 'Sierra Morena as Labyrinth: From Wildness to Christian Knighthood', *Forum for Modern Language Studies*, 17 (1981), 55–67 (56). He further notes that the inn also is described (following the argument over Mambrino's helmet) as a 'caos, máquina y laberinto de cosas' [this chaos, this mass, and labyrinth of things] (I. 45).

20. This idyllic setting conforms almost exactly to Curtius's definition of the *locus amoenus*: 'It is [...] a beautiful, shaded natural site. Its minimum ingredients comprise a tree (or several trees), a meadow, and a spring or brook. Birdsong and flowers may be added' (Ernst Robert Curtius, *European Literature and the Latin Middle Ages*, trans. Willard E. Trask (Princeton: Princeton University Press, 1990), 195). Cardenio's song here clearly provides a substitute for the birdsong to which Curtius alludes.

21. A goatherd also notices that 'no hay camino ni senda que a este lugar encamine' [there is no road nor path that leads to this place] (I. 23).

22. El Saffar, *Distance and Control in 'Don Quixote'*, 27.

23. Where 'tout nouveau personnage signifie une nouvelle intrigue' (Todorov, *Poétique de la prose*, 82).

24. Gilman, *The Novel According to Cervantes*, 99. The Byzantine narrative to which Gilman alludes is the Captive's tale, in which 'the Byzantine pattern of Mediterranean wanderings, escapes, adventures, and eventual reunion in perfect love is subtly combined in Cervantes's own memories of combat and captivity'.

25. This is, of course, in marked contrast to *Tom Jones*, where, with the exception of Tom's dinner with Mrs Whitefield, only the servants of guests eat with the staff, while their masters dine in their own quarters.

26. The library provides a modern equivalent to the treasure trove of Trojan stories exploited by a series of hosts in the *Odyssey*—and, like these, provides a form of after-dinner entertainment.

27. Cf. the traveller's tale left behind by a friend of the author at the inn in the *Furioso* (see above, Ch. 1, 'Orlando furioso').

28. Martinez-Bonati, *'Don Quixote' and the Poetics of the Novel*, 182.

29. Gilman, *The Novel According to Cervantes*, 51.

30. Which, by its similarity to Lucius' battle with wineskins in *The Golden Ass*, reveals Cervantes's familiarity with Apuleius.

31. As opposed to the inn featured in Aristomenes' story, the setting for action rather than interpolation.

32. Hutchinson, *Cervantine Journeys*, 158.
33. Close, *Don Quixote*, 32. Murillo similarly notes in his edition of the *Quijote* that Palomeque's inn is tied to 'la larga tradicíon en la literatura amorosa del "palacio de Venus", donde se reúnen diversas y desencontradas parejas de enamorados' [the great tradition in the literature of love of the 'palace of Venus', in which various separated pairs of lovers are reunited] (I. 456; my translation).
34. It is, however, repeatedly exploited to just such an effect in the *Roman comique* (see below, Ch. 3, 'Inside the *Biche*: Upstairs, Downstairs').
35. Vladimir Nabokov, *Lectures on 'Don Quixote'*, ed. Fredson Bowers (London: Weidenfeld & Nicolson, 1983), 36. Nabokov notes that at one point there are as many as thirty-five people in the inn, excluding the staff.
36. Close, *Don Quixote*, 13.
37. Note that by this point in Part I, the romanesque has invaded to such an extent that Clara's beauty does not have quite the impact it would certainly have enjoyed earlier: the judge 'traía de la mano a una doncella, al parecer de hasta diez y seis años, vestida de camino, tan bizarra, tan hermosa y tan gallarda, que a todos puso en admiracíon su vista; de suerte que, *a no haber visto a Dorotea y a Luscinda y Zoraida*, que en la venta estaban, creyeran que otra tal hermosura como la desta doncella difícilmente pudiera hallarse' [led by the hand a young lady, seemingly about sixteen years of age, in a riding dress so genteel, so beautiful, and so gay, that her presence struck them all with admiration, insomuch that, *had they not seen Dorothea, Lucinda, and Zoraida*, who were in the inn, they would have believed that such another beautiful damsel could hardly have been found] (I. 42; emphasis added).
38. Guzmán's first encounter as he takes to the road is with a muleteer, who takes him to an inn (*G.* I. I. 3).
39. Note also the appearance of the Yanguesian carriers.
40. To adapt the term of Michael McKeon in *The Origins of the English Novel.*
41. The curate and the barber also disguise themselves in order to lure Don Quijote out of the Sierra Morena; the episodes in the ducal castle, moreover, all revolve around the *topos* of disguise.
42. Cf. the *Roman comique*, in which one member of the troupe after another proves not to be an actor but someone of (uncertain) nobility in disguise. The distinction here is simply that Don Quijote transforms objects into the impossible whereas Cervantes keeps within the boundaries of the possible (if improbable).
43. 'Novels' is, of course, a misleading translation of *novelas*, which would perhaps be better rendered here as 'novellas'.
44. Edward Dudley, 'Don Quijote as Magus: The Rhetoric of Interpolation', *Bulletin of British Hispanic Studies*, 44 (1972), 355–68 (356–7).
45. Cf. Parson Adams in *Joseph Andrews* (see below, Ch. 5, 'The Reader as Travelling Companion'). Cervantes is, moreover, not the only author to impose such distance between his hero and his interpolations: the eponymous hero of Fielding's *Joseph Andrews* contrives to miss almost all of the interpolated stories.
46. Martínez-Bonati, *'Don Quixote' and the Poetics of the Novel*, 63.
47. Murillo, *A Critical Introduction to 'Don Quixote'*, 100.
48. Harriet Frazier, in an extremely thorough examination of the subject, concludes, however, that 'though Shakespeare clearly might have read Shelton's translation

of *Don Quixote, Part I* (1612), one can scarcely urge more than this' and that there is insufficient evidence to support the existence of a Shakespearian *Cardenio* play; see Harriet C. Frazier, *A Babble of Ancestral Voices: Shakespeare, Cervantes and Theobald* (The Hague: Mouton, 1974), 151.

49. There is arguably in Don Quijote's desire to resume his journey an echo of the restlessness of both Telemachus and his father in the *Odyssey*.

50. Six chapters later, we are told 'ya le pareció a don Quijote que era bien salir de tanta ociosidad como la que en aquel castillo tenía; que se imaginaba ser grande la falta que su persona hacía en dejarse estar encerrado y perezoso entre los infinitos regalos y deleites que como a caballero andante aquellos señores le hacían, y parecíale que había de dar cuenta estrecha al cielo de aquella ociosidad y encerramiento' [Don Quixote now thought it high time to quit so idle a life as that he had led in the castle, thinking he committed a great fault in suffering his person to be thus confined, and in living lazily amidst the infinite pleasures and entertainments the duke and duchess provided for him as a knight-errant; and he was of opinion he must give a strict account to God for this inactivity] (II. 57). It is not clear exactly how long Don Quijote spends at the castle following his decision to leave; Cervantes simply states that 'un día' he asks leave to depart.

51. El Saffar, *Distance and Control in 'Don Quixote'*, 83. The most notable exception to this rule is, of course, Don Diego, who is unaware of the fame of his guest. Nevertheless, he also exploits Don Quijote's madness for his own entertainment.

52. El Saffar, *Distance and Control in 'Don Quixote'*, 83.

53. Note that Don Quijote arrives at this decision after another chance encounter (with two gentlemen) at an inn.

54. 'A plot is not unified, as some think, if built round an individual [...] an individual performs many actions which yield no unitary action' (Aristotle, *Poetics*, trans. Stephen Halliwell, Loeb Classical Library (Cambridge, MA: Harvard University Press, 1995), 1451a.161–18).

55. El Saffar, *Distance and Control in 'Don Quixote'*, 83.

56. Gilman, *The Novel According to Cervantes*, 99.

57. Martínez-Bonati, *'Don Quixote' and the Poetics of the Novel*, 128.

58. Javier Salazar Rincón, *El mundo social del 'Quijote'* (Madrid: Gredos, 1986), 29 (my translation).

59. Ibid. 39 (my translation).

60. Murillo, *A Critical Introduction to 'Don Quixote'*, 185.

61. Karl-Ludwig Selig alternatively suggests that 'Sancho's blanket tossing is a simple prank, but can also be considered initiatory, a rite of passage and a referent; this flight through the air will have its counterpart in the pranks performed during the maritime games and ceremonies in Barcelona' ('*Don Quixote* and the Exploration of (Literary) Geography', *Revista canadiense de estudios hispanicos*, 6 (1982), 341–57 (351)).

62. Howard Mancing, *The Chivalric World of 'Don Quijote': Style, Structure, and Narrative Technique* (Columbia, MO: University of Missouri Press, 1982), 160.

63. As Cide Hamete is reported to remark, the duke and the duchess take such pains in their manipulation of Don Quijote that they are in danger of appearing to be mad themselves (II. 70).

64. El Saffar, *Distance and Control in 'Don Quixote'*, 92.

65. Cf. the game of cause and effect in *Jacques le Fataliste et son maître*, where Diderot repeatedly presents the reader with similarly bewildering riddles—such as the horse that bolts towards gallows—which ultimately prove to have rational explanations.

66. See above, Ch. 1, '*Orlando furioso*'.

67. Shklovsky, *Theory of Prose*, 87.

❖

CHAPTER 3

Le Roman comique
Town, Country and the Provincial Inn

The geographical vagueness of the *Furioso*, and indeed of chivalric romance more generally, places the emphasis on localized topographical features such as castles and forests. As P. E. Russell notes, the romances 'took great care to avoid localizing the actions they described in any recognizable geographical milieu, for to do so would inevitably be an upsetting intrusion into their secluded world of the imagination, diminishing and de-activating it by unwelcome contact with verifiable reality'.[1] The *Quijote*, although less extreme than its chivalresque model in the geographical freedom it displays, reveals a similar reticence concerning the specifics of place. Cervantes notably refuses to specify the name of Don Quijote's village in the opening paragraph, and, aside from those that unfold in the Sierra Morena and Barcelona, few of the episodes he narrates are assigned a precise, recognizable location. Henri Chardon finds this form of imprecision particularly frustrating in his effort to decipher Scarron's *Roman comique*: 'Il en est des localités du Roman comme des personnages: elles ont été empruntées à la réalité. Malheureusement, Scarron n'en a guère cité. A part celles de Bonnétable, de Sillé, on n'en rencontre pas dans son œuvre. Il s'est borné à de vagues désignations tout-à-fait approximatives, sans préciser aucun nom.'[2] This is peculiarly frustrating for Chardon, whose attempt to demonstrate that Scarron's novel is a *roman à clef* requires him to relate the fictional re-creation of Le Mans and the Mançois to their alleged originals. The only actual location that does in fact appear undisguised in the *Roman comique* is the *Tripot de la Biche*, concerning which Chardon reveals: 'En 1620 la maison de la *Biche* [...] se composait d'un grand corps de logis où pendait pour enseigne la *Biche*, et d'un autre petit corps de logis joignant au susdit, derrière lesquels il y avait un jeu de paume, le tout

devant les Halles.'³ At the time the *Roman comique* was written, the
Biche was run by Gabriel Despins and his wife, Françoise Boutevin;
although neither is named by Scarron, the opening chapter describes
'la Maistresse du Tripot' as someone 'qui aimoit la Comédie plus que
Sermon ni Vespres', and her generosity, 'inouïe en une Maistresse de
Tripot', is immediately demonstrated by her allowing the oxen
drawing the troupe's cart to feed freely (I. 2).⁴

Scarron is not always imprecise in his approach to locality; one may
consequently infer that, when he is vague, he is so for a reason. The
opening of the work, which is often rather casually cited as an
example of mock-epic parody, thus warrants a closer glance here:

> le soleil avoit achevé plus de la moitié de sa course et son char, ayant attrapé
> le penchant du monde, roulloit plus viste qu'il ne vouloit. Si ses chevaux
> eussent voulu profiter de la pente du chemin, il eussent achevé ce qui restoit
> du jour en moins d'un demy-quart d'heure [...] Pour parler plus humaine-
> ment et plus intelligiblement, il estoit entre cinq et six quand une charrette
> entra dans les Halles du Mans. Cette charrette estoit attellée de quatre bœufs
> fort maigres, conduits par une Jument Poulliniere [...] (I. 1)

Scarron executes his deflation of elevated language by subverting a
metaphor of travel with travel itself: while the 'char', driven by horses,
speeds across the sky, the 'charrette', drawn by four scrawny oxen and
a brood mare and 'pleine de coffres, de malles et de gros paquets de
toiles peintes' (I. 1), makes slow progress to a far from epic destination.

Jean Serroy has argued persuasively that the *Roman comique* is based
upon a 'principe de dualité', which produces a series of binary oppositions, such as 'burlesque et héroïque' and 'réaliste et romanesque'.⁵
The juxtaposition of epic and ordinary language in its opening
paragraph precedes a series of further oppositions in the opening
chapter: Le Destin is said to be 'aussi pauvre d'habits que riche de
mine' (I. 1), and the description of his clothes indeed evokes a
burlesque, degraded version of a distant heroic original: 'Son pour-
point estoit une casaque de grisette ceinte avec une courroye, laquelle
luy servoit aussi à soustenir une épée qui estoit si longue qu'on ne s'en
pouvoit aider adroitement sans fourchette. Il portoit des chausses
troussées à bas d'attache, comme celles des Comediens quand ils
representent un Heros de l'antiquité' (I. 1). The as yet unnamed Le
Destin, whose sword is too long and whose 'chausses' resemble not
those worn by the heroes of antiquity but those worn by the actors
playing those heroes, approaches a walking parody of the romanesque,

and consequently appears on this occasion to be closer to Don Quijote than to an Odysseus or even an Amadís.[6] In the same chapter, La Caverne is introduced as being 'habillée moitié ville, moitié campagne' (I. 1), and the juxtaposition of town and country that La Caverne here parades is at the heart of the *Roman comique*. (It is furthermore exploited in the same opening in more physical terms with the 'quelque coups de poing et juremens de Dieu' (I. 1) that mark the arrival of the troupe in Le Mans.) The internal and external geography of the *Biche*—its role within the journey undertaken by the troupe, and within the topographical design of the narrative— provides the basis for this exploration of the duality of Scarron's text.

The Journey of the Troupe as Narrative Frame

In order to appreciate the function and importance of Le Mans and the *Biche* in the *Roman comique*, it is essential that one understand the kind of journey upon which the members of the troupe have embarked, and where, if anywhere, it will ultimately lead them. Criticism of the novel continues to be plagued by misinterpretations of the structural function of the journey, and, in particular, of the kind of frame it provides. The relationship between frame and inter-polation is particularly complex in the *Roman comique*, and raises issues of unity common to interpolating fictions. It is perhaps inevitable that a work that displays the influence of Cervantes so clearly should attract both condemnations and defences of its structural unity reminiscent of those prompted by the first part of the *Quijote*. Where critics have tended to differ is on the narrative priority of the *Roman comique*, a disagreement that may be traced to opposing conceptions of what actually constitutes the framing situation of the text.

A number of critics have assumed that Scarron's frame is the chronotope of Le Mans and the Maine—that the frame is confined temporally and spatially to the present experiences of the troupe in Le Mans. Jacques Morel argues that after the interrogation of La Rappinière (II. 15) 'tout s'explique, tous les mystères sont éclairés', and that 'l'histoire de Destin, née dans le roman à partir du voyage comique, se résout dans ce même voyage', with Saldagne, 'son puissant persécuteur, réduit maintenant, selon toute apparence, à l'impuissance'. He thus concludes, 'tout cela fait un roman certes imparfait, comportant des incertitudes, mais non sans doute un roman inachevé'.[7] Barbara Merry remarks with some justification that 'Morel seems to suggest that Scarron could have written an excellent novel, had he excluded the burlesque scenes and the digressions', and argues alternatively, 'it is just as reasonable to take Ragotin's disgraces as the central thread of the novel. Moreover, the situation of Le Destin and L'Étoile remains unresolved: at the novel's close there has been no talk of marriage'.[8] These conflicting opinions in fact mask a shared perception about Scarron's text: when Morel suggests that the story of Le Destin and L'Étoile is concluded, and when Merry remarks that Ragotin's story has, in any case, an equally good claim to being the 'central thread', they reductively limit the events and adventures of the troupe prior to Le Mans to the status of 'hors-d'œuvre' (a term repeatedly used by Morel in particular).

These views of the *Roman comique* fail to distinguish adequately between the disconnective *nouvelles* and the connective personal histories told by members of the troupe; critical opinion seems to have changed remarkably little since Chardon wrote in 1903 that the actors' stories 'ne font pas, à vrai dire, partie intégrante du Roman' and consequently resemble the 'quatre nouvelles espagnoles qui viennent interrompre le récit et qui aujourd'hui nous semblent un hors d'œuvre nuisant à l'unité de la composition'.[9] Even the most recent criticism of the *Roman comique* has failed to recognize the structural role played by the connective interpolations. Scarron does not simply begin *in medias res*: the opening, and the retrospective narrations that follow, demonstrate a strategy of *ordo artificialis*[10] that in turn incontrovertibly implies a defined *telos*: such a beginning demands an ending even if it does not receive one.

The narrative situation that frames the internal storytelling is not confined to the present nor to Le Mans but to the journey undertaken by the troupe, of which Le Mans constitutes only a stage. Le Destin's narration is framed by the present, but the present is framed by the past that this narration recounts: his history, like those of the other members of the troupe, generates the framing narrative in which it is embedded. If one fails to grasp this, the actors' stories do indeed, as Chardon suggests, start to resemble the comparatively autonomous Spanish tales. The *Roman comique* consequently no longer seems 'inachevée' to a critic such as Morel, while others have regarded the issue of its completeness as a virtual irrelevance.[11] Merry remarks, 'perhaps Scarron would have written a final version which left no narrative structure open, but there is scant basis for this sort of speculation'. In search of an alternative reading model, Merry alludes to the 'Several scholars [who] have suggested that the novel is a forerunner of modern-day soap operas, or the seventeenth-century equivalent of a pulp novel, given the *Roman comique*'s episodic nature'.[12] The soap opera analogy, however, has been better applied to certain heroic or chivalric romances, such as the almost interminable *Amadís* cycle, in which knights may perform a seemingly infinite number of heroic deeds. It is worth noting that marriage does not provide a natural resolution in such works (and nor does death, as the protagonists are not allowed to die[13]): when, for example, Amadís and Oriana marry, the *Amadís* does not end but shifts its focus to the next generation of knights. In contrast to this type of romance, the *Roman comique* cannot structurally be likened to a soap opera, as the personal histories assigned to the various actors in the troupe are crucially all teleological in structure.

The Offray *Suite* to the *Roman comique* makes a mistake similar to that of recent critics when it marries Le Destin with L'Étoile, and Léandre with Angélique, without first establishing an essential prerequisite, the noble birth of all four characters. In structural terms, there appears to me to be no doubt that Le Destin and L'Étoile are the central characters of the *Roman comique*, while the other actors in the troupe provide complementary if secondary storylines: Ragotin's burlesque adventures, like the Spanish *nouvelles*, are, by contrast, not structurally indispensable. The issue is one of narrative priorities: the troupe's journey does not provide the same kind of frame as, for example, the pilgrimage of *The Canterbury Tales*: its function is not limited to the creation of a hypodiegetic space that comprises the main body and *raison d'être* of the work. The common practice of referring to it simply as a *récit cadre* is potentially misleading, as it implies a greater degree of subordination to the various narrations it accommodates than is actually the case. An interesting point of comparison in this context is offered by the first part of the *Quijote*: while Don Quijote's burlesque journey provides a frame for the romanesque episodes of the Cardenio quartet, Scarron reverses the situation, using his troupe's romanesque journey to frame the burlesque episodes in which Ragotin plays a leading part. Furthermore, Cervantes allows his hero to be sidelined by the other guests at Palomeque's inn to such an extent that the *telos* of his journey virtually evaporates. Scarron's troupe by contrast rarely cedes the centre stage of the narrative to Ragotin or to the *nouvelles* for more than a single chapter at a time. It should be added, however, that, although Ragotin is not part of the central romanesque plot that provides the narrative with its basic structure, he is no disposable 'hors d'œuvre'. The aforementioned duality of the *Roman comique* depends upon Ragotin to provide a burlesque counterpoint to the romanesque invasion of his town and milieu.

The structural importance of the troupe's journey is evident only when one recognizes that each of the various storylines regarding the members of the troupe has a firmly established *telos*: the revelation of the true identity of each of the actors, and their restoration to their rightful place in society (which, in the respective cases of Le Destin and L'Étoile, and Léandre and Angélique, will evidently end in marriage). The stage-names by which they are known are designed to allow the author to withhold their true identities until a suitable time appears for the revelatory scenes of *anagnorisis* or recognition. It is likely that the only member of the troupe to be called by his real name, the poet Roquebrune, is the only member of the troupe whose identity is not an issue.[14] Although Parish acknowledges Serroy's opinion that Le Destin was to be revealed as a nobleman in a subsequent part of the *Roman comique*, he maintains that Le Destin, 'Despite his humble origins', has become a nobleman 'by inclination and contamination' rather than birth, and adds that 'it still seems quite plausible within the confines of the extant novel simply to see him as the beneficiary of his upbringing, and thus as a triumph of nurture over nature'.[15] I would argue that this is too early in the history of prose fiction for a *paysan parvenu*, however; Le Destin has in fact a greater affinity with Marianne than Jacob, and the reader infers Le Destin's noble birth as surely as he does that of Marivaux's heroine. Lyall Powers has indeed noted some striking resemblances between *Tom Jones* and the *Paysan parvenu*;[16] I would suggest that Fielding (whose admiration of Scarron is in fact suggested alongside 'the History of *Marianne* and *Le Paisan Parvenu*' (*JA* III. 1) in *Joseph Andrews*) may have followed the example of Scarron rather than Marivaux in his choice of a hero who initially appears to be of low birth, but whose true identity finally reveals him to be of sufficient breeding to marry his beloved.[17]

There is, in any case, a considerable amount of textual evidence to support the suggestion of Le Destin's nobility, as well as clues to the true identities of Angélique, La Rancune and possibly even L'Olive. In an article that should arguably have rendered further discussion of this issue unnecessary, Robert Garapon accurately notes, 'Il suffit de lire attentivement le roman et de remarquer les préparations aux-quelles Scarron s'est livré pour se convaincre que Destin est en réalité un jeune homme de la première noblesse, victime d'une misérable substitution d'enfants. De son vrai nom, Destin s'appelle des Glaris; il est le fils du comte des Glaris.'[18] Although Le Destin is oblivious to his own nobility, and La Caverne is interrupted before she can reveal that of Angélique, the personal histories of both internal narrators prepare the ground for future revelations regarding the identities of members of the troupe. As Garapon correctly deduces, 'Angélique doit être la fille du baron de Sigognac, qu'elle soit la fille de La Caverne[19] ou seulement sa sœur [...] selon les règles romanesques, si Léandre est de bonne naissance, Angélique doit avoir, elle aussi, du sang noble.'[20] Further evidence for this is provided by Angélique's combative temperament, displayed on her first encounter with the Mançois: 'les mains d'Angélique estoient quelquefois serrées ou baisées, car les provinciaux sont fort endemenez et patineurs; mais un coup de pied dans l'os des jambes, un soufflet ou un coup de dent, selon qu'il estoit à propos, la delivroient bien tost de ces galans à toute outrance' (I. 8). La Caverne reveals the source of this pugnacious streak in her description of the baron as one who was 'violent dans toutes ses actions comme un Gouverneur de Place frontiere et qui avoit la reputation d'estre vaillant autant qu'on le pouvoit estre' (II. 3).

La Caverne follows the example of Le Destin in revealing more as a narrator than she knows as a character. While she holds the key to Angélique's identity, she is unaware that La Rancune is her brother, although enough information is again provided for the reader to predict another scene of *anagnorisis*: 'Mon frère et le plus jeune de nos comédiens s'enfuirent, et, depuis ce temps-là, je n'ai pas oüy parler de mon frère' (II. 3). This I would suggest holds a clue to the identity of L'Olive as well as that of La Rancune: although he features little in the unfinished *Roman comique*, it seems likely that Scarron would ultimately have revealed L'Olive to be 'le plus jeune de nos comédiens'—there would otherwise seem to be no reason for La Caverne to introduce another potential mystery into the narrative. The past connection between him and La Rancune is also suggested by the fact that they spend the majority of the novel together, and the limited impression L'Olive makes is as a sidekick to La Rancune. Furthermore, given the principle of delayed decoding behind the author's use of stage names, it seems reasonable to suppose that L'Olive's true identity would have been revealed before the narrative was allowed to conclude.

It is difficult to determine precisely how long the troupe's journey, and consequently the *Roman comique* itself, would have been in its final version; it seems unlikely, however, even allowing for the addition of further *nouvelles* and the continuing adventures of Ragotin, that it would have taken any more than two further *parties* at most to conclude. Garapon asserts with surprising confidence that the troupe's journey would have ended in Bourbon: 'C'est sans doute aux eaux de Bourbon,[21] rendez-vous de la belle société égrotante, que ne seraient opérées les retrouvailles de Destin, et du comte de Glaris, de L'Étoile et de son père l'ambassadeur.'[22] While this may be quite plausible, it is possible that Bourbon may simply have provided another stage on the troupe's journey rather than its ultimate destination, although Garapon's view that it may provide the setting for the final denouement may be supported by Le Destin's foreboding that it will be some time before he will see Verville again: 'Verville fut enfermé le reste du jour avec Le Destin, ayant peine à le quitter après une si longue absence qui, possible, devoit estre bientost suivie d'une autre plus longue encore' (II. 12). It is nevertheless clear that the troupe may not have to travel far—and perhaps not at all—in order to find the resolution to their various storylines. In contrast to the enormous distances covered by Le Destin and L'Étoile prior to becoming actors, the physical progress of the troupe since this time is virtually non-existent—they seem unable to leave Le Mans behind, having originally intended to stay there for only four or five days. The conclusion of the narrative does not depend therefore on the mobility of the troupe—indeed it may conversely be accelerated by their slow progress. In contrast to the knights of chivalric romance, Le Destin, as the protector of L'Étoile, does not pursue adventures but is pursued by them. In order for the narrative to progress, his past must catch up with his present, and, consequently, Saldagne and Verville must come to Le Mans. Le Destin's evasiveness is furthermore reflected, apparently coincidentally, by the recent progress of the troupe, who arrive in Le Mans having been forced to leave one town over a fight, and having been diverted from their intended destination by an outbreak of plague (I. 7).

Inside the *Biche*: Upstairs, Downstairs

As the examples in the *Furioso* and the *Quijote* demonstrate, the inn provides the scene for diversifying confrontations between distinctive types of discourse; in Bakhtin's terms, one might therefore define it as a fundamentally 'dialogic' chronotope.[23] In the *Furioso*, the appearance of knights in wayside inns reflects a chivalresque invasion of a sub-chivalresque setting—a situation reversed in Part II of the *Quijote* with the eponymous hero's burlesque invasion of the chivalresque castle *topos*. The *Biche*, however, more closely resembles Palomeque's inn in its evocation of a romanesque invasion of a burlesque location, and in the numerous burlesque rearguard actions this occasions. As Parish remarks, 'There can be few more rowdy novels than the *Roman comique*'[24] and a considerable proportion of this rowdiness is triggered by the friction between the troupe and the local Mançois. Although the hostess of the inn is initially hospitable, the actors' arrival is nevertheless marked by 'quelques coups de poings et juremens de Dieu' as the 'valet du Tripot' assaults the 'Charretier' (I. 1). Angélique's reaction to the attentions of the locals is, as mentioned above, similarly hostile, while the troupe's first performance is notably interrupted by 'mille coups de poing, autant de soufflets, un nombre effroyable de coups de pieds, des juremens qui ne se peuvent compter' (I. 2) when two *jeu de paume* (or real-tennis) players discover their clothes have been stolen in order to provide the actors with costumes.

The numerous inns of the *Roman comique* follow their Cervantine model by exerting powers of attraction that are almost too much for them: when, for example, Angélique is reunited with Léandre after her abduction, there is no room for her at the local inn, and she is consequently taken to a neighbouring house owned by the local curate's sister (II. 11). Le Destin's rescue of L'Étoile takes place at an inn that also (conveniently) turns out to be 'pleine d'hostes et de beuveurs' (II. 12). When the inebriated La Rancune arrives at another inn and is obliged to share a bed with another guest, shortage of space at the inn is moreover exploited to comic effect as it is on only one occasion in the *Quijote* (when, during his first stay at Palomeque's inn, Don Quijote shares a garret with a carrier who is visited by Maritornes during the night (*DQ* I. 16)). On this occasion in the *Roman comique*, the troupe's influence over the narrative is more picaresque (or, possibly, even Rabelaisian) than romanesque, as the actor pours a chamber pot full of urine over the guest sleeping beside him (I. 6).

In contrast to Palomeque's inn, the *Biche* and the other inns of the *Roman comique* attract the custom of locals as well as travellers, and are seen to provide a focal point for their surrounding communities. The aforementioned inn where Le Destin rescues L'Étoile is thus full of drinkers rather than travellers, while, at the 'assez bonne hostellerie'

(II. 4) where Le Destin meets Léandre, the host's imminent death brings the 'Magister du village' and the 'Sergent du mesme village' (II. 6) to the inn, where they subsequently come to blows. Their brawl prompts a brief local history of the innkeeper's wife, a 'Nymphe taverniere' soon to be widowed for the second time, and who had once been 'recherchée par les plus riches fermiers du pays, non tant pour sa beauté que pour le bien qu'elle avoit amassé avec son deffunt Mary à vendre bien cher et à faire mauvaise mesure de vin et d'avoine' (II. 6). The success of her business has therefore made the 'hostesse' as attractive to the local community as the inn she keeps.[25]

This last inn is in 'un gros bourg' as well as being 'sur le grand chemin' (II. 4); it is therefore tied to both the local town and the open road, and, consequently, serves both its immediate neighbours as well as travellers from further afield. The *Biche*, however, is in the centre of a large town, and its primary role as the social hub of a rather lowly *milieu* reflects its physical situation:

Dans toutes les Villes subalternes du royaume, il y a d'ordinaire un Tripot, où s'assemblent tous les jours les faineans de la ville, les uns pour jouer, les autres pour regarder ceux qui jouent; c'est là que l'on rime richement en Dieu, que l'on épargne fort peu le prochain et que les absens sont assassinez à coups de langue. On n'y fait quartier à personne, tout le monde y vit de Turc à Maure et chacun y est receu pour railler selon le talent qu'il en a eu du Seigneur. (I. 3)

As Chardon notes, one of the main attractions of the actual *Biche* for the Mançois was its highly popular *jeu de paume*[26]—Scarron's inn is also first and foremost a place of entertainment. Émile Magne furthermore suggests that other forms of recreation than the *jeu de paume* were available there when he rather severely remarks of Le Mans's *tripots*, 'C'étaient lieux de débauches de mauvais garçons et de filles.'[27] In contrast to Palomeque's inn, and the inns of *Joseph Andrews* and *Tom Jones*, there is, however, no sign of illicit sex or prostitution at the *Biche*; drunkenness is the only vice in which the clientele of the inn explicitly indulge.

Each part of Scarron's *Biche* is assigned a specific literary as well as practical function: the former may indeed be seen to derive directly and logically from the latter. In this respect, Scarron surpasses Cervantes's exploitation of the inn's internal geography by a considerable margin, investing it with a duality—or dialogism—reflective of the narrative that forms in and around it. The opposition between the upstairs and the downstairs is the clearest expression of this 'double-voicedness' (signified by Bakhtin's use of the term 'dialogism' in *The Dialogic Imagination*), with each floor having its own distinctive forms of discourse and intercourse. Scarron does not, however, employ material detail to reinforce the internal oppositions at work in the inn—like all the other inns that are paid a visit in these pages, the *Biche* is never described in physical terms, as if a location as disreputable as the inn were universally deemed to be unworthy of description. The ground floor of the *Biche* (and of the other inns of the *Roman comique*) provides an open, essentially public space, in which the local community congregates, generally to share a drink. In contrast to those featured in the fiction of Cervantes or Fielding, Scarron's inns are plagued by drunkenness,[28] and this largely explains the anarchic tendency exhibited by this part of the inn. This lawlessness is the source of much of the work's rowdiness, and is epitomized rather ironically by the lawyer, Ragotin, a man who tells Le Destin, 'Un homme comme moy peut faire des reigles quand il voudra' (I. 10). This bold statement, which reverses Cide Hamete's explicit submission to neoclassical poetics in Part II of the *Quijote*, has a rather surprising affinity with some of the narratorial pronounce-ments made by Fielding, Sterne and Diderot.[29] Ragotin's remark, which arises during the course of a conversation regarding the rules of classical comedy, reveals that he is no actor; in contrast to Le Destin, he would be unwilling to submit himself to the prescriptions a script would impose upon him.

In the context of the *Roman comique*'s structure, Ragotin's role is hence to disrupt the order that the romanesque storyline seeks to impose upon the rest of the narrative. The anarchic downstairs life of the inn that he may be said to champion follows his example in this regard, as it is clearly incapable of accommodating any sustained story-telling; anyone attempting to tell a story downstairs would inevitably be subject to countless interruptions. This part of the inn therefore accommodates conversational discourse, such as gossip and 'raillerie', rather than narrative discourse. The problem with anarchy, of course, is that it is difficult to confine or restrain; consequently, the downstairs life of the *Biche* is constantly trying to escape upstairs as if in defiance of the subordinate hierarchical role it has been assigned. When the male actors of the troupe return to the *Biche* after the 'brancards' episode, they find therefore that the rooms they had taken are no longer their own:

Quand nos Comediens arriverent, la chambre des Comediennes estoit desja pleine des plus eschauffez godelureaux de la ville dont quelques-uns estoient desja refroidis du maigre accueil qu'on leur avoit fait. Ils parloient tous ensemble de la Comedie, des bons vers, des Autheurs et des Romans. Jamais on n'ouït plus de bruit en une chambre, à moins que de s'y quereller [...] (I. 8)

Both troupe and inn are essentially public property, belonging to the clientele and spectators each respectively serves and entertains; the bedrooms upstairs thus repeatedly fail to deliver the privacy they are designed to afford, and fail to insulate the actors from their potential audience. The troupe's appropriation of the upstairs rooms is thus countered by the locals' appropriation of the troupe.

The various spaces at the inn are defined by those who occupy them, as the burlesque impact of the rabble downstairs demonstrates. The presence of the 'godelureaux' in the actresses' bedroom therefore constitutes a burlesque invasion of a space conditionally defined as romanesque by the arrival of the troupe. This invasion proves to be both constructive and destructive as Ragotin inflicts his 'Histoire de l'amante invisible' on an unwilling audience, his desire to narrate the *nouvelle* illustrating his aspirations to accede to the romanesque level of the troupe: Ragotin wishes to become an actor or poet as Don Quijote yearns to becomes a knight, and his failure to recognize that he belongs downstairs not upstairs repeatedly ends in humiliation. His telling of a *nouvelle*, however, might in certain respects be considered a success: after some initial resistance he is, after all, allowed to finish his story uninterrupted, showing once again the difference between the kinds of discourse accommodated upstairs and downstairs at the inn. He would certainly not have been allowed to complete such an extensive narration below, and the romanesque subject matter is evidently better suited to the kind of audience the troupe provides above. The private rooms upstairs, particularly the bedroom, are the only part of the inn in which sustained storytelling is possible, although even these fail to protect the storytelling process from outside intrusions, as the interruptions to Le Destin's own narration demonstrate. It may indeed seem peculiar that Le Destin is interrupted when Ragotin is not, were it not for the fact that the latter is responsible for the interruption to the former's story.[30] Ragotin can evidently interrupt the act of narration only if he is external to it; by turning him into a narrator, one of the most significant interruptive forces in the *Roman comique* is nullified, and the *nouvelle* thus secured from external interference.

Other factors, however, contribute to the uninterrupted progress of Ragotin's 'Histoire de l'amante invisible': the intercalated *nouvelles* enjoy a privileged status in the *Roman comique* relative to the actors' personal histories, and, while the narration of the former is never disrupted, the latter are by contrast prone to intrusion. The only interference regarding the introduction of these stories is apparently authorial, as Scarron appropriates first Ragotin's story with the assertion 'Ce n'est donc pas Ragotin qui parle, c'est moy' (I.8), suggesting that the lawyer and his romanesque tale are incompatible and thus require separation) and then Inézilla's tale, on the grounds that her grasp of French is insufficient. The other *nouvelles* are moreover expressly presented as texts, and are thus perceptibly separable from the internal narrator who delivers them—Mary-Jo Muratore may thus describe them as 'orphaned tales', suggesting that, though 'adopted' by the parent narrative that frames them, they never entirely belong to it.[31] These stories consequently acquire a dual existence, and simultaneously function on both hypodiegetic and extradiegetic levels, or, put more simply, as both internal narrations and authorial interventions respectively.

Having stated that Ragotin's invasion of the troupe's quarters might be described as a qualified success, I should qualify this further still by adding that this success has more to do with the authorial desire to introduce his *nouvelle* than with Ragotin himself. Ragotin, whose personality is erased from our experience of the narration he delivers in the bedroom of the *Biche*, reasserts himself as soon as it is concluded. The applause that he immediately receives for his contribution is short-lived, and his initial perseverance in resisting the earlier interruptions to it is ultimately punished as, in the context of the other *nouvelles*, Ragotin's narration constitutes a transgression. The initial resistance to his story derives, not only from the unfavourable impression Ragotin makes on his prospective audience, but also from the moment he chooses to tell it: his 'Histoire de l'amante invisible' is the only *nouvelle* not to be told as after-dinner entertainment in the *Roman comique* and his storytelling is thus premature. The punishment for this infringement of traditional storytelling ritual is severe, and Ragotin's qualified success quickly turns to unmitigated disgrace as soon as it leads him to forget his place: 'il commença à traiter les Comediens de haut en bas et, s'approchant des Comediennes, leur prit les mains sans leur consentement [...] Mademoiselle Angélique, luy déchargea un grand coup de busc sur les doigts' (I. 10). Having had his *nouvelle* stolen by his author, Ragotin is now separated from it once again, as the book from which it came is taken from him and juggled between the other Mançois in the room. In the ensuing catalogue of violence, he is restored to a more humble position—'le cul au pied des Comediennes, aprés une retrogradation fort precipitée' (I. 10)—to be further humiliated by his fellows.

Ragotin's Quixotic credentials are immediately evident: his enjoyment of chivalric romance is even demonstrated by his desire to put on a play entitled 'les Faicts et Gestes de Charlemagne, en 24 journées'; he is moreoever introduced as 'le plus grand petit fou qui ait couru les champs depuis Roland' (I. 8). This remark is not as straightforward as it may seem, for the implication here is that the (heroic) Roland is a comparable figure to the (comic) Don Quijote, and that the former's madness is equivalent to the delusions of the latter. The juxtaposition of Roland and Ragotin shows that the mock-heroic can be a two-way process in which the heroic original rather than the trivial modern is mocked. Although Scarron thus reverses the procedure as it is used by Cervantes in his portrayal of his hero, the role of Ragotin in the *Roman comique* nevertheless resembles that of Don Quijote in that it allows the author to introduce the burlesque element into his narrative. In the inn scene described above, the part Ragotin plays is reminiscent of that of Don Quijote in the ducal castle—the inadvertent fool who entertains the court; Scarron's actors thus temporarily assume the role of spectators as they observe his 'disgraces'.

In the world of the *Roman comique*, one's place in the literary rather than social hierarchy determines the part of the inn to which one belongs. If this were not the case, the positions of Ragotin and the troupe would be reversed, as even a lowly provincial lawyer would be deemed more respectable than a troupe of travelling actors.[32] Ragotin's humiliations, like those that befall Cervantes's knight, generally stem from his attempts to escape from one literary mode and space to another—from the burlesque to the romanesque, and from downstairs to upstairs. It is, therefore, not surprising that there are several echoes of Don Quijote's madness in the *Roman comique*, particularly in its early chapters. Although Ragotin's extreme vanity surpasses that of Cervantes's *hidalgo*, the manner in which he consciously decides to fall in love clearly recalls a Spanish precedent: in the humiliating scene following his reading of the *nouvelle*, the narrator remarks,

Representez-vous, je vous prie, quelle doit estre la fureur d'un petit homme plus glorieux luy seul que tous les Barbiers du Royaume, en un temps où il se faisoit tout blanc de son épée, c'est-à-dire de son histoire, et devant des Comediennes dont il vouloit devenir amoureux; car, comme vous verrez tantost, il ignoroit encore laquelle luy touchoit le plus au cœur. (I. 10)

The use of the expression *se faire tout blanc de son épée*,[33] which one might loosely (if anachronistically) translate as 'to shoot oneself in the foot', takes on an extra resonance here with the chivalresque associations of 'épée', and the suggestion that Ragotin humiliates himself with his story rather as Don Quijote does with his sword (and the chivalric pursuits it connotes).

Ragotin, 'qui se trouva dans l'hostellerie et qui ne s'en pouvoit eloigner depuis qu'il estoit amoureux de L'Étoile' (I. 15), is drawn to the *Biche* (rather as a moth to a flame) by the magnetic qualities of the troupe rather than the inn itself. Whenever he seeks to enter the romanesque space upstairs, however, the consequences are disastrous. When Ragotin escorts La Caverne and Angélique back to the *Biche* from their rehearsals in another 'tripot', for example, his attempt to climb the stairs with them ends with all three in a crumpled heap at the foot, almost as if the upstairs had physically repelled him (I. 17). Immediately prior to this minor catastrophe, with La Caverne on the one hand and Angélique on the other, Ragotin had already demonstrated his potential to bring others down in a literal sense: 'le petit homme, qui ne leur venoit qu'à la ceinture, tiroit si fort leurs mains en bas qu'elles avoient bien de la peine à s'empescher de tomber sur luy' (I. 17). Such is his impact on the narrative that he is able to violate the romanesque space of the inn bedroom (and the romanesque narrative that it accommodates) even without entering it, as the discordant serenade that interrupts Le Destin's history proves. Ragotin is generally confined downstairs, and to the company of La Rancune, who occupies a middle ground between the troupe and the lawyer. La Rancune is in fact tied inextricably to both the burlesque and romanesque strands of the *Roman comique*: he plays an active, often directorial part in Ragotin's misadventures, and a lesser part in Le Destin's adventures (when he comes to his aid in Paris (I. 18)); he is furthermore, one anticipates, a key element in the romanesque subplot that will ultimately reveal him to be La Caverne's brother.

Bedtime Stories

In contrast to all the other interpolations in the *Roman comique*, Le Destin's story is delivered in three parts.[34] Its opening in the thirteenth chapter marks a transition from the apparently haphazard burlesque adventures that dominate the opening of the novel to the settled pattern of a romanesque plot. After the introduction of Ragotin and the interlude of his 'Histoire de l'amante invisible', Le Destin's interpolation begins to assert itself as the primary narrative. As stated earlier, this narration both frames and is framed by the present, and the two episodes that interrupt its progress, the curé de Domfront's abduction and Ragotin's serenade, assume in relation to it a subordinate role. Scarron thus inverts the conventional association of interpolation and deviation, turning the present of Le Mans into something resembling a digressive interlude from Le Destin's adventures. This impression is arguably compounded by the arrival, during one of these interludes in Le Destin's story, of the Operateur's own troupe, 'qui estoit composé de sa femme, d'une vieille servante More, d'un Singe et de deux valets' (I. 15). These new guests at the *Biche* play only a peripheral part in the *Roman comique*; Inézilla alone has any formative impact on the narrative, and this impact is exclusively digressive, limited solely to the introduction of two *nouvelles*.

None of the autobiographical interpolations of the *Roman comique* is positioned at random—each is in fact triggered by a particular event in the narrative. The pattern of *ordo artificialis* creates a strong rippling effect throughout the work, generating a succession of retrospective narrations as the action progresses to a point of crisis at which the present can be decoded only by recourse to the past. When this past catches up with the present through retrospective interpolation, the narrative may progress intelligibly once more. In Le Destin's case, the crisis is the revelation that Saldagne is in the vicinity of Le Mans, as the sighting of one of his servants implies; the stories of La Caverne and Léandre are meanwhile prompted by the more pressing emergency of Angélique's abduction (for which Saldagne is also responsible). One is moreover given the impression that at the point of their narration all of these personal histories are already long overdue, as La Caverne indeed suggests: 'Enfin, La Caverne [...] reprocha à Destin et à L'Étoile que, depuis le temps qu'ils estoient ensemble, ils avoient pu reconnoistre jusqu'à quelle point elle estoit de leurs amies; et toutesfois qu'ils avoient si peu de confiance en elle et en sa fille qu'elles ignoroient encore leur veritable condition' (I. 12). La Caverne, in an aside that opens the way to her own autobiographical narration, 'adjousta qu'elle avoit esté assez persecutée dans sa vie pour conseiller des malheureux tels qu'ils paroissoient estre' (I. 12). This remark furthermore demonstrates that she and her daughter provide a fitting audience for Le Destin's story; in contrast to the *nouvelles*, 'contées, le plus souvent lues à haute voix devant une compagnie nombreuse',[35] the histories told by the troupe are personal, and therefore narrated in private. This marks a departure from the storytelling at Palomeque's inn, where a single space accommodates both *nouvelles* and autobiographies, and in which a character recounts his past to a room of strangers; as Jean Rousset notes, in the *Roman comique*, 'ceux qui parlent sont aussi ceux qui écoutent': 'les cinq autobiographies ne sortent donc pas du cercle des comédiens; la troupe forme, conformément à la nature du milieu théâtrale, un petit monde séparé aux secrets duquel les autres, les non initiés, n'ont pas accès'.[36]

The setting for Le Destin's narration, and the spatial demarcation of this 'petit monde', is the actresses' bedroom at the *Biche*; although, as we have already seen, this room is prone to invasion and intrusion, it is the most secure space available to the actors. Consequently, Le Destin tells the longest and most leisurely of the autobiographical narrations there and, in contrast to La Caverne, is given plenty of space and time to finish. It should in addition be specified that the locals gain admittance to the actresses' quarters only during the day (or at least before dinner). Le Destin, by contrast, has privileged access to the actresses' bedroom even late in the evening: while all the troupe are free to have dinner there (even if, like La Rancune, they may prefer to eat elsewhere), after the meal only he remains with the actresses; he soon begins his narration, and continues until 'deux heures après minuit sonnerent' (I. 13). He resumes his story the next evening when, after the arrival of the Operateur, 'Les Comediennes [...] se retirerent ensuite dans leur chambre, où Le Destin les conduisit pour achever son histoire, que La Caverne et sa fille mouroient d'impatience d'entendre' (I. 15); their interest, and the suspense it implies, provide further indications of the teleological drive behind Le Destin's adventures. The story concludes the following evening, after dinner once again, when 'Le Destin s'enferma avec les Comediennes pour continuer son Histoire' (I. 17).

Despite the tears that precede and succeed it, Le Destin's narration is not uncompromisingly romanesque, and its narrator is surprisingly keen to entertain his audience. Even more unexpected is the comic relief that finds its way into La Caverne's interpolation; although distraught at the abduction of Angélique, she manages like Le Destin to rise above her distress in order to amuse her audience: 'Quelque grand sujet que j'aye d'estre fort triste, je ne puis songer à ce jour-là que je ne rie de la plaisante façon dont le grand Page s'acquitta de son rôle. Il ne faut pas que ma mauvaise humeur vous cache une chose si plaisante' (II. 3). Laughter soon returns to tears, however, as the page's humiliation has fatal consequences for La Caverne's father. Le Destin's story, in contrast to Léandre's hasty summary of events, begins playfully—and in a far from romanesque manner—with two exemplary comic anecdotes that illustrate the farcical meanness of his supposed father (I. 13). The association of the comic and the 'low' that is characteristic of the *Roman comique* is accentuated by the manner in which Le Destin's announcement of his apparent low birth prepares the ground for these short *divertissements*. The comic soon gives way to the romanesque, however, to mirror the transition Serroy observes from the burlesque to the romanesque in the *Roman comique* as a whole.[37] The account of Le Destin's youth confirms this sense of progression from one mode of discourse to its inverse, with an account of his childhood reading that merits quoting at length:

Le Baron d'Arques avoit une Bibliotheque de Romans fort ample. Nostre Precepteur, qui n'en avoit jamais leu dans le pays Latin, qui nous en avoit d'abord defendu la lecture et qui les avoit cent fois blasmez devant le Baron d'Arques, pour les luy rendre aussy odieux qu'ils les trouvoit divertissans, en devint luy-mesme si feru qu'après avoir devoré les vieux et les modernes, il avoua que la lecture des bons Romans instruisoit en divertissant et qu'il ne les croyoit pas moins propres à donner de beaux sentimens aux jeunes gens que la lecture de Plutarque. Il nous porta donc à les lire autant qu'il nous en avoit destounez et nous proposa d'abord de lire les modernes; mais ils n'estoient pas encore selon nostre goust, et jusqu'à l'âge de quinze ans, nous nous plaisions bien plus à lire les Amadis de Gaule que les Astrées et les autres beaux Romans que l'on a faits depuis [...] Nous donnions donc à la lecture des Romans la plus grande partie du temps que nous avions pour nous divertir. (I. 13)

There are evident echoes here of the reading habits of Cervantes's *hidalgo*, as well as Sorel's more recent *Francion*, in which the hero professes his childhood admiration for chivalric romance in his account of his 'advantures scholastiques':

tousjours j'avois un Roman caché dessus moy, que je lisois en mettant mes autres livres au devant, de peur que le Regent ne l'apperceust: Le courage m'estant alors creu de beaucoup, je souspirois en moy mesme de ce que je n'avois encore faict aucun exploit de guerre, bien que je fusse à l'aage où les Chevaliers errans avoient desja defaict une infinité de leurs ennemis.[38]

With both Francion and Le Destin, as with Don Quijote, a link is clearly implied between the hero's enthusiasm for romance and his subsequent search for adventures. The question therefore arises—is Scarron's hero more Quixotic than romanesque?

I noted earlier that Le Destin's appearance on his arrival in Le Mans could be taken to hint at a parody of the romanesque hero. Although it would seem reasonable to deduce that this undistinguished entrance is designed to undermine his heroic status, in the ensuing narrative he is allowed to play the part of hero without being subjected to the kind of humiliations that plague Ragotin or Don Quijote. As we have already seen, however, he is not entirely insulated from the burlesque component of the *Roman comique*: the *Biche* provides the setting for an interplay of the burlesque and romanesque in which each contaminates the other. When, for example, Le Destin leaves the actresses' bedroom to investigate 'une grande rumeur dans la chambre voisine' (I. 11), he becomes embroiled in a burlesque episode— 's'estant acharné sur une grosse servante qu'il avoit troussée, [il] luy donna plus de cent claques sur les fesses' (I. 11).[39] Scarron does not protect his protagonist from comic or burlesque interference, but uses these to modulate or temper the romanesque streak that runs through both the *Roman comique* and its hero. The burlesque thus grounds the romanesque in an appropriately earthy representation of contemporary (provincial) reality, and thereby acts as a guarantor of the actuality—or at least plausibility—of Le Destin's adventures.

Scarron's hero provides a model of chivalry that is neither straightforward nor straightforwardly parodic. One may infer that Le Destin's reference to the *Amadís* in the passage cited above serves as a badge that identifies the work rather than the character himself: rather than implying that his hero is a Quixotic reader, this allusion indicates instead the author's desire to place his work in the same tradition as the *Quijote*, rather as Fielding does more explicitly when he describes *Joseph Andrews* as being 'Written in Imitation of The *Manner* of CERVANTES, Author of *Don Quixote*'. This self-conscious procedure of Cervantine self-alignment is followed by many of Cervantes's admirers, from Sorel to Diderot: Marivaux, whose Pharsamon rather anachronistically reads 'les anciens romans, les Amadis de Gaule, l'Arioste, et tant d'autres livres'[40] previously read by Don Quijote, provides an interesting counterpoint to the *Roman comique*, as his hero's reading of chivalric romance does in fact indicate a characteristically Quixotic imagination. Scarron, by contrast, apparently suggests, not that Le Destin is a Quixotic figure, but that his childhood admiration of these works reflects an innate nobility of spirit.[41] Le Destin moreover presumably outgrows chivalric romance—he remarks that modern novels are not *yet* to his taste, and one is left to assume that, after the age of 15, 'les *Astrées*' replaced 'les *Amadis de Gaule*' in his affections.

Le Destin is thus no Quijote, although his narration raises questions that anticipate those prompted in Prévost's *Manon Lescaut* by the Chevalier des Grieux—another character who arguably inherits Don Quijote's tendency to transform reality into romance. When her identity is revealed in the course of Le Destin's narrative, L'Étoile responds to Angélique's surprise by remarking 'que sa compagne avoit raison de douter qu'elle fust cette Leonore dont Le Destin avoit fait une beauté de Romant' (I. 18)—although Angélique insists this is not the reason for her incredulity ('Ce n'est point par cette raison-là, repartit Angélique, mais c'est à cause que l'on a toûjours de la peine à croire une chose que l'on a beaucoup desirée' (I. 18)). L'Étoile thus queries Le Destin's reliability as a narrator, although the reader is presumably led to infer her modesty rather than his inaccuracy. In contrast to the Chevalier's narration in *Manon Lescaut*, Le Destin's idealized account of his beloved is supported by a considerable amount of external corroboration; L'Étoile is indeed introduced by the narrator with similar hyperbole: 'il n'avoit pas au monde de fille plus modeste et d'une humeur plus douce' (I. 8).

In contrast to these connective interpolations, the *nouvelles*, like the *jeu de paume*, form part of the public entertainment on offer at the inn, which consequently is represented as a place of recreation rather than rest. The apparent gratuitousness of these stories paradoxically renders them indispensable to the construction of the *Roman comique*: like the burlesque episodes in which Ragotin features so prominently, they divert the narrative away from its romanesque *telos*. In this respect the disconnective interpolation provides the narrative equivalent of an inn for the reader, allowing a pause or rest from the progress of the protagonists; for the protagonists themselves, it mimics the location in which it is generally told, fulfilling the innlike function of providing a distracting break from their own troubled adventures. The topographical role of the inn thus provides direct parallels to the topological function of an interpolation.

Given that one of the *nouvelles* and one of the troupe's narrations are not told at an inn, it would appear that the inn in the *Roman comique* is not unique in the opportunities for storytelling it provides. The two interpolations in question are nevertheless incorporated according to the pattern established at the inn: the home of 'un des plus riches Bourgeois de la ville' (I. 19) provides the setting for both public and private narrations, and, although it is not clear precisely where the former of these is told,[42] the latter, La Caverne's story, is delivered in the privacy of the actresses' temporary bedroom. Both are related in circumstances that approximate to the environment offered by the inn; even when the inn does not provide the venue for storytelling in the *Roman comique*, it thus provides a model for the location that replaces it. Although they take place elsewhere, the narrations told by Inézilla and La Caverne nevertheless demonstrate why the inn is indispensable to the incorporation of internal narrations in the comic fiction of the seventeenth and eighteenth centuries. 'A Trompeur, trompeur et demi' is generated by the sociability of the *Biche* even though it is told in a house outside Le Mans, while La Caverne's interpolation springs from the new intimacy (signalled by Le Destin's story) that materializes between the actresses and Le Destin at the *Biche*.

The unnamed Bourgeois's house—'une maison des plus belles du païs' (I. 19)—may seem more appropriate than the inn to a story set for the most part in the equally private household of a baron's chateau, particularly given the parallels to be drawn between the situation La Caverne narrates and the present context in which it is narrated. The presence of one troupe at the Baron de Signognac's castle is, for example, evidently complemented by the presence of another in the Bourgeois's home, while the disappearance of Angélique in the present echoes that of La Caverne's brother in the past. What is perhaps more interesting, however, is how innlike the Bourgeois's house proves to be; the privacy that one might have expected relative to a public house does not in fact materialize, and La Caverne's story, like Le Destin's narration in the *Biche*, is subject to a comic interruption. While Le Destin is interrupted by the lowly Ragotin, La Caverne's account is halted by a lowly dog, whom the actresses at first fear to be a ghost. The nature of this incident provides further evidence of the marked influence of the *Quijote* on the *Roman comique*. Don Quijote is, as we saw in the previous chapter, plagued by a series of burlesque nocturnal encounters and misadventures; at Palomeque's inn one of these moreover leads Sancho to suspect the presence of the supernatural in his sleeping quarters (in the guise of the 'encantado moro'), while in a bedroom at the ducal castle his master is subject to an animal intrusion when he is mauled by cats.[43]

Town and Country, Burlesque and Romanesque

Ragotin's often violent catastrophes in and around the *Biche* emphasize the fact that the inn belongs to his burlesque world rather than the romanesque world of Le Destin. The only episodes that actually occur there are burlesque in character, and romanesque incident enters only indirectly by interpolation. This is clearly not the case in the *Quijote*— the romanesque narrative of Cardenio and Dorotea unfolds in the inn and is finally resolved there. By contrast, the plotting of the romanesque storyline of the *Roman comique* is confined entirely to the world outside the *Biche*; Henri Bénac's remark that 'depuis *Don Quichotte* et le roman picaresque, l'auberge était un décor international où se déroulait l'aventure' is therefore slightly misleading.[44] As the centre of storytelling in the *Roman comique*, the inn contrasts with the route that leads there: the road, and the open country to which it provides access, are never used as interpolatory frames, and serve exclusively as a setting for adventures rather than storytelling.

The *Biche* is insulated from romanesque incident in part by its location in a town rather than on the wayside of a country road; furthermore, in contrast to the relatively exotic locations of Le Destin's narration and of the *nouvelles*, Le Mans is a provincial town that is recognizably part of the actual world inhabited by Scarron's contemporary readership. When the troupe leaves the inn for other locations in Le Mans, no romanesque adventures occur—the actors return unscathed, for example, from their rehearsal at another inn in the town. During their brief stay at La Rappinière's home, the inn once again provides the model for a private household, as another burlesque nocturnal encounter with an animal is introduced: with the discovery of a goat, 'toute la maison fut en rumeur' (I. 4).[45] It is only when the troupe leaves Le Mans entirely that the opportunity for romanesque events arises.[46] With each excursion from the town the main romanesque storyline progresses another stage: after the 'brancards' episode, in which Le Destin narrowly misses meeting Saldagne, comes the latter's abduction of the Curé de Domfront (and the consequent encounter between Le Destin and one of Saldagne's minions). The Curé is accosted by Saldagne's men 'à une lieu et demie de la ville [...] dans un chemin creux' (I. 14), indicating that one does not have to stray far from the town for the door to the romanesque to be opened. This is confirmed by the fact that the troupe's next venture from Le Mans, which ends with the highly romanesque

abduction of Angélique, is set at only 'une lieu de la ville, je n'ay pas
bien sceu de quel costé' (I. 19) at the Bourgeois's house. The
specificity of the town thus gives way in the latter case to deliberate
imprecision—this self-conscious adoption of geographical vagueness,
which, as we have seen, heralds the imminent approach of a decisive
stage in the romanesque plot of Scarron's narrative. The door to
romanesque adventures is in fact opened in literal as well as
metaphorical terms at the Bourgeois's home, as Angélique explains:

> Vous vous pouvez bien figurer quelle fut la surprise de ma mere et de moy,
> lors-que, nous promenant dans le Parc de la maison où nous estions, nous en
> vismes ouvrir une petite porte qui donnoit dans la campagne et entrer par là
> cinq ou six hommes qui se saisirent de moy sans presque regarder ma mere et
> m'emporterent demy-morte de frayeur jusqu'auprez de leurs chevaux. (II. 11)

The *Biche* resembles Palomeque's inn in the *Quijote* in that it
functions more like a home to its new arrivals than a hostelry, and this
derives in part from the type of journey the troupe has undertaken.
As we have already seen, the romanesque storyline of the *Roman
comique* demonstrates a clear teleology; the same cannot be said,
however, of the troupe's physical progress. While the *telos* of the plot
implies a journey that will end, the movements of Le Destin and his
company are not consciously driven by their pursuit of such an end
(or of such an ending). The slowness of their progress, as noted above,
would only inadvertently accelerate the conclusion of the narrative
given that, even if the members of the troupe are not the actors they
seem to be, they do take to the road in order to perform: they do not
travel in order finally to arrive, and any ultimate destination is
therefore irrelevant to them. As the stops on the journey are its *raison
d'être*, and as the troupe is presumed to stay for approximately four or
five days in most towns (as they originally aim to stay in Le Mans), it
follows that a little more than simply overnight accommodation is
required. The *Biche* thus provides a home base for the actors,
somewhere for them to eat, sleep, perform and, perhaps most
significantly, tell stories; although it proves unable to insulate
interpolations from interruption, its relative security makes it a logical
setting for the insertion of internal narrations.

Le Destin's excursions from the inn—in particular his pursuit of
Angélique's abductors and subsequent rescue of L'Étoile—bring the
Roman comique close to that which Frank Pierce describes as the
'circular pattern' and Edwin Williamson as the 'cyclical crises' of the

Amadís—a design as noted earlier emulated by the *Quijote*.[47] The *Roman comique* comprises a series of journeys that begin and end at the *Biche*, and Le Destin's previously noted resemblance to a knight errant thus extends to his movements: his trips from the inn represent a modern, gently parodic counterpart to the sallies of a knight errant from his castle. The narrative circularity that the *ordo artificialis* elicits is thus reflected in the spatial circularity of the hero's journeys from the inn in Le Mans. Like those undertaken by Amadís and Don Quijote, each of Le Destin's sallies covers more ground than the last, with his last sally occupying almost all of the second part of the *Roman comique*. This is significant because, the further Le Destin travels from Le Mans, the further he enters into the realm of romance.

Rather like Don Quijote, whose entry into the Sierra Morena marks the introduction of romanesque elements to the narrative, Le Destin abandons the ordinary, quotidian road for the winding, uncertain paths of romance in his pursuit of Angélique; once again, however, there is a parodic component to these trails through the countryside, as they produce adventures that amount to rather less than Le Destin might have envisaged. When he trusts to chance—as all knights errant should—he encounters a madman with none of Orlando's heroic stature:

il enfila au hazard un chemin creux, comme le sont la plupart de ceux de Mayne [...] Il maudissoit interieurement un si mechant chemin quand il se sentit sauter en croupe quelque homme ou quelque Diable qui luy passa les bras à l'entour du col [...] La Lune luisoit alors assez pour luy faire veoir qu'il avoit un grand homme nud en croupe et un vilain visage auprés du sien. (II. 1)

The topographical specificity of the town is not entirely left behind, as Scarron provides a deflatory local detail concerning the path chosen by Le Destin—the second 'chemin creux' of the *Roman comique*. Although Le Destin's meeting with a village idiot is hardly the material of romance, he notably retains a greater degree of dignity than Ragotin achieves upon his typically catastrophic encounter with the same character later in the narrative. The episode furthermore ends on a note that is perhaps less overtly anti-romanesque than it is self-consciously romanesque: 'il suffit que vous sçachiez qu'il s'égara dans un bois et que, tantost ne voyant goutte et tantost estant éclairé de la Lune, il trouva le jour auprés d'une Metairie où il jugea à propos de faire repaistre son cheval et où nous le laisserons' (II. 1). The 'bois' or wood is a uniquely romanesque *topos* as it is employed in the *Roman comique*; this is indeed implied by an authorial aside in the 'Histoire de l'amante invisible', in which Scarron distinguishes himself from 'quelques faiseurs de Romans' who implausibly have their heroes tell their stories all day and 'apres disner reprendre leur Histoire ou s'enfoncer dans un bois pour y parler tous seuls' (I. 9). Another wood provides yet another romanesque marker at a decisive stage in Angélique's abduction when 'l'entrée d'un bois' (II. 11) is the scene of a second *enlèvement*, namely that of L'Étoile.

Having spent a night outdoors, the following day Le Destin 'trouva une assez bonne hostellerie, parce qu'elle estoit sur le grand chemin' (II. 4), and thus returns from the open country of romance to the burlesque inn, in which he is reunited with Léandre. As if to demonstrate the fundamental incompatibility of the inn and the romanesque in the *Roman comique*, when Le Destin and L'Étoile manage to trick their pursecutors into taking them to an inn, the romanesque threat is temporarily averted as Saldagne's men drink themselves unconscious, thereby allowing the two lovers to escape. The denouement of the abduction plot nevertheless marks a unique occasion in the *Roman comique* in that it constitutes a romanesque incident in an inn. This unnamed inn performs a different function from the 'home from home' of the *tripot* in Le Mans: it is linked to the open road, not the town, and in the *Roman comique* this brings it into the realm of chance and of romanesque adventures. The evolution from the burlesque to the romanesque that Serroy observes in the novel is thus accompanied by a transition from one kind of inn to another.

The Reader and the *Roman comique*

If the *Roman comique* is incomplete, it is not because it lacks a (classical) *telos* but because its author was not sufficiently committed to its execution. Scarron is not alone in this regard, for the same may be said of a considerable proportion of French prose fiction in the seventeenth and eighteenth centuries—including, of course, the novels of Marivaux. Rousset remarks that the *Roman comique* exhibits 'une macédoine très éloignée de l'uniformité de style tenue pour "classique"', and adds, 'c'est cependant au XVIIe siècle que triomphe ce système des multiples détenteurs de la narration'.[48] This impression is reinforced by the burlesque episodes and disconnective inter-polations that defer (endlessly, in the extant version) the resolution of the narrative. Scarron's text evidently lacks the unity of action and the uniformity of tone prescribed by classical and neoclassical poetics. The issue of unity in the *Roman comique* continues to be contentious, with debate focusing primarily on the intercalated *nouvelles*. Muratore claims to speak for the majority of readers when she asserts, 'the embedded fictions appear to the reader as intrusive supplements inserted to frustrate the reader's progress and break his concentration'. She refers to 'real readers'—a category that is presumably intended to exclude critics—who

find the tales not only excessively long, but more significantly, textually irrelevant. The fact that the chapters in which they are contained are the book's longest makes them appear even more tedious than they actually are [...] Readers labour in vain to uncover a connecting thread that might fuse inner and outer fictions [...] They discover only a trivial diversion that the main narrator has thrust deliberately in their path to slow the novel's progress towards closure.[49]

This image of the impatient reader is not new: Du Plaisir, for example, wrote in 1683, 'Nous haïssons tout ce qui s'oppose à notre curiosité; nous voudrions presque commencer la lecture d'un volume par la fin.'[50]

Although she never states so explicitly, Muratore presumably finds the Spanish tales as 'excessively long' and 'textually irrelevant' as her alleged readers. She would certainly not be alone in doing so, for, as we have already seen, the *Quijote*'s use of interpolation has attracted similar criticism. Furthermore, both *Joseph Andrews* and *Tom Jones* have also, from the time of their publication to the present day, continued to attract criticism that one might loosely describe as classically inflected. J. Paul Hunter, for example, observes with some justification that critics have tended to try too hard to reconcile the interpolations in *Joseph Andrews* to the concept of unity, and that 'critical haste to justify them has simplified their contributions in such a way that they remain, on balance, defects'.[51] Like Muratore (or her reader), Hunter disparages Fielding's deviations from unity as 'boring' and 'soporific' and asserts that, along with Joseph and Fanny, 'many readers [...] tend to doze off'[52] during Wilson's autobiographical story; he seems, therefore, to take Fielding's suggestion that his digressions are places of rest a little too literally.

Muratore justifiably argues that, of the several attempts to bridge the gap between the *nouvelles* and the rest of the *Roman comique*, 'none

are [*sic*] wholly convincing'.[53] Such efforts include the most ex-
haustive (indeed exhausting) defence by Frederick de Armas, whose
conclusions are characterized by such vague pronouncements as 'the
first part of the *Roman comique* can then be seen as a work dealing with
attitudes toward love' and that 'the *Roman comique*, then, is a work
unified by the ideas of love and justice'.[54] While this may well be true,
it is too vague to be of any interest, given, as in fact Aristotle
insisted,[55] that thematic unity does not equate to structural unity—
one could, for example, argue that any pile of books on the same
subject was thematically unified. While there are certainly
correspondences between the *nouvelles* and the rest of the narrative,
these should not diminish our awareness of the formal separateness of
these stories. Muratore may well be correct in her assumption that
most readers today find the *nouvelles* irrelevant or tedious, but she is
clearly mistaken in her assumption that this demonstrates a failing in
the text itself. All she has demonstrated is the classical 'baggage' these
readers bring to the text. She, moreover, dubiously assumes that
models of reading have not changed since the seventeenth century,
and that twentieth-century readers approach the *Roman comique* with
the same values as those of Scarron's contemporaries.

Other critics have conversely suggested that the *Roman comique*
should not be judged according to classical poetics and have offered
alternative aesthetic criteria: Joan DeJean, for example, writes that 'all
of the so-called compositional weaknesses and peculiarities of the
Roman comique can also be viewed as strengths when re-examined
from the perspective of Menippean satire'[56] and Barbara Merry has
indeed further explored the Menippean aspect of Scarron's text.
Henri Coulet, on the other hand, has suggested that 'ces prétendus
défauts sont des qualités si l'on adopte l'esthétique baroque'.[57] That
the *Roman comique* may be regarded by one critic as a Menippean
satire and another as a baroque novel arguably indicates that neither
category is categorical enough.[58] Both of these terms moreover have
themselves been the subject of controversy over recent years. Both
DeJean and Coulet have at least shown, however, that alternative
criteria for the critical assessment of a work of literature do exist and
may productively be applied, although neither appears to question
why the disconnective interpolations in the *Roman comique* have
persistently attracted such evaluative and normative criticism.

Muratore admits that the 'unsuccessful merger between primary
and secondary narratives appears to be the result of authorial design';[59]

she thus rather oddly suggests that Scarron deliberately failed in his attempt to fuse frame and interpolation, when there is no evidence of any attempt on his part to execute such a merger. The duality of the *Roman comique* extends beyond the binary oppositions Serroy delineates, and its form very clearly suggests a tension between two conflicting aesthetics. As we have already seen, the classically tinged criticism that the interpolation of *nouvelles* tends to attract offers a constrictive, incomplete view of the text in which Ragotin and the *nouvelles* appear as flaws. The alternative aesthetic criteria DeJean or Merry apply inevitably also suffer from limitations of their own: if viewing the *Roman comique* as a baroque or Menippean text turns its weaknesses into strengths, it is not entirely facetious to ask whether it also turns its strengths into weaknesses or, at the very least, diminishes our appreciation of them. Among these classical strengths one might, for example, include the *ordo artificialis* plot arrangement, while the intercalation of the *nouvelles* that interrupt its progress might be regarded as a Menippean or baroque strength. As this apparently contradictory combination of narrative materials suggests, the *Roman comique* cannot adequately be located within a single aesthetic. It is a text that seems truly of its time in that it reflects the tension between the emerging neoclassicism, with its emphasis on unity, and the continuing influence of a prior aesthetic of diversity and variety that previously dominated a variety of genres (from the many forms of romance to the framing fictions in the tradition of Boccacio) but that is not so easily named. It is this difficulty of appellation that arguably induces critics to invoke such terms as Menippean satire or, in the context of the seventeenth century, the baroque.

The *Roman comique* shows that the rise of one aesthetic does not necessarily imply the immediate fall of another; with its incomplete plot execution, Scarron's work appears to look towards neoclassicism without wholly wishing to embrace it. The *Roman comique* is not alone in this respect, for the insertion of disconnective interpolations within teleological narratives endures well into the eighteenth century, as one may see from the practice of such popular novelists as Lesage, Marivaux and Fielding. This phenomenon suggests that an older model of reading survives alongside its neoclassical counterpart far longer than is generally recognized. Parish indeed argues that, in the case of the *Roman comique*, 'the interplay of the different strands of the novel, by frustrating any desire to proceed rapidly towards a conclusion, promotes a non-progressive reading pleasure'.[60] While this desire for resolution remains in an attenuated form, Scarron's novel (in common with the others examined in these pages) repeatedly diverts the reader's attention away from the narrative *telos*. One might also suggest, however, that this approach may reflect as well as promote the 'non-progressive reading pleasure' of Scarron's contemporary readers: the text may, in other words, be an effect rather than a cause of reading practices in the mid-seventeenth century. Muratore's frustrated 'real reader' is distinctly modern, and ill-suited to the kind of reading experience offered by a digressive text such as the *Roman comique*.

Notes to Chapter 3

1. P. E. Russell, *Cervantes* (Oxford: Oxford University Press, 1985), 32.
2. Henri Chardon, *Scarron inconnu et les types des personnages du 'Roman comique'* (Paris: Champion, 1903), 221.
3. Ibid. 193. The *Biche* is described in a bill of sale dated 1 October 1612: 'Une maison manable, composée de salle basse, cave voûtée dessous, cuisine au côté, chambres haultes sur la dicte salle et cuisine, grenier dessus et monté pour exploitation;—*item* un autre petit corps de logis y joignant, composé de deux chambres basses à cheminées, avecque le jeu de courte paulme par darrière, couvert de bardeau et toutes les issues et commodités d'icelle maison et jeu de paulme qui en dépend.' By the time of the *Roman comique*, however, 'la *Biche* fut de bonne heure partagée en deux moitiés, dont l'une fit dès lors partie de la maison voisine' (ibid. 196, 198).
4. Quotations are from the Pléiade edition of Paul Scarron, *Le Romant comique*, published in *Romanciers du XVIIe siècle*, ed. Antoine Adam (Paris: Gallimard, 1958), 531–797. References are to part and chapter. Characters' names have been modernized throughout.
5. Jean Serroy, *Roman et réalité: Les Histoires comiques au XVIIe siècle* (Grenoble: Presses Universitaires de Grenoble, 1980), 446.
6. See below, 'Bedtime Stories'.
7. Jacques Morel, 'La Composition du *Roman comique*', *L'Information littéraire*, 5 (1970), 212–17 (215–16).
8. Barbara Merry, *Menippean Elements in Paul Scarron's 'Roman comique'* (New York: Peter Lang, 1991), 43–4.
9. Chardon, *Scarron inconnu*, 264, 257.
10. The *Aethiopica*, via Jacques Amyot's French translation of 1547, was in this regard a hugely influential model of narrative construction in the seventeenth century; Scarron's contemporary Sorel, who followed this model of *ordo artificialis* in his *Francion*, criticizes the poor practitioners of this technique in his treatise on literature *De la connoissance des bons livres*: 'pour commencer une Histoire de cette maniere, il faut que cela se fasse avec ordre, & que l'on descouvre petit à petit qui sont ceux dont l'on veut raconter les avantures. C'est à faux qu'ils se vantent d'imiter l'Histoire Ethiopique d'Heliodore' (Paris: André Pralard, 1671), 123. In *Le Berger extravagant*, the deluded Lysis remarks, 'Il faut que mon histoire commence par le milieu [...] c'est ainsi que sont les plus celebres Romans'), and

Clarimond, Sorel's mouthpiece in the same work, cites Heliodorus as an example of a well-executed *in medias res* opening, and refers to 'l'histoire Æthiopienne que tant d'autres ont prise pour patron' (*Le Berger extravagant*, 3 vols. (Rouen, 1640 edn.), ii. 134, 135). For a discussion of the impact of Amyot's Heliodorus on narrative order in the sixteenth and seventeeenth centuries, see Terence Cave, 'Suspense and the Pre-History of the Novel', *Revue de littérature comparée*, 70 (1996), 507–16. See also A. D. Nuttall, *Openings: Narrative Beginnings from the Epic to the Novel* (Oxford: Clarendon Press, 1992), 31–2.

11. This, for example, is the view of Richard Parish: 'we have little or no impression of the *récit cadre* having any sense of impetus towards a resolution [...] The incompleteness of the *Roman comique* is not just contingent, therefore, it is definitional. The 'nonteleological' writing and the deliberate tone of unfinality with which it ends (irrespective of any putative third book) all point to the business of completion as an irrelevance' (*Scarron: 'Le Roman comique'* (London: Grant & Cutler, 1998), 103).

12. Merry, *Menippean Elements*, 121, 33.

13. Except in the notable exception of Juan Díaz's contribution to the *Amadís* series, the eighth book, in which the author kills off the hero—an act that Henry Thomas humorously describes as the 'most unpardonable offence of all'. As Thomas also notes, the author of the following volume 'will not hear of the death of Amadís' and carries on regardless (*The Romance of 'Amadís of Gaul'* (Oxford: Bibliographical Society, 1912), 265, 266).

14. Parish accurately notes, however, that, 'in the cases of Ragotin, Roquebrune, and later and most strikingly, La Garouffière, the names are introduced after the characters, seeming to suggest that types are more important than individuals' (*Scarron*, 40); thus even La Rappinière's identity is subject to a small degree of 'delayed decoding'.

15. Parish, *Scarron*, 30.

16. Lyall H. Powers, 'Tom Jones and Jacob de la Vallée', *Papers of the Michigan Academy of Science, Arts, and Letters*, 47 (1962), 659–67.

17. Fielding, however, may well have known Scarron through the highly popular translation by Tom Brown and John Savage, published in 1700, and reprinted five times before 1760.

18. Robert Garapon, 'Les Préparations dans le *Roman comique* de Scarron', *Actes du colloque Renaissance-classicisme du Maine, Le Mans 1971* (Paris: A.-G. Nizet, 1975), 11–18 (12).

19. By far the less probable of the two alternatives.

20. Garapon, 'Les Préparations', 16.

21. Where Le Destin arranges to meet Verville.

22. Garapon, 'Les Préparations', 18.

23. And consequently, a characteristically novelistic chronotope. See 'Discourse in the Novel', in Bakhtin, *The Dialogic Imagination*, particularly 260–75. Bakhtin argues that 'the style of a novel is to be found in the combination of its styles; the language of a novel is the system of its "languages" [...] Authorial speech, the speeches of narrators, inserted genres, the speech of characters are merely those fundamental compositional unities with whose help heteroglossia [*raznorecie*] can enter the novel; each of them permits a multiplicity of social voices and a wide variety of their links and interrelationships (always more or less dialogized).

These distinctive links and interrelationships between utterances and languages, this movement of the theme through different languages and speech types, its dispersion into the rivulets and droplets of social heteroglossia, its dialogization— this is the basic distinguishing feature of the stylistics of the novel' (*The Dialogic Imagination*, 262–3).

24. Parish, *Scarron*, 44.
25. Cf. the *hôtesse* of the *Grand Cerf* (and her admittedly distant prototype, the *Odyssey*'s Penelope).
26. 'Les Jeux de Paume abondaient au Mans dès le XVIe siècle' (Chardon, *Scarron inconnu*, 191).
27. Émile Magne, *Scarron et son milieu* (Paris: Émile-Paul, 1924), 52–3.
28. As Parish notes of the *Roman comique*, 'Drinking, as in Rabelais, leads to drunkenness' (*Scarron*, 39); see e.g. I. 10.
29. Note, for example, Tristram's rhetorical question, 'is a man to follow rules——or rules to follow him' (*TS* IV. 10).
30. Ragotin's serenade is the only interruption forced on Le Destin's story: the prior break in its narration is by contrast determined by Le Destin and his audience themselves, as they choose, given the lateness of the hour, to defer its conclusion until the next day.
31. Mary-Jo Muratore, *Mimesis and Metatextuality in the French Neo-Classical Text* (Geneva: Droz, 1994), 113. This is true of disconnective interpolations generally, see above, Ch. 1, 'Connective and Disconnective Interpolations'.
32. In his edition of the *Roman comique*, Magne notes, 'Pour Tallemant des Réaux, comédien était, au début du XVIIe siècle, synonyme de vaurien' (*Le Roman comique*, ed. Émile Magne (Paris: Garnier, 1973), 416). This perhaps oversimplifies the case, but Tallemant does recollect that, at this time, 'Il y avoit deux troupes alors à Paris; c'estoient presque tous filous, et leur femmes vivoient dans la plus grande licence du monde' (Gédéon Tallemant des Réaux, 'Mondory ou l'histoire des principaux comediens françois', in *Historiettes*, ed. Antoine Adam, 2 vols. (Paris: Gallimard, 1970), ii. 773).
33. Adam cites Leroux: 'On dit qu'un homme se fait tout blanc de son épée. C'est-à-dire qu'il se promet de faire bien de choses où souvent il ne peut réussir' (*Romanciers du XVIIe siècle*, 1425).
34. It is certainly possible, however, that La Caverne's narration would have been resumed in a subsequent part.
35. Jean Rousset, 'Insertions et interventions dans le *Roman Comique*', *l'Esprit créateur*, 11/2 (1971), 141–53 (144).
36. Ibid. 144.
37. Serroy, *Roman et réalité*, 466.
38. Charles Sorel, *Histoire comique de Francion*, in *Romanciers du XVIIe siècle*, ed. Antoine Adam (Paris: Gallimard, 1958), 183.
39. His dinner with Mme Bouvillon provides a similar example of the manner in which Scarron places his romanesque hero in unromanesque situations.
40. This citation is taken from the Pléiade edition of Pierre Carlet de Chamblain de Marivaux, *Pharsamon ou les Nouvelles Folies romanesques*, in *Marivaux: Œuvres de Jeunesse*, ed. Frédéric Deloffre (Paris: Gallimard, 1972), 393.
41. Rather as Montaigne describes in the *Essais* his childhood love of chivalric romance: 'Quant aux *Amadis* et telles sortes d'escrits, ils n'ont pas eu le credit

d'arrester seulement mon enfance [...] cette vieille ame poisante ne se laisse plus chatouiller, non seulement à l'Arioste, mais encores au bon Ovide, sa facilité et ses inventions, qui m'ont ravy autresfois, à peine m'entretiennent elles à cette heure' (*Essais*, ed. Maurice Rat, 2 vols. (Paris: Garnier, 1962), II. 10.

42. 'A Trompeur, trompeur et demi' arises directly from the encounter between the troupe (including the 'Operateur' and his wife) and La Garouffière, which takes place after dinner: 'On leur donna deux chambres pour mettre leurs hardes et pour se preparer en liberté à la Comedie, qui fut remise à la nuit. On les fit aussi disner en particulier et, aprés disner, ceux qui voulurent se promener eurent à choisir d'un grand bois et d'un beau jardin. Un jeune Conseiller du Parlement de Rennes, proche parent du maistre de la maison, accosta nos Comediens et s'arresta à faire conversation avec eux' (I. 21).

43. See above, Ch. 1, and *DQ* I. 17 and II. 46. It may furthermore be pertinent to note a similarity between the function of the troupe and that of Don Quijote and Sancho: the role of both is to entertain, although the knight and his squire are invited by the duke and duchess for the inadvertent comedy they provide their court while the troupe are solicited by the unnamed Bourgeois for their more deliberate, scripted form of entertainment. Ironically, the accidental theatre of Don Quijote is successful in its execution while the troupe's scripted form of theatre is aborted before it can even begin when Angélique is abducted.

44. In his edition of *Le Roman comique*, 2 vols. (Paris: Les Belles Lettres, 1951), i. 41.

45. The influence of the inn on this particular household is further underlined by the author's remark that La Rappinière 'mangeoit d'ordinaire au cabaret aux despens des sots' (I. 4) and is thus fed by a local inn rather than his own kitchen.

46. In Paris, however, La Rappinière had played a minor role in Le Destin's adventures with his robbery of the latter.

47. Frank Pierce, *Amadís de Gaula* (Boston: Twayne, 1976), 26; Edwin Williamson, *The Half-way House of Fiction: 'Don Quixote' and Arthurian Romance* (Oxford: Clarendon Press, 1984), 40.

48. Rousset, 'Insertions et interventions', 142.

49. Muratore, *Mimesis and Metatextuality*, 107.

50. L'abbé Du Plaisir, *Sentiments sur les lettres et l'histoire*, ed. Philippe Hourcade (Geneva: Droz, 1975), 44. Du Plaisir's remarks closely follow those of Valincour in his 1678 commentary on *La Princesse de Clèves*: 'L'esprit qui s'est fait un plaisir de voir la suite d'une histoire qui luy paroist agréable, se haste d'aller jusques au bout, et souffre avec impatience, et quelquefois mesme avec dégoust, tout ce qui le retarde dans sa course, et qui lui paroist étranger à ce qu'il cherche' (Valincour, *Lettres à Madame la Marquise *** sur le sujet de la Princesse de Clèves*, facsimile of the 1678 edn. (Tours: Université de Tours, 1972), 19).

51. J. Paul Hunter, *Occasional Form: Henry Fielding and the Chains of Circumstance* (Baltimore: Johns Hopkins University Press, 1975), 152.

52. Ibid. 156, 160.

53. Muratore, *Mimesis and Metatextuality*, 105, 107.

54. Frederick de Armas, *Paul Scarron* (New York: Twayne, 1972), 87, 91.

55. See above, Ch. 2 n. 54.

56. Joan DeJean, *Scarron's 'Roman comique': A Comedy of the Novel, a Novel of Comedy* (Bern: Peter Lang, 1977), 95.

57. Henri Coulet, *Le Roman jusqu'à la Révolution* (Paris: Armand Colin, 1967), 207.

58. Merry indeed admits that Menippean satire is 'a literary tradition that is most often used to describe prose works that resist classification' (Merry, *Menippean Elements*, 3).

59. Muratore, *Mimesis and Metatextuality*, 105.

60. Parish, *Scarron*, 101. Daniel Javitch makes a similar argument for the interruptive interweaving of the *Furioso* ('*Cantus interruptus* in the *Orlando furioso*', *MLN* 95 (1980), 66–80). See below, Ch. 7 n. 50.

CHAPTER 4

Fielding I
The Topography of Travel

James Boswell noted of Samuel Johnson, 'If (said he) I had not duties [...] I would spend my life driving briskly in a post-chaise with a pretty woman; but she should be one who could understand me, and would add something to the conversation.'[1] In both *Joseph Andrews* and *Tom Jones*, however, travel is categorically presented as a trial rather than a pleasure. In contrast to the knight of chivalric romance, or indeed of the *Quijote*, few of Fielding's characters in these works leave the comfort and security of their home for the uncertainties of the road unless they are obliged to do so—uncertainties that remain even in the comparatively modern world of turnpikes and coaching inns.[2] A number of characters, including of course the eponymous heroes themselves, are in fact punished for alleged malfeasance by expulsion from their community or employment. Partridge and Jenny Jones set an early example for their alleged son in this regard when they are (unfairly) banished from Allworthy's parish. Ironically, while Partridge and Jenny Jones are punished for an assumed sexual transgression, Joseph is dismissed for his failure so to transgress. Joseph, of course, is banished from his place of work rather than his home; his homeward journey, with all the obstacles and impediments it entails, evidently brings him closer than Tom to an Odyssean model. Joseph still has a home to which he may return; part of Tom's aimlessness when he first takes to the road derives from the fact that his home exists not at the end of a road but in his future. Tom must venture into the world in order to regain the possibility of a future home; in contrast to Joseph, he must choose his own path and his own destination—choices that initially seem irrelevant given that it can only lead him away from his ultimate goal. Tom's initial projects, such as taking to the sea or joining the army, seem to be intended primarily as means of passing the time until he may once again return home. In this respect, Tom is closer to a chivalresque model than Joseph, keenly pursuing adventures rather than involuntarily being plagued by them.

Domesticity and the Road

The domestic sphere frames the journeys of both Joseph Andrews and Tom Jones. The intended parody of *Pamela* in *Joseph Andrews* evidently demands that the hero be initially placed in a household analogous to that of his alleged sister, Pamela. Joseph's rejection of his mistress, and her consequent dismissal of him, reflect the gulf between the narrative interests of Fielding and Richardson. Whereas the *Quijote* outgrows its original parodic function but maintains throughout the structure this function necessitated, *Joseph Andrews* breaks dramatically from all that its target text presents and represents. The domestic sphere in which Richardson operates is too confined for Fielding: it is, as Nancy Armstrong argues, a 'specifically feminine space'[3] in the seventeenth and eighteenth centuries, the counterpart to the public, male, space that dominates most of Fielding's fiction. This sphere is also, it should be added, too restrictive for many of Fielding's female characters, including the heroines of *Joseph Andrews* and *Tom Jones*. The roads travelled by Joseph and Tom are far from being exclusively male, as the examples of Fanny, Sophia, Mrs Waters and Mrs Fitzpatrick illustrate. While the road proves potentially dangerous to women (as, for example, Northerton's attack on Mrs Waters demonstrates), it is hardly any safer for the men—Joseph, after all, is brutally attacked almost as soon as he has begun his journey. Although a degree of male protection often seems prudent in Fielding's fiction for women travelling alone, it should be noted that male over-protectiveness more than once provides the incentive for women to take to the road in the first place: for Sophia and Mrs Fitzpatrick, the road provides an escape from the father and husband who have respectively sought to impose intolerable domestic situations upon them.

The marked differences between the worlds inhabited by the heroines of *Pamela* and *Clarissa* and the women of *Joseph Andrews* and *Tom Jones* amply illustrate the distinctive concerns of their authors. Ian Watt reveals that Richardson, in a letter to Miss Westcomb, 'contrasts the "goose-like gabble" of social conversation with the delights of epistolary intercourse for the lady who makes "her closet her paradise". His heroines do not and cannot share the life of the street, the highways and the places of public resort with Defoe's Moll Flanders and even Fielding's Miss Western'.[4] Richardson indeed, as Watt notes, describes the heroine of *Tom Jones* with evident indignation as 'inn-frequenting Sophia'.[5]

The contrast in the worlds evoked by Richardson and Fielding echoes closely the distinctions offered in conduct books between the roles of men and women; in an early seventeenth-century Puritan marriage pamphlet entitled *A Godly Forme of Householde Gouernment*, the following divisions are made: while the husband is urged to 'Travel, seek a living [...] Deal with many men [...] Be entertaining [...] Dispatch all things outdoors', the wife is advised that her role is to 'Keep the house [...] Talk with few [...] Be solitary and withdrawn [...] Oversee and give order within'.[6] Fielding's heroes, and the narrators who tell their stories, resemble the Puritan husband as strikingly as their female counterparts in Richardson seek to imitate the example of his Puritan wife. Indeed, the authorial personalities that infuse the contrasting approaches of Richardson and Fielding suggest that our two authors might themselves have made a highly complementary married couple. It is, therefore, particularly apt that, as William Warner suggests, a 'fable of origins' long established in novelistic and critical practice has placed Richardson and Fielding in the role of parents of the English novel: 'This fable casts Richardson and Fielding as the first coherent, self-conscious practitioners of what would become the modern novel, as rival inventors of two diametrically opposed, yet complementary types of novelistic writing, one that explores psychic depths, and another that narrates the diverse forms of the social: in short, as the two fathers of the novel.'[7] Although Warner's position that this 'double paternity' for the novel is a fable rather than a true story may be contentious in some quarters, the opposition in the narrative approaches of Richardson and Fielding conversely seems relatively uncontroversial. While, as Watt remarks, the drama in Richardson 'unrolls in a flow of letters from one lonely closet to another' and 'an opening door threatens some new violation of a cherished privacy',[8] in Fielding there is a strong sense in which the adventures truly begin only once the heroes have left their respective households. The opening door that promises danger for Richardson's heroines promises freedom and adventure for those who take to the road in *Joseph Andrews* and *Tom Jones*. As Warner suggests above, however, there remains a reductive tendency in much of the criticism of eighteenth–century fiction to present the worlds

represented by Richardson and Fielding as being diametrically
opposed.

The view that the Richardson–Fielding relationship may be represented in terms of the contrasting indoor/outdoor arenas in which they
ostensibly operate is suggested by Coleridge's expression of his preference for Fielding: 'To take him up after Richardson is like emerging
from a sick room heated by stoves into an open lawn on a breezy day
in May.'[9] Watt, who would evidently disagree with Coleridge, nevertheless formulates his comparison of these two authors in terms of a
similarly spatially conceived contrast when he argues that Fielding's
fiction, 'far from being an intimate drama which we peep at through a
keyhole, is a series of reminiscences told by a genial raconteur in some
wayside inn—the favoured public locus of his tale'.[10] It is easy to forget,
however, the amount of time one actually spends in domestic settings
in both *Joseph Andrews* and *Tom Jones*. While Joseph is ejected from Lady
Booby's household after only nine chapters, Tom spends the first third
of his narrative, and by far the longest span of time, happily settled in
Paradise Hall. The journeys undertaken by Joseph and Tom moreover
end, as they begin, in the domestic sphere; it should nevertheless be
added that *Joseph Andrews* and *Tom Jones* both end as soon as the two
heroes are established in their new domestic situations. The return home
provides little more than the requisite formulaic closure to Fielding's
two narratives; as stated earlier, the domestic sphere provides a frame
rather than the unique setting for the adventures of Joseph and Tom.
Richardson's *Pamela* conversely continues long after the marriage
between Pamela and Mr B. with the much-ignored second part of 1741.

While Richardson's *Pamela* almost entirely isolates the household
from the world outside, Fielding's representations of domesticity
characteristically invest the home with openness and instability. In
Joseph Andrews this openness soon manifests itself in the two-way
traffic of the 'downstairs' life of the Booby's residence. Adams first
appears 'drinking a Cup of Ale in Sir *Thomas's* Kitchin' (*JA* I. 2);[11] we
later learn that Lady Booby did not think the parson's 'Dress good
enough for the Gentry at her Table' (*JA* II. 8). The kitchen—of both
private homes and public inns—proves to be Adams's natural habitat:
when the stagecoach in which he is travelling makes a brief stop at an
unnamed inn he, 'as was his Custom, made directly to the Kitchin'
(*JA* II. 5). As the domain to which servants (except in the course of
their duties) are normally confined, the modest Fanny is not
comfortable anywhere else, and therefore refuses the invitation to eat

at the Squire's own table (*JA* III. 7). Conversely, other characters reveal their social aspirations by their desire to be promoted from kitchen to parlour: at Mrs Whitefield's dinner table in *Tom Jones*, a guest who 'stiled himself a Lawyer, but was indeed a most vile Petty-fogger',[12] is observed to have 'often visited in [Allworthy's] Kitchin': 'He therefore took Occasion to enquire after the good Family there, with that Familiarity which would have become an intimate Friend or Acquaintance of Mr. *Allworthy*; and indeed he did all in his Power to insinuate himself to be such, though he had never had the Honour of speaking to any Person in that Family higher than the Butler' (*TJ* VIII. 8). The kitchen provides an interface with the world outside, an intermediary space between private and public spheres that is neither entirely private nor entirely public. The door is open for guests such as Adams to enter—as long as they do not displease their host (as indeed Adams does, with the result that Lady Booby warns, 'my Doors will no longer be open to you' (*JA* IV. 2)). It is also open for servants to be dismissed, as Joseph learns to his cost.

The influence of the journey motif in *Joseph Andrews* appears to extend beyond the hero's *nostos* and into the domestic frame that ostensibly contains it. The Booby and Adams households succeed the inns of the preceding journey in more ways than one might expect. Aside from providing accommodation for the homecoming travellers, they take on many of the characteristics one would normally associate with the comic tradition of fictionalized inns: they provide the setting for two fights (both of which feature Beau Didapper), and for '*curious Night-Adventures*' (*JA* IV. 14) of the kind one sees in inns from the *Quijote* to the *Pickwick Papers*[13]—including, of course, the inn at Upton in *Tom Jones*. A private house rather than an inn moreover provides a location for storytelling in *Joseph Andrews*, with the tale of Leonard and Paul told at Adams's house.

The two country households represented in *Tom Jones* (those of Allworthy and Western) extend the rudimentary courtesies offered to Adams by the Boobys to almost inn- or almslike proportions.[14] While Western's home is particularly welcoming to those, like Parson Supple, who share at least one of the host's two main interests—drinking and hunting—Allworthy is described as a model of hospitality, providing his guests with a highly inviting 'eleemosynary Abode' (*TJ* I. 10): 'Neither Mr *Allworthy*'s House, nor his Heart, were shut against any Part of Mankind, but they were both more particularly open to Men of Merit. To say the Truth, this was the only

House in the Kingdom where you was sure to gain a Dinner by deserving it' (*TJ* I. 10). While the alcohol-fuelled entertainment on offer at Western's home duplicates to some degree the appeal of an inn, Allworthy's generosity has a chivalric or even courtly quality: his house is transformed into a modern version of the castle *topos*, providing a haven for these alleged 'Men of Merit'. The problem, of course, is that such men are harder to find in Allworthy's Somerset than they appear to be in the realms of chivalric romance. With the exception of his adopted son, none of those to whom Allworthy extends his generosity proves worthy of it. Neither the Blifil brothers nor Thwackum and Square demonstrate any 'Merit' whatsoever; Tom, with 'some Heroic Ingredients in his Composition' (*TJ* VII. 11), is the only member of the household with the innate nobility Allworthy's courtly model demands, and is ironically the first to be banished by his benefactor.

Fielding and the Romanesque Landscape

The appearance of merit rather than merit itself ensures Allworthy's hospitality, and Tom's status in the Allworthy household is thus never entirely secure. In both *Joseph Andrews* and *Tom Jones*, Fielding creates insecure domestic situations for his heroes, which in turn provoke the journeys central to each narrative. While Adams's naivety has traditionally led to him being identified as a Quixotic figure, one could argue that Tom also has more in common than one might expect with Cervantes's knight. Fielding's narrator occasionally presents the young hero with such ironic distance that the reader is unsure whether or not Tom is implicated by the parodic re-creation of romance motifs. The famous '*Battle sung by the Muse in the* Homerican *Stile*', which the narrator asserts '*none but the classical Reader can taste*' (*TJ* IV. 8), actually concludes with a *clin d'œil* to the reader of romances and anti-romances:

Having scoured the whole Coast of the Enemy, as well as *Homer's* Heroes ever did, or as *Don Quixote*, or any other Knight-Errant in the World could have done, he [Tom] returned to *Molly*, whom he found in a Condition, which must give both me and my Reader Pain, were it to be described here. *Tom* raved like a Madman, beat his Breast, tore his Hair, stamped on the Ground, and vowed the utmost Vengeance on all who had been concerned. (*TJ* IV. 8)

One may reasonably ask the same question of Tom that was posed in the previous chapter regarding Scarron's Le Destin: is he an Orlando or a Quijote here? The same doubts are raised by the manner in which Tom's reaction to his banishment is narrated: upon leaving the house, Tom immediately (and conveniently) finds 'a little Brook' beside which 'he threw himself down [...] Here he presently fell into the most violent Agonies, tearing his Hair from his Head, and using most other Actions which generally accompany Fits of Madness, Rage, and Despair' (*TJ* VI. 12). The romanesque parody implied by this introduction of the *locus amoenus* and the lamenting hero arguably inflects Tom with a degree of Quixotism.[15] While his 'Fits' arise from genuine distress and therefore fall short of Don Quijote's gratuitous imitation of Orlando, the romanesque connotations are evidently exploited deliberately by Fielding. The real violence of Tom's 'Agonies' implicitly resists the casual brevity with which they are reported: the reference to '*most* other Actions which *generally* accompany Fits' (emphasis added) implies the vagueness of a narrator who does not take his hero's grief too seriously.

In 1750, Pierre-Antoine de La Place published a hugely successful translation of *Tom Jones*, having only recently completed his French edition of plays by Shakespeare, Jonson, Dryden, Otway and others in his *Théâtre anglais* (8 vols., 1745–9). His translation of *Tom Jones* was an immediate and remarkable success: the marquis d'Argenson, a signatory of the Arrêt de Conseil of February 1750, which failed in its attempt to suppress it, noted 'tout le monde lit ce livre à Paris'. In the survey of 500 private library catalogues undertaken by Daniel Mornet, *Tom Jones* was the third most widespread novel or romance in France (appearing seventy-seven times). No other French translation appeared until after the Revolution, and La Place's version remained the most popular for almost a century after its first publication. It also became the sole source for the first Italian and Spanish versions of *Tom Jones* (in 1756 and 1796 respectively). Chéron, who translated *Tom Jones* in 1804, wrote of La Place's version: 'il a un succès qui, je l'avoue, me fait un peu trembler pour ma traduction.'[16]

La Place transforms the original *Tom Jones* into a *roman romanesque* of contrasting *bienséance*. An example of this process is pertinent here, however, for part of La Place's transformation of Fielding involves turning Tom into the kind of hero that belongs in a *roman romanesque* rather than a 'History'. The remark cited above that '*Jones* had some Heroic Ingredients in his Composition' is rendered by La Place in inadvertently Quixotic terms as 'Notre Héros étoit né courageux; on a même déjà apperçû qu'il avoit des idées un peu romanesques'.[17] For La Place, 'romanesque' is not the dirty word it was for the majority of his contemporaries; the heroic romanesque is his goal as clearly as it was Fielding's target. With generally opposing intentions and results, both Fielding and La Place incorporate the topographical features of various forms of romance in their versions of *Tom Jones*. As Shelly Charles notes, La Place does most of his cutting during the first two sections of the narrative;[18] the final part, which Tom spends in the relatively high London society of Lady Bellaston, is more or less untouched by the translator and therefore occupies a disproportionate amount of the French version: London is the setting for a third of the original, but approximately half of the French *Tom Jones*. The increased part given to London by La Place is doubly ironic if one agrees with David Goldknopf that Fielding is less comfortable with the milieu of London than with those of the country or the road, and that the 'final section is the least satisfactory in the novel'.[19] The wayside inn, Fielding's 'favoured public locus', is incompatible with the tone of the 'intrigue patétique' the translator seeks to create from the original text. It is hardly surprising, therefore, that La Place is in a hurry to get to London, nor that the reader of the French *Tom Jones* spends far less time in the kitchens of country inns than his English counterpart.

While La Place aims to naturalize the topographical elements of the English *Tom Jones* that are foreign to the landscape of the *roman romanesque*, Fielding repeatedly introduces romanesque motifs to distance himself from the tradition with which his translator conversely seeks to align himself. He repeatedly incorporates the most hackneyed *topoi* of romance within both *Joseph Andrews* and *Tom Jones* in order to expose some of the stylized conventions endemic to the genre. The little brook noted above is not the first to appear in *Tom Jones*; Fielding earlier paints a similarly romanesque *locus amoenus* in preparation for a highly unromanesque encounter: 'our Heroe was walking in a most delicious Grove, where the gentle Breezes fanning the Leaves, together with the sweet Trilling of a murmuring Stream, and the melodious Notes of Nightingales formed all together the most enchanting Harmony' (*TJ* V. 10). The pastoral scene provides a fitting backdrop for Tom's ensuing soliloquy on the merits of Sophia, delivered 'by the Side of a gently murmuring Brook', and concluding with the young hero vowing to engrave Sophia's name onto 'every Tree' (*TJ* V. 10).[20] Into this setting appears, 'in a Shift that was somewhat of the coarsest, and none of the Cleanest', and with a pitchfork in her hand, a less than idealized pastoral vision in the form of Molly Seagrim.[21] Tom and Molly retire to 'the thickest Part of the Grove' (*TJ* V. 10) with rather less discretion than the comparatively chaste Amadís and Oriana had demonstrated on their own retreat into a similarly opportune thicket.[22] Fielding interrupts the coitus of Tom and Molly as rudely as an Ariosto or a Sterne,[23] with the battle occasioned by the arrival of Blifil and Thwackum, followed by Squire Western and his party. The parodic subversion of romance topography is typically made explicit by Fielding:

The Reader may remember, that in our Description of this Grove, we mentioned a murmuring Brook, which Brook did not come there, as such gentle Streams flow through vulgar Romances, with no other Purpose than to murmur. No; Fortune had decreed to enoble this little Brook with a higher Honour than any other of those which wash the plains of *Arcadia*, ever deserved. (*TJ* V. 12)

The 'Honour' in question is the reviving of Sophia, who had previously fainted upon the sight of so much blood.

The knights of chivalric romance rarely have to wander far into a forest before encountering new adventures; indeed the forest seems on occasion so crowded with incident that its connotations of solitude or isolation may appear to be compromised.[24] The forest retains its role as the supplier of adventures in Fielding's fiction in a manner that does not always imply parody so much as a self-conscious adherence to formal convention. When Tom, accompanied by the Man of the Hill, is admiring the views afforded by Mazard Hill, the appearance of a wood immediately precedes the introduction of a damsel in distress: 'They now walked to that Part of the Hill which looks to the North West, and which hangs over a vast and extensive Wood. Here they were no sooner arrived, than they heard at a Distance the most violent Skreams of a Woman, proceeding from the Wood below them' (*TJ* IX. 2).

As we have also seen in the *Quijote* and the *Roman comique*, leaving the beaten track or road signifies opening the door to adventure. In an episode of *Joseph Andrews* that provides a prototype to Tom's rescue of Mrs Waters, Adams loses his way and meets an unnamed gentleman; as night overtakes them 'near some Bushes' they hear the 'most violent Shrieks imaginable in a female Voice' (*JA* II. 9). Just as the Man of the Hill lends Tom no assistance in the rescue of Mrs Waters, so Adams's companion, ironically badged 'the Man of Courage' (*JA* II. 9) for his professed hatred of cowardice, makes his way home rather than risk injury to himself. Once again, Fielding apparently distinguishes his own fictional world from its romance precedents, observing that Adams's antagonist has no regard for 'the Laws of Heroism' (*JA* II. 9); as in the *Quijote*, chivalry is noticeable chiefly for its absence from the modern world. The truth is inevitably a little more complex, however, for Tom's rescue of Mrs Waters, an initial act of chivalry that leads to a less than chivalrous act of infidelity to his beloved, recalls, as Miller suggests, Ruggiero's rescue of Angelica in the *Furioso*, 'wherein the hero finds the naked body mounted behind him on his horse'—which finds a modern parallel in Mrs Waters's unconvincing attempt to preserve her modesty by walking behind Tom on the road to Upton—'far too seductive to resist and, forgetting his proper love, decides to enjoy the rescued maiden himself'.[25] Chivalry is not exclusively confined to the realm of the chivalric romance, nor is its absence uniquely the province of the early modern novel.

Leaving the Road: The House as Storytelling *Locus*

There are, as we have seen, peculiarly innlike properties to the various households that frame the journeys undertaken by both Joseph and Tom. While Fielding separates both his heroes from their domestic situations, the road they travel does not provide a clean break from scenes of domesticity. Having apparently sought to escape from the private to the public spheres through the medium of the journey, Fielding occasionally punctuates the road travelled with a temporary return to the intimacy of a private home. The most surprising aspect of these domestic intrusions is the manner in which the inn is robbed of one of its traditional functions: given the highly prominent role assigned to the inn in *Joseph Andrews* and *Tom Jones*, it seems curious that Fielding does not follow his predecessors by exploiting its potential as a *locus* for storytelling. In *Joseph Andrews*, none of the numerous interpolated stories is told at an inn—a setting that seems positively antagonistic to the storytelling process: when the stagecoach, the literal and metaphorical vehicle for the telling of the 'History of Leonora', pulls into an inn, the narration is interrupted, and resumes only when the coach continues its journey. In *Tom Jones*, the inn is less hostile to the telling of stories: these, however, are not the disconnective entertainments one would hear in Palomeque's inn or the *Tripot de la Biche* but brief autobiographical accounts, such as those given by the Quaker (*TJ* XI. 7), Mrs Fitzpatrick (*TJ* XI. 4 ff.), those exchanged by Partridge and Tom (*TJ* VIII. 6), or the biographical gossip in which Partridge in particular indulges.

In *Joseph Andrews* and *Tom Jones*, Fielding generally chooses a domestic backdrop for the interpolation of internal narrations. Wilson and the Man of the Hill tell their stories in the comfort and privacy of their own home rather than a wayside inn. Such apparent digressions from the main action are appropriately occasioned by deviations from the main road or thoroughfare. Each of these episodes opens as night falls, and, while this would normally herald the imminent appearance of an inn, the reader senses that the conventional inn–road narrative syntax that punctuates the travellers' progress is to be abandoned by the author. Joseph and Tom (and their respective companions) each leave the relative comfort of inns at a late stage in the day, and subsequently leave the road altogether. As we have already seen with the *Quijote* and the *Roman comique*, the act of leaving the road inevitably produces either adventures or accidents. At one point in *Joseph Andrews*, Fanny's tiredness prompts a break in her journey with Joseph and Adams; as they are resting by the side of the road, they encounter some sheep-stealers (whom they mistake for murderers). They make their escape, and finally see 'several Lights scattered at a small distance from each other, and at the same time found themselves on the descent of a very steep Hill' (*JA* III. 2)— down which Adams promptly falls. The cross-country excursion continues across fields, meadows, a river, and, finally, a 'little Orchard, which led them to a House' (*JA* III. 2), and consequently to the telling of Wilson's history.

Tom and Partridge are also on a hillside when they see 'a glimmering Light through some Trees' (*TJ* VIII. 10) much to Partridge's delight: 'Oh, Sir! Heaven hath at last heard my Prayers, and hath brought us to a House; perhaps it may be an Inn' (*TJ* VIII. 10). The home of the Man of the Hill does indeed function as an inn in one respect—as David Goldknopf notes, 'the old man's house serves as a kind of inn [...] sheltering Jones and Partridge for the night'; he adds, however, that 'the experience it offers is of course quite different from the life of the inn; the openness and human interaction of inn-life is set off against the motif of alienation and misanthropy which the old man's life illustrates'.[26] The contrast that Goldknopf perceives between the inn and the old man's home ignores the fact that Tom and the old man interact in a manner comparable to two strangers meeting at an inn—indeed Fielding's inns are not always, as we shall see, as open or as sociable as Goldknopf assumes. In any case, the inn is evidently an unsuitable place for the narration of the old man's history—and not simply because a misanthrope would seem out of place in an inn. The contrast that Fielding emphasizes here is not, however, as Goldknopf suggests, between the inn and the old man's life, but between the old man's past and present.

Wilson's story, for similar reasons, is equally ill-suited to narration in a public setting; both he and the Man of the Hill have isolated themselves from society as much as possible. With the exception of our respective heroes, when the outside world intrudes, it does so with violence, as the assault of the old man in *Tom Jones* demonstrates; Joseph, as we later learn, was furthermore abducted from Wilson's home by gypsies, while, more recently, the local squire shoots the spaniel that belongs to Wilson's daughter (*JA* III. 4). Like Voltaire's Candide, Wilson has decided that, in order to escape the ills of the modern world, *il faut cultiver notre jardin*. As the manner of their incorporation suggests, the autodiegetic histories told by Wilson and the Man of the Hill have much in common: they each tell the story of a rake's progress, and guide the reader through the less respectable strata of London society. Wilson's tour begins in the fashionable coffee houses of St James's Street, takes in Covent Garden, where he 'shone forth in the Balconies of the Play-houses, visited Whores, made love to Orange-Wenches, and damned Plays' (*JA* III. 3), and taverns in which the 'best Conversation was nothing but Noise' (*JA* III. 3). Wilson's debts finally result in his imprisonment, of which he remarks, 'as I had not Money sufficient to procure me a separate Apartment, I was crouded in with a great number of miserable Wretches' (*JA* III. 3); this detail is noteworthy because it epitomizes the emphasis on the public sphere in Wilson's narration; Wilson drifts from one haunt to another, around each of which a different social circle gathers. Even the private house has been subsumed into this public sphere, as Wilson's affair with a married woman, and his flirtation with Saphira, the '*Coquette achevée*' (*JA* III. 3), suggest.

The social intercourse described in the story of the Man of the Hill is similarly inflected with decadence, from the debauchery of Exeter College, to 'the Friars, which you know is the Scene of all Mirth and Jollity' (*TJ* VIII. 12), and the various other gaming taverns of London. Whereas Wilson actively seeks to attach himself to a succession of social groups, the Man of the Hill initially goes to London to hide rather than to socialize: 'London, the best Retirement of either Grief or Shame, unless for Persons of a very public Character; for here you have the Advantage of Solitude without its Disadvantage, since you may be alone and in Company at the same Time' (*TJ* VIII. 12). A setting as public as an inn for the narration of these histories would have seriously undermined their impact: the private, country homes that these reformed rakes now inhabit provide a vital counterpoint to the urban dens of iniquity they both describe. The inn is an inappropriate venue for these interpolations because it does not sufficiently contrast with the scenes they portray: the social exposition that characterizes each of these histories produces highly mobile protagonists, and the wayside inn owes its existence to the same mobility and even errancy that one associates with the former lives of Wilson and the Man of the Hill. Like each successive circle of Wilson's acquaintances, it provides a stage on a journey. The conclusion of Wilson's adventures, and his transformation from protagonist to narrator, require a setting that suggests contented stasis—something that an inn evidently cannot provide. The association of stillness with happiness is, as we have seen, prominent in *Tom Jones*, with the domestic resolution of the eponymous hero; in the case of the Man of the Hill, however, the solitary retirement of the former traveller indicates resignation rather than contentment. For him too—but in his own way—it seems it is better to arrive than to travel hopefully.

The histories told by Wilson and the Man of the Hill have a confessional quality that renders their narration particularly unsuitable for the inn, a setting in which guests demand entertainment rather than instruction, and that rarely in Fielding's fiction provides the secure intimacy that such personal histories demand (and receive, for example, in Cervantes and Scarron). In a variety of ways, therefore, these two episodes of internal narration demonstrate how interpolations determine the setting of their own narration, and hence the topographical design of the work that frames them. The relationship between these two narrations and their respective frames is not, however, the same. In contrast to the story of the Man of the Hill, a disconnective interpolation that is resolutely autonomous and separate from the rest of *Tom Jones*, Wilson's tale proves to be a classic example of a connective interpolation masquerading as a digression. An ostensibly accidental, physical deviation in the hero's journey thus proves crucial to the resolution of his story; this exemplifies Fielding's method in *Joseph Andrews* of advancing his narrative by impeding the physical progress of his protagonists.

Joseph Andrews: Progress Barred

Marie-Luce Chênerie's remark that 'tout le développement du conte merveilleux marchait avec les arrêts'[27] could as easily be applied to the kind of journey that provides the structure for such works as *Joseph Andrews*. Joseph spends remarkably little of the narrative actually on the road: his progress is repeatedly disrupted, forcing him off it—and generally into inns. After briefly hesitating 'whether he should leave the Town that Night, or procuring a Lodging, wait 'till the Morning' (*JA* I. 10), Joseph decides (at seven in the evening) to begin his journey immediately. His initial good progress is interrupted after four hours by 'a violent Storm of Hail', which obliges him to take shelter in 'a famous House of Hospitality well known to the western Traveller' (*JA* I. 11). Fielding uses the inn to introduce a note of contemporary reality as well as realism, as he describes the *Red Lion* at Egham, and presents its keeper, Timothy Harris, as '*Timotheus*'.[28] Given the brevity of Joseph's stay there, the reader learns a considerable amount about this model innkeeper, 'a Person well-received among all sorts of Men, being qualified to render himself agreeable to any; as he is well versed in History and Politicks, hath a smattering in Law and Divinity, cracks a good Jest, and plays wonderfully well on the *French* Horn' (*JA* I. 11). Complimentary images of inns and innkeepers are rare in Fielding's fiction unless, of course, he is paying a compliment to those of his actual acquaintance, as is the case here and in his account of *The Bell* at Gloucester in *Tom Jones*. Joseph, who seats himself by the 'Kitchin-Fire' (*JA* I. 11), is joined by Timotheus (and an excellent observation of his on 'the Certainty of Death') and his wife, and finally a fellow-traveller also taking shelter from the storm. The weather thus conspires with the inn to produce a coincidental encounter that in turn provides Joseph with a travelling companion and a horse to the next inn. In fact, the weather repeatedly gives Fielding the means with which to forge similarly fortuitous encounters between his characters. A 'violent Shower of Rain' (*JA* II. 3) thus keeps Adams from leaving an inn long enough for him to be joined there by Mrs Slipslop and Joseph; the reunion of Joseph and Fanny is brought about in a similar fashion, as when Adams and Fanny take to the road to meet Joseph at one inn, they are within a mile diverted to another, 'by a most violent Storm of Rain' (*JA* II. 12), where, of course, Joseph turns out to be after all.[29]

In both *Joseph Andrews* and *Tom Jones*, the inn produces a series of meetings between people who are already acquainted or (unknowingly) connected in some way. The connection may initially seem insubstantial, but ultimately proves to have a formative impact on the hero's progress: Joseph, for example, recognizes the aforementioned guest of the *Red Lion* as 'the Servant of a neighbouring Gentleman, who used to visit at their House' (*JA* I. 10); this tenuous link, cemented by 'a loving Pot', subsequently provides Joseph with a free ride to the next stage of his journey. As we have seen above, the inn also provides the setting for more significant encounters, most notably those between Joseph and Adams (*JA* I. 14), and between Joseph and Fanny. While some of the inns through which the narrative passes do introduce new characters (such as the inn staff themselves), the hero's journey is dominated by a small cast, many of whom are introduced in the opening chapters. When Joseph leaves London behind, it does not stay left behind: Mrs Slipslop and Peter Pounce both cross Joseph's path and travel with him some of the way home, and Lady Booby also follows him back to the country, finally overtaking him as he arrives in her parish. The characters we meet at one wayside inn moreover often reappear at another: thus the 'two Gentlemen who were present at Mr *Tow-wouse's* when *Joseph* was detained for his Horse's-Meat, and whom we have before mentioned to have stopt at the Alehouse with *Adams*' (*JA* II. 5), turn up at the inn that provides a break from the History of Leonora. In *Tom Jones*, the hero's departure also creates a domino effect, precipitating the journeys of one character (Western) after another (Sophia); in partial consequence of this, the inns of *Tom Jones* are as likely to accommodate close relations as total strangers. Some of the characters Tom meets on his way to London furthermore appear at more than one inn; most notable among these is Dowling, the lawyer, who remains a murky presence in the background of the narrative until the final denouement.

By contrast to the inn, the road generally provides the setting for—often unwelcome—encounters with strangers in both *Joseph Andrews* and *Tom Jones*, from Joseph's meeting with his assailants to Tom's confrontation with an incompetent highwayman. The road consequently seems more authentic in its openness to chance than the inn, wherein the coincidental meetings between characters are transparently orchestrated by the author. The road also seems more naturalistic in that Fielding does not use it solely as a cue to introduce adventures or accidents; for much of *Joseph Andrews*, it may be accurately represented as a blank space in which no discrete events are allowed to intrude. One might therefore say that Fielding's famous metaphor of the inn for the spaces between chapters[30] is inverted by the pattern of his narrative. While the inn provides an interval for the travellers on their journey, the road performs a similar function for the narrative itself; the reader hence encounters such phrases as 'Nothing remarkable happened on the Road, 'till their arrival at the Inn' (*JA* I. 12), which exemplify this opposition between the two. When Joseph and his companions continue on their way immediately after the Wilson episode, the reader is informed that they 'travelled many Miles before they met with any Adventure worth relating' and adds that 'in this Interval, we shall present our Readers with a very curious Discourse' (*JA* III. 5); the road thus frames a conversation between Joseph and Adams on public schools.

On the rare occasions when our travellers make substantial progress on their journey, the absence of obstacles this implies diminishes the presence of the road to the extent that it becomes virtually invisible. We have already seen how the road generally provides no more than the space between adventures; for those obliged to travel, as opposed to tourists, a *good* journey is one of which one has barely been aware—that is over before one knows it.[31] In these circumstances, however, the experience of travelling has been virtually erased as a subject of interest in its own right; consequently, as both travellers and readers of fictional travelogues, one becomes most conscious of the process of travelling when it has become problematic. In the 1760s, Sterne's seventh volume of *Tristram Shandy* and his *Sentimental Journey* thus become memorable not for their descriptions of French towns but for their accounts of a traveller's difficulties with his post-chaise, and the many other impediments to his progress.[32]

Although the road of *Joseph Andrews* allows its travellers occasional bursts of rapid, uninterrupted progress, it ordinarily offers them a variety of obstructions instead. When Joseph leaves the second inn of his journey, he gets no further than two miles before he is 'met by two Fellows in a narrow Lane' (*JA* I. 12)[33] who rob him, then physically remove him from the road by tossing him into a ditch; he is therefore obliged to delay his journey and rest at *The Dragon*, where he meets Parson Adams. Adams's experience of travel is also far from encouraging, as, like his Cervantine predecessor, he abandons his intended destination (having forgotten the sermons he intended to sell in London), and decides to accompany Joseph instead. From Palomeque's inn in the *Quijote* to the *Grand Cerf* in *Jacques*, leaving an inn rarely proves as straightforward as finding one. In contrast to the road, which repels and deflects, the inn attracts and detains both characters and narrators: when Joseph is accidentally stranded with an unpaid bill at *The Dragon*, the narrator thus remarks, 'we cannot therefore at present get Mr *Joseph* out of the inn' (*JA* II. 2).[34] *The Dragon*'s magnetism, which contrasts directly with the unwelcoming bearing of Mrs Tow-wouse, is equally evident in bringing about Adams's timely arrival as well as the return of one of Joseph's assailants.

The Dragon is not the only inn to exert such remarkable powers of attraction. The unnamed public house that sees the reunion of Joseph and Fanny is less cooperative when it comes to their departure: 'when they were ready to set out, an Accident a little retarded them' (*JA* II. 13)—namely, another bill. Rather than continue on their way, Joseph and Fanny thus wait at the inn, while Adams has meanwhile had an unsuccessful interview with Trulliber then 'sallied all around the Parish, but to no purpose' (*JA* II. 15). When the trio is finally rescued by a charitable pedlar, the narrator explicitly suggests a Cervantine parallel when he refers to 'that Inn, which they had more reason to have mistaken for a Castle, than Don *Quixote* ever had any of those in which he sojourned; seeing they had met with such Difficulty in escaping out of its Walls' (*JA* II. 16). Adams, like Don Quijote, underestimates the value of money; he thereby twice causes delays to his companions' progress, and three times embarrassment.[35]

The journeys of Joseph and Adams are plagued by a number of practical difficulties involving the two means of transport upon which they depend: the horse and the stagecoach. Horses repeatedly cause their riders problems: after his departure from *The Dragon*, Joseph is injured for the second time when Adams's horse succumbs to its violent 'Propensity to kneeling' (*JA* II. 5) while he is riding it; when he and Fanny later mount the same horse, it 'discovered much Uneasiness at this double Load, and began to consider his hinder as his Fore-legs, moving the direct contrary way to that which is called forwards. Nor could *Joseph* with all his Horsemanship persuade him to advance' (*JA* III. 12).[36] The politics of the stagecoach is another recurrent source of contention, as each successive group of passengers decides who may gain admittance and who must seek alternative transport. When Joseph is found in a ditch, he is allowed into the coach only because a young lawyer among the passengers fears they may be held responsible for his death if they leave him there. When his injured leg renders him incapable of continuing on horseback, his social rank becomes a bar to his admission into the coach, with 'Miss

Grave-airs insisting, against the Remonstrances of all the rest, that she would not admit a Footman into the Coach [...] A young Lady, who was, it seems, an Earl's Grand Daughter, begged it with almost Tears in her Eyes' (*JA* II. 5). This *impasse* is finally resolved by Miss Grave-airs's exchange of the stage for a recently arrived private coach of her own. Her haughtiness regarding this form of public transport—'I am not much used to Stage-Coaches, I seldom travel in them' (*JA* II. 5)— outdoes even Richardson's disparaging allusion to 'inn-frequenting Sophia'.[37] While Miss Grave-Airs's remark is clearly satirically intended as an attack on snobbery, it at the same time suggests that the stagecoach suffered in some quarters from the same poor reputation as the inns between which it transported its guests. Indeed John Cresset, an innkeeper, poses the question in 1672,

Is it for a Mans pleasure, or advantagious to their healths and Business, to travel with a mixt Company that he knows not how to converse with; to be affronted by the rudeness of a surly, dogged, cursing, ill-natured Coachman; necessitated to Lodge or Bait at the worst Inns on the Road, where there is no accommodation fit for a Gentleman; and this merely because the Owners of the Inns, and the Coachmen, are agreed together to cheat the guests?[38]

It should be added, however, that Cresset is far from being an objective witness; as Douglas Chambers remarks, 'as an inn-keeper, [he] was deprived of part of his trade'[39] by the proliferation of stagecoaches.

In some ways, the stagecoach in *Joseph Andrews* provides a mobile version of the inn. It accommodates a broad variety of social types and classes, from servants like Mrs Slipslop to the aforementioned 'Earl's Grand Daughter', and various comic caricatures, including the lawyer, the 'Man of Wit' and the discreetly alcoholic 'Lady' of the first stagecoach. In contrast to the inn, the stagecoach is not compartmentalized but comprises a single, cramped space,[40] in which everyone is forced to share the company of his fellow-passengers. As the 'History of Leonora' demonstrates, however, the stagecoach partially replaces the inn as a storytelling *locus* in *Joseph Andrews*. While the inn is a static site, relying upon the mobility of its guests to realize its storytelling potential, the mobility of the stagecoach is seen directly to prompt the act of narration. The only interpolation in *Joseph Andrews* that is not told in a domestic setting is nevertheless occasioned by a passing view of a domestic setting—'a great House which stood at some Distance from the Road' (*JA* II. 3). By the matter it narrates it furthermore constitutes, like the subsequent story of Leonard and

Paul, a return to a domestic setting. The circumstances in which this story is incorporated demonstrate the virtue of leisurely travel, which Tristram Shandy later espouses: by not travelling too quickly, the passengers of the stagecoach open their eyes to potentially interesting 'views and prospects' (*TS* I. 14). Their attention turns from their own journey to a story whose (disconnective) separateness is underlined by the remark that the house is 'at some Distance' from the road. At the same time that the coach continues its linear progress, the narrative conversely deviates radically from its hitherto straight path.[41]

Joseph Andrews and *Tom Jones*: Home and Away at the Inn

Having suggested that the households in *Joseph Andrews* and *Tom Jones* have certain innlike qualities, one should add that the reverse is also the case: the domestic dimension is prominent in Fielding's representations of the inn. The literary inn is not adequately described or categorized as a *topos* of travel alone. In a figurative as well as a literal sense, it is a halfway house; Goldknopf's remark, however, that 'the inn is a settlement on the bank of the road, intermediate in its sociological openness between a rural and urban environment',[42] conveys only one aspect of this intermediacy. Goldknopf represents the inn as if it *belonged* uniquely to the road, and hence to the travellers from urban and rural communities who pass through it. The inn is not, however, a neutral or empty space defined exclusively by its guests, but a setting in which the domestic and the foreign interact. This foreign element includes the reader himself, whose attention is initially focused upon the hero's progress rather than the stages that mark a pause in that progress. As we have already seen, the inn resists narrative subordination to the road, and to the traveller who follows the road seeking only the briefest visit there before moving on to more adventures. It does not merely provide a backdrop to the traveller-centred narrative that temporarily invades it, but seeks to force it off course and to subject it to its own rules. I earlier alluded to the magnetic powers of the inn; these attract not only the traveller, but also those who live within its immediate surroundings; as with the *Roman comique*, the inn is not just on the bank of the road but at the heart of the local community. *The Dragon* thus provides a single stage upon which a number of local characters may gather, including Mr Barnabas the clergyman and the surgeon, both of whom remain at the inn long after their presence is required, as they seek their own entertainment. The domestic aspect of the inn, which includes this local component, is most prominently represented by those for whom the inn is a home: the keepers and staff continually deflect the narrative away from the guests whose stories are ostensibly the main priority of the narrative.

Throughout *Joseph Andrews* and *Tom Jones*, the inn provides the reader with diverse views of domestic life as the relationships between various keepers and their wives are successively delineated. When Tom arrives at Hambrook,[43] the reader is given a summary of the recent marital history of the innkeeper, Robin, which rather resembles a magistrate's report:

'... his Wife was gone from home, and had locked up almost every Thing, and carried the Keys along with her.' Indeed, the Fact was, that a favourite Daughter of hers was just married, and gone, that Morning, home with her Husband; and that she and her Mother together, had almost stript the poor Man of all his Goods, as well as Money: For tho' he had several Children, this Daughter only, who was the Mother's Favourite, was the Object of her Consideration, and to the Humour of this one Child, she would, with Pleasure, have sacrificed all the rest, and her Husband into the Bargain. (*TJ* VII. 10)

With the notable exceptions of the actual inns Fielding incorporates in his fiction, such as *The Red Lion* in *Joseph Andrews*, or *The Bell* in *Tom Jones*, in most of the inns that Joseph or Tom visit there seems to be a story of marital disharmony waiting to be told. At the second inn of *Tom Jones*, where Tom sustains his injuries at the hands of Northerton, another materialistic landlady is 'absolute Governess' (*TJ* VIII. 7) of the house, while 'the Landlord of the House, or rather Husband of the Landlady' has a more passive role:

He had but lately made his Descent down Stairs, after a long Fit of the Gout, in which Distemper he was generally confined to his Room during one half of the Year; and during the rest, he walked about the House, smoked his Pipe, and drank his Bottle with his Friends, without concerning himself in the least with any Kind of Business. He had been bred, as they call it, a Gentleman, that is bred to do nothing, and had spent a very small Fortune, which he inherited from an industrious Farmer his Uncle, in Hunting, Horse-racing, and Cock-fighting, and had been married by my Landlady for certain Purposes, which he had long since desisted from answering: For which she hated him heartily. But as he was a surly Kind of Fellow, so she contented herself with frequently upbraiding him by disadvantageous Comparisons with her first Husband, whose Praise she had eternally in her Mouth. (*TJ* VIII. 7)

Fielding specializes in shrewish landladies; he consequently finds it necessary to defend the similarity between the above hostess and her counterpart in Upton in one of his introductory essays, on the basis that 'there are certain Characteristics, in which most Individuals of every Profession and Occupation agree' (*TJ* X. 1). Arguably the most memorable of Fielding's inhospitable hostesses, however, is Mrs Towwouse, whose personality is evidently reflected in Fielding's choice of *The Dragon* as a suitable name for her inn.[44]

The Dragon dramatically illustrates the manner in which the domestic life of the inn tends to displace the guests as the focus of the narrative. A 'pleasant Discourse' between Adams, Barnabas and the bookseller is interrupted by 'a most hideous Uproar' (*JA* I. 17) when Mr Tow-wouse is discovered in bed with Betty, the chambermaid. This leads the narrator 'to open to the Reader the Steps which led to a Catastrophe, common enough, and comical enough too, perhaps in modern History, yet often fatal to the Repose and Well-being of Families' (*JA* I. 17), and to devote the following chapter to the '*History of* Betty *the Chambermaid, and an Account of what occasioned the violent Scene in the preceding Chapter*' (*JA* I. 18). The narrative is thus temporarily diverted from the guests of the inn to its staff as the domestic sexual politics of the inn take centre stage. In *Tom Jones*, a similarly 'violent Uproar' (*TJ* XII. 6) occurs at an inn when Grace, a maid, is discovered in a compromising position with a Merry Andrew. Fielding's chambermaids seem to share 'certain Characteristics' with their Cervantine antecedent, Maritornes; of these, Susan, the chambermaid at Upton, perhaps resembles her most closely, her physical appearance being portrayed in similarly grotesque terms (*TJ* IX. 3).[45] Like Maritornes, Susan unsuccessfully plans a liaison at her inn—albeit not with a carrier but with an ostler (*TJ* X. 2).[46]

Illicit sexual encounters provide one example of the way in which the emphasis of inn life may temporarily switch from the foreign or extrinsic to the domestic. As the often violent disputes between the hosts and guests suggest, such contrasting elements coexist uneasily in both *Joseph Andrews* and *Tom Jones*.[47] Hospitality may easily turn to hostility: even the initially amicable dialogue between Adams and the 'kind Host' (*JA* II. 16) who offers him a free pot of beer '*by the Disagreement in their Opinions seemed to threaten an unlucky Catastrophe*' (*JA* II. 17). When Adams insists that 'travelling [...] in Books' (*JA* II. 17) is preferable to physical travel, he indirectly calls into question part of the *raison d'être* of the host and his inn; it is not surprising, therefore, that the host should react so angrily. The poor reception of Tom and Mrs Waters at Upton arises from a rather more concrete challenge to the innkeeper's trade. In the eighteenth century, the inn, like the works of fiction in which it tends to feature, has a generally poor reputation against which it must defend itself: it is revealed that the landlady at Upton has worked hard to safeguard the name of her own inn, described as

a House of exceeding good Repute, whither *Irish* Ladies of strict Virtue, and many Northern Lasses of the same Predicament, were accustomed to resort in their Way to *Bath*. The Landlady therefore would by no Means have admitted any Conversation of a disreputable Kind to pass under her Roof. Indeed so foul and contagious are all such Proceedings, that they contaminate the very innocent Scenes where they are committed, and give the Name of a bad House, or of a House of ill Repute, to all those where they are suffered to be carried on.

Not that I would intimate, that such strict Chastity as was preserved in the Temple of *Vesta* can possibly be maintained at a public Inn. My good Landlady did not hope for such a Blessing [...] But to exclude all vulgar Concubinage, and to drive all Whores in Rags from within the Walls, is within the Power of every one. This my Landlady very strictly adhered to [...] (*TJ* IX. 3)

Mrs Waters's dishevelled appearance constitutes a threat to the good name the landlady has sought to cultivate for her inn. The landlady of the inn where the puppet show is performed[48] is equally concerned with the reputation of her establishment, and when she discovers the Merry Andrew with her maid, complains to her husband that her house is being made 'a Bawdyhouse of by such lousy Vermin' (*TJ* XII. 6).

If one were to construct a hierarchy of public houses or places of entertainment according to their reputation, one would certainly find the inn well below, for example, the fashionable coffee house. One of the few establishments to be ranked beneath the inn, however, would be the alehouse—although the distinction between these is often unclear in *Joseph Andrews* and *Tom Jones*. Referring to the house where Adams and Joseph are held captive by the Squire's men, Fielding remarks, 'This Inn, which indeed we might call an Ale-house, had not the Words, *The New Inn*, been writ on the Sign' (*JA* III. 8). The keepers of alehouses prefer to be seen as the keepers of inns, while the latter enjoy a sense of superiority over the former. When Mrs Towwouse learns that the penniless Joseph is being looked after at her inn, she asks, 'Why doth not such a Fellow go to an Ale-house?' (*JA* I. 12).

The narratorial hesitation about the *New Inn* is typical of the narrators of *Joseph Andrews* and *Tom Jones*, both of whom appear uncertain what they should call the public houses where their travellers rest on their respective journeys. The unnamed public house in which Joseph and Fanny are reunited is said to be 'an Inn, or rather Ale-house' (*JA* II. 12), while the aforementioned inn in *Tom Jones* where the puppet show is performed is described as 'an Inn, or indeed, an Ale-house' (*TJ* XII. 5). In each case, the correction bears the tone of an admission, as if the author were reluctant to reveal that his hero and heroine could frequent such lowly establishments. A deliberately crestfallen downward spiral may be observed in the very process of narration here, as it corrects itself to subtly bathetic effect.

Whereas the alehouse may be beneath the inn in the hierarchy of public houses, the lodging house at which Tom stays in London may conversely be regarded as being superior to both. While, as we shall see below, Partridge 'was never better pleased than when he arrived at an Inn, nor ever more dissatisfied than when he was again forced to leave it' (*TJ* XII. 13), it is clear that his companion, like Sophia, is not naturally at home in the same environment.[49] When Tom arrives in London, he temporarily takes a room at the *Bull and Gate* in Holborn but soon moves to 'a very reputable House, and in a very good part of Town' (*TJ* XIII. 5). The narrator is swift to reassure the 'gentle Reader' who may have 'some Concern, should it be apprehended, that during this unhappy Separation from *Sophia*, he took up his Residence either at an Inn, or in the Street' (*TJ* XIII. 5) that Tom is in more respectable lodgings. This respectability is confirmed by the announcement that Tom is now in the house where Allworthy also stays on his visits to London, kept by the widow of a clergyman.

It soon transpires nevertheless that any public house is susceptible to the same problems as those suffered by the wayside inn. Mrs Miller's house is, for example, the scene of another 'mistaken room' nocturnal misadventure when Nightingale mistakes Tom's apartment for his own (*TJ* XV. 7), and is subject more than once to a 'violent Uproar' (*TJ* XIII. 5, XIV. 6), the second of which is similarly occasioned by an illicit sexual relationship. Like the landlady at Upton, Mrs Miller shows considerable regard for the reputation of her house, twice rebuking Jones for having female company in his room late at night (*TJ* XIV. 3, XIV. 5). This concern, however, ultimately proves to be insufficient to prevent the pregnancy of her daughter by her only other guest, Nightingale, disparagingly described as one of those

'Men of Wit and Pleasure' who frequent 'Play-Houses, Coffee-Houses, and Taverns' (*TJ* XIII. 5). While illicit sex at a wayside inn is far from unusual and consequently causes only a temporary furore that is soon resolved (as at *The Dragon*), the affair between Nightingale and Nancy is represented as a far more serious proposition. Such a shift in perspective derives from the manner in which the transitory aspect of inn life, whereby guests stay only briefly before moving on, is almost entirely eliminated in Mrs Miller's house—Nightingale, for example, is said to have lodged there for two years. The domestic sphere seems to subsume the guests, turning them into more permanent fixtures of the lodging house—indeed Nightingale literally becomes a part of the family. It does not take long for Jones to be promoted from guest to member of Mrs Miller's household: following his rescue of Nightingale from the hands of his footman, he spends 'a very chearful Evening' (*TJ* XIII. 5) in the company of his fellow-lodger, Mrs Miller and her two daughters, and is subsequently invited to breakfast, tea and dinner with them. He moreover comes to the rescue of Mrs Miller's family on two occasions, providing further financial aid to Mr Anderson, the husband of her cousin, and helping to bring about the marriage of Nancy. Jones in fact becomes so embroiled in the domestic life of Mrs Miller's family that, having brought the affair of Nightingale and Nancy to a happy resolution, the narrator fears that certain of his readers will wish it had been 'spared as impertinent to the main Design' (*TJ* XV. 8).

Joseph Andrews and *Tom Jones*: The Topography of the Inn

Although the domestic and the foreign in Fielding's inns are often presented in terms suggesting conflict, there is an underlying complementarity in their relationship that is the product of the author's highly dynamic construction of his narrative. In contrast to Cervantes and Scarron, both of whom assign to the domestic life of the inn a genuinely disruptive role—allowing it, for example, repeatedly to interrupt the guests' storytelling—the domestic aspect of Fielding's inns generally takes centre stage without displacing events (narrated or otherwise) of substantial importance to the reader. The discovery of Betty the chambermaid with Mr Tow-wouse, and of Grace with the Merry Andrew, interrupts not stories but conversations that appear in any case to be on the point of petering out. The narrators of *Joseph Andrews* and *Tom Jones* are as restless as their interweaving antecedents in chivalric romance, and even the inn fails to provide the temporary stasis one would identify as one of its natural functions. Since the *Quijote*, the inn is no longer one place but many places concurrently, and thus has the same ability to accommodate internal *entrelacement* as the forest of romance.

Fielding's narrator moves from room to room, switching from one narrative thread to another: when Joseph is in the bedroom of *The Dragon* relating his recent misfortunes to Adams, the narrative avoids unnecessary repetition by moving to the kitchen—a move repeated in *Tom Jones* for less innocent reasons when Fielding leaves Tom and Mrs Waters to their amorous exchange for the company of Partridge. When characters are confined to one room, the narrator compensates by becoming mobile himself (in anticipation of Sterne's approach in *Tristram Shandy*). Thus, when Joseph goes to bed at *The Dragon*, the narrator follows Adams downstairs, where he joins Barnabas and the bookseller for the aforementioned '*pleasant Discourse*', which is in turn interrupted when it has lost impetus by the 'hideous Uproar' in the Tow-wouses' bedroom. Fielding's narrator is like a roving reporter hungrily pursuing the action as it moves from one part of the inn to another. When Tom is literally immobile, having been knocked un-conscious by Northerton, the narrator professes to have difficulty keeping up with the pace of events, claiming that he could not describe 'every Particular' unless he had 'forty Pens, and could, at once, write with them all together' (*TJ* VII. 12).

Although Fielding's inns fall short of the labyrinthine *Great White Horse*, the setting for another famous 'mistaken room' episode in English fiction when Mr Pickwick meets with the lady in yellow curl papers,[50] they are usually large enough to accommodate the various narrative strands required to occupy the restless narrator and his reader. In the case of the inn at Upton, each room seems to contain a narrative of its own, from 'the *Rose*' where Sophia rests to 'the *Wild-goose*' (*TJ* X. 3) that Fitzpatrick shares with Mr Macklachlan.[51] The number of guests the inn at Upton is able to accommodate unquestionably indicates a Cervantine model: when Sophia arrives there, the landlady tells her, 'all my best Rooms are full' (*TJ* X. 3). Where Palomeque's inn provides encounters that lead to the resolution of various storylines, however, the Upton inn complicates rather than resolves the central love plot by engineering a missed meeting as clearly orchestrated as all the contrived encounters typical of Fielding's inns. This failure to meet is as formative as any meeting in *Tom Jones*: as Goldknopf notes, 'Sophia's pursuit of

Tom is reversed' at Upton and 'the subordinate chases, Fitzpatrick's pursuit of his wife and Squire Western's of his daughter, are dovetailed into the main pursuit'.[52] The manner in which Tom and Sophia, and Mr and Mrs Fitzpatrick, evade each other moreover suggests an Ariostan model to complement the Cervantine one, recalling Atlante's enchanted castle in the *Furioso* even if, at Upton, those pursued are no longer illusory presences.[53]

Fielding continually imposes immobility upon his characters to pursue other narrative threads, or to create the space for an interlude. He once again parodically invokes one of the most romanesque of procedures at potentially the most dramatic point in *Joseph Andrews*: Fanny's abduction by the squire.[54] When Adams and Joseph are held captive upstairs by the squire at the *New Inn*, Fielding abandons them with Ariostan detachment:[55] as they remain tied to the bedposts, the narrative moves downstairs for '*A Discourse between the Poet and the Player; of no other Use in this History but to Divert the Reader*': 'Before we proceed any farther in this Tragedy we shall leave Mr *Joseph* and Mr *Adams* to themselves, and imitate the wise Conductors of the Stage; who in the midst of a grave Action entertain you with some excellent piece of Satire or Humour called a Dance' (III. 10). The romanesque abduction of Fanny is thus deflated by comic dialogue, while the imprisonment of Joseph and Adams at the inn moreover suggests another modern equivalent to the episode of Atlante's castle, in which the knights are imprisoned by the enchanter's magic. Fielding's justification of this highly unclassical use of antithesis and juxtaposition here anticipates his defence of the introductory chapters in *Tom Jones*, but once again the stated terms of the contrast are evident distortions. The discourse between poet and player is followed by another dialogue, as the narrative returns upstairs in the following chapter in order to report the concurrent conversation between Joseph and Adams. Fielding typically signposts the contrast between these two dialogues, noting that 'the next Chapter [...] is a sort of Counterpart to this' (*JA* III. 10). The comic *divertissement* is thus followed by 'some of the best and gravest Matters of the Book' (*JA* III. 10), '*calculated for the Instruction and Improvement of the Reader*' (*JA* III. 11), and the *utile* hence provides a neat counterpart to the *dulce*.

As the juxtaposition of dialogues at the *New Inn* suggests, there is a strong sense of pattern and design in Fielding's exploitation of the internal geography of the inn. Some of the upstairs/downstairs oppositions noted of the *Roman comique* in the previous chapter may equally be applied to *Joseph Andrews* and *Tom Jones*. Fielding's inns follow the example of the *Tripot de la Biche*, the accommodation upstairs providing a degree of privacy for its guests, the downstairs area offering by contrast a public space in which the local community as well as passing travellers may congregate. These distinctive functions have a direct impact on the manner in which Fielding exploits the inn; it is no coincidence, for example, that the comic dialogue between the poet and player takes place downstairs while the grave dialogue between Joseph and Adams is situated upstairs. In both *Joseph Andrews* and *Tom Jones*, the distinctive roles of the upstairs and downstairs curiously reflect their literal physical relationship to produce a hierarchy of *high* and *low* not dissimilar to that of the romanesque and burlesque in Scarron's *tripot*. In *Tom Jones*, the bedrooms upstairs thus accommodate the '*serious*' autobiographical narrations of characters, such as those of Mrs Fitzpatrick (*TJ* XI. 4), Sophia (*TJ* XI. 8), Partridge (*TJ* VIII. 6) and Tom himself (*TJ* VIII. 5) (although, to avoid repetition, only the personal histories of Mrs Fitzpatrick and Partridge are directly related in the text).

Whereas the kitchen is invisible in Palomeque's inn or in the *Biche*, in Fielding's fiction it provides a direct counterpart to the bedroom in numerous ways. While the inn exerts magnetic powers of attraction over those outside, the kitchen attracts those who have already entered. In the kitchen of *The Dragon*, for example, the reader is informed that 'a great Variety of Company were now assembled from all the Rooms of the House, as well as the Neighbourhood' (*JA* I. 14). As we have already seen, the kitchen is where both Joseph and Adams automatically head for upon arrival; it is also Partridge's natural habitat. Partridge indeed appears to confine himself to the kitchen out of choice rather than social necessity; his presence there, however, conveys an impression of his relationship to Tom that he is repeatedly obliged to correct: he thus informs the company gathered in the kitchen of *The Bell*, 'That tho' he carried the Knapsack, and contented himself with staying among Servants, while *Tom Jones* (as he called him) was regaling in the Parlour, he was not his Servant, but only a Friend and Companion, and as good a Gentleman as Mr *Jones* himself' (*TJ* VIII. 8). The social hierarchy of the inn mimics that of the private household, with the kitchen primarily, although not exclusively, the domain of the staff and servants. When Adams is seen to favour the kitchen over other rooms or apartments, he is thereby revealed to be admirably free of arrogance or pretension and, as a result, to be a worthy parson. Sophia's graciousness is similarly illustrated by her conduct in the kitchen of a country inn: 'with a Smile of great Condescension' she tells the landlady at Upton, 'If you will give me Leave, Madam, I will warm myself a few Minutes at your Kitchin Fire; for it is really very cold; but I must insist on disturbing no one from his Seat' (*TJ* X. 3). When Sophia is later resting in her apartment, Honour returns to the kitchen and displays all the snobbish arrogance her mistress so conspicuously lacked:

While the Supper was preparing, Mrs *Abigail* began to lament she had not ordered a Fire in the Parlour; but she said, that was now too late, 'However,' said she, 'I have Novelty to recommend a Kitchin; for I do not believe I ever eat in one before.' Then turning to the Post-boys, she asked them, 'Why they were not in the Stable with their Horses? If I must eat my hard Fare here, Madam,' cries she to the Landlady, 'I beg the Kitchin may be kept clear, that I may not be surrounded with all the Black-guards in Town [...]' (*TJ* X. 4)

However reluctantly, Honour submits to the hierarchical symmetry Fielding imposes on the inn at Upton, sharing the kitchen with Partridge while Tom and Sophia enjoy the seclusion of their private apartments.

Partridge, like Adams, is evidently drawn to the sociability of the kitchen. Following the fight that marks his arrival at Upton with Jones and Mrs Waters, he joins the 'good People' who 'now ranged themselves round the Kitchen-Fire, where good humour seemed to maintain an absolute Dominion' (*TJ* IX. 4), while Tom accompanies Mrs Waters to her apartment, where their dinner has been prepared. The social intercourse of the kitchen subsequently takes place concurrently with the sexual intercourse in the bedroom, and once again the inn proves to be different things to different people. In contrast to the private and personal histories exchanged in the bedroom, the storytelling of the kitchen constitutes public entertainment—usually at the expense of the guests upstairs. Jones is repeatedly the victim of (kitchen-)table talk: at the inn at Hambrook, 'the Guide had no sooner taken his Place at the Kitchin-Fire, than he acquainted the whole Company with all he knew, or had ever heard concerning *Jones*' (*TJ* VII. 10); at the next inn, while he is in 'the Sun', the landlady is in the kitchen 'entertaining a Circle that she had gathered round her with the History of poor *Jones*' (*TJ* VIII. 4). Partridge is similarly indiscreet, and while Jones interviews a guide who had previously travelled with Sophia 'in Whispers in an inner Room, *Partridge*, who had no such Delicacy in his Disposition, was in the Kitchin very openly catechising the other Guide who had attended

Mrs *Fitzpatrick*' (*TJ* XII. 8). Partridge's indiscretion proves particularly costly to Jones as it excites Sophia's disapproval: 'in reality, *Sophia* was much more offended at the Freedoms which she thought, and not without good Reason, he had taken with her Name and Character, than at any Freedoms, in which, under his present Circumstances, he had indulged himself with the Person of another Woman' (*TJ* XII. 8).[56] The loose talk of the kitchen has a formative impact on the course of the narrative: the reader is told that Honour could never have prevailed on Sophia to leave the inn at Upton without seeing Jones 'had it not been for those two strong Instances of Levity in his Behaviour' (*TJ* XII. 8).

Between the sociability of the kitchen and the privacy of the bedroom the various parlours and apartments form a middle ground that assumes some of the functions of each. Tom is refused a bedroom by Robin at Hambrook on the grounds that he is 'but a poor Parish Bastard' and hence unworthy of such accommodation; he is obliged to sleep in the 'Parlour, or rather Hole' (*TJ* VII. 10) instead, which is consequently revealed to be inferior to the bedroom in the social hierarchy according to which the inn caters for its guests.[57] In relation to the kitchen, however, the parlours and apartments of Fielding's inns offer more elevated and comfortable surroundings. At *The Bell*, Partridge's conversation in the kitchen with Mr Whitefield runs parallel to the comparatively private exchange at the dinner to which Tom is invited by Mrs Whitefield in another room of the inn. The parlour, as its name suggests, offers an opportunity for dialogue—not the public chatter of the kitchen, however, but relatively private conversation.[58] Tom's aforementioned conversation with Sophia's former guide is thus conducted in a parlour or 'inner Room', while he later tells his story to Dowling in a parlour over a bottle of wine (*TJ* XII. 10), thereby breaking the monopoly on personal histories enjoyed by the bedrooms of Fielding's inns. The narrator of *Tom Jones* also reveals he is writing his history in a 'little Parlour' (*TJ* XIII. 1), thereby suggesting an intimate dialogue between himself and the reader that duplicates the one taking place between Jones and Dowling in the parlour of an unnamed inn.

Although the inn's kitchen may be characterized by its powers of attraction, these are not complemented by equal powers of retention: while characters such as Adams and Partridge may be happy to join the servants and staff who are confined to the kitchen, the majority of those with a choice, such as Sophia, prefer to retire either to a parlour or to a bedroom as soon as possible. In *The Dragon*, Mr Tow-wouse thus hopes 'so large an Assembly' in the kitchen would 'shortly adjourn into several Apartments' (*JA* I. 14) as indeed Barnabas, Adams and the surgeon do 'to take part of a Bowl of Punch' (*JA* I. 16). Appearances determine to which part of the inn a guest will be welcome, and this is the reason Tom causes such confusion at the various houses through which he passes. The ambiguity of his social rank repeatedly affects the manner of his reception, as the various innkeepers seek to determine what part of their house is appropriate to him. Fielding describes one host in *Joseph Andrews* as a man who 'always proportioned his Respect to the Appearance of a Traveller' (*JA* II. 5). Having, as we have already seen, been refused a bedroom in Hambrook, Tom encounters similar resistance when he tries to go upstairs with Mrs Waters at Upton. On most occasions his noble bearing initially attracts hospitable treatment from his hosts, which subsequently evaporates with reports of his poor birth. When Tom arrives at *The Bell*, Mrs Whitefield's 'Sagacity soon discovered in the Air of our Heroe something which distinguished him from the Vulgar' (*TJ* VIII. 8). She consequently orders a room to be prepared and a place at her dinner table to be kept for him; when Tom, however, attempts to return the compliment with his own invitation to tea, his reputation has already been tarnished by both the 'Petty-fogger' and Partridge, and Mrs Whitefield hence 'refused, and with a Manner so different from that with which she had received him at Dinner, that it a little surprized him' (*TJ* VIII. 8).

I suggested earlier that Goldknopf overestimates, or at least over-simplifies, the sociability of the inn when he alludes to 'the openness and human interaction of inn-life' as if this were its only aspect. In fact, the social interaction to which Goldknopf alludes is far less conspicuous in Fielding's inns than it is in either the *Quijote* or the *Roman comique*, and is confined largely to the socializing between the staff of the inn and the guests' servants in the kitchen. The guests themselves generally wish to avoid the kind of society an inn affords, and prefer to stay in their own apartments;[59] when they do interact with other guests they do so either privately, such as behind the closed door of Mrs Waters's bedroom at Upton, or accidentally, such as on the occasion Fitzpatrick mistakenly opens this door in his search for his wife. As I noted earlier, the characters who meet at the inns of *Joseph Andrews* and *Tom Jones* tend to be previous acquaintances or relations who consequently interact relatively little with strangers. Thus, while the social interaction of the kitchen may spill over into the parlour, it fails to take over the inn in the same way as it does, for example, at Palomeque's *venta*. Although a number of the characters at Palomeque's inn prove, like those at the inns of *Joseph Andrews* and *Tom Jones*, to be coincidentally connected or related in some way, they form a community there that extends beyond these bonds to embrace the other guests at the inn.

Bakhtin's subgeneric category, the 'adventure novel of everyday life', suggests if not a paradoxical then at least a curious combination of opposites, as appropriate to Fielding's fiction as to the classical works of fiction to which he applies the term. Joseph, Tom and the numerous others who take to the road in *Joseph Andrews* and *Tom Jones* travel a course that is simultaneously familiar and foreign, and that inflects an essentially realistic topography with magical qualities. Goldknopf notes that

the inns in *Tom Jones* are much more than busy buildings with doors that can be opened at the wrong time; their power to stir the imagination lies far beyond that of mere mad-cap contrivance. Inns in general have rich symbolic overtones [...] In strange surroundings our basic needs recover their primitive supremacy, and the ordinary *gasthaus* assumes the aura of the dubious castle where the wayfarer seeks his nervous night's shelter.[60]

The inn serves basic needs in a basic form: when the three travellers in *Joseph Andrews* settle down to a meal at one such house, the narrator remarks that they 'fell to eating with Appetites infinitely more voracious than are to be found at the most exquisite Eating-Houses in the Parish of *St. James's*' (*JA* II. 16). As we see elsewhere, however, Fielding's inns are often reluctant to cater to the needs they are intended to serve, and decent food and rest are rarely available there.[61] Equally striking is the reluctance of Fielding's travellers to be catered for by the inn, and, moreover, to follow the conventional pattern of literary travels. There is an almost carnivalesque inversion of everyday life in their progress: they tend to travel at night rather than rest, and, in the case of Sophia, to rest during the day rather than to travel. At one inn therefore, 'The Sun [...] had been some time retired to Rest, when *Sophia* arose greatly refreshed by her sleep' (*TJ* XI. 3), while, as we saw earlier, Joseph embarks from London at night, and continues until his violent encounter with the robbers. Tom in particular appears to relish the romance of nocturnal travel, with the moon rising (rather as Sophia does) to light his way:

the dirty Fingers of Night would have drawn her sable Curtain over the Universe, had not the Moon forbid her, who now, with a Face as broad and as red as those of some jolly Mortals, who, like her, turn Night into Day, began to rise from her Bed, where she had slumbered away the Day, in order to sit up all Night. *Jones* had not travelled far before he paid his Compliments to that beautiful Planet, and turning to his Companion, asked him, If he had ever beheld so delicious an Evening. (*TJ* VIII. 9)[62]

Perhaps La Place's perception of Jones as a romanesque hero is not quite as misplaced as it first appeared. Although Fielding parodies many of the procedures his translator was later to adopt, and his fiction is incompatible with the latter's project of *bienséant* romancification, it is clear that he seeks to reform and modernize rather than annihilate the practices of romance. Goldknopf is clearly justified in pointing to the obvious parallels between the castle and the inn; Fielding, how-ever, exploits the inn *topos* in a manner that also suggests a parallel with the forests of chivalric romance. The manner in which he weaves between rooms, with characters narrowly evading each other, recalls Ariosto's technique in the *Furioso*; with Fielding, the inn has expanded yet further, succeeding labyrinthine romances to become both a labyrinth and a romance of its own. Like the labyrinth or forest, the inn is not a place of resolution or conclusion as it was in the *Quijote*—in contrast to *Tristram Shandy*,[63] no one is allowed to die there, or even have uninterrupted sex—but a *locus* through which the hero must pass in order to gain *sophia* or, indeed, Sophia.

Notes to Chapter 4

1. James Boswell, *Boswell's Life of Johnson*, ed. G. Birkbeck Hill, rev. L. F. Powell, 6 vols. (Oxford: Clarendon Press, 1934–64), 19 September 1777, iii. 162. Mrs Hester Thrale (later Mrs Piozzi) once asked Johnson why he enjoyed riding in a coach so much, to which he responded, 'That in the first place, the company was shut in with him *there*; and could not escape, as out of a room: in the next place, he heard all that was said in a carriage, where it was my turn to be deaf' (Samuel Johnson, *Johnsonian Miscellanies*, ed. G. Birkbeck Hill, 2 vols. (Oxford: Clarendon Press, 1897), i. 329).

2. Roy Porter observes of the turnpikes, 'These Georgian "motorways" produced their own booming sub-economy of inns, ostlers, coachmen and coaching services, highwaymen, and illicit game-dealers'—a cast of characters many of whom feature in the background of *Joseph Andrews* and *Tom Jones*; see Porter, *English Society in the Eighteenth Century*, 2nd edn. (London: Penguin, 1990), 191.

3. Nancy Armstrong, *Desire and Domestic Fiction: A Political History of the Novel* (Oxford: Oxford University Press, 1987), 251.

4. Watt, *The Rise of the Novel*, 188.

5. Letter to Miss G[rainger], 22 Jan. 1750, in *Notes and Queries*, 4th ser., 3 (1869), 276.

6. From John Dod and Robert Cleaver, *A Godly Forme of Householde Gouernment: For the Ordering of Private Families according to the Direction of God's Word* (London, 1614), quoted in Kathleen M. Davis, 'The Sacred Condition of Equality—How Original were Puritan Doctrines of Marriage?', *Social History*, 5 (1977), 563–80 (570).

7. William B. Warner, 'The Elevation of the Novel in England: Hegemony and Literary History', *ELH* 59 (1992), 577–96 (578).

8. Watt, *The Rise of the Novel*, 189.

9. Samuel Taylor Coleridge, *Table Talk*, ed. Carl Woodring, 2 vols., in *The Complete Works of Samuel Taylor Coleridge*, Bollingen Series LXXV (London: Routledge, 1990), i. 496.

10. Watt, *The Rise of the Novel*, 285.

11. Quotations are from Henry Fielding, *Joseph Andrews*, ed. Martin C. Battestin (Middletown, CT: Wesleyan University Press, 1967). References are to book and chapter.

12. 'one of those who may be termed Train-bearers to the Law [...] and will ride more Miles for half a Crown than a Post-boy' (*TJ* VIII. 8). (Quotations are from Henry Fielding, *Tom Jones*, ed. Martin C. Battestin and Fredson Bowers, 2 vols. (Oxford: Wesleyan University Press, 1975). References are to book and chapter.)

13. See below, n. 50.

14. Cf. Goldsmith's *She Stoops to Conquer: or the Mistakes of a Night* (1773), in which the running joke is the mistaking of a private house for an inn (in *Collected Works*, ed. Arthur Friedman, 5 vols. (Oxford: Clarendon Press, 1966), v. 101–217).

15. An originally epic *topos* has clearly by this time become identified with romance.

16. For further details of the contemporary reception of La Place's translation, see Shelly Charles, 'Le *Tom Jones* de La Place ou la fabrique d'un roman français', *Revue d'histoire littéraire*, 6 (1994), 931–58.

17. *HTJ* VII. 6. (Quotations are from Henry Fielding, *Histoire de Tom Jones, ou l'enfant trouvé*, trans. Pierre-Antoine de La Place, 4 vols. (London: Nourse, 1750). References are to book and chapter.)

18. Charles, 'Le *Tom Jones* de La Place', 948–9.

19. David Goldknopf, 'The Failure of Plot in *Tom Jones*', *Criticism*, 11 (1969), 262–74 (269). Goldknopf adds, 'It is curious that Fielding, who spent most of his adult life in or near London, was unable to recreate that milieu with vividness or conviction.'

20. Cf. the scene in the *Furioso* where Angelica and Medoro inscribe each other's names in the bark of trees, prompting Orlando's descent into madness—notably by an idyllic stream (*OF* XXIII. 100–5).

21. Cf. Sancho's similarly anti-idealistic portrait of Dulcinea in the *Quijote* (*DQ* I. 38).

22. Note that Tom requires less encouragement than Amadís, who must be urged on by his squire, Gandalín, in order to consummate his relationship with Oriana (*A*. I. 35). On the remarkable analogues between the plots of the *Amadís* and *Tom Jones*, see Miller's compelling evidence (*Henry Fielding's 'Tom Jones'*, 18).

23. See, for example, Ruggiero's failed rape of Angelica (*OF* X. 113 ff.); this is further explored below in Chapter 7, 'Jacques le Fataliste *ou* son maître: Whose Storyline is it Anyway?' *Tristram Shandy*, of course, opens with the interrupted coitus of Tristram's parents.

24. This phenomenon led C. S. Lewis to remark, 'as the (improbable) adventure which we are following is liable at any moment to be interrupted by some quite different (improbable) adventures, there steals upon us unawares the conviction that adventures of this sort are going on all around us, that in this vast forest (we are nearly always in a forest) this is the sort of thing that goes on all the time, that it was going on before we arrived and will continue after we have left' (in his introduction to Spenser, in G. B. Harrison (ed.), *Major British Writers*, 2 vols. (London: Harcourt, Brace, 1954), i. 98).

25. Miller, *Henry Fielding's 'Tom Jones'*, 68.

26. Goldknopf, 'The Failure of Plot in *Tom Jones*', 268.

27. Chênerie, *Le Chevalier errant*, 503–4.

28. Note, however, that the modern reference is accompanied by the latinate name, '*Timotheus*'.

29. Fielding's 'comic Epic-Poem in Prose' (JA, preface) thus invites yet another epic parallel as a storm brings the hero and heroine together. The inn proves to be the modern counterpart of the cave in which Dido and Aeneas meet in *Aeneid* IV, ll. 160–8 (Virgil, *Aeneid*, Budé edition, ed. and trans. Jacques Perret, 3 vols. (Paris: Les Belles Lettres, 1981), i. 116). Note also the encounter with the gypsies in *Tom Jones*, which is precipitated by precipitation as Tom and Partridge 'deviated into a much less frequented Track' in the rain and darkness only to stumble upon the community of gypsies with whom they pass the rest of the storm (*TJ* XII. 12).

30. See below, Ch. 5, 'Fielding and the Rhetoric of Travel'.

31. As Fielding suggests in *Tom Jones* when he remarks that Sophia and her fellow-travellers have 'made such good Expedition, that they performed a Journey of ninety Miles in two Days', arriving in London 'without having encountered any one Adventure on the Road' (*TJ* XI. 9) worth relating.

32. See below, Ch. 6, 'The Journey through France'.

33. Cf. Dr Slop's meeting with Obadiah 'in the dirtiest part of a dirty lane' (*TS* II. 9) in *Tristram Shandy*.

34. Cf. the narrator's apparent difficulty with a hill in *Tom Jones* (below, Ch. 5, 'The Reader as Travelling Companion'), Tristram's genuine troubles with a staircase in *Tristram Shandy* (below, Ch. 6, 'The Miniaturization of the Digressive Landscape') and an *impasse* in *Jacques* (below, Ch. 7, 'Two Narrative Metaphors: The Road and the Horse'). The case of Joseph characteristically suggests an epic source, as the hospitality of the inn reveals, in its detention of one of its guests, a modern, commercial equivalent to that of the hosts of the *Odyssey*.

35. At the following alehouse, Adams and his companions again run up a debt that they are unable to pay (*JA* II. 16).

36. Cf. Jacques's difficulty with the hangman's horse, below (Ch. 7, 'Two Narrative Metaphors: The Road and the Horse').

37. As Rosamond Bayne-Powell observes, 'English people of the upper classes generally travelled in their carriages, drawn by their own horses, or when posting had been established, by post-horses' (*Travellers in Eighteenth-Century England* (London: John Murray, 1951), 8).

38. *A Copy of a Letter*, reprinted in Joan Parkes, *Travel in England in the Seventeenth Century* (Oxford: Oxford University Press, 1925), 93.

39. Douglas Chambers, *The Reinvention of the World: English Writing 1650–1750* (London: Arnold, 1996), 36.
40. 'This crowding of the coaches was a common complaint' (Bayne-Powell, *Travellers in Eighteenth-Century England*, 11).
41. Fielding is not the first to use the stagecoach as a narrative frame for the interpolation of stories: Percy Adams notes the precedent of Mrs Manley's *A Stage-Coach Journey to Exeter* (originally published in 1696 as *Letters to a Friend*) in which among the narrator's companions are 'a fop who ogles her and tells a story of catching his mistress in bed with another man; the wife of a major, very talkative, whose story is of her second husband; and two virgin travellers'; new characters join the narrator at Salisbury, including 'a pregnant wife, her roving husband, and a friendly Mrs Stanhope, who also has a story, hers sentimental, of an unfaithful lover' (Percy G. Adams, *Travel Literature and the Evolution of the Novel* (Lexington, KY: University Press of Kentucky, 1983), 217).
42. Goldknopf, 'The Failure of Plot in *Tom Jones*', 266–7.
43. One learns the name of the village when Sophia passes through it (*TJ* X. 9).
44. The *OED* records this sense of the word *dragon*, 'a fierce violent person; *esp.* a fiercely or aggressively watchful woman: a duenna', and cites Johnson's dictionary of 1755: '*Dragon* [...] 3. A fierce violent man or woman'. This sense of the word was therefore in common usage in the mid-eighteenth century.
45. See *DQ* I. 16.
46. The Maritornes episode of the *Quijote* moreover unquestionably provides the prototype for the mistaken bed scene at Booby Hall in *Joseph Andrews* (*JA* IV. 14)
47. The most notable of which are the bloody fight between Adams and the host (*JA* II. 5), the 'violent Dispute' over the reckoning between Robin and his guests (*TJ* VII. 11), and the '*Battle of* Upton', in which Tom, Partridge and Mrs Waters defend themselves against the landlady, landlord, and Susan (*TJ* IX. 3).
48. An episode that inevitably echoes the puppet-show scene in the *Quijote* (*DQ* II. 26).
49. Tom also notably refuses to go to a tavern with Nightingale (*TJ* XIII. 6).
50. 'The Great White Horse is famous in the neighbourhood, in the same degree as a prize ox, or county paper-chronicled turnip, or unwieldy pig—for its enormous size. Never were such labyrinths of uncarpeted passages, such clusters of mouldy, badly lighted rooms, such huge numbers of small dens for eating or sleeping in, beneath any one roof, as are collected together between the four walls of the Great White Horse at Ipswich' (*The Pickwick Papers* (Oxford: Oxford University Press, 1986), ch. XXII, pp. 271–2).
51. Note the careful choice of room names; elsewhere Tom's identity is perhaps more subtly hinted at when he stays in a room called 'the Sun' (*TJ* VIII. 4).
52. Goldknopf, 'The Failure of Plot in *Tom Jones*', 268.
53. See *OF* XII. 1–22, and below, Ch. 5, 'Fielding and the Rhetoric of Travel'. Henry K. Miller suggests other models for the inn at Upton: 'Don Quixote took an inn to be a castle; but Fielding, drawing with equal comic force upon the romance tradition, has metamorphosed the humble inn at Upton into Circe's Isle and the enchanted Bower of Bliss' (Miller, *Henry Fielding's 'Tom Jones'*, 51).
54. The abduction of the heroine is one of the stock situations of French romance throughout the seventeenth and eighteenth centuries. Sorel tells the story of a girl who, when asked how far she had advanced in the *roman* she was reading,

replied that she was at the fourth abduction or 'enlèvement' (*De la connoissance des bons livres*, 114). Five years earlier, Antoine Furetière had remarked in his *Roman bourgeois*, 'Il ne tiendroit qu'à moi de faire icy une héroïne qu'on enleveroit autant de fois que je voudrois faire de volumes' (in *Romanciers du XVIIe siècle*, ed. A. Adam (Paris: Gallimard, 1958), 917); cf. *Jacques*: 'Vous voyez, Lecteur, que je suis en beau chemin, et qu'il ne tiendrait qu'à moi de vous faire attendre un an, deux ans, trois ans, le récit des amours de Jacques, en le séparant de son maitre et en leur faisant courir à chacun tous les hazards qu'il me plairait' (*JF* 5). Quotations are from Denis Diderot, *Jaques le Fataliste et son maitre*, ed. Simone Lecointre and Jean Le Galliot (Paris: Droz, 1976). References are to page only.

55. Miller also draws attention to the 'irony and air of benign attachment' that the *Furioso* shares with 'the ethos of the Narrator of *Tom Jones*' (*Henry Fielding's 'Tom Jones'*, 19).

56. Sophia earlier tells Honour (in reference to Jones), 'I can forgive all rather than his exposing my Name in so barbarous a Manner' (*TJ* X. 5) while Honour, at another inn, had told her Mistress, 'he must be a very pitiful Fellow, and could have no Love for a Lady, whose Name he would thus prostitute in an Alehouse' (*TJ* VIII. 9).

57. Once again one may observe in the manner in which 'Hole' succeeds 'Parlour' a comic downward spiral akin to that noted above with 'Alehouse' and 'Inn'.

58. 'Parlour' (from the old French form of *parler*) is defined in this context by the *OED* as 'a room in an inn more private than the taproom, where people may converse apart'.

59. Tom, for example, wishes to avoid the quaker he meets at the inn in Hambrook.

60. Goldknopf, 'The Failure of Plot in *Tom Jones*', 266.

61. See, for example, Fielding's description in *Tom Jones* of 'some Maxims, which Publicans hold to be the grand Mysteries of their Trade': 'The first is, if they have any Thing good in their House (which indeed very seldom happens) to produce it only to Persons who travel with great Equipages' (*TJ* VIII. 7).

62. A few pages later, at the foot of a hill, Tom tells Partridge, 'I wish I was at the Top of this Hill; it must certainly afford a most charming Prospect, especially by this Light: For the solemn Gloom which the Moon casts on all Objects, is beyond Expression beautiful, especially to an Imagination which is desirous of cultivating melancholy Ideas' (*TJ* VIII. 10). There is unquestionably here a strong suggestion of Quixotism in Tom's cultivation of his own distress.

63. Le Fever dies at an inn not far from the Shandys (*TS* VI. 10).

CHAPTER 5

Fielding II
The Topology of Travel

The journey has long provided one of the dominant metaphors of literary discourse, and Fielding is evidently far from being the first author to exploit the language of travel in order to describe the narrative process.[1] An examination of the topology of Fielding's fiction reveals the precise influence a narrated journey may exert on the metaphors by which the idea of narrative is explored. Cervantes's fiction provides a good example of this phenomenon: as Hutchinson notes in his valuable study, 'land travel, especially walking, dominates Cervantes's imagery of narrative movement' in the *Quijote*, while the travel metaphors in the *Galatea* and *Persiles y Sigismunda* generally and appropriately relate to the sea.[2] In order to determine the extent to which Fielding is original in his rhetorical approach, some of the claims of Hutchinson's thesis merit some preliminary consideration.

Hutchinson uses an example of Sancho's idiosyncratic storytelling in Part I of the *Quijote* (*DQ* I. 20) to illustrate Cervantes's metaphorical use of travel:

The story is exemplary for the ways it fuses and confuses telling with traveling. The tale gets sidetracked immediately by the opening formulas whose purpose is normally to lead into the story, not out of it: to Sancho, however, the phrase 'may evil come to those who seek it out' seems applicable to Don Quixote's stubborn bent for seeking out danger, and prompts him to suggest they take another route, to which the knight replies: 'Follow your story Sancho, and leave the road we are to follow to me.' Sancho's discourse has transgressed from his narrative track to the spatial route of his journey with Don Quixote [...] In this passage, as in nearly all passages where Cervantine characters, narrators, or authors speak or write about narrative, the language of commentary represents narration primarily as a kind of journey.[3]

Hutchinson's insistence that Cervantes presents narration as a journey in the *Quijote*, however, rests primarily on the fact that the narrative process is described through verbs of motion, such as '*pasar, seguir, proseguir, volver, ir, andar,* and *llegar*'[4] and the repeated use of nouns such as *camino* and *paso*. While this undoubtedly depicts narration as a process of travelling, it does so on such a rudimentary level that it hardly distinguishes the rhetoric of the *Quijote* from that of other fiction. Nor is Cervantes's use of metaphor as precise as that which characterizes Fielding's fiction: while the travel metaphors of the *Quijote* are indeed confined to 'land travel, especially walking', one should note that Don Quijote spends more time travelling on horseback than on foot.

Hutchinson tends to use 'movement' and 'travel' as if they were entirely synonymous. While the verbs he catalogues evidently entail movement, they do not in any properly realized sense convey the magnitude implied in 'travel' or 'journey'.[5] Cervantes's metaphors of movement are furthermore generally confined to the verbs and nouns cited above. With very few exceptions, such metaphors do not invoke the topography of travel other than the basic *camino* itself: of these, the most striking occurs when Sancho's narrations draw attention to themselves by their failure to make progress. In the previous chapter, it was noted that the visibility of the fictionalized journey increases in inverse proportion to the smoothness of its progress, and consequently virtually disappears unless impeded. The same may be said of the process of narration: the waywardness of Sancho's storytelling shifts the attention of both the fictive listener and the actual reader from its content to its form, a transition that leads to the further and more sustained elaboration of metaphors relating to the topography of travel. The rhetorical apparatus of Fielding's fiction nevertheless develops such metaphors to a far greater extent than its counterpart and antecedent in the *Quijote*. Perhaps more significantly, Fielding's rhetoric of travel employs the same *topoi* his fiction shares topographically with the *Quijote*. In other words, while Cervantes restricts himself to simple metaphors of movement, Fielding develops the metaphorical potential of the journey to accommodate the inn, a *topos* that represents stasis as clearly as it implies travel.

Fielding and the Rhetoric of Travel

In a number of digressive fictions, a struggling authorial persona is presented as the reason for his narrative's errancy. In, for example, Swift's *Tale of a Tub*, the disorderly text is seen to be rooted in the disorderly imagination of the narrator. Narratorial incompetence may also be presented as the product rather than the source of difficult narrative material: the narrator of Ariosto's *Furioso* thus appears to be perpetually straining to keep up with the movements of his numerous errant protagonists. Conversely, the various narratorial intrusions and interpolations in Fielding's *Joseph Andrews* and *Tom Jones* are designed to reflect the author's absolute control of his subject—and, indeed, his 'Subjects' (*TJ* II. 1).[6] Chance, which generates interpolations through the motif of encounter in each of the fictions so far reviewed, continues to play a key role in the works of Fielding: the history of Wilson, for example, is introduced to the reader as the product of a chance meeting (which later turns out to be more fateful than accidental). In both *Joseph Andrews* and *Tom Jones*, however, deviations from the diegesis or main narrative are increasingly and transparently identifiable as the products of authorial interference rather than Providence. The systematic intercalation of extradiegetic material in the introductory chapters of *Joseph Andrews* and *Tom Jones* creates an impression of authorial control that is unprecedented in digressive fiction. Fielding's originality lies not only in the introduction of the 'initial Essays' (*TJ* V. 1), however, but in the use he puts them to. While Fielding himself suggests a theatrical parallel for his 'Prefatory Chapter' with the dramatic 'Prologue' (*TJ* XVI. 1), I would argue that the *Furioso* provides him with a prototype in this context. Ariosto begins each canto of his poem with a preface or proem; moreover, like Fielding, he uses this introductory matter to project a particular image of authorship—albeit one that contrasts sharply with that found in *Joseph Andrews* and *Tom Jones*.

An Ariostan inspiration for Fielding's prefatory chapters is in particular suggested by the metaphor adopted by each author in his final address to his readership. Ariosto begins the lengthy proem of his final canto with his own variation on the nautical metaphor:

> Or, se mi mostra la mia carta il vero,
> non è lontano a discoprirsi il porto;
> sí che nel lito i voti scitoglier spero
> a chi nel mar per tanta via m'ha scorto;
> ove, o di non tornar col legno intero,
> o d'errar sempre, ebbi già il viso smorto.
> Ma mi par di veder, ma veggo certo,
> veggo la terra, e veggo il lito aperto.
> (*OF* XLVI. 1. 1–8)[7]

[Now if my chart tells me true, the harbour will soon be in sight and I may hope to fulfil my vow ashore to One who has accompanied me on so long a voyage. Oh, how I had paled at the prospect of returning with but a crippled ship, or perhaps of wandering forever! But I think I see ... yes, I do see land, I see the welcoming shore.]

On the shore, waiting for him to land, are the poet's friends. In the last of *Tom Jones*'s prefatory chapters, Fielding also bids his reader farewell with the aid of a travel metaphor:

We are now, Reader, arrived at the last Stage of our long Journey. As we have therefore travelled together through so many Pages, let us behave to one another like Fellow-Travellers in a Stage-Coach, who have passed several days in the Company of each other; and who, notwithstanding any Bickerings or little Animosities which may have occurred on the Road, generally make all up at the last, and mount, for the last Time, into their Vehicle with Chearfulness and Good-Humour; since after this one Stage, it may possibly happen to us, as it commonly happens to them, never to meet more. (*TJ* XVIII.1)

The differences in the type and style of metaphor adopted by each author are revealing: while Ariosto portrays the poet-narrator here as an anxious, solitary figure accompanied only by divine inspiration, Fielding presents the author and reader as fellow-travellers; furthermore, whereas Ariosto's poet presents his enterprise as a perilous maritime expedition, Fielding decides upon the less heroic metaphor of the stagecoach.[8] In each case, the chosen metaphor is particularly appropriate: the dangerous and difficult voyage evoked by Ariosto's narrator evidently recalls the arduous journeys undertaken by those whose adventures he has narrated. Not for the first time in the poem, the experience of the eponymous hero and his fellow-knights is reflected in the trials of the narrator: the latter admits his fear that he might have been doomed to 'errar sempre'. The *Furioso* itself resembles Atlante's castle, in which the entrapped knights seem sentenced to wander endlessly until the arrival of Astolfo. Atlante's castle, a 'palazzo altiero' constructed from 'vari marmi con suttil lavoro' [stately edifice [...] built of many kinds of marble, a work of intricate design] (*OF* XII. 8) may indeed be construed as a metaphor for the poem. Italo Calvino hints at this when he notes the effect of Astolfo's breaking of the spell:

To those he had captured, Atlante grants freedom to roam the roads of the poem once more. Is this Atlante or Ariosto? The enchanted palace stands revealed as an astute structural stratagem on the part of the narrator [...] The enchanter who wants to delay the accomplishment of destiny and the poet-strategist who now swells, now thins the ranks of the figures on the stage, first regrouping and then dispersing them, merge until the two are virtually identical.[9]

Fielding's metaphor of the stagecoach reflects the topography and register of his work as clearly as Ariosto's ship coming into harbour; the image of an epic or romanesque journey across the seas would appear incongruous in a work in which the action is landlocked. Fielding's authorial persona thus adopts a metaphor compatible with the experiences available to his characters. While none of the protagonists in *Tom Jones* travels by stagecoach (in contrast to their counterparts in *Joseph Andrews*), the topology of coaches and inn nevertheless conforms to the topography Fielding delineates. As Hunter remarks, 'soon the idea of journey takes control of the book's rhetoric as well as its narrative'.[10] The vocabulary of eighteenth-century travel thus frames the journey of the reader as well as of the heroes of *Joseph Andrews* and *Tom Jones*. While Ariosto hints at a metaphorical connection between Atlante's labyrinthine palace and his own poem, Fielding expressly identifies another, less romanesque edifice as an appropriate metaphor for his work: in the '*Bill of Fare to the Feast*', which opens *Tom Jones*, he famously likens his role to that of the keeper of a 'public Ordinary' (*TJ* I. 1) in which every chapter is a course and the food to be consumed is 'HUMAN NATURE'.[11] As we have already seen, Fielding is not the first to use such culinary metaphors;[12] he nevertheless explores their potential in greater depth than any previous author. What makes the 'Bill of Fare' interesting to the reader is the deftness with which the author juggles with the image he has created, and the extent to which he is willing to force the comparison: he thereby brings a new meaning to Pope's famous couplet by framing it within a culinary context: 'But the Whole, to continue the same Metaphor, consists in the Cookery of the Author; for as Mr *Pope* tells us, "True Wit is Nature to Advantage *drest*, | What oft' was thought, but ne'er so well exprest"' (*TJ* I. 1).[13]

Fielding opens *Tom Jones* with the following declaration: 'An Author ought to consider himself, not as a Gentleman who gives a private or eleemosynary Treat, but rather as one who keeps a public Ordinary, at which all Persons are welcome for their Money' (*TJ* I. 1). This distinction between the private and public domain resonates beyond its immediate metaphorical significance here to suggest Fielding's topographical preference for the open road over the closed, domestic sphere favoured by Richardson. His announcement that all paying customers are welcome clearly alludes to his readership; at the same time, however, Fielding suggests something about the variety of *dramatis personae* his metaphorical tavern is able to accommodate. The 'Ordinary' is open to a broader cross-section of society than is likely at the 'Treat' offered by a gentleman—an impression compounded by the author's insistence upon the 'prodigious Variety' (*TJ* I. 1) of cuisine he is to serve his reader. Fielding concludes his introduction with another topographical pointer when he reveals he will begin his feast 'in that more plain and simple Manner in which it is found in the Country, and shall hereafter hash and ragoo it with all the high *French* and *Italian* Seasoning of Affectation and Vice which Courts and Cities afford' (*TJ* I. 1). As we have seen in the previous chapter, La Place evidently preferred the '*French*' seasoning to the plain country cuisine served in the first part of *Tom Jones.*

Through his 'Ordinary' metaphor, Fielding presents *Tom Jones* as a work that will refresh and entertain the reader (ordinaries were often gambling houses as well as eating houses). The general 'Bill of Fare, which all Persons may peruse at their first Entrance into the House' is, he announces, to be accompanied by 'particular Bills to every Course which is to be served up in this and the ensuing Volumes' (*TJ* I. 1). This image curiously conflicts with the travel metaphor of the final prefatory chapter: whereas the reader to whom Fielding bids farewell is described as his travelling companion, the reader of this opening chapter is a diner preparing not for a journey but for a meal (the scale of which, in any case, would presumably render him incapable of leaving the table, let alone climbing into a stagecoach). Fielding presents himself and his narrative in a variety of different guises during the course of *Tom Jones*, and is not afraid to mix metaphors; as Robert Chibka observes, 'the innkeeper who owns the place (I: 1) and the passenger who travels on an equal footing (XVIII: 1) do not resolve into one "character" without distortion, though each image suggests parallels with certain characters in the novel'.[14]

The 'Ordinary' metaphor, and the stasis it implies, in fact suit *Tom Jones* rather less well than another image that performs a similar function in *Joseph Andrews*. In the introductory chapter to book II of *Joseph Andrews*, Fielding declares, 'What are the Contents prefixed to every Chapter, but so many Inscriptions over the Gates of Inns [...] informing the Reader what Entertainment he is to expect, which, if he likes not, he may travel on to the next'.[15] The reader is warned 'not to travel through these Pages too fast: for if he doth, he may probably miss the seeing some curious Productions of Nature which will be observed by the slower and more accurate Reader' (*JA* II. 1);[16] he is once again embarked on a textual journey, apparently following in the footsteps of Joseph and Adams by travelling from inn to inn. Fielding, however, is as guilty here as he is in *Tom Jones* of mixing his inn metaphors: in the same prefatory chapter he informs his reader, 'those little Spaces between our Chapters may be looked upon as an Inn or Resting-Place, where he may stop and take a Glass' (following the example of Adams in particular) and 'those Pages which are placed between our Books [...] as those Stages, where, in long Journeys, the Traveller stays some Time to repose himself' (*JA* II. 1). The inn, the narrator implies, constitutes a blank space or vacuum in which no events or incidents may enter, and in which the traveller may enjoy a complete rest from the episodes thrown up by a journey. In this respect, Fielding's inn metaphor bears little relation to its topographical model in either his own fiction or that of such predecessors as Cervantes and Scarron. The inns of *Joseph Andrews* and *Tom Jones*, we have already seen, rarely provide the rest a traveller seeks: while Joseph and Tom frequently pause at wayside inns, their adventures never surrender as easily to stasis; as Hunter notes, 'the inns for us, as for Joseph and Tom, are sometimes no more restful than a footrace or an ambush'.[17]

In the final prefatory chapter of *Tom Jones*, Fielding informs his reader that they are 'arrived at the last Stage' (*TJ* XVIII. 1) of their journey (by which he means an inn rather than the distance between inns which a stage may also signify[18]). Fielding's metaphorical inn has thus graduated from representing a blank page in *Joseph Andrews* to an introductory chapter in *Tom Jones*. This transition is ironically belittled by Fielding's minimalist descriptions of certain prefatory chapters such as those '*Containing little or nothing*' (*TJ* III. 1) or '*Containing five pages of paper*' (*TJ* IV. 1). Notwithstanding this false modesty, Fielding chooses in these essays to preserve the characteristics mentioned above of an enveloping vacuum, external to the narrative whose progress they interrupt. These 'textual inns' are not, however, intended as dull places in which the reader may nod off: they are no more designed for rest than the inns that punctuate the roads travelled by Joseph and Tom. One might say that these essays have more in common with Fielding's 'Ordinary' than with his 'Stage': they are designed to rouse and refresh the reader rather than put him to sleep. In the last of these

'Prologues', for example, the narrator expresses his hope that his 'ludicrous Observations' may have 'prevented thee from taking a Nap when it was beginning to steal on thee' (*TJ* XVIII. 1). In an earlier 'Essay', he distinguishes his work from those histories that 'should always be attended with a Tankard of good Ale' (*TJ* IV. 1):

That our Work, therefore, might be in no Danger of being likened to the Labours of these Historians, we have taken every Occasion of interspersing though the whole sundry Similies, Descriptions, and other kind of poetical Embellishments. These are, indeed, designed to supply the Place of the said Ale, and to refresh the Mind, whenever those Slumbers which in a long Work are apt to invade the Reader as well as the Writer, shall begin to creep upon him. Without Interruptions of this Kind, the best Narrative of plain Matter of Fact must overpower every Reader. (*TJ* IV. 1)

In keeping with the 'ordinary' metaphor of the opening chapter, the narrator represents the 'Embellishments' (which presumably include the prefatory chapters) as the 'Ale' with which the reader may wash down the many courses of his feast. The interruptions to the 'plain Matter of Fact' are therefore presented as refreshing diversions on an otherwise potentially monotonous journey.

The Introductory Chapters: The Case of La Place

Fielding's suggestion that one of his introductory chapters contains '*little or nothing*' is in keeping with his other ironically disparaging comments regarding such essays in both *Joseph Andrews* and *Tom Jones*. In the former of these works, for example, the narrator remarks that 'a Chapter or two (for Instance this I am now writing) may be often pass'd over without Injury to the Whole' (*JA* II. 1). In an introductory chapter of *Tom Jones*, entitled '*Of* THE SERIOUS *in writing, and for what Purpose it is introduced*', Fielding claims to follow the example of 'that most exquisite Entertainment, called the *English* pantomime' by adopting the pantomime convention of dividing the spectacle into '*the Serious* and *the Comic*'—or, as he subsequently puts it, between the '*Duller* and *Dullest*' (*TJ* V. 1). Fielding then turns from John Rich's pantomime to Homer's *Odyssey*, which he defends from Horace's famous accusation, '*Indignor quandoque bonus dormitat* Homerus, | *Verum Opere longo fas et obrepere Somnum*' (*TJ* V. 1).[19] Fielding insists that Homer should not be understood to fall asleep while he is writing: 'these soporific Parts are so many Scenes of *Serious* artfully interwoven, in order to contrast and set off the rest'; consequently, he asks the reader to consider his 'initial Essays' in the same light ('or rather in this Darkness' (*TJ* V. 1)). He concludes this chapter with a comment reminiscent of *Joseph Andrews*, informing the reader that, 'if he shall be of Opinion, that he can find enough of Serious in other Parts of this History, he may pass over these, in which we profess to be laboriously dull, and begin the following Books, at the second Chapter' (*TJ* V. 1).

Few readers would question the premiss that a strong sense of contrast operates in the relationship between the introductory chapters and the narrative that they both frame and interrupt. The terms 'Serious' and 'Comic', however, are evidently and deliberately inadequate to describe the kind of antithesis that operates either in Homer's poetry or in Fielding's own fiction—comic moments in the *Odyssey*, for example, are few and far between. Fielding's refusal to provide a considered defence of his method of intercalating essays is, of course, all the more ironic given the label of seriousness he teasingly applies to them. The joke, however, notably backfires with the decision of one of his readers to do exactly what Fielding suggests, and begin each book of *Tom Jones* at the second chapter. The reader in question, La Place, called Fielding's bluff by taking his advice at face value and omitting the introductory chapters from his translation.

La Place prefaces his *Tom Jones* with a letter ostensibly addressed to Fielding, but whose inclusion evidently demonstrates it to be primarily intended for his own readership. The letter predictably serves chiefly to justify the translator's strategy: La Place puts forward the rather dubious assertion that he has done only what Fielding himself would have done had he been writing for a French audience:

Si M. Fielding [...] avoit écrit pour les François, il eut probablement supprimé un grand nombre de passages très excellens en eux-mêmes, mais qui leur paraîtroient déplacés. Une fois échauffé par l'intérêt résultant d'une intrigue patétique & adroitement tissuë, ils supportent impatiemment toute espece de digressions, de Dissertations, ou de Traités de Morale, & regardent ces ornemens, quelque beaux qu'ils soient, comme autant d'obstacles au plaisir dont ils sont empressés de jouir. J'ai fait ce que l'Auteur eût fait lui-même. (*HTJ*, preface, pp. viii–ix)[20]

Fielding's self-conscious assertions of his authority over his 'Subjects' in *Tom Jones* are inverted by La Place, who subjugates himself to the presumed will of his (French) readers and critics rather than to his (English) author. Thus, while Fielding ostentatiously turns a deaf ear to the voice of the critic, La Place may be imagined to be studiously taking notes. All of the alterations he makes to his target text reveal a classically underpinned aesthetic that has evolved little since the influential criticism of Huet, Valincour and Du Plaisir in the 1670s and 1680s.[21] La Place's remarks echo Du Plaisir's pronouncement, 'Le mélange d'histoires particulières avec l'histoire principale est contre le gré du lecteur'. Du Plaisir, who claims to speak for all readers, would certainly not have reacted more positively than La Place to the attempts by Fielding and Sterne to slow the reader's progress. The success of La Place's translation arguably reflects that little had changed in the intervening seventy years: the French reader allegedly continued to demand a smooth and preferably quick ride to the end of the *roman* he was reading.[22] It is, moreover, revealing that La Place perceives the narrative of *Tom Jones* to be 'une intrigue patétique & adroitement tissuë', or love story, rather than a comic romance. This in fact describes his *Tom Jones* rather better than Fielding's original: La Place's translation seeks to transform Fielding's 'History' into one of those 'monstrous Romances' (*TJ* IX. 1) from which the author is at such pains to distance himself; in other words, to make it less novel and, some would argue, less a novel.

La Place thus removes all of Fielding's introductory chapters, or 'Dissertations', with the exception of approximately half of the 'Invocation' (*TJ* XIII. 1).[23] He adds in a footnote to his prefatory letter that these chapters could subsequently be published separately, in 'un petit volume détaché aussi instructif qu'amusant'. His perception of these prefatory essays as entirely distinct and autonomous ornaments recalls Fielding's own remark regarding 'these several initial Chapters; most of which, like Modern Prologues, may as properly be prefixed to any other Book in this History as to that which they introduce, or indeed to any other History as to this' (*TJ* XVI. 1).[24] La Place omits Fielding's observations and intrusions for the same reason that Marivaux conversely provides *La Vie de Marianne* with an unusually contemplative narrator: reflections have little if any place in the conventional *roman romanesque*. Marianne's musings, like Fielding's 'ludicrous Observations', provide Marivaux with a 'Mark or Stamp' (*TJ* IX. 1) by which his work may be distinguished from those of his less respected contemporaries. The fictive editor of *La Vie de Marianne* may, therefore, point to the inclusion of the heroine's reflections as an indication that the work in question is not a *roman* at all: 'si c'était une histoire simplement imaginée, il y a toute apparence qu'elle n'aurait pas la forme qu'elle a. Marianne n'y ferait ni de si longues ni de si fréquentes réflexions.'[25]

La Place does not simply cut out the majority of Fielding's essays and observations. Like the good neoclassicist he tries to be, he eliminates all of those other 'poetical Embellishments' in which the author's presence is most strongly felt in the original: Fielding's mock-epic '*Battle sung by the Muse in the* Homerican *Stile*' is thus reduced to a brief, non-parodic summary, while his '*Description of a Battle of the amorous Kind*' (*TJ* IX. 5) between Tom and Mrs Waters is similarly transformed: 'Les sentimens d'une reconnoissance très légitime, de la part de la Dame, ouvrirent la scène. *Jones* y répondit avec chaleur: le dialogue fut vif & pressant, l'amour & l'occasion le dictoient; point de raisonnemens, point de digressions inutiles, rien qui s'écartât du but' (*HTJ* IX.3). The brevity and haste with which both La Place and the lovers at the inn pursue sexual resolution reflect the translator's approach to his task as a whole, and his decision to include 'rien qui s'écartât du but' in his version of *Tom Jones*. In this respect, La Place may be said to stand at the opposite end of the spectrum from Ariosto or Sterne, each of whom repeatedly (and sometimes endlessly) defers or interrupts the attempted coitus of their characters.[26] As this example also demonstrates, La Place seeks to turn Fielding's originally comic 'Battle' into a romanesque episode not so far from the very type that the English author sought to parody. This process of romanesque transformation becomes explicit in La Place's abbreviated rendering of Fielding's '*short Hint of what we can do in the Sublime, and a Description of Miss* Sophia Western' (*TJ* IV.2). The '*Hint*' was evidently not short enough for La Place, who writes,

Le véridique Auteur de cette histoire, a fait un portrait en grand, & très-détaillé des charmes de la figure, du caractére, & des talens de notre Héroïne; & moi, pour épargner à nos François, moins patients que nos voisins, l'ennui toujours inséparable des longueurs, je dirai tout simplement,
   Que Sophie était belle, & qui plus est aimable. (*HTJ* IV.1)

This last sentence almost completely replaces about three pages of the original, in which the author waxes lyrical over his heroine. La Place does not quite leave it there, however: he steers his readers along a quite different path from that chosen by Fielding, inviting them to conjure up the old clichés of certain 'vieux Romans' and to super-impose them on Sophia:

Ceux de mes Lecteurs dont l'imagination, pour s'échauffer, a besoin d'être fixée sur un objet particulier, peuvent ouvrir celui de nos vieux Romans qui leur tombera le plûtôt sous la main: le portrait de la première Princesse, pourvû qu'elle ait de grands yeux noirs bien coupés, vifs & pleins de douceurs, tous les autres traits du visage dignes d'accompagner de si beaux yeux, une peau blanche plusque l'albâtre, une taille de Nymphe, la noble modestie de Diane, & les graces de Vénus: pourvû, dis-je, qu'il trouve à peu près ce portrait-là, dans *Cyrus* ou dans *Clélie*, c'est d'aprés nature celui de notre Héroïne; & ma besogne est faite. (*HTJ* IV.1)

This appeal to a romanesque context is highly reminiscent of an episode in Furetière's *Roman bourgeois*, in which the narrator refuses to give an account of a conversation between two lovers because there already exist so many equivalent dialogues in other romances: 'vous devez savoir 20 ou 30 de ces entretiens par cœur', he tells his reader, inviting him instead to insert his own favourite 'entretien' from any romance he chooses.[27] La Place's intervention, in contrast to Furetière's, is not intentionally parodic, although it is clearly humorous. Were the reader to insert an 'entretien', one might, however, presume this contribution to constitute an inadvertent *parodos* or 'singing in imitation' of the numerous original romances.

La Place's allusion to the French romances of the previous century demonstrates that he does not always adhere to the principle of narratorial invisibility upon which an ostensible neoclassicist should insist. He occasionally follows the example of Fielding by intruding into his narrative in order to reinforce the new (but contrastingly conventional) context he seeks to establish for his version of *Tom Jones*, while his relocation of Sophia within a French tradition of romance heroines reflects his general enterprise of romanesque reappropriation. In his abbreviated portrait of Sophia, La Place retains from the original only her black eyes and skin whiter than alabaster. He gives her 'une taille de nymphe', but predictably omits Fielding's admission that her forehead 'might have been higher without Prejudice to her' (*TJ* IV.2) as this would compromise the idealized image appropriate to a heroine of romance.[28] As we saw earlier, a similar transformation is wrought on Tom. La Place cannot simply leave his reader to wander unaccompanied through his translation; having removed the introductory chapters by which Fielding had guided his reader, he is obliged to intervene himself in order to keep his reader on the right track. He in fact comes out of the translator's closet on more than one occasion—his explicit reference to the 'véridique Auteur', for example, is equally an admission of his own influence on the narrative in question. His concern for his French reader, moreover, leads him to add to as well as cut from the original: to ensure that his reader recognizes the name Dowling upon the lawyer's reappearance at *The Bell* at Gloucester in book VIII, he inserts a chapter of his own entitled 'Où le Traducteur Français parle seul' (*HTJ* VIII. 7). Having omitted the introductory chapters, in which Fielding speaks directly to his reader, La Place finally resorts to similarly intrusive chapters of his own. When the translator makes an appearance, it is inevitably to justify his radical alterations—generally by pointing out alleged weaknesses in Fielding's original.

La Place does not simply cut out the most evidently innovative and novel aspects of *Tom Jones*: as we saw in the previous chapter, he does a considerable amount of cutting during the picaresque-inflected middle section of the narrative, which Tom spends on the road, but leaves the final London section more or less intact. The tripartite balance of Fielding's work is thus sacrificed by La Place, who relegates the inn and the road from their central and pivotal role to a comparatively fleeting appearance. Fielding's original seems both too old and too new for his translator: the metaphorical inns of the introductory chapters and the actual inns of Tom's journey are both regarded as unwelcome diversions from the 'intrigue patétique'. La Place's decision to include such a clearly defined digression as the personal history of the Man of the Hill may, therefore, seem puzzling. The inclusion of this internal narration suggests that La Place's cuts were not simply motivated by a concern for formal unity, particularly given that the inn in *Tom Jones* (as in *Joseph Andrews*) does not provide the setting for any such disconnective interpolations. La Place's approach to editing his source appears to be guided by a desire for uniformity of tone rather than unity of action. It is, therefore, hardly surprising, for example, that La Place does not seek to incorporate such radical variations in tone as the mock-epic—or, indeed, the colourful vernacular of Squire Western. The inn, as a *locus* that accommodates and promotes polyphony over uniformity, is evidently incompatible with La Place's classical mindset.

As noted above, Fielding states that the purpose of his introductory chapters is to provide a contrast; the 'Art of Contrast' (*TJ* V. 1) is, however, alien to La Place's monotonizing strategy. It is for this reason above all that he eliminates these chapters and all the other antitheses and oppositions that are integral to Fielding's design: the French version loses the force of the country/city opposition that operates in the original, while the 'upstairs/downstairs' and 'kitchen/bedroom' juxtapositions that characterize Fielding's inns inevitably also disappear. It should be added, however, that La Place's decision to romancify *Tom Jones* was an undeniable factor in the enormous contemporary success his translation enjoyed. By contrast, the abbé Desfontaines's extremely faithful 1743 translation of *Joseph Andrews* was unanimously condemned on its publication as being too English and, consequently, unreadable. The abbé, however, has had the latest, if not the last, word: while La Place's *Tom Jones* is no longer read except by literary historians, Desfontaines's *Joseph Andrews* has recently made a comeback with a new edition.[29] The La Place translation nevertheless provides a fascinating insight into what *Tom Jones* is not: the omission of the introductory chapters and the shift of emphasis from road and inn to town reflect where the greatest differences between Fielding's fiction and those 'foolish Novels' reside.

The Introductory Chapters: The 'Art of Contrast'

Fielding's game of bluff and double bluff regarding the purpose of the introductory chapters masks his refusal in either *Joseph Andrews* or *Tom Jones* to provide any truly convincing reasons for their inclusion. In the fifth prologue of *Tom Jones*, the narrator promises 'to lay before the Reader, the Reasons which have induced us, to intersperse these several digressive Essays, in the Course of this Work'. The only reason he in fact gives at this point is a 'new Vein of Knowledge':

This Vein is no other than that of Contrast, which runs through all the Works of the Creation, and may, probably, have a large Share in constituting in us the Idea of all Beauty, as well natural as artificial: For what demonstrates the Beauty and Excellence of any Thing, but its Reverse? Thus the Beauty of Day, and that of Summer, is set off by the Horrors of Night and Winter. (*TJ* V. 1)

Fielding's conception of his introductions as 'the Horrors of Night and Winter' is evidently to some degree ironic. One suspects that Sterne may speak for Fielding as well as himself when he inverts this metaphor in *Tristram Shandy*: Tristram, in contrast to the implied author who presides over *Tom Jones*, insists that his digressions are the 'sun-shine' and the 'life' of his work, and that 'one cold eternal winter would reign in every page of it' if they were removed' (*TS* I. 22). Neither Fielding's image nor Sterne's, however, may be construed to be either straightforward or straightforwardly ironic. It would seem as perverse to interpret Fielding's magisterially plotted narrative as the darkness that allows these essays to shine, as it would be to assume he included these simply, as he suggests, as a foil to the rest of his work.

There are few works of fiction that confound the reader's attempt to distinguish between actual and implied authors as much as those of Fielding. It is perhaps idle to speculate whether Fielding himself was fonder of his introductory chapters or of his narrative. One may detect, however, beneath the easily dismissed self-deprecating assertions of the dullness and irrelevance of the 'initial Essays', the particular attachment of his authorial persona for these chapters of his work, even if, as he remarks, he can 'with less Pains write one of the Books of this History, than the Prefatory Chapter to each of them' (*TJ* XVI. 1). Fielding's narrator-essayist evidently revels in the opportunity these chapters afford to distance himself from less learned contemporaries;[30] this enjoyment apparently derives from a certain contempt for those writers incapable of managing anything other than 'mere Narrative only' (*TJ* IX. 1), and, implicitly, for 'plain Narrative' (*TJ* XVIII. 1) itself. Goldknopf's confidently categorical assertions that Fielding is a neoclassicist[31] (a designation that no doubt would have puzzled La Place) is in this respect highly questionable: both *Joseph Andrews* and *Tom Jones* systematically invert the classical stance regarding the silence of the authorial voice.[32] Indeed, the authorial persona of Fielding's work arguably has a greater affinity with the aesthetics of medieval romance. Eugène Vinaver writes that 'a good romance writer' was expected to reveal the meaning of his story with 'such embellishing thoughts as he considers appropriate; by doing this he would raise his work to a level of distinction which no straightforward narration could ever reach'.[33] It is here implied, as it is in *Tom Jones*, that anyone can tell a story, but only a genuine poet can, with considered elaboration, transform the adventures of his characters into a work of art; as Fielding puts it, 'to the Composition of Novels and Romances, nothing is necessary but Paper, Pens and Ink, with the manual Capacity of using them' (*TJ* IX. 1).[34] The *Furioso* is not the only romance to provide a potential source for Fielding's essays; while the precise definition of *conjoincture* in the work of Chrétien de Troyes has long been contentious,[35] the term apparently alludes to the narratorial commentary that connects events in the narrative. It is in the *conjoinctures* of his poem that the poet may display his learning and erudition and consequently set himself apart from humbler writers—

Chrétien de Troyes may therefore write that 'cil ne fet mis savoir | Qui sa science n'abandone | Tant con Deus la grace l'an done' [he is not wise who does not demonstrate his learning so long as God gives him grace].[36] A far later example of chivalric romance, the *Amadís*, attaches an importance to narratorial commentary that could be described as Fieldingesque were it not for Montalvo's apparent seriousness: in his preface to the first volume, he presents his narratorial intrusions as the highest form of his art, while the narrative matter itself is represented as comparatively coarse:

los cuales cinco libros como quiera que hasta aquí más por patrañas que por crónicas eran tenidos, son con las tales enmiendas acompañados de tales enxemplos y doctrinas, que con justa causa se podrán comparar a los livianos y febles saleros de corcho, que con tiras de oro y de plata son encarcelados y guarnescidos, porque así los cavalleros mancebos como los más ancianos hallen en ellos lo que a cada uno conviene. (*A.* I. 225)

[The said five Books, although up to now they have been considered fictions rather than chronicles, by virtue of the said emendations are augmented with moralizations and teachings of such a kind that they properly can be compared with cheap, coarse, cork salt shakers encased and adorned with bands of silver and gold—thus augmented in order that gentlemen, both old and young, may find in them what pertains to each.]

Montalvo, however, intrudes very little during the course of the *Amadís* and confines his occasional commentary to simple and repetitive moralizations against human vices (particularly pride) rather than displays of erudition.

Fielding's metaphor of 'Night and Winter' for his introductory chapters resonates beyond its immediate context as the ostensibly negative counterpart to 'Day' and 'Summer'. In works dominated by the topography and topology of journey, from the physical progress of the hero to the textual progress of the narrator and reader, both night and winter take on particular significance. As we have seen in each of the previous chapters, nightfall almost inevitably brings the travelling hero to an inn (as it once brought the knight to a castle); on the rare occasions that it does not, Fielding generally has an ulterior motive: in both *Joseph Andrews* and *Tom Jones*, travelling by night (or sleeping outdoors[37]) generally leads either to adventures or to misadventures, such as Joseph's meeting with two thieves (*JA* I. 12) or Tom's less violent encounter with a highwayman (*TJ* XII. 14). By representing his introductory chapters as the nights between the days of his narrative, Fielding reinforces the connotations of shelter and rest elicited elsewhere by his use of the inn as a metaphor for these 'digressive Essays'. The ambivalences and ambiguities of Fielding's metaphors of contrast are such, however, that the image of the inn may be seen to be represented by light as well as by darkness. The inn, and other places of shelter (such as the house of the Man of the Hill), often appear in Fielding's narratives as the light perceived from a distance by the traveller making his way at night. According to this interpretation, the inn may simultaneously be metaphorically associated with the apparent opposites of light and night. This does not alter the fact that the introductory chapters are to the reader what night is to the various characters who take to the road in *Joseph Andrews* and *Tom Jones*: cyclically recurring, enforced interruptions that oblige the traveller to pause on his journey. As metaphorical night—or winter—these chapters may be seen as part of Fielding's professed imitation of a divine model in his own 'great Creation' (*TJ* X. 1); the seasonal metaphor in particular suggests they may provide the textual counterpart to Nature's own time of rest—or stasis—until it rises again in spring. After nightfall, the inclement weather that winter implies is furthermore the most frequently given reason for the traveller breaking his journey at an inn: Tom's travels take place in winter, as the numerous references to the Jacobite rebellion of 1745 (and, of course, Partridge's persistent complaints about the cold) inform us; although Fielding does not state precisely the time of year at which Joseph embarks on his journey, the weather, which includes a hailstorm (*JA* I. 11), is clearly wintry, and therefore plays a key part in diverting Joseph from road to inn.

There is a further connotation of Fielding's winter metaphor that deserves a mention in this context. Winter had for a long time before Fielding been associated with the storytelling that its long evenings invited: a winter's tale signified 'an old trivial tale of some length suitable for nothing better than to while away a winter evening'.[38] The oral and communal characteristics of these stories are evident in many of the examples of the term's use: aside from the most obvious instance, *The Winter's Tale* in which Mamillus comments 'A sad tale's best for winter', in *Macbeth* an uncharacteristically cosy picture is painted when Lady Macbeth remarks, 'O these flawes and starts [...] would well become | A woman's story, at a Winter's fire'.[39] Whitlock similarly evokes a fireside setting when he observes, 'A pretty upshot of all ambitious Designes [...] to be made at length a Winter's Tale, and Chimney-corner Discourse' (1654).[40] The image these examples evoke is entirely appropriate to the tales exchanged around the 'Kitchin/Kitchen Fire' (*JA* I. 11; *TJ* IX. 6) of Fielding's country inns, from the story of Joseph's misfortune which Adams overhears at *The Dragon* (*JA* I. 14) to Partridge's account of his encounter with the mysterious Man of the Hill (*TJ* IX. 6).

The Reader as Travelling Companion

With the notable exception of the preface to *Joseph Andrews*, Fielding generally speaks of his fiction in metaphorical terms; with his images of stagecoaches and inns, the manner in which the topology of *Joseph Andrews* and *Tom Jones* emulates the landscape through which his characters travel is evident. Despite the spatial metaphor of a 'new Province of Writing' (*TJ* II. 1), the rhetoric of *Tom Jones* is familiar rather than foreign to the reader. It is striking, however, that Fielding appears to find the basic narrative syntax of inn and road so compelling that he introduces it in the most unlikely of contexts. In a manner that may recall Ariosto, Fielding places inherently ordinary *topoi* (such as inns and coaches) in an alien landscape: in *A Journey from this World to the Next* (1743), the narrator discovers to his surprise that death has not made his spirit able to fly. He learns from Mercury, 'the Porter', that he must take a stagecoach from a nearby inn to reach the 'other World'. The first stop on his journey is the '*City of Diseases*', the suburban streets of which are lined with 'Bagnio's, Taverns, and Cooks Shops', where the coach pauses at another inn before carrying its passengers first to the '*Palace of Death*' and finally to the banks of 'the great River *Cocytus*' (*JWN* I. 1; I. 2; I. 4; I. 5).[41] Having crossed the river, the narrator and his fellow–travellers continue on foot. The topography of this journey hence embraces the *loci* of romance and classical mythology as well as those commonly found in Fielding's own, longer fiction, as the narrator travels from inn to palace to '*Elysium*' (*JWN* I. 7 ff.). Once again travel invades the narrator's rhetoric; following the description of the coach ('this extraordinary Vehicle' (*JWN* I. 1)), the first chapter concludes thus: 'Such was the Vehicle in which I set out, and now those who are not willing to travel on with me, may, if they please, stop here; those who are, must proceed to the subsequent Chapters, in which this Journey is continued' (*JWN* I. 1). Fielding, six years before *Tom Jones*, hence places his narrator in a stagecoach and invites the reader to be his travelling companion. The stagecoach here duplicates itself on a metaphorical level to become the vehicle for both the journey and its narration; it therefore takes the narrator on an excursion with the reader that retraces (both rhetorically and spatially) his prior expedition with his fellow-deceased.

This double role for the stagecoach merges narrative and rhetoric in a manner that is rare but not unprecedented. In Alemán's *Guzmán de Alfarache*, a work as laden with travel metaphors as *Tom Jones*, the narrator's uncertain, digressive progress mimics the wayward path of his past life and travels; this *rapprochement* of diegetic and extradiegetic levels of narrative creates the impression that the reader has become the travelling companion of the hero as well as the narrator.[42] Towards the end of the first part, while the young Guzmán and his fellow-rogues entertain themselves at an inn, the older Guzmán advises his reader, 'Descansa un poco en esta venta; que en la jornada del capítulo siguiente oirás lo que aconteció en Florencia con un pobre que allí falleció' [Rest thy selfe a while in this Inne; for in that our journey, which we are to make to the Chapter following, you shall heare what hapned in Florence to a poore man that died there] (*G.* I. III. 4). The reader is thus placed in the same inn as the protagonist, as if he were part of the *vida* being recorded by the narrator, and, consequently, as if he were part of the narrator's own past—perhaps even a rogue himself. When it is time to move on from the inn, the reader is hailed once more to accompany Guzmán on his journey; the question is, however, which Guzmán: 'Comido y reposado has en la venta. Levántate, amigo, si en esta jornada gustas de que te sirva yendo en tu compañía' [Come, let us away. Thou hast now bayted and refresht thy selfe in thy Inne; Come, I say: Arise, and let us be gone, if thou beest willing to have my Company, and that I should doe thee service in this journey] (*G.* II. I. 1). As the distinction between the orders of narrative is blurred, Guzmán the protagonist and Guzmán the narrator become virtually indistinguishable.

The apparent merging of narrative levels that Alemán achieves in the *Guzmán* largely derives from the ambivalence inherent to the (autodiegetic) first-person voice of the picaresque *vida*. Fielding's heterodiegetic narrator, by contrast, allows neither himself nor his reader to travel on the same journeys as those undertaken by his protagonists. He nevertheless depicts the reader's progress in terms that emulate the travels of Joseph and Tom with more precision than that offered by any stagecoach metaphor. At one point in *Tom Jones*, for example, the reader's experience of a chapter is seen to duplicate that of the unfortunate character whose misadventure the author records: the chapter in which the bloodied and bandaged Tom terrifies a 'Centinel' appointed to guard the disgraced Northerton is entitled '*A most dreadful Chapter indeed; and which few Readers ought to venture upon in an Evening, especially when alone*' (*TJ* VII. 14). Fielding thus playfully suggests the reader's journey may be vulnerable to the same dangers as those faced by the characters whose adventures he relates. Elsewhere in *Tom Jones*, reading is portrayed as having dangers of its own: in a chapter entitled '*The Reader's Neck brought into Danger by a Description; his Escape, and the great Condescension of Miss* Bridget Allworthy' (*TJ* I. 4), the narrator once again depicts one of his 'poetical Embellishments' with the aid of a spatial metaphor: 'Reader, take care, I have unadvisedly led thee to the Top of as high a Hill as Mr *Allworthy's*, and how to get thee down without breaking thy Neck, I do not well know. However, let us e'en venture to slide down together' (*TJ* I. 4). The 'Hill' in question is the mock-heroic description in the preceding paragraph, the heightened tone of which is ironically translated as a physical elevation. In contrast to the guide who leads Jones in circles (*TJ* VII. 10), Fielding's narrator is a reliable escort for the reader and has no difficulty in guiding him to safety. This brief pretence of a narratorial *impasse* illustrates perfectly the difference between the authorial personae created by Fielding and Sterne. While Tristram, unable to get Walter and his uncle Toby down the stairs in book IV, is finally reduced to seeking the aid of a '*day-tall* critick' (*TS* IV. 13), the narrator of *Tom Jones* feigns similar difficulty only to resume his narrative at will.

Variations in the pace as well as tone of the journey undertaken by the hero and heroine of *Tom Jones* have a formative impact on the kind of travels upon which Fielding's narrator accompanies his reader. When Sophia and her fellow-travellers (Mrs Fitzpatrick and the Irish peer) have 'made such good Expedition, that they performed a Journey of ninety Miles in two Days', and arrive in London 'without having encountered any one Adventure on the Road worthy the Dignity of this History to relate' (*TJ* XI. 9), the absence of any deviations or interruptions to their progress provides an example that the narrator elects to follow: 'Our Pen, therefore, shall imitate the Expedition it describes, and our History shall keep Pace with the Travellers who are its Subject. Good Writers will, indeed, do well to imitate the ingenious Traveller in this Instance, who always proportions his stay at any Place to the Beauties, Elegancies, and

Curiosities, which it affords' (*TJ* XI. 9). Fielding's narrator deviates only in order to explain that this is no time for deviation, and, as the momentum of Sophia's progress increases, so does the narrative that reports it. As Hutchinson notes, 'when movement is sustained and varied, as in a journey, narrative more than follows the movements it narrates, it accompanies them, in some sense it moves with them'.[43] The narrator of *Tom Jones* demonstrates himself once again to be the antithesis of Sterne's Tristram, who is unable to determine narrative priorities and thus to keep up with his own narrative. Tristram, and the Yorick of *A Sentimental Journey*, are clearly poles apart from Fielding's 'ingenious Traveller':

> The Woods, the Rivers, the Lawns of *Devon* and of *Dorset*, attract the Eye of the ingenious Traveller, and retard his Pace, which Delay he afterwards compensates by swiftly scouring over the gloomy Heath of *Bagshot*, or that pleasant Plain which extends itself Westward from *Stockbridge*, where no other object than one single Tree only in sixteen Miles presents itself to the View [...] (*TJ* XI. 9)[44]

While Tristram relishes the opportunities offered by the Languedoc plain, noting that 'There is nothing more pleasing to a traveller——or more terrible to travel-writers, than a large rich plain' (*TS* VII. 42),[45] Fielding's narrator is faithful to his characters; he does not allow himself to deviate here from the path that they lay before him.

Fielding's metaphor of the stagecoach, although happily echoing the forms of transport materially available to the characters within the fiction, is inadequate to describe the freedom of movement his narratives enjoy. The manner in which he alternates between hero and heroine, and between one scene and another, may fairly be described as the *entrelacement* or interweaving normally associated with chivalric romance. The adoption of this technique indeed leads to certain superficial similarities between the narrators of the *Furioso* and *Tom Jones*: in particular, both of them appear on certain occasions to follow characters rather than direct them. Ariosto's Angelica, for example, is pursued not only by her numerous suitors, but also by her narrator, who tells the reader in the eighth canto 'Alquanto la sua istoria io vo *seguire*' [I shall *pursue* [or *follow*] her story a little] (*OF* VIII. 30; emphasis added). Fielding's narrator is also on one occasion said to follow rather than accompany or lead his heroine, Sophia, as she leaves the inn at Upton: 'we shall now, therefore, pursue the Steps of that lovely Creature, and leave her unworthy Lover a little longer to bemoan his ill Luck, or rather his ill Conduct' (*TJ* XI. 2). This would seem utterly atypical of the narrator of *Tom Jones* were it not for the obvious mastery that underlies the switch from Tom to Sophia. While the urgent and abrupt interweaving of the *Furioso* suggests a narrator (as opposed to an author) on the verge of losing control, forced by circumstances into urgent changes of tack,[46] Fielding's authorial persona is free to make his own decisions, one of which is to be seen to punish Tom by obliging him to contemplate his own misbehaviour. In fact, the tone of such a narrative shift also indicates an affinity with Cervantes, whose interweaving in the *Quijote* appears more controlled than its Ariostan model. When, for example, Palomeque is attacked by two guests attempting to leave his inn without paying, Cide Hamete abandons him to pursue the ongoing story of Don Luis: 'Pero dejémosle aquí, que no faltará quien le socorra, o si no, sufra y calle el que se atreve a más de a lo que sus fuerzas le prometen, y volvámonos atrás cincuenta pasos, a ver qué fue lo que don Luis respondió al oidor' [But let us leave him there awhile; for he will not want somebody or other to relieve him; or, if not, let him suffer and be silent, who is so foolhardy as to engage in what is above his strength; and let us turn fifty paces back, to see what Don Luis replied to the judge] (*DQ* I. 44). Cervantes, like Fielding, presents interweaving as a form of punishment for characters who have acted foolishly. In the case of Fielding, however, the image of the narrator chasing after the heroine belies the absolute control the former enjoys over the latter; this power is displayed more clearly eight chapters later in *Tom Jones*: when, following his pursuit of Sophia, the narrator wishes to return to Jones, he notes, 'we have now brought *Sophia* into safe Hands' (*TJ* XI. 10). On this occasion, he is no longer chasing his heroine but delivering her to safety (rather as a knight errant might); in contrast to the knights who vainly pursue Angelica in the *Furioso*, Fielding's narrator succeeds in catching up with the lady he pursues.

The freedom of movement enjoyed by the narrator of *Tom Jones* reveals a debt to the narrators of such romances as the *Furioso* and *The Faerie Queene*; the dynamism of these narrators may be said to re-create on a diegetic level the remarkable mobility of the riders of the hippogriff in the *Furioso*. Fielding, however, sought this freedom as much for his temporal approach to *Tom Jones* as for his spatial manœuvrings. His narrator's rejection of those travel-writers who do not 'swiftly scour' over unarresting landscapes is echoed by his apparent impatience with the 'painful and voluminous Historian', who 'thinks himself obliged to keep even Pace with Time, whose Amanuensis he is; and, like his Master, travels as slowly through Centuries of monkish Dulness' (*TJ* II. 1). The narrator therefore warns his reader not to be surprised if his 'History sometimes seems to stand still, and sometimes to fly' (*TJ* II. 1)—one might even specify, 'fly' like a hippogriff.

The impact of Fielding's systematic implementation of the topology of travel as an interpretative framework for his work was such that a number of contemporary readers expressed their own experience of *Tom Jones* through the same metaphors. Despite the romanesque temporal freedom Fielding's narrator enjoys, one reader notes that 'for chrystal Palaces and winged Horses, we find comely Cots and ambling Nags; and instead of Impossibility, what we experience every Day'.[47] Other readers respond specifically to Fielding's metaphor of the reader as travelling companion—Captain Lewis Thomas, for example, expresses his reading of *Tom Jones* in the following terms: 'to use a Metaphor in the Foundling, I have been these four or five days last past a fellow Traveller of Harry Fieldings, & a very agreeable Journey I have had.'[48] Orbilius similarly remarks, 'in attending my Author in every Stage, and through every Inn he drives [...] I shall at least be sure of good Chear'.[49] While La Place may not have enjoyed Fielding's authorial intrusions, nor the camaraderie between author and reader that such intrusions may promote, other (English) imitators of *Tom Jones* followed the example of Fielding in appropriating the vocabulary of travel. Perhaps the most notable of these is William Goodall, whose *Captain Greenland* Wayne Booth notes to be 'more completely dominated by an intruding narrator than any previous novel';[50] Goodall compares his reader to 'a Man who is riding a long Journey, through strange and uncertain Roads', and adds:

we therefore, as the whole Track of this Circuit is cut and marked out by us [...] have erected all modern Conveniences, except Post-Chaises, for him to travel by [...] as a Reward for his Toil, and to refresh him we shall immediately present him with a Tavern [...] or Ginshop; in the Shapes of a Digression, a Poem, a Song, or a Story. The Number of our Pages may serve for Mile-stones, and when he is weary, and has travelled by Day, at the end of our Chapter he may put up his Horse, and so now we'll suppose him to be gone to his Rest.[51]

The manner in which Fielding's contemporaries describe reading as travelling may be described as playfully self-conscious—the self-referential author of *Joseph Andrews* and *Tom Jones* therefore prompted similarly self-referential commentary from his peers. Fielding himself, however, provides an example of reading that contrastingly verges on the Quixotic; I noted earlier the dispute that arises in *Joseph Andrews* when Adams asserts to a 'kind Host' (*JA* II. 16) that travelling 'in Books [is] the only way of travelling by which any Knowledge is to be acquired' (*JA* II. 17).[52] Adams here resembles Don Quijote by the extremity of the position he takes, which entirely discounts the value of first-hand experience of the world in favour of the world of the imagination:

'Do you imagine sailing by different Cities or Countries is travelling? No
    Cælum non Animum mutant qui trans mare currunt.[53]
I can go farther in an Afternoon, than you in a Twelve-Month. What, I suppose you have seen the Pillars of *Hercules*, and perhaps the Walls of *Carthage*' [...] 'Then I suppose,' cries the Host, 'you have been at the *East Indies*, for there are no such [places], I will be sworn, either in the *West* or the *Levant*'. 'Pray where's the *Levant*?' quoth *Adams*, 'that should be in the *East Indies* by right'.—'O ho! you are a pretty Traveller,' cries the Host, 'and not know the *Levant*'. (*JA* II. 17)

As Martin Battestin notes in his edition of the novel, 'Adams understands the etymology, but mistakes the location' of the Levant and conse-quently gives himself away. While he indeed learns nothing by his journey in *Joseph Andrews*, his erudition is of no help to him either—rather like Don Quijote, Adams is unable to learn progressively from experience.[54] By contrast, Joseph, his travelling companion, is a walking argument against Adams's position that one can acquire knowledge only through the text, not through the world. In *Tom Jones*, Fielding provides further arguments for the dangers of abandoning the world for the library: among the 'Qualifications' he demands of his critics is 'another Sort of Knowledge beyond the Power of Learning to bestow, and this is to be had by Conversation': 'So necessary is this to the understanding of the Characters of Men, that none are more ignorant of them than those learned Pedants, whose Lives have been entirely consumed in Colleges, and among Books; For however exquisitely human Nature may have been described by Writers, the true practical System can be learnt only in the World' (*TJ* IX. 1). As we shall see below, Diderot, despite being as enthusiastic a conversationalist as Fielding, does not share his enthusiasm for exploring the world outside; Sterne's *Tristram Shandy*, by contrast, repeatedly shows the dangers of confinement, and of a life 'consumed' by books alone.

Notes to Chapter 5

1. Curtius, in his examination of the nautical *topos*, cites a range of examples from Virgil to Spenser that renders protracted discussion of the matter redundant here (*European Literature and the Latin Middle Ages*, 128–30). It may, however, be worth adding to Curtius's list an example from Rabelais's *Gargantua*, in which Alcofrybas ends the chapter '*Les couleurs et livrée de Garagantua*' with the remark: 'Mais plus oultre ne fera voile mon equif entre ces gouffres et guez mal plaisans: je retourne faire scale au port dont suis yssu' (*Gargantua*, in *Œuvres complètes*, ed. Pierre Jourda, 2 vols. (Paris: Garnier, 1962), i, ch. 10, p. 42).

2. Hutchinson, *Cervantine Journeys*, 49.

3. Ibid. 44.

4. Ibid. 45.

5. This sense of magnitude is clear in the various definitions the *OED* gives for *travel*, the first pertinent one of which is 'the act of travelling or journeying'. The *OED* further notes the old French source of *journey* (*journee*), and its former meanings—a day, and thus a day's travel; the modern definition it gives underlines the sense of scale and distance to which I have referred: 'A "spell" or continued course of going or travelling, having its beginning and end in place or time, and thus viewed as a distinct whole; a march, ride, drive, or combination of these or other modes of progression *to a certain more or less distant place, or extending over a certain distance or space of time*; an excursion or expedition to some distance; a round of travel' (emphasis added).

6. This control is evident despite the occasional ironic authorial disclaimer, such as when he claims to be unsure of Blifil's motives in concealing Tom's name: 'As to the Name of *Jones* he thought proper to conceal it, and why he did so must be left to the Judgement of the sagacious Reader: For we never chuse to assign Motives to the Actions of Men, when there is any Possibility of our being mistaken' (*TJ* V. 11).

7. Cf. Spenser's comparable use of the nautical metaphor in *The Faerie Queene*: 'Behold I see the hauen night at hand, | To which I meane my wearie course to bend; | Vere the main shete, and beare up with the land, | The which afore is fairely to be kend, | And seemeth safe from stormes, that may offend; | There this faire virgin wearie of her way | Must landed be, now at her iourneyes end: | There eke my feeble barke a while may stay, | Till merry wind and weather call her thence away' (Edmund Spenser, *The Faerie Queene*, ed. A. C. Hamilton (London: Longman, 1977), I. xii. 1. 1–9).

8. This is not the only occasion upon which Fielding (inconsistently) compares *Tom Jones* to a stagecoach: 'Such Histories as these [...] may likewise be compared to a Stage-Coach, which performs constantly the same Course, empty as well as full' (*TJ* II. 1). An implicit reference to a stagecoach may also be inferred in Fielding's assertion that his 'History' was 'obliged to turn about and travel backwards' (*TJ* XI. 2).

9. Calvino, 'The Structure of *Orlando furioso*', 173.

10. Hunter, *Occasional Form*, 143.

11. An 'Ordinary' is defined in the *OED* as 'an eating-house or tavern where public meals are provided at a fixed price'. A possible inspiration for Fielding's metaphor of the Ordinary may be found in Horace's *Epistles*: 'denique non omnes eadem

mirantur amantque: carmine tu gaudes, hic delectatur iambis, ille Bioneis sermonibus et sale nigro. tres mihi convivae prope dissentire videntur, poscentes vario multum diversa palato. quid dem? quid non dem?'[After all, men have not all the same tastes and likes. Lyric song is your delight, our neighbour here takes pleasure in iambics, the one yonder in Bion's satires, with their caustic wit. 'Tis, I fancy, much like three guests who disagree; their tastes vary, and they call for widely different dishes. What am I to put before them? What not?] (Horace, *Satires, Epistles, Ars Poetica*, trans. H. Rushton Fairclough, Loeb Classical Library (Cambridge, MA: Harvard University Press, 1929), II. ii. 57–63).

12. See e.g. *OF* XIII. 80, quoted above in Ch. 1.

13. Cf. his use of a similar culinary metaphor in *The Covent-Garden Journal*: he writes, for example, to Mr Censor, 'I have related to you the plain Fact, which, when drest by a little of your cookery, will make a palatable Dish' (*The Covent-Garden Journal*, 28: 181).

14. Robert L. Chibka, 'Taking "The Serious" Seriously: The Introductory Chapters of *Tom Jones*', *The Eighteenth Century: Theory and Interpretation*, 31 (1990), 23–45 (30).

15. Cf. the aforementioned opening chapter of *Tom Jones*, in which the reader, if unimpressed by the bill of fare, is free to 'depart to some other Ordinary better accommodated to their Taste' (*TJ* I. 1).

16. Cf. *TS* I. 20, discussed below, Ch. 6, 'The Travel of Language'.

17. Hunter, *Occasional Form*, 151.

18. 'A place in which rest is taken on a journey; a roadside inn for the accommodation of travellers riding post or by stage-coach' (*OED*).

19. Quoted by Fielding from the *Ars Poetica* (ll. 359–60).

20. Quotations are from *Histoire de Tom Jones, ou l'enfant trouvé*, trans. Pierre-Antoine de La Place, 4 vols. (London: Nourse, 1750). References are to book and chapter.

21. See above, Ch. 3, 'The Reader and the *Roman comique*'.

22. Cf. an earlier image of the impatient listener in *Guzmán de Alfarache*: 'Que quien desea saber una cosa, querría que las palabras unas tropellasen a otros para salir juntas y presto de la boca' [he that hath a longing desire to know a thing, would willingly have one word come treading on the heeles of another; and with a quick and nimble pace come (if it were possible) huddling all at once out of the mouth] (*G.* I. I. 4).

23. La Place's reasoning for cutting the invocation echoes his comments in the prefatory letter: referring to himself in the third person, he remarks, 'plus occupé de l'intérêt qu'inspirent *Jones* et son amante, que des brillans détails dont leur Histoire est semée, il se flatte que les Lecteurs, affectés du même sentiment, lui pardonneront ce défaut d'exactitude, en faveur du plaisir de perdre moins souvent de vuë des personnages que l'Auteur Anglois a rendu si dignes d'être aimés' (*HTJ* XIII. 1).

24. Cf. Cervantes's remarks on the writing of prefaces in his own preface to the *Quijote*.

25. Pierre Carlet de Chamblain de Marivaux, *La Vie de Marianne* (Paris: Garnier, 1957), 5.

26. See above, Ch. 4 n. 23, and below, Ch. 7, 'Jacques le Fataliste ou son maître: Whose Storyline is it Anyway?'

27. 'Vous entrelarderez icy celuy que vous trouverez le plus à vostre goust, et que vous croirez mieux convenir au sujet. J'ay pensé mesme de commander à l'imprimeur de laisser en cet endroit du papier blanc, pour y transplanter plus commodément celuy que vous auriez choisi, afin que vous puissiez l'y placer' (Furetière, *Roman bourgeois*, 1018). A similar invitation to the reader to contribute to the work he is reading is made by Sterne, who invites his reader to paint his own likeness of Widow Wadman (*TS* VI. 38) and, unlike Furetière, actually does leave him a blank page in order to do so.

28. Fielding's incorporation of a flaw in his heroine's appearance may be seen as the eighteenth-century equivalent to Chaucer's remark that Criseyde was beautiful save for the fact that 'hire browes joyneden yfeere' (*Troilus and Criseyde*, in *The Riverside Chaucer*, 3rd edn. (Oxford: Oxford University Press, 1987), V. 813). A more distant precedent is constituted by Odysseus' famous scar.

29. Henry Fielding, *Joseph Andrews*, trans. abbé Desfontaines, ed. Serge Soupel (Paris: Flammarion, 1990).

30. 'I have now secured myself from the Imitation of those who are utterly incapable of any degree of Reflection, and whose Learning is not equal to an Essay' (*TJ* IX. 1).

31. Goldknopf refers to the 'already decaying neo-classical set of values' ('The Failure of Plot in *Tom Jones*', 272) Fielding displays in *Tom Jones*.

32. 'The poet should say as little as possible in his own voice' (Aristotle, *Poetics*, 1460a6–7).

33. Eugène Vinaver, *The Rise of Romance* (Oxford: Clarendon Press, 1971), 17.

34. Cf. Diderot's equally scornful pronouncements regarding the *roman* and the *conte* in *Ceci n'est pas un conte* and *Jacques*.

35. See Anne Berthelot, 'The Romance as *Conjoincture* of Brief Narratives', *L'Esprit créateur*, 33 (1993), 51–60.

36. Chrétien de Troyes, *Erec et Enide* (Paris: Flammarion, 1994), Prologue, ll. 16–18.

37. See e.g. *JA* III. 2.

38. J. H. P. Pafford, in his preface to the Arden edition of *The Winter's Tale* (London: Routledge, 1963), p. liii.

39. *The Winter's Tale* II. i. 25; *Macbeth* III. iv. 63–5.

40. Recorded in the *OED*, which also quotes from Jenkinson's *Triumph of Faith* (1613):'Let our mirth be [...] spiritual mirth [...] not winter tales, and foolish stories, the divel's chronicles, which *neuer need printing* we can so well remember them' (emphasis added); note once again the quintessential orality of these tales.

41. Quotations are from Henry Fielding, *A Journey from this World to the Next*, in vol. ii of *Miscellanies*, ed. Hugh Amory and Bertrand A. Goldgar (Oxford: Wesleyan University Press, 1993). References are to book and chapter.

42. Cf. *Jacques*, in which the narrator rather than the reader is presented at certain points as the travelling companion of Jacques and his master—again, at an inn.

43. Hutchinson, *Cervantine Journeys*, 46.

44. Cf. Fielding's preface to *The Journal of a Voyage to Lisbon*: 'To make a traveller an agreeable companion to a man of sense, it is necessary, not only that he should have seen much, but that he should have overlooked much of what he hath seen' (Oxford: Oxford University Press, 1997), 122.

45. See below, Ch. 6, 'The Journey through France'.

46. The apparent incompetence of Ariosto's narrator is repeatedly seen to endanger the lives of his characters: Angelica is left tied to the rock on Ebuda for almost two cantos, while Ruggiero is almost drowned by his creator's restless narrative shifts: 'Ma mi parria, Signor, far troppo fallo, | se, per voler di costor dir, lasciassi/ anto Ruggier nel mar, che v'affrogessi' [But would it not be unpardonable, my Lord, if in my urge to pursue their story, I left Ruggiero in the sea so long that he drowned?] (*OF* XLI. 46. 6–8).
47. Anon., *An essay on the new species of writing founded by Mr. Fielding, 1751* (London: W. Owen, 1751); reprinted by the Augustan Reprint Society, ed. Alan D. McKillop (Los Angeles: William Andrews Clark Memorial Library, University of California), 95 (1962), 6.
48. From a letter dated 3 April 1749, in J. P. Feil, 'Fielding's Character of Mrs Whitefield', *Philological Quarterly*, 39 (1960), 508–10 (509).
49. 'Orbilius', 'An Examen of *The History of Tom Jones, a Foundling*' (London: W. Owen, 1750), Letter I.
50. Wayne C. Booth, 'The Self-Conscious Narrator in Comic Fiction before *Tristram Shandy*', *PMLA* 67 (1952), 163–85 (183).
51. William Goodall, *The Adventures of Captain Greenland, Written in Imitation of all those Wise, Learned, Witty, and Humorous Authors, who either already have, or hereafter may Write in the same Stile and Manner* (London, 1752), i. 30–2.
52. Note the alleged remark by Fielding's bookseller that his author is 'well travelled in the Greek and Roman Authors' (*The Covent-Garden Journal*, 17).
53. A quotation from Horace, *Epistles*, I. xi. 27.
54. See above, Ch. 2. Adams's impressive erudition also recalls Don Quijote, whose discourse on arms and learning (*DQ* I. 38–9) impresses his audience at Palomeque's inn.

CHAPTER 6

Tristram Shandy
Narrative as Travelogue

At first, the generally sedentary Tristram, working on his '*Life and Opinions*' in his study, would seem the antithesis of the compulsively errant heroes of the *Furioso* and *Quijote*, or indeed of the travellers whose journeys are depicted by Scarron and Fielding. In a physical sense, with the important exception of the journey through France in volume VII, the topography of *Tristram Shandy* is intimately—perhaps even claustrophobically—confined to Shandy Hall and its immediate environs. Sterne's narrative, however, is characterized by its irrepressible dynamism: Tristram flits from one subject to another as easily as Don Quijote moves from one misadventure to the next. The physical errancy of the hero, in other words, has been almost entirely displaced by the intellectual or imaginative errancy of the narrator. The connection between these two forms of errancy is at its most striking in the figurative language adopted by Sterne, but is not confined to the metaphorical level. Each of the works examined above uses to varying degrees the journey *topos* as a frame into which interpolations and digressions may be inserted; in *Tristram Shandy*, the '*Life*' of the narrator, the writing of his autobiography, constitutes the journey and therefore frame through which Sterne subverts the topographical conventions of interpolating narrative.

The Language of Travel

Tristram's writing of his own life is consistently expressed in terms that illustrate the influence of the *Quijote* (further reinforced by Sterne's numerous allusions to Cervantes). Don Quijote's sallies find a modern counterpart in Tristram's embarking on his autobiography:

my dear friend and companion,——if you should think me somewhat sparing of my narrative on my first setting out,——bear with me,——and let me go on, and tell my story my own way:————or if I should seem now and then to trifle upon the road,————or should sometimes put on a fool's cap with a bell to it, for a moment or two as we pass along,—don't fly off,——but rather courteously give me credit for a little more wisdom than appears upon my outside;——and as we jogg on, either laugh with me, or at me [...] (I. 6)[1]

Like the reader of *Tom Jones*, the reader of *Tristram Shandy* is presented as the narrator's travelling companion. While Fielding's reader and narrator are strangers sharing a stagecoach, Sterne implies an even greater familiarity between his 'travellers'—one might even liken their relationship to that of Don Quijote and Sancho Panza, with Tristram as the knight errant and the reader as his squire. Ironically, given his insistence that his reader should not 'fly off', Tristram later admits that he cannot stop himself from doing the same: 'I fly off from what I am about, as far and as often too as any writer in *Great-Britain*; yet I constantly take care to order affairs so, that my main business does not stand still in my absence' (I. 22). Tristram's freedom of movement within his narrative, like that exercised by the narrator of *Tom Jones*,[2] echoes temporally the spatial mobility of the knights errant of romance. Tristram rides his hobby horse, the writing of his '*Life*', as freely as Ariosto's knights errant ride the hippogriff—and, more tellingly perhaps, as freely as Don Quijote rides the wooden Clavileño. Indeed, Don Quijote's imagined travels on Clavileño may be seen as a striking intermediary phase (or, if the pun may be excused, 'half-way *horse*') in the transition from hippogriff to hobby horse: the physical immobility of both Don Quijote and Tristram does not impede either from wandering imaginatively or intellectually on his respective mount.

Tristram resembles the narrator of that most self-conscious of chivalric romances, the *Furioso*, as strongly as any of the knights errant who feature in it. As we have already seen, the errancy of Ariosto's knights forces the narrator into a similarly errant approach to the organization of his narrative; when the poem shifts from one storyline to another, the reader is given the impression that the action of each narrative thread continues without him.[3] When Tristram remarks that his main business does not stand still in his absence, however, he is not quite the struggling narrator we see in the *Furioso* and elsewhere in *Tristram Shandy*. In contrast to the knights of chivalric romance, the members of Tristram's family are unable to wander very far; as we shall see below, physical displacement of any kind proves to be inherently problematic in *Tristram Shandy*. Toby in particular requires Tristram's help as a narrator in order to make any progress:

whilst *Obadiah* has been going those said miles and back [to meet Dr Slop], I have brought my uncle *Toby* from *Namur*, quite across all *Flanders*, into *England*:——That I have had him ill upon my hands near four years;——and have since travelled him and Corporal *Trim*, in a chariot and four, a journey of near two hundred miles down into *Yorkshire* [...] (II. 8)

As Hutchinson remarks, 'writers (or narrators) *travel* their characters: "travel" becomes a transitive verb whose object is the traveller.'[4] In this respect Tristram has the opposite problem to Ariosto's narrator. As the difficulties he faces in getting his father and uncle down a flight of stairs demonstrates,[5] Tristram's compulsive digressiveness runs the risk of paralysing those who appear in his narrative: Walter is thus left 'upon the bed for half an hour' (III. 30), and Mrs. Shandy is left in the corridor outside the parlour to 'stand for five minutes: till I bring up the affairs of the kitchen [...] to the same period' (V. 5). Henri Fluchère accurately describes time in *Tristram Shandy* as being 'comme les morceaux d'un puzzle frappés de la même apparente immobilité';[6] Tristram's errancy therefore creates temporal stasis, which in turn gives him the freedom to wander in (but not alter) the past.

Tristram famously describes Locke's *Essay concerning Human Under-standing* as 'a history-book [...] of what passes in a man's own mind' (II. 2), a description that has widely been regarded as equally appropriate to *Tristram Shandy* itself. Tristram's desire to be his own historian produces instead a form of intellectual travelogue, in which history is explored through metaphors that express spatial errancy:

when a man sits down to write a history,——tho' it be but the history of *Jack Hickathrift* or *Tom Thumb*, he knows no more than his heels what lets and confounded hinderances he is to meet with in his way,——or what a dance he may be led, by one excursion or another, before all is over. Could a historiographer drive on his history, as a muleteer drives on his mule,——straight forward;——for instance, from *Rome* all the way to *Loretto*, without ever once turning his head aside either to the right hand or to the left,——he might venture to foretell you to an hour when he should get to his journey's end;——but the thing is, morally speaking, impossible: For, if he is a man of the least spirit, he will have fifty deviations from a straight line to make with this or that party as he goes along, which he can no ways avoid. He will have views and prospects to himself perpetually solliciting his eye, which he can no more help standing still to look at than he can fly [...] (I. 14)[7]

Like Don Quijote, Tristram is here presented as being caught between two incompatible visions of the world—a knight errant trapped in a muleteer's reality. The muleteer, a staple character of picaresque fiction and a prominent figure in Part I of the *Quijote*, must avoid any distractions that might delay his arrival at his destination.[8] Tristram's desire to enjoy the 'views and prospects' that deviations afford evinces the same spirit of enquiry that led Dampier, in the preface to his *New Voyage* (1697), to argue that 'one who rambles about a Country can give usually a better account of it, than a Carrier who jogs on to his Inn, without ever going out of his Road'.[9] Tristram, by contrast, presents himself as a traveller of leisure (determined 'to go on leisurely' as long as he is alive) embarked on a romantic adventure, rather than a worker obliged to travel for a living. He cannot, however, divorce himself entirely from the order of reality that the muleteer represents. When subjective errancy gives way (or, more precisely, runs parallel) to its objective counterpart in his travels through France, he does not jump from his hobby horse to a real horse: he crosses the 'rich plains of *Languedoc*' (VII. 42), for example, on a mule, and elsewhere admits, 'I have not a horse worth riding on' (III. 12). Paradoxically, the only time he rides a real horse is when it is not real: he metaphorically expresses the progress he has made in his narrative as the rider of a galloping horse:

What a rate have I gone on at, curvetting and frisking it away, two up and two down for four volumes together, without looking once behind, or even on one side of me, to see whom I trod upon!——I'll tread upon no-one,——quoth I to myself when I mounted——I'll take a good rattling gallop; but I'll not hurt the poorest jack-ass upon the road——So off I set——up one lane——down another, through this turn-pike——over that, as if the arch-jockey of jockeys had got behind me. (IV. 20)

Even though Tristram here compliments himself on his rapid progress, and in particular for his refusal to turn backwards or sideways, going forwards does not necessarily imply straight linearity. He cannot prevent his horse from 'curvetting and frisking', nor from leading him 'up one lane——down another'; his steed constantly pulls him off 'the king's highway' (IV. 20; IX. 12), to use Tristram's own metaphor, its friskiness being the metaphorical expression of the narrator's digressiveness.[10] Sterne may well have been inspired by Mabbe's translation of Alemán's *Guzmán de Alfarache*—even if this were not the case, Tristram's metaphors of travel bear a striking resemblance to those adopted by Alemán's (and Mabbe's) narrator: Guzmán, unable to curb his own digressiveness, remarks that 'no hay hombre cuerdo a caballo' [there is no man that is Master of himselfe, when he is on horsebacke] (G. I. I. 3) and provides another image of the narrator-as-muleteer:

¿No ves mi poco sufrimiento, cómo no pude abstenerme y cómo sin pensar corrió hasta aquí la pluma? Arrimáronme el acicate y torcíme a la parte que mi picaba. No sé qué disculpa darte, sino es la que dan los que llevan por delante sus bestias de carga, que dan con el hombre que encuentran contra una pared o le derriban por el suelo y después dicen: «Perdone.» (G. I. I. 3)

[Perceivest thou not how impatient I am? Seest thou not that I can not containe my selfe? and how that my pen, before ever I thought of lashing out so farre, hath slipt upon this Theame. They gave mee the yarke with the spurre, and I turned my head to strike where they pricked me. I know not what excuse to make thee, but to tell thee, that I doe as Carriers doe, that drive their beasts of burthen before them, who rush the man that meetes them against the wall, or throwes him to the ground, and then say, I cry you mercy, Sir.]

Tristram's muleteer and Guzmán's carrier provide metaphors of linear progress: just as Tristram's muleteer keeps his eyes fixed on the road ahead, ignoring all the views to the side, Guzmán's carrier refuses to give up the road to those travelling in the opposite direction and thus knocks them over in his path or pushes them aside. Guzmán's mule, however, is rather like Tristram's galloping horse (which, however, will 'tread upon no-one'): forward progress is not the same as straight-forward progress.[11]

The Travel of Language

In the first volume of *Tristram Shandy*, the narrator orders a careless (female) reader to re-read an earlier chapter: '——'Tis to rebuke a vicious taste which has crept into thousands beside herself,——of reading straight forwards, more in quest of the adventures, than of the deep erudition and knowledge which a book of this cast, if read over as it should be, would infallibly impart with them' (I. 20). Sterne, like Fielding before him,[12] is keen to slow his reader down, and presents *Tristram Shandy* as a *Bildungsroman* in which the reader, not the hero, is to be educated. The fictive reader addressed by Sterne is held to be misguided because she approaches reading as a quest rather than as an end in itself. While Tristram generally perceives and presents himself as resolutely purposeful—committed to presenting the reader with his entire '*Life and Opinions*'—he proves in practice to be not a questing narrator but an errant narrator. Like Don Quijote, for whom any sense of destination is undermined to such a degree that it is unable to assert itself, Tristram is intent on the journey upon which he has embarked with his readers rather than on where it may ultimately lead him, as the comparison cited above between the historiographer and the muleteer suggests. As he cannot possible arrive, Tristram must be content to travel if not hopefully, then at least cheerfully. Elizabeth Harries remarks accurately that Tristram's situation takes to an extreme the paradoxical problem posed by Ginés de Pasamonte in the *Quijote*; when Don Quijote asks Ginés if his autobiography is finished, he responds, '¿Cómo puede estar acabado [...] si aún no está acabada mi vida' [How can it be finished? [...] since my life is not yet finished?] (*DQ* I. 22). As Harries also notes, 'Tristram will always grow up faster than Walter Shandy can formulate the *Tristra-poedia*—or than he himself can compose his autobiography.'[13] Furthermore, as Tristram twice declares his intention to continue writing his autobiography until he dies, the end of his '*Life*' implies the end of his life.[14]

In both *Tristram Shandy* and the *Quijote*, movement is symbolically identified with life, and stasis with sickness or death—Tristram indeed states at one point, 'so much of motion, is so much of life, and so much of joy——and that to stand still, or get on but slowly, is death and the devil' (VII. 13). When Don Quijote leaves the chronotope of the road on his last sally, he dies almost immediately: as soon as he comes to his senses he therefore loses them permanently. When death knocks on Tristram's door, Sterne's hero decides to flee while his 'two spider legs' (VII. 1) are still able to support him, and he thereby strikingly seeks refuge from time in space. Tristram's geographical flight from death, which reflects Sterne's own flight from closure in his narrative, provides an objective counterpoint to the subjective errancy of the rest of the work. For the rest of *Tristram Shandy*, the hero-narrator is confined to his study; like Don Quijote in his library, Tristram creates a world into which he may escape:

But in this clear climate of fantasy and perspiration, where every idea, sensible and insensible, gets vent——in this land, my dear Eugenius——in this fertile land of chivalry and romance, where I now sit, unskrewing my ink-horn to write my uncle Toby's amours, and with all the meanders of JULIA's track in quest of her DIEGO, in full view of my study window——(VIII. 1)[15]

In both the *Quijote* and *Tristram Shandy*, physical confinement is seen to lead almost inevitably to intellectual errancy. Other than Tristram himself, the most obvious illustration of this principle in Sterne's work is uncle Toby. When Toby is confined to his bedroom by his injury[16]—reinforcing the association of stasis with illness—the reader is on this occasion explicitly referred to Don Quijote's library: Toby is said to have as many 'books of military architecture, as Don *Quixote* was found to have of chivalry, when the curate and barber invaded his library' (II. 3).

Like Tristram, Toby travels without moving: 'my uncle *Toby* was able to cross the *Maes* and *Sambre*; make diversions as far as *Vauban*'s line, the abbey of *Salsines*, &c.' (II. 3), while, 'in a period of fifteen or sixteen years', he 'seldom went further than the bowling-green' (IX. 2). Toby's 'desire for knowledge' becomes as strong as a knight errant's desire for adventures, and his quest is again expressed in terms that suggest a parallel with the heroes of chivalric romance: Tristram impotently implores his uncle to '——stop!——go not one foot further into this thorny and bewilder'd track,——intricate are the steps! intricate are the mases of this labyrinth! intricate are the troubles which the pursuit of this bewitching phantom, KNOWLEDGE will bring upon thee' (II. 3).[17] A sense of stasis underlies Tristram's portrait of the various members of his family—they all appear to be 'stuck in their ways', incapable of evolving or shifting from their positions. The restless mobility of the narrative, with its constant deviations and changes of direction, offsets the immobility of the characters it seeks to portray.[18] We have already noted, for example, that Toby requires Tristram's help in order to travel from Namur to Yorkshire. It may consequently seem odd that this impression of stasis is expressed metaphorically in terms of movement: Toby is said to *ride* his hobby horse: 'now the HOBBY-HORSE which my uncle *Toby* always rode upon [...] you might have travelled from *York* to *Dover*,——from *Dover* to *Penzance* in *Cornwall*, and from *Penzance* to *York* back again, and not have seen such another on the road' (I. 24). When put in these terms, the hobby horse would seem to represent mobility. However, aside from the fact that it apparently signifies movement without a rational purpose (or intellectual errancy), the hobby-horse crucially represents not 'real horse-ness' but an artificial, farcical illusion of 'horse-ness' and, consequently, of mobility.[19]

While Don Quijote and Toby are doomed to ride their respective mounts until death, Tristram is doomed to err among words: in each case, the errancy of the hero is prompted by his reading. Tristram's wayward intellect is presented by Sterne as the inevitable consequence of his education—and, in particular, of his exposure to his father's 'Tristra-pœdia'; when Tristram finds himself lost in his own narrative, he blames Walter:

when a man is telling a story in the strange way I do mine, he is obliged continually to be going backwards and forwards to keep all tight together in the reader's fancy [...] and now you see, I am lost myself!——
        ——But 'tis my father's fault [...] (VI. 33)

This kind of self-exculpation is typical of Tristram—in the celebrated opening of the first volume he similarly places the blame for his unhappy existence on his parents' interrupted coitus. In his own way, Walter is as extravagantly Quixotic as Uncle Toby; he might indeed be described as a Quijote of rhetoric, and Don Quijote's fights at country inns are thus succeeded by Walter's verbal sallies: 'My father had such a skirmishing, cutting kind of a slashing way with him in his disputations, thrusting and ripping, and giving every one a stroke to remember him by in his turn——that if there were twenty people in company——in less than half an hour he was sure to have every one of 'em against him' (VIII. 34). Just as Don Quijote continually seeks opportunities to demonstrate his courage (as, for example, when he confronts the lion (*DQ* II. 17)), Walter repeatedly adopts ridiculous positions in order to test his wit.[20] Both are in continual conflict with their surroundings: in contrast to Cervantes's knight, however, Walter enjoys and deliberately cultivates this conflict.

Tristram's own struggle with his narrative might be regarded as Walter's legacy to his son. When one examines some of the principles from the Tristra-pœdia expounded by Walter, it is clear that Sterne intended it to provide a Lockean explanation of Tristram's narratorial errancy. Walter demonstrates his ability to discourse on nothing other than discourse itself when he explains the pedagogic potential of the auxiliary verb: 'Now the use of the *Auxiliaries* is, at once to set the soul a going by herself upon the materials as they are brought her; and by the versability of this great engine, round which they are twisted, to open new tracks of enquiry, and make every idea engender millions' (V. 42). Language is presented by Walter as self-sufficient and self-propagating as well as providing the key to new realms of learning; he proves to his audience (Uncle Toby and Parson Yorick) that he can discourse intelligently on a randomly chosen subject— namely, that of a white bear.[21] Tristram swiftly brings the curtain down on his father's oration, although the reader is informed in the next volume that Walter 'had danced his white bear backwards and forwards through half a dozen pages' (VI. 2). This Rabelaisian lesson in discourse, in which a word may explode into an essay or a book, suggests that the Tristra-pœdia inadvertently constitutes a systematic lesson in digression:

Tristram [...] shall be made to conjugate every word in the dictionary, backwards and forwards the same way;——every word, Yorick, by this means, you see, is converted into a thesis or an hypothesis;——every thesis and hypothesis have an offspring of propositions;——and each proposition has its own consequences and conclusions; every one of which leads the mind on again into fresh tracks of enquiries and doubtings. (VI. 2)

As Melvyn New observes, 'The theory of auxiliary verbs is the *reductio ad absurdum* [...] of the fate of words in *Tristram Shandy*'.[22] The snowball effect that Walter elaborates implies the impossibility of linear progress: Tristram is doomed to go 'backwards and forwards', and each proposition becomes the narrative equivalent of a romance episode, compelling the knight/narrator to abandon his intended destination in favour of the adventures promised by 'fresh tracks'. Words have taken on the attributes of the 'homme-récit' by which romance narratives are amplified: each proposition contains a history to be explored. Just as the *topoi* of forest or inn are used to open a narrative to new possibilities, Tristram's intellect is trained not to select or prioritize, but to follow blindly the paths of his countless associations. It is Toby, not Walter, who recognizes the danger of the latter's system: '——The force of this engine, added my father, is incredible, in opening a child's head.——'Tis enough, brother *Shandy*, cried my uncle *Toby*, to burst it into a thousand splinters——' (VI. 2). Just as Toby's life is 'put in jeopardy by words' (II. 2), Tristram's 'Life' continually appears to be on the verge of collapse as its narrator struggles to order words rather than be ordered by them.[23] Like the characters of the *Furioso* and the wandering chess pieces in Lewis Carroll's *Alice through the Looking-Glass*, Tristram's words seem to have a life of their own.

The impression of a narrator losing control is strongest in *Tristram Shandy* at a micro-narrative level, with the apparently haphazard construction of its sentences: as Sigurd Burckhardt remarks, 'scarcely a sentence in *Tristram Shandy*, far less a chapter or episode, and least of all the book as a whole, ever runs straight'.[24] Tristram, diverted from his main clause by a lengthy parenthesis, is often obliged to abort a sentence and try again in the next:

I had just time, in my travels though *Denmark* with Mr *Noddy's* eldest son, whom, in the year 1741, I accompanied as governor, riding along with him at a prodigious rate thro' most parts of *Europe*, and of which original journey perform'd by us two, a most delectable narrative will be given in the progress of this work. I had just time, I say [...] (I. 11)

In this case, Tristram's physical errancy finds its perfect expression in the verbal errancy of his narrative: his sentences are as cyclical as the sallies of Amadís and Don Quijote—and, indeed, as his own excursions abroad.[25] Tristram himself explicitly associates digression with parenthesis when he expresses his desire to 'go on straight forwards, without digression or parenthesis, in my uncle *Toby's* amours' (VII. 43).

Tristram's inability to pursue a linear narrative is graphically represented in volume VI by the lines he draws to show his progress through the previous volumes (VI. 40):

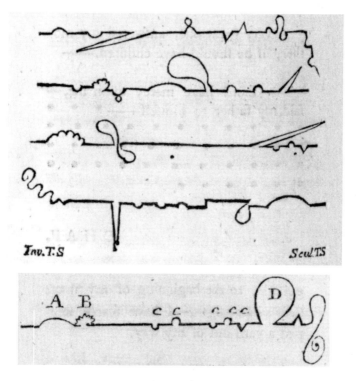

Fig. 1: *Tristram's lines of progress*
(Reprinted by kind permission of the British Library)

He continues to aim at a straight line 'turning neither to the right hand or to the left' (VI. 40), despite his stated desire to distinguish himself from the blinkered, sterile perspective symbolized by his muleteer. He hardly appears to pursue this goal enthusiastically, however, particularly when one considers that he expressly refers to the moral associations implied by the straight line:

This *right line*,—the path-way for Christians to walk in! say divines————
————The emblem of moral rectitude! says *Cicero*————
————The *best line*! say cabbage-planters————is the shortest line, says *Archimedes*, which can be drawn from one given point to another.————
(VI. 40)

It is a pity that Tristram does not deliver the 'chapter upon straight lines' he promises on the same page, for the implications of his inability or refusal to pursue a straight line in his narrative remain unexplored. The absence of such a chapter, however, is arguably a statement in itself.

Two interpretations of Tristram's digressiveness in this context are possible. One may assume that the (religious) association of errancy with error (exemplified paradigmatically by the biblical story of the wandering Jew) is expressed either only to be dismissed, or to provide the reader with a moral framework in which to judge the narrator. There are reasonable grounds to suggest the former: one may sense, perhaps, some authorial contempt behind the reference to 'divines', while the mention of 'cabbage-planters' that follows the allusion to Cicero is deliberately bathetic. It would also seem peculiar of Sterne to imply that his narrator's verbal errancy may reflect moral delinquency. Nevertheless, the common identification of errancy with error or vice often appears to inform both *Tristram Shandy* and *A Sentimental Journey*. When, in the latter work, Yorick is tempted to accept Mme de L***'s invitation to visit her in Brussels, the geographical deviation this would require implies moral errancy: to go to Brussels would be to stray from Eliza as well as his intended route through Europe. Yorick's desire to see Mme de L*** is, he insists, sentimentally rather than carnally motivated: he wishes above all to hear the apparently tragic tale she has to tell. Infidelity—even if it is merely sentimental—is nevertheless suggested by Yorick himself: 'Why should I dissemble the matter? I had sworn to her [Eliza] eternal fidelity—she had a right to my whole heart—to divide my affections was to lessen them—to expose them, was to risk them: where there is risk, there may be loss' (*SJ* I. 36). *A Sentimental Journey* thus implies an association between interpolation and infidelity that unites all the interpolating fictions so far examined. In *Tristram Shandy*, despite all the parallels between sex and writing (which, as Frank Brady remarks, are 'too well known to need discussion'[26]), infidelity is not so explicitly identified with verbal or physical errancy. Tristram does, however, remark on the danger of sidling into 'some bastardly digression' (VIII. 1), and thereby associates digressions with illicit sex.[27] Aside from the intriguing fact that the majority of inter-polations incorporated by Cervantes, Scarron and Fielding are stories of infidelity, the connotations of error are at their most striking in the critical reception of interpolating narratives: the criticism of disunity that these works have tended to attract seems to be rooted in a moral perception of the interpolating author as one who is *unfaithful* in some way to the main body/wife of his narrative. The geographical errancy of the hero, which normally generates the necessary conditions for interpolation, and the diegetic errancy of his narrator seem in the mind of such critics to hint at the moral errancy of the author.

The possibility that Tristram deviates morally as he deviates narratorially may therefore deserve more attention than it has generally received. Digressions may be the 'sun-shine' of reading (I. 22), but Tristram also perceives them as 'transgressions' (VI. 40) into which he is led by various 'devils'.[28] Brady notes that Sterne's reference to Bunyan at the outset of *Tristram Shandy* (I. 4) has received far less interest than the accompanying allusion to Montaigne because the differences between Sterne's work and *Pilgrim's Progress* are far more striking than the similarities: 'In spite of Christian's deviations from the highway, *Pilgrim's Progress* is the most "progressive" of works; its journey framework stands out like the backbone of an armadillo, while the plot line of *Tristram* is hidden and twisted. Yet Tristram too is embarked on life's journey, several of them, and he too encounters misery and disaster.'[29] While Christian's journey is infinitely less circuitous than Tristram's own wanderings, the latter may be seen to perpetuate (or, alternatively, to undermine parodically) the same associations of physical and moral errancy. *Tristram Shandy* generates ambivalence as easily as it produces (sexual/textual) ambiguities, and the ambivalence regarding the moral implications of Tristram's deviations is nowhere more evident than in the intercalation of Yorick's sermon in volume II: in this case, the narrative errs but does so in order to give the reader a moral lesson. This would appear to reverse the conventional association upon which the allegory of *Pilgrim's Progress* rests.[30] The theme of the sermon, however, is peculiarly appropriate to its status within *Tristram Shandy* as an inserted narration. Sterne's moral lesson leads the reader to the 'right path' by showing him how man has previously erred from it in the name of religion. In implicit contrast to the harmless exploits of Cervantes's knight errant, Yorick's sermon rhetorically asks, 'In how many kingdoms of the world has the crusading sword of this misguided saint-errant [the "*Romish* church"] spared neither age, or merit, or sex, or condition?' (II. 17). Tristram thus errs to show the dangers of 'misguided' errancy rather than errancy *per se*, although the idea of 'guided' errancy may in any case seem to verge on the oxymoronic.

The Miniaturization of the Digressive Landscape

Physical displacement, as suggested above, is presented as inherently problematic by Sterne. This is as true of the micro-journey of the Homunculus as it is of Tristram's journey through France. The Homunculus, deprived by Mrs Shandy's interruption of the animal spirits 'whose business it was to have escorted and gone hand-in-hand with [him], and conducted him safe to the place destined for his reception' (I. 2), must undertake his perilous journey alone: 'what if any accident had befallen him in his way alone?——or that, thro' terror of it, natural to so young a traveller, my little gentleman had got to his journey's end miserably spent' (I. 2). Tristram's Homunculus is a microscopic picaro, (literally) thrust alone and unprotected into a dangerous world. From the outset, Sterne uses the journey *topos* customary to interpolating and digressive fiction but radically reduces the scale of physical displacement. The account of the Homunculus thus sets the tone for Sterne's miniaturization of the conventional digressive landscape. Tristram in his study resembles in this respect his confined uncle, whose injury leads him to reduce Europe to the size of a bowling green. Tristram (who also suffers injuries and ill health) takes this process of miniaturization even further, reducing the seemingly boundless expanses of romance to the scale of a small country village.

With the important exception of volume VII, *Tristram Shandy* is, as suggested above, essentially confined to Shandy Hall and its immediate surroundings. The home of the Shandys inherits many of the characteristics of the inn as it appears in the works of Cervantes,

Scarron and Fielding. Although it is a relatively closed environment, in which the only guests are those who are invited, it remains open to accident and chance. Chance, however, may be regarded as an uninvited guest—an intruder from the outside world, who upsets the fixed patterns of the household; when the door opens for Dr Slop, the potential for accident follows him inside. From his first appearance in the narrative, Dr Slop is indeed presented as a victim of chance: the open road of picaresque narrative, now reduced to a narrow country lane, sees him mounted on his 'little diminutive pony' and colliding with Obadiah 'upon a strong monster of a coach-horse, prick'd into a full gallop, and making all practicable speed the adverse way' (II. 9) (narrated, as we have already seen, with all the sexual innuendo Sterne can muster in this 'dirtiest part of a dirty lane'). Even a short journey such as that undertaken by Dr Slop to Shandy Hall thus proves as vulnerable to 'pitiful misadventures and cross accidents' (I. 5) as Tristram's life and narrative. Dr Slop, as his undignified entrance suggests, introduces a strong element of burlesque into both *Tristram Shandy* and Shandy Hall. A 'little, squat, uncourtly figure [...] of about four feet and a half perpendicular height, with a breadth of back, and a sesquipedality of belly' (II. 9), Dr Slop is to medicine what Scarron's Ragotin is to law. The 'beluted' (II. 9) doctor indeed resembles the frequently humiliated lawyer of Le Mans: this resemblance is accentuated by the innlike internal geography of Shandy Hall. As we saw earlier, Ragotin's burlesque role ties him to the downstairs life of the inn, and disaster inevitably follows whenever he enters the space upstairs. Dr Slop's exploits upstairs are even more catastrophic, as he botches Tristram's delivery and by so doing compounds the disaster of Tristram's conception—a disaster that, it may be added, is prompted by a previous (double) masculine invasion of a feminine space. Dr Slop is not the only man in *Tristram Shandy* who does not belong upstairs, however: Tristram's unhappy life, and Bobby's unfortunate death, suggest that Walter's efforts to enter his wife's bedroom and indeed his wife are equally doomed, and that he should never have left the parlour downstairs.

While the bedrooms of Shandy Hall offer none of the romanesque possibilities that the rooms of Scarron's *Tripot* accommodate, they remain an inherently private (and feminine) space. During the course of Tristram's delivery, the only member of the Shandy family to have unrestrained access to all the rooms is Tristram himself, as he observes not only his own birth but his own conception. For the other men of the Shandy household, the upstairs becomes a largely forbidden and consequently mysterious zone during Tristram's delivery. Until Tristram is actually born, Walter and Toby confine themselves to the parlour, where they sit and listen to the goings-on above stairs: '————I wonder what's all that noise, and running backwards and forwards for, above stairs, quoth my father, addressing himself after an hour and a half's silence, to my uncle *Toby* [...] ——What can they be doing brother? quoth my father,——we can scarce hear ourselves talk' (I. 21). Unable to leave the parlour, Walter continues to listen for clues regarding the welfare of his wife and child: he later remarks, perhaps a little anxiously, 'All is quiet and hush [...] at least above stairs,—— I hear not one foot stirring' (III. 23). News of the accident to Tristram, however, does not come directly from upstairs but from the kitchen, where Susannah has related the latest events to Trim, and where Dr Slop is attempting to build a bridge for the infant's squashed nose. Walter, on hearing the news, is immediately led to his own room by Toby to recover from the shock in private: while the parlour provides a place for Walter to converse with his guests, his bedroom is the room he chooses in order to grieve in private. With the temporary reversal of the domestic hierarchy occasioned by Tristram's difficult arrival, Walter is the last to know what is happening upstairs. As the two brothers later return downstairs to the parlour, Walter is reminded of his new position at the foot of this temporary hierarchy when he calls to Susannah to ask 'how does your mistress?': '"As well", said *Susannah*, tripping by, but without looking up, "as can be expected"' (IV. 12). The fact that Susannah looks up to her master neither literally nor figuratively leads Walter to observe

——that from the very moment the mistress of the house is brought to bed, every female in it, from my lady's gentlewoman down to the cinder-wench, becomes an inch taller for it; and give themselves more airs upon that single inch, than all the other inches put together.

I think rather, replied my uncle *Toby*, that 'tis we who sink an inch lower. (IV. 12)

Walter may nevertheless enjoy the sanctuary of his parlour, the one room of Shandy Hall where he retains his authority. The parlour is a place for words, not deeds, and provides the setting for almost all Walter's conversations and debates with Toby (and thus a considerable part of *Tristram Shandy*). During Tristram's delivery, when Mrs Shandy is otherwise occupied, the parlour is an exclusively masculine space;

although Sterne makes it clear that Mrs Shandy has been there in the past,[31] in the timespan covered by Tristram's narrative she goes no further than 'opening the door' (V. 13) until the very last page of *Tristram Shandy*.[32] Shandy Hall offers no more privacy than an inn; even the parlour, however, offers little in the way of insulation from the rest of the house. Not only does the noise from the rest of the house seep in (causing Walter to complain): private discussions also leak out. Mrs Shandy is not the only member of the household to eavesdrop outside the parlour door:

> whenever an extraordinary message, or letter, was delivered in the parlour,——or a discourse suspended till a servant went out——or the lines of discontent were observed to hang upon the brows of my father or mother——or, in short, when any thing was supposed to be upon the tapis worth knowing or listening to, 'twas the rule to leave the door, not absolutely shut, but somewhat a-jar——as it stands just now,——which, under covert of the bad hinge, (and that possibly might be one of the many reasons why it was never mended) it was not difficult to manage [...] my mother stands at this moment profiting by it.——*Obadiah* did the same thing [...] (V. 6)

The parlour is thus connected to the rest of the house, and above all to the kitchen, by the go-between, Obadiah. The social hierarchy observed in the inns of *Tom Jones*, in which the servants chat with the inn staff downstairs while their masters converse upstairs, therefore finds its domestic equivalent in Shandy Hall in the relationship between parlour and kitchen: 'whatever motion, debate, harangue, dialogue, project, or dissertation, was going forwards in the parlour, there was generally another at the same time, and upon the same subject, running parallel along with it in the kitchen' (V. 6). The kitchen, in both *Tristram Shandy* and *A Sentimental Journey*, is a place for entertainment as well as work: Yorick's servant La Fleur, for example, having taken the Count de L***'s servant to 'a back parlour in the Auberge', is in turn invited back to the kitchen of the Count's *hôtel*. In under five minutes, La Fleur 'set the *fille de chambre*, the *maitre d'hotel*, the cook, the scullion, and all the household, dogs and cats, besides an old monkey, a-dancing: I suppose there was never a merrier kitchen since the flood' (*SJ* I. 37).

Both parlour and kitchen have their champions in *Tristram Shandy*, and Sterne's comparison of his two orators, Walter and Trim, thereby reflects the parallels and differences in the social functions of the two rooms. The contest Tristram hypothesizes between Walter, a man of 'deep reading——prompt memory——with *Cato*, and *Seneca*, and *Epictetus*, at his fingers ends' (V. 6), and Trim, 'with nothing——to remember', is a battle between 'nature and education' (V. 6), between learned spontaneity and intuitive straightforwardness:

> The one proceeding from period to period, by metaphor and allusion, and striking the fancy as he went along, (as men of wit and fancy do) with the entertainment and pleasantry of his pictures and images.
>
> The other, without wit or antithesis, or point or turn, this way or that; but leaving the images on one side, and the pictures on the other, going strait forwards as nature could lead him, to the heart. O *Trim*! would to heaven thou hadst a better historian! (V. 6)

Straightforwardness is once again perceived to reflect natural virtue— in this case, Trim's honesty and sincerity, although Walter's more ornate style is not seen conversely to imply any vice.[33] One may sense nevertheless that Tristram's admiration of Trim is tinged with envy for his ability to reach the 'heart' of the matter without diversions. When Tristram remarks that Trim deserves 'a better historian', he implies that his own literary style, as 'bent' by learning as his father's rhetoric, cannot do justice to the corporal's natural eloquence.

Both parlour and kitchen provide willing audiences for the skilled orator. Trim's effectiveness as a speaker promotes him in the hierarchy of Shandy Hall, and his position as manservant does not therefore restrict him to the kitchen. Trim, welcome in both parlour and kitchen, demonstrates his wide appeal and his adaptability as a speaker, while Walter, by contrast, has difficulty attracting an interested audience. Yorick and Slop appear to be the only characters consistently to listen closely to him: Toby's mind is often elsewhere, while Mrs Shandy generally appears to take little interest in her husband's philosophizing. The parlour and the kitchen invite different forms of verbal exchange: while the parlour is the setting for Walter's learned monologues and for the debating of various issues, the audience in the kitchen require more accessible forms of expression. This distinction is illustrated by the locations chosen for two of the most substantial of *Tristram Shandy*'s interpolations: the sermon and the story of Le Fever. In the relatively learned atmosphere of the parlour, the sermon finds an appreciative audience (with the exception of the persistently burlesque Dr Slop, who repeatedly interrupts its narration); the kitchen staff, however, are presented as being more interested in entertaining than improving themselves, and thus (like the inattentive lady reader of *Tristram Shandy*) to prefer anecdotes and stories to sermons or lessons. Susannah declares, 'I like to hear *Trim's* stories about the captain', and the rest of the staff evidently concur: '*Susannah*, the cook, *Jonathan*, *Obadiah*, and corporal *Trim*, formed a circle about the fire; and as soon as the scullion had shut the kitchen door,——the corporal begun' (V. 10).

Both the sermon and the story of Le Fever recall the introduction of the *novela* told by the curate in the *Quijote* and the interpolated tales of the *Roman comique*: in each case, the act of relation implies a sense of community, and of shared experience. Even when the speaker or storyteller is reading from a manuscript, the emphasis remains on the orality of narration, with the audience participating actively with their own commentary. Both Sterne, who famously asserts that 'Writing, when properly managed [...] is but a different name for conversation' (II. 11), and subsequently Diderot, in *Jacques*, evidently seek to preserve this sense of orality in the construction of their own narratives. It may seem surprising, therefore, that Sterne does not allow Trim to tell the story of Le Fever himself. Indeed, neither the sermon nor the story of Le Fever is told by the person who first related it: the sermon, originally delivered by Yorick to his congregation, is retold in the parlour by Trim, while the story of Le Fever, originally related by Trim in the kitchen, is later retold by Tristram. Sterne, who lessens the 'ready-made' quality of the sermon by subjecting it to repeated interruption, chooses not to subject the ostensibly spontaneous story of Le Fever to what would appear more naturally to be the same kind of faltering progress. This decision is reminiscent of Scarron's 'hijacking' of Ragotin's *novela*, whereby the author intrudes into his fiction in order to assert his *auctoritas*—'Ce n'est donc pas Ragotin qui parle, c'est moy' (*RC* I. 8). Whereas Scarron prefers directly to narrate the story as an author, without the intermediary mouthpiece of one of his characters, Tristram, if not Sterne, gives the impression that he deeply regrets not allowing Trim to narrate the story himself: '——fool that I was! nor can I recollect, (nor perhaps you) without turning back to the place, what it was that hindered me from letting the corporal tell it in his own words;——but the occasion is lost,——I must tell it now in my own' (VI. 5). Sterne's decision not to use Trim as the teller of a sentimental episode may suggest an authorial perception of his character as an inherently comic narrator in the vein of Sancho Panza. When Sancho tells a story, the reader's interest resides in the manner of its telling rather than the matter told; although Sterne does not entirely deflect the reader's attention from the sermon to its narrator, Trim nevertheless provides a comic frame for Yorick's lesson to make it *dulce* as well as *utile*. Trim, whose relationship to his master clearly suggests a Cervantine model, inherits Sancho's love of talking—'The fellow lov'd to advise,——or rather to hear himself talk [...] set his tongue a-going,——you had no hold of him' (II. 5). When Trim comes to narrate a story in his own words (as opposed to reading from another's script), his Sanchoesque function is evident: his 'story of the king of Bohemia' is as doomed to repeated interruption and correction as Sancho's own aborted narrations, and almost as vulnerable to deviation. The story, which starts out itself as a *divertissement*, is in turn diverted to become the story of Trim's falling in love (VIII. 19). Trim is evidently not, however, the incompetent narrator that Sancho appears to be: Toby holds his servant's storytelling to be not the least of his 'many excellencies' (VIII. 19), and if his story fails to progress the fault lies rather with his master. In this respect there are evident parallels with *Jacques*.

The relative immobility of the Shandys and their entourage forces Sterne into a highly innovative approach to the incorporation of interpolations. Whereas its digressive precedents rely heavily on the physical errancy of their protagonists to produce opportunities for interpolation, Sterne must create his opportunities within a much more restricted space. His digressive landscape shrinks the conventional topography of digressive fiction to such an extent that a stage on a journey is reduced to a step on a staircase, and a knight's sally to a short stroll in the village. The travels of Walter and Toby upon the staircase of Shandy Hall are as fraught with problems as any in *Tristram Shandy*: the reader joins them on the 'first landing', as Walter remarks to his brother, 'what a long chapter of chances do the events of this world lay open to us! Take pen and ink in hand' (IV. 9). Walter hence reverses Tristram's habit of using the world as a metaphor for the text, turning the text into a metaphor for the world. The staircase is subsequently shown to be as prone to accident as the open road, as Toby accidentally hits Walter 'a desperate blow souse upon his shin-bone' with his crutch: ''Twas a hundred to one [...] a meer chance, said my uncle *Toby*' (IV. 9).

The chapter ends with Walter and Toby still standing on the first landing, and Tristram begins the next with little confidence of progress:

Is it not a shame to make two chapters out of what passed in going down one pair of stairs? for we are got no farther yet than to the first landing, and there are fifteen more steps down to the bottom; and for aught I know, as my father and my uncle *Toby* are in a talking humour, there may be as many chapters as steps;——let that be as it will, Sir, I can no more help it than my destiny:——a sudden impulse comes across me——(IV. 10)

Tristram's difficulty with his father and uncle on the staircase also frames the famous counterpart to this declaration on the impossibility of ever making progress in his autobiography: 'I am this month one whole year older than I was this time twelve-month; and having got, as you perceive, almost into the middle of my fourth volume——and no farther than to my first day's life——'tis demonstrative that I have three hundred and sixty-four days more life to write just now, than when I first set out' (IV. 13).[34] When each step has the potential to generate an episode or frame a digression, the shortest journey may produce an almost limitless narrative; as the journey shrinks, so does the space required to intercalate other material. The lack of progress made by Walter and Toby down the stairs, and its implications for Tristram's writing of his autobiography, create a sense of paradox reminiscent of the fable of Achilles and the tortoise.[35] Sterne similarly demonstrates that infinite subdivisions may be made within a finite space: as Peter Conrad remarks, 'the Shandy house is elastic, at times narrowing into a cell constricting the characters as Toby is squeezed in his sentry-box, elsewhere swelling to enclose the whole of an imagined Europe. It is a nutshell, but an infinite space.'[36] Tristram, unable to get his father and uncle to the foot of the stairs, finally gives up and pays a '*day-tall* critick' (IV. 13) to do the job for him. Even the 'critick', however, cannot get Toby and Walter there by conventional means: he is obliged instead to perform a *coup de théâtre*, dropping 'a curtain at the stairs foot' (IV. 13). An *impasse* is thus averted by abandoning the rules of narrative for those of drama.[37]

In *Tristram Shandy*, virtual stasis rivals mobility as a stimulus for interpolation, as the inertia of the characters repeatedly provokes the narrator's counterbalancing errancy. The staircase thus creates a frame for Tristram's 'chapter upon chapters' (IV. 10) as well as a conversation between Walter and Toby. The progress of the two brothers is reduced to the textual equivalent of a slow-motion replay: chapter 11 sees Walter 'setting his foot upon the first step from the landing' only to be then 'drawing his leg back' (IV. 11) as he turns towards Toby; in chapter 12 this forwards-backwards motion is repeated[38] (Walter 'taking the same step over again from the landing' then 'drawing his leg back again' (IV. 12)) and succeeded by a further retreat as Walter crosses 'the landing, in order to set his back against the wall' (IV. 12). In each case, the physical regression appears to be prompted by the turn of the conversation: Walter, it seems, has difficulty walking and talking at the same time (in contrast to his son, who '*wrote-galloping*' (VII. 4)). The landing, as reluctant to relinquish Walter and Toby as the *Grand Cerf* is to release Jacques and his master, indeed punctuates the staircase rather as the inn traditionally punctuates the road: the landing provides Walter and Toby with a resting place on their short but slow journey and an opportunity to converse in greater depth.

The sallies of Don Quijote and his knight-errant models are parodically reduced in scale by Sterne to Yorick's 'several sallies about his parish' upon 'a lean, sorry jack-ass of a horse [...] full brother to *Rosinante*' (I. 10), and the expedition of Toby (who is compared favourably to 'the most courteous knight of romance' (IX. 3)) to Widow Wadman's house. This latter journey, one of many to progress slowly and end unhappily, is as circuitous as Tristram's narrative. Toby and Trim are said to 'sally forth' to see Widow Wadman at the end of the eighth volume, although Tristram postpones his account to the next volume as it is 'worth more, than to be wove into the fag end of the eighth volume of such a work as this' (VIII. 35).[39] In fact, Toby and Trim do not enter the Widow's house until the displaced eighteenth chapter of volume IX, even though the narrative leaps proleptically ahead to the 'sopha' upon which Toby is seated with his beloved (IX. 20). Tristram declares at the opening of the ninth volume that 'I could never yet get fairly to my uncle Toby's amours, till this very moment' (IX. 1), and his deferment of their narration evidently reflects his uncle's own hesitancy. Toby, after extensive preparations to his apparel,[40] leaves for Widow Wadman's house accompanied by Trim; on his way there he 'turn'd his head more than once behind him' (IX. 3), seeking moral support from his manservant, who 'march'd three paces distant from his master' (IX. 2). He comes to a halt 'within twenty paces of Mrs *Wadman*'s door', afraid that she might 'take it amiss' (IX. 4), a fear that prompts Trim to launch once again into the story of his unfortunate brother, Tom. Toby, stranded between his own cottage and Widow Wadman's house, is simultaneously stranded between two possible ways of life. Trim's remark that 'Nothing [...] can be so sad as confinement for life—or so sweet, an' please your honour, as liberty' (IX. 4) becomes, in his master's mind, a choice between Widow Wadman (whose house he looks at 'gravely') and his cottage and bowling green (which he looks at 'earnestly' (IX. 4)). Toby, loath to give up the freedom of errancy represented graphically by Trim's spiralling flourish of his cane, can neither advance nor retreat on his journey: as progression and regression are thus ruled out, Trim temporarily averts the *impasse* through digression, as he continues the tale of his brother. Tristram's metaphor of the earth's orbit of the sun (I. 22) for the narrative's rotation about its characters thus finds an echo in Toby's circling of Widow Wadman's house. Trim's digression and the discussion it stimulates liberate Toby from physical as well as intellectual paralysis: the verbal evasiveness of the interpolation prompts a physical deviation as Toby, unable to go either forwards or backwards, goes sideways. The conversation between the two veterans almost inevitably turns to the importance of 'the knowledge of arms',[41] and Toby's military metaphor carries him away:

as the knowledge of arms tends so apparently to the good and quiet of the world [...] whenever that drum beats in our ears, I trust, Corporal, we shall neither of us want so much humanity and fellow-feeling as to face about and march.

In pronouncing this, my uncle Toby faced about, and march'd firmly as at the head of his company———and the faithful Corporal [...] march'd close behind him down the avenue.

———Now what can their two noddles be about? cried my father to my mother———by all that's strange, they are besieging Mrs Wadman in form, and are marching round her house to mark out the lines of circumvallation. (IX. 8)

A metaphor of travel thus engenders travel itself, as Toby's hobby horse leads him away from his intended goal. While Toby and Trim head down the avenue, Tristram also 'faces about': instead of following his uncle, he turns his attention to his parents and he replays the previous scene from their perspective. Walter and Mrs Shandy intend to stop only for the moment they think it will take to see 'with what ceremonies my brother Toby and his man Trim make their first entry' (IX. 10). Walter's frustration at his brother's delayed entry unites him with the implied reader of the previous chapters:

The Corporal was just then setting in with the story of his brother Tom and the Jew's widow: the story went on———and on———it had no episodes in it———it came back, and went on———and on again; there was no end of it———the reader found it very long———

———G—help my father! he pish'd fifty times at every new attitude, and gave the corporal's stick, with all its flourishings and danglings, to as many devils as chose to accept of them. (IX. 10)

Toby is allowed to ride his hobby horse for the next seven chapters, as the narrator indulges in digression upon digression; when he and Trim reach the end of the avenue, they at last remember that 'their business lay the other way' (IX. 16), and head once again for Widow Wadman's house. The closer they come, the more Tristram delays their arrival, raising the suspense not just for the readers (actual and implied) and Walter and Mrs Shandy, but also for Bridget, who stands 'perdue' inside, 'her finger and her thumb upon the latch, benumb'd with expectation' (IX. 16), and Widow Wadman herself, who watches their painfully slow approach behind the curtain of her bedroom. Indeed, Toby enters the house only by accident, as Trim, standing 'with the rapper of the door suspended for a full minute in his hand' (IX. 16), lets it fall just as Toby is about to call him back for another conference. The destination is reached, but the narrative produces confusion rather than a climax, as the next two chapters are left blank and the reader is plunged proleptically into the middle of Toby's interview with Widow Wadman. This sense of disorientation, in which the end is no sooner reached than it is simultaneously left behind and deferred, underscores the impossibility of any successful resolution in *Tristram Shandy*: Toby's affair with Widow Wadman is as doomed to fail as Tristram's disorderly account of it.

Sterne's narrative, in which the shortest of journeys may provide a frame for an interpolation or a digression, nevertheless employs *topoi* that allow it to escape from its confined topographical space. Sterne, despite his reduction in scale, retains some of the familiar landmarks of conventionally digressive fictions: alongside the motifs of road, horse and travel that are preserved in metaphorical form in *Tristram Shandy*, he includes the inn not as a metaphor but as an actual *locus* in his village landscape. In the village inhabited by the Shandys, the inn is the only location of significance to the narrative outside Shandy Hall and the respective homes of Toby and Widow Wadman. The inn in question, located within the village rather than on the open road, serves both the local community and the passing traveller, and this double function prompts its role in *Tristram Shandy* as the setting for the story of Le Fever. Sterne, however, inverts the usual practice of digressive fiction: the story begins, not with Toby going to an inn, but with an inn coming to Toby, as a local landlord arrives 'to beg a glass or two of sack' (VI. 6) for a guest who has taken ill. This process of inversion continues, for, while the inns of the *Quijote*, and their successors in Scarron and Fielding, are places that abound with life and action, Sterne's local inn is the scene of Le Fever's death. This distinction masks, however, an underlying similarity to Palomeque's inn and the *Tripot de la Biche*: like the inns of Cervantes and Scarron (and later Diderot), Sterne's inn seems reluctant to release its guests. The semi-permanence that characterizes Don Quijote's stay in Palomeque's inn, or that of Scarron's troupe of actors in their *Tripot*, here gives way to permanence with Le Fever's death. Le Fever, who, like so many characters in *Tristram Shandy*, is unable to reach his appointed destination, ironically thus passes away in a place he intended only to pass through. It is pertinent in this context to note that Tristram, who flees from death by travelling, nevertheless expresses the desire to die in an inn—to 'die-galloping' as he '*wrote-galloping*'; he wishes 'that the Disposer of all things may so order it, that it happen not to me in my own house————but rather in some decent inn' (VII. 12).[42]

The village inn provides Sterne with a means of diversifying his narrative, as it allows an outsider to penetrate the enclosed environment of the Shandy household: it therefore performs a similar function to the frames into which Sterne introduces his interpolations. Tristram's family is so self-contained that few outsiders seem welcome to Shandy Hall, and Sterne must consequently adopt unusual measures in order to introduce interpolations into his fiction. Yorick's sermon, for example, is smuggled into Shandy Hall, and into Tristram's narrative, within Toby's copy of '*Stevinus*': it is therefore literally, as well as figuratively, embedded in another book. The sermon notably travels as badly as everything else in *Tristram Shandy*: having eluded its fictive author and owner to become part of another's story, it is lost a second time 'thro' an unsuspected fissure in thy master's pocket, down into a treacherous and tatter'd lining' while Yorick is riding upon 'his Rosinante'. The journey of the sermon does not end here, however, but follows a picaresque path of its own as it is 'trod deep into the dirt by the left hind foot' (II. 17) of Yorick's horse, where it lies buried for ten days until it is found by a beggar. Like a picaro, the sermon serves many masters: the beggar sells it for a halfpenny to a parish-clerk, who passes it onto his parson; it is then read by a prebendary in York Minster 'before a thousand witnesses', and later printed.

Although Slawkenbergius's Tale is not embedded quite as literally within another work as Yorick's sermon, it is nevertheless a quintessentially framed text. It is ostensibly taken from one narrative frame, Slawkenbergius's 'decads', and placed into another, Tristram's autobiography; like the sermon, it is presented as a text that exists prior to its appearance in Tristram's opus (it does not, however, have to travel as far as the sermon, as it comes from Walter's own library). Although Slawkenbergius is German and the setting for the ninth tale of his tenth decad is French, it has an unmistakably Spanish flavour to it: underlying the caricatural and satirical qualities of the tale is a highly sentimental intrigue reminiscent of the romanesque *novelas* interpolated by both Cervantes and Scarron, and a topography that increasingly reflects the Spanish identity of its protagonists. Diego thus enters Strasbourg 'mounted upon a dark mule', and 'chance brought him to the great inn in the market-place over-against the church' (IV, 'Slawkenburgius's Tale').[43] It is not until the last few pages of the tale that Diego's name is revealed, as he happens by chance to stay at the same inn as Julia's brother, Fernandez (having earlier crossed his path on the road to Strasbourg). Diego, oblivious to the furore he has left behind him in Strasbourg, thus returns with Julia and Fernandez to their home in '*Valadolid*' (IV, 'Slawkenburgius's Tale') and, in contrast to Tristram's narration of his own journey through France, is revealed to arrive at his destination.

The Journey through France

Tristram's tour of France in volume VII is a journey through more than one type of fictional landscape; his physical flight from death provides a frame that accommodates diverse literary modes, from the parodical to the picaresque and romanesque. Although Tristram's journey is clearly quite different from the one that the troupe undertakes in the *Roman comique*, Sterne posits a conceptual opposition between town and country that recalls the fiction of both Scarron and Fielding. In *Tristram Shandy*, the city or town is more firmly rooted in contemporary reality than the open countryside, although this is not to suggest that Tristram provides the reader with a strong impression of any of the towns he visits—as Arthur Cash notes, neither *Tristram Shandy* nor *A Sentimental Journey* 'gives any sense of the village of Montreuil with its beautiful medieval buildings and walls. Sterne's Montreuil passages might as well have been placed in any village in France so long as it had a posting inn'.[44] If Tristram's account appears contemporary, it has less to do with his powers of description than his implied parody of recent travelogues. Sterne consequently depends both upon the reader's recognition of the towns he describes as a part of his own world, and upon his familiarity with contemporary travel literature. Tristram in the narration of his travels is preoccupied more by the mechanics of travel than any particular location he visits, and the journey imagery that pervades the rest of the narrative here, in its more concrete manifestation, subordinates all the other aspects of the intercalated travelogue. His account, like that of Yorick in *A Sentimental Journey*, is dominated by the practical aspects of travelling, such as inns and chaises, perhaps because his progress is too difficult to allow him to concentrate on higher matters. Tristram's travels by chaise, for example, soon lead him to the conclusion '*That something is always wrong in a French post-chaise upon first setting out*' (VII. 8); later, on his arrival in Lyon, his chaise 'broke into a thousand pieces' (VII. 28), forcing him to find another means of transport.[45] The focus on the practicalities of travel may also be attributed to the urgency of the situation: Tristram is, after all, not a tourist but a man literally running for his life.

Among the accessories of travel that feature prominently in Tristram's journey are the various maps and guides that he carries with him. Tristram errs not just as a narrator but as a reader on his journey through France. When he notes, 'There is not a town in all *France*, which in my opinion, looks better in the map, than MONTREUIL; ———I own, it does not look so well in the book of post roads; but when you come to see it——to be sure it looks most pitifully' (VII. 9). Tristram again appears less interested in the France outside his chaise than the France of his maps and guidebooks. He indeed refers the reader to the 'Book of French post-roads, page 36, edition of 1762' (VII. 10) in a footnote to the following chapter, which comprises little more than a list of the posts between Montreuil and Abbeville. Even Paris fails to inspire Sterne's traveller, whose first comment is 'The streets however are nasty' (VII. 17), and who goes on to note that they are 'so villainously narrow, that there is not room in all Paris to turn a wheel-barrow' (VII. 17). Tristram's interest in the streets of Paris leads him to cite another of his books, a 'survey' of 1716, which states that '*Paris* doth contain nine hundred streets' (VII. 18); he goes on to state the precise number of streets in twenty of Paris's 'quarters' or *quartiers*. This reinforces the impression of a reader in his study rather than a traveller on a journey— or perhaps a traveller who 'reads-galloping' to the extent that he barely looks up from his books.[46] Once again one is invited to infer the influence of Walter Shandy (another of *Tristram Shandy*'s great readers) as Tristram's journey provides a parallel with his father's earlier planning of Bobby's Grand Tour. When he receives the news of Bobby's death, Walter is in the process of 'calculating the expence of his riding post from *Calais* to *Paris*, and so on to *Lyons*'. The progress of his planning of the route is narrated as if it constituted a journey in its own right, and an 'inauspicious journey' at that: when Obadiah interrupts, Walter 'had every foot of it to travel over again', and is subsequently said to be 'pursuing his journey' while conversing with Obadiah. When Obadiah enters the parlour a second time, Walter, 'who had a map of *Sanson's*, and a book of the post roads before him', lets slip his compasses, leaving 'nothing for him to do, but to return back to *Calais* (like many others) as wise as he had set out' (V. 2).

Walter's preparations for his elder son's journey are not far removed from his younger son's experience as a traveller: both father and son travel within travel literature, and the text appears in each case to overwhelm the world. Tristram alludes to one reference work after another, from the 'accounts of Lyon', and of 'Spon and others' (VII. 31) to the 'large set of provincial maps now publishing at Paris' (VII. 21) and the 'history of China in Chinese characters' he initially wishes to visit in the Jesuit library in Lyon (VII. 39). Tristram's journey is resolutely literary throughout: having led the reader on a parodic tour of recent travel writing, most notably in his account of (accounts of) Calais, he eventually leaves such urban(e) contemporary satire behind for an open road into a landscape far closer to the world of fiction. The sense of contemporaneity that informs Tristram's journey from Calais to Lyon fades as he arrives in the south of France and, for the first time on his journey, turns his attention from town to country. This shift in the narrative is marked by another change in modes of transport: having travelled by post-chaise to Lyon, Tristram decides to continue by boat to Avignon and then by mule. Tristram convinces himself that this is a blessing in disguise; aside from the money he will save, he is particularly taken with the prospect of seeing 'the castles of romance, whence courteous knights have whilome rescued the distress'd' (VII. 29). Rather like Don Quijote, he is drawn to romance but unable to escape the mundane reality symbolized by his humble means of transport, the mule.

Having left Death behind him, Tristram may now travel at a more leisurely pace, and his resolution to 'traverse the rich plains of *Languedoc* upon his [mule's] back, as slowly as foot could fall' (VII. 42) simultaneously suggests the adventurous spirit of the knight errant and the relative poverty of the picaro.[47] Tristram's journey through the plain would appear to provide the most naturalistic frame in his entire work for any interpolated stories or adventures, and Sterne's traveller indeed makes it clear that he is aware of the opportunities offered by the apparently featureless plain. As we saw earlier, Tristram observes that 'There is nothing more pleasing to a traveller——or more terrible to travel writers, than a large rich plain', and adds,

especially if it is without great rivers or bridges; and presents nothing to the eye but one unvaried picture of plenty: for after they have once told you that 'tis delicious! or delightful! (as the case happens)——that the soil was grateful, and that nature pours out all her abundance &c. ... they have then a large plain upon their hands which they know not what to do with——and which is of little or no use to them but to carry them to some town [...] (VII. 42)

The plain, which provides an unwelcome challenge to the descriptive powers of the travel writer, is the kind of blank canvas that digressive and interpolating fictions generate in order to expand or diversify the main action of the narrative. In *A Sentimental Journey*, for example, the road to Versailles creates a valuable space for Yorick to fill: 'As there was nothing in this road, or rather nothing which I look for in travelling, I cannot fill the blank better than with a short history' (*SJ* II. 63); a digression inevitably ensues. The blank of the 'barren' Languedoc plain is not, however, filled by an authorial intrusion: Tristram tells the reader,

by seizing every handle, of what size or shape soever, which chance held out to me in this journey——I turned my *plain* into a *city*——I was always in company, and with great variety too; and as my mule loved society as much as myself, and had some proposals always on his part to offer to every beast he met——I am confident we could have passed through Pall-Mall or St James's-Street for a month together, with fewer adventures——and seen less of human nature. (VII. 43)

As greedy for experience as any knight errant, Tristram takes every opportunity to delay his progress that presents itself: 'by stopping and talking to every soul I met who was not in a full trot——joining all parties before me——waiting for every soul behind——hailing all those who were coming through cross roads——arresting all kinds of beggars, pilgrims, fiddlers, fryars——not passing by a woman in a mulberry-tree without commending her legs, and tempting her into conversation with a pinch of snuff' (VII. 43). If this comes as no surprise to the reader of *Tristram Shandy*, what is unexpected is Tristram's omission from his travelogue of all but one of these 'adventures': his dance with the peasant girl, Nanette. Tristram, 'hastening to the story of my uncle *Toby's* amours' (VII. 43), reveals the digressive potential of his journey only to refuse to exploit it,[48] and, rather than incorporate his traveller's tales in his autobiography, promises to publish these separately in a collection entitled 'PLAIN STORIES' (VII. 43).[49]

Tristram actually takes advantage of relatively few of the opportunities for interpolation he creates in the narration of his journey through France. The most striking refusal to interpolate occurs in an episode that provides a form of coda to volume VII and 'trailer' for *A Sentimental Journey*: Tristram's encounter with Maria in volume IX. Maria is introduced in a manner that is typical of interpolating journeys generally: the hero's progress on the road is interrupted by a roadside distraction, and his journey thus deviates from its intended path with the promise of an entertaining (romanesque) interlude. Although Tristram is travelling by chaise rather than on horseback, the encounter with this 'poor damsel' (IX. 24) unquestionably indicates a romance model. The particular influence of the *Quijote* upon the Maria episode in *Tristram Shandy* may be inferred from a number of echoes of Cervantes's text: the pastoral figure of Maria, sitting 'upon a bank playing her vespers upon her pipe, with her little goat beside her' (IX. 24), bears some resemblance in this respect to Cervantes's shepherdess, Marcela; the fact that she is 'unsettled in her mind' but is 'sensible for short periods' (IX. 24) moreover recalls the character of Cardenio (as does the motif of thwarted marriage as a cause of insanity). The use of music to announce a digressive episode signals a further Sternean affinity with Cervantes: the mournful song of Don Luis at Palomeque's inn provides the introduction to the story of his love for Doña Clara into the narrative of the *Quijote*.[50] Sterne, having thus created all the expectations of an interpolation, refuses to satisfy them: in contrast to Yorick, who almost travels all the way to Brussels to hear the story of Mme de L***, Tristram seems keen to leave Maria behind:

Adieu, Maria!——adieu, poor hapless damsel!——some time, but not *now*, I may hear thy sorrows from thy own lips——but I was deceived; for that moment she took her pipe and told me such a tale of woe with it, that I rose up, and with broken and irregular steps walk'd softly to my chaise.
————What an excellent inn at Moulins! (IX. 24)

Tristram neither wishes to hear Maria's story nor, once heard, to include it in his narrative, as his author whets the reader's appetite for his *Sentimental Journey*.

The Maria episode of *Tristram Shandy* in fact provides a potential frame for two inserted histories; aside from Maria, Tristram's postillion also has a promisingly romanesque air about him: when he tells Tristram a little of Maria's circumstances, he does so 'with so much discretion and natural eloquence' that Tristram remarks, 'I could not help decyphering something in his face above his condition, and should have sifted out his history, had not poor Maria's taken such full possession of me' (IX. 24). The familiar motif of a character whose present circumstances belie his nobility (or formerly elevated 'condition')[51] is invoked by Sterne only to be dismissed. This created and rejected opportunity, which finds a close equivalent in Diderot's *Jacques*,[52] may suggest the parodying of a well-worn device. In any case, Sterne's refusal to interpolate his 'plain stories', or the histories of Maria and the postillion, demonstrates his rejection of the conventional journey as a frame for interpolated narrations. The only digression framed by Tristram's Grand Tour is that of the abbess of Andoüillets, and this is a narratorial intrusion rather than a character's interpolation; for all of Tristram's claims to '*write-galloping*', this tale never seems to belong to the journey that allegedly inspired it. Once again one can sense more strongly the author writing in his study than the narrator scribbling in his chaise. This impression is compounded by the lack of correspondence between the length of the story of the abbess and the ground Tristram covers during his reader's perusal of it: immediately prior to the point at which the tale is inserted, he is leaving Chantilly for Fontainebleau; immediately after it (six chapters later) he is approaching Lyon,[53] and congratulating himself with 'what a tract of country have I run [...] during the time you have been reading, and reflecting, Madam, upon this story!' (VII. 26). Sterne consistently undermines the convention of the journey as a narrative frame—in this case, by his deliberately poor execution of it. As we have already seen, he elsewhere subverts the tradition of interpolating fictions by his deflating miniaturization of the journey frame upon which it depends: the only travels that frame deviations and digressions in *Tristram Shandy* are confined to the microcosm of Shandy Hall and its environs. Sterne thereby achieves the opposite of his digressive antecedents: Tristram's digressiveness appears to frame his journey rather than vice versa.

Just as Tristram's past is always present in *Tristram Shandy*, so the tradition of interpolating and digressive fiction that exists prior to the eighteenth

century is as much a part of Sterne's present as the works of his
contemporaries. As suggested earlier, Sterne's eighteenth-century
consciousness embraces far more than eighteenth-century England; the
Quijote and the *Roman comique* are neither English nor eighteenth
century, but they must be allowed to have equal, if not greater, relevance
to Sterne than any of the works of either Defoe or Richardson.
Consequently, the continental tradition of digressive comic fiction offers
an instructive perspective from which to view *Tristram Shandy*. Sterne's
debts to the *Quijote* in *Tristram Shandy* (and to the *Roman comique* in *A
Sentimental Journey*[54]), and his manifest admiration of the authors of
these works, should not be seen to diminish our understanding of his
remarkable originality. Sterne, as his inventive approach to interpolation
demonstrates, plays with the conventions of digressive fiction—and, as
we have seen, even parodies them. His great innovation in this respect
is his virtual substitution of the domestic world for the external
topography of errant narratives.

The domestic sphere dominates in two different forms: in the
closed environment of Shandy Hall (and its immediate surroundings),
and in the study in which Tristram writes his autobiography. The
locations of road and inn are no longer pre-eminent as narrative
frames; as Sterne shifts the focus of attention from audience to
narrator, the emphasis changes from the internal narrations of the
former to the various intrusions of the latter. While *Tristram Shandy*
does allow the interpolation of a 'personal history' in, for example,
the story of Le Fever or of Trim's brother, Tom, the interiorization of
conventional digressive topography substantially diminishes the part
this form of digression, favoured by all of Sterne's digressive antecedents, plays in disrupting the progress of the narrative. Confined for
the most part to his study, with no one else to interrupt him,[55] the
narrator interrupts himself; and even when he flees from death in his
chaise, Tristram continues to intervene in his own narrative and evade
the intrusions of others.

Having distanced his own use of topography from those of his
digressive predecessors, Sterne does not, however, abandon the
familiar motifs of digressive fiction but transforms them from physical
locations to metaphorical markers. Although the language of travel
and movement largely replaces travel itself as a frame for digressive
narratives, the ascendancy of the verbal does not signify the disappearance of the physical. Throughout *Tristram Shandy* the material
provides a standing (or walking) critique of the abstract and verbal:

Toby and Trim tend to take Walter's abstractions—such as radical heat and moisture or the auxiliaries (V. 33 ff.; V. 42)—in a literal way, while the manner in which Tristram's failure to reach some sort of narrative resolution has a physical (or genetic) cause in Walter's failure to reach a satisfying sexual resolution with Mrs Shandy. Thus, while narratorial errancy largely succeeds physical errancy in *Tristram Shandy*, the physical element survives in order to mock these more modern wanderings. The journey through France might therefore be seen (in Toby's terms) as a rearguard action, with Sterne's 'mental picaresque'[56] being displaced by its physical original. The model of physical errancy proves remarkably resilient, and in both *Tristram Shandy* and *Jacques* coexists uneasily with the narratorial errancy it engendered.

Notes to Chapter 6

1. Quotations are from Laurence Sterne, *The Life and Opinions of Tristram Shandy, Gentleman*, ed. Melvyn and Joan New, 3 vols. (Gainesville, FL: University of Florida Press, 1978–84).
2. Whose 'History' is also said 'sometimes to fly' (*TJ* II. 1).
3. See above, Ch. 1, '*Orlando furioso*'.
4. Hutchinson, *Cervantine Journeys*, 207.
5. See below, 'The Miniaturization of the Digressive Landscape'.
6. Henri Fluchère, *Laurence Sterne, de l'homme à l'œuvre* (Paris: Gallimard 1961), 312.
7. Cf. *A Sentimental Journey*, in which Yorick criticizes in similar terms travel-writers like 'Mundungus', who 'made the whole tour [...] without one generous connection or pleasurable anecdote to tell of; but he had travell'd straight on looking neither to his right hand or his left, lest Love or Pity should seduce him out of his road' (*SJ* I. 24). (Quotations are from Laurence Sterne, *A Sentimental Journey through France and Italy*, ed. Tom Keymer (The Everyman Library; London: J. M. Dent, 1994), I. 24. References are to volume and page.)
8. As Frank Brady notes, 'the muleteer–mule analogy adds an overtone that [to journey straight ahead] is sterile, since the mule, in contrast to the ass, usually exemplifies sterility in *Tristram*' ('*Tristram Shandy*: Sexuality, Morality, and Sensibility', *Eighteenth-Century Studies*, 4 (1970), 41–56 (45)).
9. William Dampier, *A New Voyage Round the World*, reprint of 1729 edn., ed. Sir Albert Gray (London: Argonaut, 1927), 4.
10. See *Tristram Shandy* (IX. 12) once again, in which digression (rather than narrative) is expressed as a 'frisky' horse: 'if it is to be a digression, it must be a good frisky one, and upon a frisky subject too, where neither the horse or his rider are to be caught, but by rebound'.
11. Cf. Burton's *Anatomy*, in which the author's 'silent, sedentary, solitary, private life' is said to have produced a 'running wit' and an 'unconstant, unsettled mind'. Burton, however, compares himself not to a horse but to a dog: 'This roving humour [...] I have ever had, & like a ranging Spaniell, that barkes at every bird he sees, leaving his game, I have followed all [...] I never travelled but in Mappe

or Card, in which mine unconfined thoughts have freely expatiated, as having ever beene especially delighted with the study of *Cosmography*' (Robert Burton, *The Anatomy of Melancholy*, ed. Thomas C. Faulkner, Nicolas K. Kiessling and Rhonda L. Blair, 3 vols. (Oxford: Clarendon Press, 1989–94), 3).

12. Cf. *Joseph Andrews*, in which the reader is warned 'not to travel through these Pages too fast: for if he doth, he may probably miss the seeing some curious Productions of Nature which will be observed by the slower and more accurate Reader' (*JA* II.1). Quoted above, Ch. 5.

13. Elizabeth W. Harries, 'Sterne's Novels: Gathering up the Fragments', *ELH* 49 (1982), 35–49 (41).

14. Tristram resolves to 'go on leisurely, writing and publishing two volumes of my life every year;——which [...] I shall continue to do as long as I live' (I. 14) and says of the 'machine' that is his autobiography that 'it shall be kept a-going these forty years, if it pleases the fountain of health to bless me so long with life and good spirits' (I. 22). Tristram refers back to these statements immediately before embarking for France (VII. 1). Cf. Montaigne's famous remark in 'De la Vanité': 'Qui ne voit que j'ay pris une route par laquelle, sans cesse et sans travail, j'iray autant qu'il y aura d'ancre et de papier au monde?' (*Essais*, III. 9).

15. The mention of 'chivalry' and 'romance' here suggests an implicit allusion to the *Quijote* to accompany the explicit reference to Uncle Toby and Slawkenbergius's tale.

16. Toby 'was four years totally confined,—part of it to his bed, and all of it to his room' (I. 25).

17. Cf. Tristram's equally despairing appeal to Dr Slop, 'Truce!—truce, good Dr Slop—stay thy obstetrick hand' (II. 11).

18. See above, Ch. 4, '*Joseph Andrews* and *Tom Jones*: The Topography of the Inn'.

19. For a description of the other connotations of Sterne's hobby horse, see Helen Ostovich, 'Reader as Hobby-Horse in *Tristram Shandy*', *Philological Quarterly*, 68 (1989), 325–42 (326–7).

20. 'What did not a little contribute to leave him thus without an ally, was, that if there was any one post more untenable than the rest, he would be sure to throw himself into it; and to do him justice, when he was once there, would defend it so gallantly, that 'twould have been a concern, either to a brave man, or a good-natured one, to have seen him driven out' (VIII. 34).

21. I am indebted to A. D. Nuttall for his convincing suggestion that the image of the white bear at the end of volume V constitutes a reference to the notorious stage direction in *A Winter's Tale*: '*Exit, pursued by a bear*' (III. 3). The Florida edition makes no mention of this probable allusion.

22. Melvyn New, *Laurence Sterne as Satirist: A Reading of 'Tristram Shandy'* (Gainesville, FL: University of Florida Press, 1969), 15.

23. Cf. 'is a man to follow rules—or rules to follow him' (IV. 10).

24. Sigurd Burckhardt, '*Tristram Shandy*'s Law of Gravity', *ELH* 28 (1961), 70–88 (80).

25. For the cyclical nature of the *Quijote*, see above, Ch. 2.

26. Brady, '*Tristram Shandy*: Sexuality, Morality, and Sensibility', 46.

27. Cf. Muratore's description of the Spanish stories in the *Roman comique* as 'orphaned tales' (see above, Ch. 3 n. 31).

28. '*John de la Casse*'s devils' and '*Benevento*'s devils' (VI. 40). Cf. the opening of

Tristram Shandy, in which the animal spirits 'presently make a road of it [...] which, when they are once used to, the Devil himself sometimes shall not be able to drive them off it' (I. 1).

29. Brady, '*Tristram Shandy*: Sexuality, Morality, and Sensibility', 45.

30. Tristram's earlier rebuke to the lady reader of his work reinforces this inversion: 'Madam' is condemned for her 'vile pruriency for fresh adventures' and for her 'vicious taste [...] of reading straight forwards', and the narrator consequently implies that the 'true path' is not straight but circuitous. Pruriency is apparently a feminine trait: Mrs Shandy both eavesdrops (V. 5) and looks through a keyhole (VIII. 35).

31. See the quotation below, in which Sterne refers to 'the lines of discontent [that] were observed to hang upon the brows of my father or mother' in the parlour (V. 6).

32. No room is assigned to the final chapter of volume IX, in which Walter, Toby, Dr Slop, and Mrs Shandy are all seated together; one may assume, however, that the parlour is the likeliest setting.

33. Tristram remarks elsewhere that 'Nature, who makes every thing so well to answer its destination, and seldom or never errs' (IX. 22).

34. Cf. the contrastingly feigned narratorial difficulties of Fielding in *Joseph Andrews* (see above, Ch. 4, '*Joseph Andrews*: Progress Barred') and *Tom Jones* (see above, Ch. 5, 'The Reader as Travelling Companion'), and of Diderot in *Jacques* (see below, Ch. 7, 'Two Narrative Metaphors: The Road and the Horse').

35. See the relevance of the same paradox in Chapter 7 below.

36. Peter Conrad, *Shandyism: The Character of Romantic Irony* (Oxford: Blackwell, 1978), 26.

37. It is no coincidence that *Tristram Shandy* abounds in theatrical metaphors, and Shandy Hall follows in the tradition of Cervantes's inn as a theatrical (comic) stage. Tristram refers to the 'exquisite scenes' offered by 'this whimsical theatre of ours' (III. 39), and elsewhere begs the reader to 'assist me here, to wheel off my uncle *Toby's* ordnance behind the scenes,——to remove his sentry-box, and clear the theatre, *if possible*, of horn-works and half moons' (VI. 29). Tristram also notes that chapters 'in a work of this dramatic cast [...] are as necessary as the shifting of scenes' (IV. 10), and repeatedly ends a chapter by dropping the curtain on a scene (see also II. 5; II. 19). Don Diego, the hero of 'Slawkenbergius's Tale', is also presented as an actor in a play: 'We left the stranger behind the curtain asleep——he enters now upon the stage' (IV, 'Slawkenbergius's Tale').

38. Cf. the 'forwards-backwards' motion of sex and thought to which Brady alludes: 'Tristram conjoins thought, story, and sex: "when a man is telling a story in the strange way I do mine, he is obliged continually to be going backwards and forwards to keep all tight together in the reader's fancy"' (Brady, '*Tristram Shandy*: Sexuality, Morality, and Sensibility', 45).

39. Sterne's use of the word 'sally' always appears to hint at the original sense of the word as an excursion or expedition. Even when Tristram employs 'sally' in the context of verbal repartee, the danger inherent in its original chivalric or military meaning remains: Yorick, for example, is warned that his 'sallies' will lead him to his downfall (I. 12).

40. Toby's 'blue and gold [...] shone so bright against the sun that morning, and had

so metallick, and doughty an air with them, that had my uncle Toby thought of attacking in armour, nothing could have so well imposed upon his imagination' (IX. 2). The parallels with Don Quijote are clear enough to render further comment unnecessary.

41. Cf. Don Quijote's discussion of the relative merits of arms and learning (*DQ* I. 37–8).

42. There is an echo here of Montaigne's expression of his desire to die while travelling: 'Si je craignois de mourir en autre lieu que celuy de ma naissance, si je pensois mourir moins à mon aise esloigné des miens, à peine sortiroy-je hors de France; je ne sortirois pas sans effroy hors de ma paroisse. Je sens la mort qui me pince continuellement la gorge ou les reins. Mais je suis autrement faict: elle m'est une partout. Si toutesfois j'avois à choisir, ce seroit, ce croy-je, plustost à cheval que dans un lict, hors de ma maison et esloigné des miens' (*Essais*, III. 9).

43. The inn is the *Maison Kammerzell*.

44. Cash, *Laurence Sterne: The Later Years*, 123.

45. See above, Ch. 4, '*Joseph Andrews*: Progress Barred'.

46. See Cash, who notes that 'Sterne wrote the travel narrative in *Tristram Shandy*, VII, and *A Sentimental Journey* while sitting in his study in Coxwold' (*Laurence Sterne: The Later Years*, 122–3).

47. A similarly Quixotic effect is produced in *A Sentimental Journey* when Yorick makes a detour in order to meet the Maria Tristram encountered near Moulins: ''Tis going, I own, like the Knight of the Woeful Countenance, in quest of melancholy adventures' (*SJ* II. 95).

48. Cf. *Jacques*, in which Diderot reveals certain paths his narrative could take only to refuse them (below, Ch. 7, 'Two Narrative Metaphors: The Road and the Horse').

49. Cf. La Place's decision to omit Fielding's introductory chapters, and his suggestion that they be published separately in a collection of their own (see above, Ch. 5, 'The Introductory Chapters: The Case of La Place').

50. See *DQ* I. 42. The use of music or song as a force for physical deviation (Tristram is distracted from his journey by 'the sweetest notes I ever heard' (*TS* IX. 24)) inevitably also recalls the sirens of Homer's *Odyssey*.

51. In the *Roman comique*, this motif forms the basis of the entire romanesque action of the narrative, with one member of the troupe after another proving to be nobler than his or her present circumstances suggest. In the eighteenth century, the most famous use of this motif occurs in the opening scene of *Manon Lescaut*: 'Parmi les douze filles qui étaient enchaînées six à six par le milieu du corps, il y en avait une dont l'air et la figure étaient si peu conformes à sa condition, qu'en toute autre état je l'eusse prise pour une personne du premier rang' (l'abbé Prévost, *Histoire du Chevalier des Grieux et Manon Lescaut* in *Romanciers du XVIII* *siècle*, ed. Étiemble (Paris: Gallimard, 1960), 1224). In both of these works, the intriguing appearance of the stranger prompts an explanatory interpolation.

52. See Diderot's non-incorporation of the history of the *Grand Cerf*'s hostess, below, Ch. 7, 'From Inn to Castle'.

53. Having passed through Fontainebleau, Sens, Joigny, Auxerre, Dijon, Châlon, Mâcon 'and a score more upon the road to LYONS' (VII. 26).

54. See the episode in *A Sentimental Journey* entitled 'THE DWARF', which is based upon an incident in the *Roman comique* (*RC* II. 17).

55. 'Jenny', the only other character to enter Tristram's study, does not play a part in interrupting or otherwise disrupting the writing of his autobiography.
56. Brady's term ('*Tristram Shandy*: Sexuality, Morality, and Sensibility', 44).

CHAPTER 7

Jacques le Fataliste et son maître
Travelogue as Narrative

There is a moment in *Jacques le Fataliste et son maître*, as there is in most of the texts examined above, when adverse weather forces the travellers to seek shelter. In contrast to these earlier works, however, Diderot's narrator refuses to specify where Jacques and his master actually stay on this occasion: 'ils furent accueillis par un orage qui les contraignit de s'acheminer ... — Où? — Où? Lecteur, vous êtes d'une curiosité bien incommode [...] Si vous insistez, je vous dirai qu'ils s'acheminerent vers ... Oui; pourquoi pas? vers un château immense' (p. 29).[1] The narrator immediately admits the chateau to be an allegorical smokescreen, but persists in his refusal to indicate where our two travellers spend the night; instead he asks the reader to choose from a catalogue of possibilities:

Je vous sacrifierai mon allégorie et toutes les richesses que j'en pourrais tirer; je conviendrai de tout ce qui vous plaira, mais à condition que vous ne me tracasserez point sur le dernier gîte de Jacques et de son maitre; soit qu'ils aient atteint une grande ville et qu'ils aient couché chez des filles; qu'ils aient passé la nuit chez un vieil ami qui les fêta de son mieux; qu'ils se soient refugiés chez des Moines mendians, où ils furent mal logés et mal repus pour l'amour de Dieu; qu'ils aient été accueillis dans la maison d'un Grand, où ils manquerent de tout ce qui est nécessaire, au milieu de tout ce qui est superflu; qu'ils soient sortis le matin d'une grande auberge, où on leur fit payer très cherement un mauvais souper servi dans des plats d'argent, et une nuit passée entre des rideaux de damas et des draps humides et repliés; qu'ils aient reçu l'hospitalité chez un Curé de village à portion congrue, qui courut mettre à contribution les bassescours de ses paroissiens pour avoir une omelette et une fricassée de poulets; ou qu'ils se soient enivrés d'excellens vins, fait grande chere et pris une indigestion bien conditionnée dans une riche Abbaye de Bernardins [...] (pp. 30–1)

The second of these locations is subsequently revealed to be the 'correct' one when Jacques is obliged to retrace his steps to recoup the watch and purse he had left behind. What is interesting about the list, however, is the variety of options it reveals to be open to the author of *Jacques* when it comes to deciding where his characters may find overnight shelter. Whereas only the inn generally seems available to the itinerant heroes of Scarron or Fielding, the journey of Jacques and his master is closer to the model offered by Cervantes in the *Quijote*, where the knight and his squire at various points also stay at 'une grande auberge', a castle and the 'maison d'un Grand'.

Diderot frequently draws his reader's attention to the almost infinite possibilities open to him as the author of a fictional journey; he notes, for example, that, by separating Jacques and his master, he could make his reader's wait for the resumption of Jacques's story last three years. The above catalogue of potential *gîtes* is distinguishable from such apparently casual authorial bravado as, with the exception of the house of the 'Curé de village', each of the locations in the list (or their close equivalents) feature in the course of the novel, from the *tripots* run by Mme d'Aisnon and her daughter, where 'un ou deux des convives restaient, passaient la nuit avec Madame et Mademoiselle, à leur choix' (p. 162), to the *Grand Cerf*, the Château de Miremont, and the monasteries described in the stories of Jacques's brother Jean and the Abbé Hudson. This list of settings therefore reflects the actual rather than potential diversity of *Jacques*, a text that includes a rich compendium of *gîtes* (from peasant cottage to aristocratic chateau) and the social *milieu* each represents. This array of locations is moreover essentially *literary*, forming a topography that reveals the formative impact of a tradition of comic fiction embracing all of the texts included in this study. A remedy once suggested by Diderot for the vapours indeed confirms the obvious presence of such precedents within the narrative fabric of *Jacques*:

J'avais toujours traité les romans comme des productions assez frivoles; j'ai enfin découvert qu'ils étaient bons pour les vapeurs; j'en indiquerai la recette à Tronchin la première fois que je le verrai. Recipe huit à dix pages du Roman comique; quatre chapitres de Don Quichotte; un paragraphe bien choisi de Rabelais; faites infuser le tout dans une quantité raisonnable de Jacques le Fataliste ou de Manon Lescaut; et variez ces drogues comme on varie les plantes, en leur substituant d'autres qui ont à peu près la même vertu.[2]

One might be reminded here of Fielding's similarly organic view of *Tom Jones* in his opening 'Bill of Fare' for the reader, as Diderot here presents *Jacques* as a medicine, infused with the *Quijote* and the *Roman comique*, with the ability to dissipate low spirits.[3] The narrative syntax of road and inn Diderot inherits from such predecessors as Cervantes and Scarron had become familiar, even conventional, however, within the context of comic or picaresque prose fiction by the time he came to write *Jacques*; he thus predictably engages with these conventions with characteristically radical playfulness. Roger Kempf remarks of *Jacques*, 'C'est l'anti-voyage, et par là-même, l'anti-roman, à une époque où tout écrivain tenait Babylone et l'Amérique au bout de sa plume.'[4] *Jacques* does more than parody the kind of *roman romanesque* to which Kempf alludes, however: in a fashion that recalls, but is not limited to, the method of Sterne in *Tristram Shandy*, the travels of Jacques and his master subvert the very idea of the journey as an organizing principle of narrative. In so doing, Diderot's 'anti-voyage' produces a narrative that marks the zenith as well as the imminent decline of the fictional travelogue in comic fiction.

Two Narrative Metaphors: The Road and the Horse

It may come as little surprise, given the explicit influence of Cervantes and Sterne (and the possible influence of Fielding), that the rhetoric of travel features prominently in *Jacques* and, indeed, in much of Diderot's other writings. In his 'Réflexions sur l'ode', for example, Diderot declares dramatically, 'Ce n'est pas une bête de somme qui suit son chemin, c'est sur un cheval fougueux et ailée que le poëte odaïque est monté';[5] this strikingly chivalresque image of the poet recalls Sterne's historiographer (as well as Ariosto's hippogriff): 'Could a historiographer drive on his history, as a muleteer drives on his mule,——straight forward;——for instance, from *Rome* all the way to *Loretto*, without ever once turning his head aside either to the right hand or the left [...]?' (*TS* I. 14). The *Lettre sur les sourds et les muets* also invites comparison with the same chapter of *Tristram Shandy*, as Diderot pleads the legitimacy of digression, arguing, 'dans une lettre les écarts sont permis, sur-tout lorsqu'ils peuvent conduire à des vues utiles',[6] rather as Tristram's historiographer 'will have fifty deviations from a straight line to make with this or that party as he goes along, which he can no ways avoid. He will have views and prospects to himself perpetually solliciting his eye, which he can no more help standing still to look at than he can fly' (*TS* I. 14). Digressions are thus expressed by both authors in spatial, scenic terms as escapes from the blinkered linearity of the straight path or road. In the same *Lettre*,[7] one moreover encounters the same image of the author and reader as fellow-travellers observed earlier in the *Furioso* and in *Tom Jones*: 'Nous avons fait assez de chemin ensemble, et je sens qu'il est temps de se séparer. Si je vous arrête encore un moment à la sortie du labyrinthe où je vous ai promené, c'est pour vous rappeler en peu de mots les détours.'[8]

In *Jacques*, whose existence is first recorded in 1771 (some twenty years after the *Lettre sur les sourds et les muets*) in a letter from Meister to Bodmer,[9] the *chemin* travelled by the master and his servant has a rhetorical equivalent in the path along which the reader is asked to follow the author.[10] It soon becomes clear, however, that these two paths do not always run parallel to each other; when the rhetorical path or course is first invoked, it is in fact in direct opposition to its topographical counterpart:

Jacques commença l'histoire de ses amours. C'était l'après diner. Il faisait lourd, son maitre s'endormit. La nuit les surprit au milieu des champs; les voilà fourvoyés. Voilà le maitre dans une colere terrible et tombant à grands coups de fouet sur son valet, et le pauvre diable disant à chaque coup: Celui-là était apparemment encore écrit là-haut.

Vous voyez, Lecteur, que je suis en beau chemin, et qu'il ne tiendrait qu'à moi de vous faire attendre un an, deux ans, trois ans, le récit des amours de Jacques, en le séparant de son maitre et en leur faisant courir à chacun tous les hazards qu'il me plairait. (p. 5)

While Jacques and his master are 'fourvoyés', the reverse is said to be true of the narrator, who confidently asserts that he is 'en beau chemin'—'beau' precisely because it diverts the narrative away from its expected course into an area in which anything can happen.

In works such as *Jacques* or *Tom Jones*, where travel dominates both the rhetoric and the narrative itself, the reader's sensitivity to the spatial terms in which he relates to narrative is heightened. Even the most ordinary, everyday expressions are inflected with new vitality: when, for example, Jacques is asked to return to his *récit*, his response, 'Je ne sais *où* j'en étais' (p. 18; emphasis added), takes on added significance to complement the narratorial suppression of geographical information elsewhere in *Jacques*. Parallels between the waywardness of the travellers' progress and that of their storytelling are similarly often expressed on a micro-narrative level: after Jacques's master has been diverted by his servant from the story he intended to tell, he asks, 'Jacques, pourquoi

m'avez-vous dérouté?' (p. 340)[11] while, at the *Grand Cerf*, Jacques asks
to be reminded as to what point in his story he had reached: 'Je vous
prie, mon Maitre, pour cette fois ci, et pour toutes les autres, de me
remettre sur la *voie*' (p. 117; emphasis added).

In *Jacques*, as at certain moments in *Tom Jones*,[12] Diderot's narrator
suffers problems with his narrative that duplicate the difficulties facing
Jacques and his master on their journey. At certain points, the narrative and the self-conscious rhetoric that accompanies it are strikingly
conflated by the simultaneous metaphorical and literal exploitation of
a locution; when Jacques has reached a point of crisis in his story, with
no apparent solution in sight, the narrator intervenes thus:

> Lecteur, si je faisais ici une pause et que je reprisse l'histoire de l'homme à
> une seule chemise, parcequ'il n'avait qu'un corps à la fois, je voudrais bien
> savoir ce que vous en penseriez.—Que je me suis fourré dans un *impasse*, à
> la Voltaire, ou, vulgairement dans un cul-de-sac d'où je ne sais comment
> sortir, et que je me jette dans un conte fait à plaisir, pour gagner du temps et
> chercher quelque moyen de sortir de celui que j'ai commencé. Eh bien,
> Lecteur, vous vous abusez de tout point. Je sais très bien comment Jacques
> sera tiré de sa détresse [...] (pp. 110–11)

(In contrast to Tristram, and in common with his counterpart in *Tom
Jones*, Diderot's narrator only feigns difficulty here.[13]) The metaphorical
impasse suggested by the interruption of Jacques's narration coincides
with a literal *impasse*: as soon as the narrator returns from his digression
to his travellers, the reader learns that the break in storytelling coincides
with a break in the journey that frames it: 'Tandis que je vous faisais
cette histoire, que vous prendrez pour un conte [...] Jacques et son
Maitre avaient atteint le gîte où ils avaient la nuit à passer. Il était tard,
la porte de la ville était fermée et ils avaient été obligés de s'arrêter dans
le faubourg' (p. 113). The shift from Jacques's narration to the story of
Gousse is thus accompanied by the transition from road to inn, as Jacques
and his master enter the *Grand Cerf*.

When Jacques asks his master to put him back on track ('de me
remettre sur la voie'), the track in question is, as we have seen, that of
his 'amours'. The manner in which the 'voie' is thereby identified
with the act of narration here takes on added significance in the
context of *Jacques*. The road occupies a privileged position throughout
in relation to the telling of Jacques's story: just as our two travellers are
unable to travel without telling stories, so they are unable to tell their
stories without travelling. It is therefore significant that in the opening

paragraph the question that directly follows 'Où allaient-ils?' is 'Que disaient-ils' (p. 3), as if travel inevitably implies dialogue.[14] It is moreover immediately striking that, although Jacques has been in his master's service for at least ten years (p. 223), the master knows very little about him. Indeed, the narrations of both master and servant arise from the mutual ignorance of each regarding the other's past: in the opening dialogue between the two travellers, the master learns for the first time that Jacques had once been in love; when he remarks, 'Tu ne m'en as jamais dit un mot', Jacques simply responds, 'C'est que cela ne pouvait être dit ni plutôt ni plus tard' (p. 4). More surprising perhaps is the master's ignorance of Jacques's previous employment, which leads to the latter revealing a lengthy list of former masters beginning (as it will eventually end) with Desglands:

JACQUES. — [...] C'est lui qui me donna au Commandeur de La Boulaye qui périt en passant à Malthe; c'est le Commandeur de La Boulaye qui me donna à son frère ainé le Capitaine, qui est peutêtre mort à présent de la fistule. C'est ce Capitaine qui me donna à son frère le plus jeune, l'Avocat général de Toulouse qui devint fou et que la famille fit enfermer. C'est M. Pascal, Avocat général de Toulouse qui me donna au Comte de Tourville, qui aima mieux laisser croître sa barbe sous un habit de Capucin que d'exposer sa vie. C'est le Comte de Tourville qui me donna à la Marquise du Belloy qui s'est sauvée à Londres avec un étranger. C'est la Marquise du Belloy qui me donna à un de ses cousins, qui s'est ruiné avec les femmes et qui a passé aux Isles. C'est ce cousin-là qui me donna à un Mr Hérissant, usurier de profession, qui faisait valoir l'argent de M. de Rusai, Docteur de Sorbonne, qui me fit entrer chez Mademoiselle Isselin, que vous entreteniez, et qui me plaça chez vous [...]
LE MAITRE. — Mais, Jacques, tu as parcouru bien des maisons en assez peu de temps. (pp. 220–1)

Ironically, this picaresque procession of former employers actually emphasizes the unpicaresque characteristics of *Jacques*. Whereas the picaresque novel typically constructs its episodic narrative around the picaro's experience of a succession of masters, in *Jacques* the narrative is based upon a single, enduring master–servant relationship. In this respect Jacques may be described as a picaro who has graduated to the role of squire, faithful to the master for whom, as he says himself, he was made: 'Jacques a été fait pour vous, et vous fûtes fait pour Jacques' (p. 221). Although there are evident differences between them, Jacques's role resembles that of Sancho rather more than that of, for example, a Lázaro or a Guzmán, as the narrator apparently confirms:

'Jacques et son maitre ne sont bons qu'ensemble et ne valent rien séparés, non plus que Don Quichotte sans Sancho' (pp. 82–3).

Jacques's list of former masters acts as both an invocation and a revocation of the picaresque, with each master or mistress, and the episodes he or she might have generated in a picaresque narrative, being reduced to an unelaborated entry in a list. This rejection of narrative possibilities, perhaps surprisingly, is in fact typical of *Jacques*, which refuses as many deviations as it embraces; its narrator often content to articulate an opportunity for expansion only to decline it. This type of rebuttal is often presented as evidence of the narrative's rejection of the romanesque—as, for example, in the case of the non-pursuit of the bandits in the opening part of the novel—and serves to illustrate the ease and frequency with which the narrator may disrupt and delay the progress of the story in which he is presently engaged.[15] Like Palomeque's collection of books in the *Quijote*, or the *nouvelles* of La Garouffière and Inézilla in the *Roman comique*, Jacques's former masters provide an almost infinite source of potential digressions.

As the *impasse* that simultaneously leads away from Jacques's narration and the road (and into the *Grand Cerf*) suggests, the progress of master and servant along the course of their journey is uniquely intertwined with that of their personal narratives. For much of *Jacques*, the road constitutes far more than a narrative metaphor: it provides an objective manifestation of linearity that not only runs parallel to, but sets the boundaries for, the subjective linearity of Jacques's story. Jacques's progress as a narrator may thus be measured according to his progress along the road. From the outset, when Jacques and his master stray from their road, they stray from Jacques's story; when Jacques 'commença l'histoire de ses amours', he and his master (in contrast to the narrator) are both spatially and diegetically 'fourvoyés', finding themselves suddenly 'au milieu des champs' (p. 5). Only when Jacques and his master are 'remontés sur leurs bêtes et poursuivant leur chemin' (p. 5) the following day is the former's narration allowed to advance. Leaving the road continues to imply abandoning Jacques's story; neither the first inn, 'la plus misérable des auberges' (p. 11), nor the *Grand Cerf* proves receptive to Jacques's *récit*: in the former of these, the 'brigands' in the adjoining room create a distraction that renders it unsuitable for storytelling, while, at the latter, the 'hôtesse' wins the battle for the master's attention with the tale of Mme de la Pommeraye.[16]

The conflation of road and narrative is not only evident in the manner in which the inn halts the progress of the travellers and their tales; even the smallest of physical transgressions from the linear road proves disruptive to the act of narration. When, for example, Jacques is in the process of describing the surgeon's visit, he is interrupted mid-sentence by his weary master:

Et le Chirurgien s'étant approché du lit de Jacques, celui-ci ne lui laissa pas le temps de parler. J'ai tout entendu, lui dit-il … Puis, s'adressant à son maître, il ajouta … Il allait ajouter, lorsque son maitre l'arrêta. Il était las de marcher, il s'assit sur le bord du chemin la tête tournée vers un voyageur qui s'avançait de leur côté à pied, la bride de son cheval qui le suivait passée dans son bras. (p. 50)

The edge of the road here constitutes the borderline between narrative progression and digression. The reason Jacques's story is largely confined to the road may partly be explained by a remark made by his master regarding two stories about Desglands. Of one of these, the story of his 'emplâtre', the master states, 'Cette aventure-là sera pour la route', and adds, 'l'autre est courte' (p. 221), as indeed proves to be the case. The difference between a tale for the road and a tale for the inn seems to be its length—the road is apparently perceived as the more suitable environment for substantial narrations. While the *conte* of Mme de la Pommeraye would normally fall into this category, the narrator to whom it is assigned confines it to the *Grand Cerf*. The master consequently makes clear to Jacques that he must for the time being cede his narratorial role to the hostess: 'Jacques, nous avons plus d'un jour à vivre ensemble, à moins que […]' (p. 132). Jacques's narration must therefore give way to any *contes* that may be told only under certain conditions and by certain narrators as well as other, shorter anecdotes that spontaneously arise from his conversation with his master. Until the conclusion of *Jacques* the servant's story is, after all, presented essentially as a *passe-temps* that comes to the fore only when no other forms of entertainment are available; indeed, much of the play of Diderot's text clearly derives from the conflicting priorities in this regard of the implied reader and Jacques's master. One should add that the intimacy of the autobiographical stories of master and servant requires a degree of privacy and tranquillity that the inns of *Jacques* are unable to provide.

Simply because the personal histories told by Jacques and his master are largely confined to the road, it does not necessarily follow that the road is largely confined to these personal histories. The travellers do not have to leave the road to find themselves interrupted, either by their intrusive author or by various encounters *en route*; it is striking, however, that, although the diversionary threat of these meetings is always clear, none of these actually alters the course of Jacques and his master, with the exception of the final confrontation with the Chevalier de St Ouin. With the aforementioned encounter with a 'Chirurgien' and his female companion, or with that of the mysterious funeral cortège, our travellers seem on the verge of a potential adventure only for it narrowly to miss them as it passes by. The author's refusal to exploit the romanesque potential of such meetings effectively means there is little difference between these and the non-event he describes of the departure of Jacques and his master from the sinister inn of the second night of their journey (pp. 17–18).[17]

As distracting as such encounters threaten to be, they cause fewer problems to the progress of Jacques's storytelling than the narrator's direct intrusions; more disruptive than either of these, however, is the manner in which the author indirectly sabotages the advancement of the narrative. The horse, the dynamic force that determines the progress of Jacques and his master, also determines the progress of their narrations. It is variously used as a metaphor of Fate and of the narrative in which it features, and at times of both: the narrator notes of Jacques and his horse,

Son usage était de le laisser aller à sa fantaisie, car il trouvait autant d'inconvénient à l'arrêter quand il galopait qu'à le presser quand il marchait lentement. Nous croyons conduire le destin, mais c'est toujours lui qui nous mène: et le destin, pour Jacques était tout ce qui le touchait ou l'approchait, son cheval, son maitre, un moine, un chien, une femme, un mulet, une corneille. (p. 40)

The undertones of romance are conspicuous in the manner in which Jacques fatalistically allows his horse to choose his path for him.[18] Whereas the stagecoach in *Tom Jones* or the horse in *Tristram Shandy* may appear at certain points as a metaphor and at others as matter, in *Jacques* the horse may take on both of these roles simultaneously.[19] These roles are moreover internally dualistic: at a metaphorical level the horse is used as a symbol both of its author's narrative and of the writing on the 'grand rouleau', while at a physical level it serves both as one of the author's 'characters' and as an instrument of Fate. The equine metaphors observed earlier in *Tristram Shandy*, like the metaphors of travel in *Tom Jones*, are no longer confined in *Jacques* to the extradiegetic realm of the self-conscious narrator; Diderot reclaims them from an abstract, rhetorical level by reintroducing them into the objective as well as the subjective world. In other words, the horse returns in Diderot's work as a physical rather than an intellectual creation—as a living horse rather than a hobby horse.

The first point at which it becomes clear that the steeds carrying Jacques and his master to their eventual destination are the instruments of their author occurs immediately following the master's rejection of Jacques's assertion that knee injuries are the most painful of all:

> Allons donc, Jacques, tu te moques ... Mais ce que je ne vous laisserais pas ignorer pour tout l'or du monde, c'est qu'à peine le maitre de Jacques lui eût-il fait cette impertinente réponse, son cheval bronche et s'abat, que son genou va s'appuyer rudement sur un caillou pointu, et que le voilà criant à tue-tête: Je suis mort! J'ai le genou cassé! ... (p. 22)

Diderot's game of (hypodiegetic) cause and (diegetic) effect here transgresses and thus erases the borders between narrative levels. This process, which, as various critics have observed, also allows the narrator to travel from extradiegetic to diegetic levels (such as when he appears to occupy the same room in the inn as Jacques and his master[20]), may equally be discerned on a typographical or syntactical level.[21] While, for example, Jacques is telling the story of his captain, the inevitable interruption is executed thus: 'Son adversaire envoie à son secours, se met à table avec ses amis et le reste de la carrossée, boit et mange gaiement. Les uns se disposaient à suivre leur route, et les autres à retourner dans la Capitale en masque et sur des chevaux de poste, *lorsque* l'hôtesse reparut et mit fin au récit de Jacques' (p. 157; emphasis added). The two levels of narrative are fused and the division between past and present blurred by the connecting 'lorsque'.

While the horse is a symbol of destiny to Jacques, to the reader it represents above all the physical incarnation of the progress of Jacques's narration: the direction of the servant's story thus correlates to the direction of the servant's servant. It soon becomes apparent that the horses in *Jacques* serve their author far better than their owners; they are generally mentioned by the narrator only when they impede either the journey or Jacques's narration. I state 'either' rather than 'both' because the disruption of the former does not imply that of the latter (and vice versa)—indeed the opposite usually proves to be the case as the first notable appearance of the master's steed demonstrates: by throwing off its rider, it illustrates an issue raised in the course of Jacques's narration while halting the advancement of the travellers on their journey. Furthermore, when the master climbs back into the saddle, the situation is reversed, with swift physical progress being made at the cost of the narration's progression:

Lorsque le maitre fut un peu revenu de sa chute et de son angoisse, il se remit en selle et appuya cinq ou six coups d'éperon à son cheval, qui partit comme un éclair: autant en fit la monture de Jacques, car il y avait entre ces deux animaux la même intimité qu'entre leurs cavaliers; c'étaient deux paires d'amis.

　　Lorsque les deux chevaux essouflés reprirent leur pas ordinaire, Jacques dit à son maitre: Eh bien, Monsieur, qu'en pensez-vous? (p. 23)

When the two horses race ahead, such rapid progress proves to be in-compatible with storytelling, or indeed dialogue, and conversation may be resumed only when they tire and return to their usual, leisurely pace.[22]

　　The more slowly the travellers advance, the greater the theoretical space between encounters or intrusions, and, consequently, the greater the hypodiegetic space that is created. Thus, when the master's horse is stolen and the two decide to continue on foot, Jacques is allowed to make considerable and uninterrupted progress in his narration until, after another narratorial intrusion, a replacement for the horse is found and the two travel on horseback once more. There may, however, be an additional reason for the smoother progress of Jacques's story while he and his master proceed on foot: with his two characters obliged to walk, one of the author's most important obstructive agents, the horse, is temporarily unavailable. As one may see most emphatically in a work like *The Canterbury Tales*, when the journey progresses easily so may the act of narration; as suggested in an earlier chapter, it is when the journey becomes problematic that it asserts its presence most strongly; conversely, when it ceases to be difficult, it becomes virtually invisible.[23] As soon as Jacques gives his own horse to his master and attempts to continue his story on a new mount, this disruptive potential is again available to the author, who thus exploits it to the full. The section of the journey where Jacques rides the hangman's horse finds the coincidence of road and narration, and of horse and narration, at its most striking. When he buys another horse, the master inadvertently buys into other stories; when Jacques climbs into the saddle of his new mount, he thus immediately digresses from his 'amours' to the story of his brother Jean,[24] a digression followed by the horse's own change of direction:

LE MAITRE. — Non, non, prenons une prise de tabac, voyons l'heure qu'il est et poursuis.
JACQUES. — J'y consens, puisque vous le voulez ... Mais le cheval de Jacques fut d'un autre avis [...] (p. 55)

When the horse bolts towards the gallows on this occasion, it leaves both road and storytelling behind and thereby simultaneously effects a physical and narrational deviation.

The narrator's extradiegetic intrusions find a diegetic counterpart in the horse's interference in his rider's tale. Moreover, by leading Jacques towards the gallows, the horse diverts the narrative to the story of its previous master rather as the 'voiture funèbre' (p. 61), which crosses their path shortly afterwards, directs the narrative towards Jacques's own former master, the captain. Jacques proves to have less influence over the course of his journey, and consequently his narration, than the horse he rides—Jacques '*mene son Maitre*' (p. 230), but his horse in turn leads him,[25] as the circumstances in which it bolts for a second time illustrate:

Jacques allait commencer l'histoire de son Capitaine, lorsque pour la seconde fois son cheval se jetant brusquement hors de la grande route à droite, l'emporte à travers une longue plaine, à un bon quart de lieue de distance, et s'arrête tout court entre des fourches patibulaires ... Entre des fourches patibulaires? Voilà une singuliere allure de cheval de mener son cavalier au gibet! (p. 75)

Rather like Diderot's aforementioned poet, the horse is no 'bête de somme qui suit droit son chemin'. Jacques wonders whether the horse is an instrument of Fate—'Est-ce un avertissement du Destin?' (p. 75)—when, as the reader knows, it is simply its author's agent. It is striking in this context that Jacques's insistence that one cannot know what is 'écrit là-haut' is reflected in his ignorance in equine matters: when the master eyes the hangman's horse for the first time and remarks 'Son cheval me parait bon', Jacques reveals, 'J'ai servi dans l'infanterie, et je ne m'y connais pas' (p. 51).

Even without leaving the road, this newly acquired horse succeeds in disrupting the act of narration by repeatedly forcing small regressions on its rider-narrator: 'Ici Jacques s'arrêta, et celui lui arriva plusieurs fois dans le cours de son récit, à chaque mouvement de tête que son cheval faisait de droite et de gauche. Alors pour continuer il reprenait sa derniere phrase, comme s'il avait eu le hoquet' (p. 77).[26] There is something rather Shandean in the fact that just looking to the side is enough to interrupt the forward momentum of Jacques's storytelling, as the faltering progress of the horse engenders the faltering of the narration. After first cursing his steed—'Maudite bête, tiendras-tu ta tête droite?' (p. 79)—Jacques soon submits himself to forces he sees are clearly beyond his control: 'Va donc où tu voudras!' (p. 79). By contrast, as Donal O'Gorman observes, the master's horse conforms obediently to its subservient role: 'Bien que le maître soit un automate qui ne fait guère preuve d'une volonté propre, son animal obéit docilement à ses ordres. Cette relation entre le maître et son cheval rappelle les romans d'aventures où le héros ne mène à bien ses projets que grâce au soutien inconditionnel de son étalon vigoureux.'[27] One should note, however, that the submissiveness of the master's horse allows him to be stolen from his owner, and thus prevents him from providing the 'soutien inconditionnel' that O'Gorman describes.

Aside from the section in which Jacques and his master proceed on foot, the horse is closely linked to the storytelling process throughout *Jacques*, and not simply as a disruptive force. Despite the problems Jacques incurs with the hangman's 'bizarre animal' (p. 81), the horse retains its privileged status as a (literal and metaphorical) vehicle for the narration and reception of interpolations. In the last section, leading from the *Grand Cerf* to Desglands's castle, the horse expedites rather than sabotages the storytelling of master and servant; in this part of the journey, horse and narration are so closely identified that mounting and dismounting respectively imply continuing and interrupting a story. As Jacques approaches the end of his story, and as he and his master simultaneously approach the village where St Ouin's son is being raised, his master indeed dismounts in order to ensure that the resolution of the narration will coincide precisely with the end of their journey:

Mais Jacques et son maitre sont à l'entrée du village où ils allaient voir l'enfant et les nourriciers de l'enfant du Chevalier de St Ouin. Jacques se tut. Son maître lui dit: Descendons et faisons ici une pause.—Pourquoi? Parceque, selon toute apparence tu touches à la conclusion de tes amours.— Pas toutàfait.—Quand on est arrivé au genou il y a peu de chemin à faire.— Mon Maitre, Denise avait la cuisse plus longue qu'une autre.—Descendons toujours. (p. 369)[28]

The nearer the anticipated conclusion, the more frequent the interruptions, and the progress of Jacques's *récit* may thus be measured now in inches rather than miles; once again Zeno's paradox comes to mind as the decisive moment is deferred.[29] The narrator moreover notes that Jacques's drinking increasingly impinges upon the progress of his story as he approaches the end: 'Ici, Jacques fit halte à son récit et donna une nouvelle atteinte à sa gourde. Les atteintes étaient d'autant plus fréquentes que les distances étaient courtes, ou comme disent les géometres, en raison inverse des distances' (p. 365).

O'Gorman remarks of the horse, 'Grâce à cet animal, le couple picaresque constitue un café ambulant et universel dont chaque endroit et chaque moment peuvent être le décor occasionnel.'[30] There are, however, clear differences between the inn and the horse as vehicles for the introduction of interpolations; while the inns in *Jacques* prove as resistant to incident as the *Biche* in the *Roman comique*, the road taken by the horse, although offering no adventures as such to Diderot's travellers, is exposed to a series of distracting encounters and events that constantly change the course of the narrative. Whereas the road consequently frames a considerable number and variety of stories and anecdotes, the *Grand Cerf* is essentially, if not quite exclusively, geared towards the telling of a single, substantial narration. The impact of the *Grand Cerf* furthermore extends beyond the residence there of Jacques and his master as, once again in contrast to the road in *Jacques*, it joins fellow-travellers together. As Kempf observes, 'La fraternité des voyageurs représente une communauté, non de l'infortune—comme dans *Candide*—mais du récit et de la confidence.'[31] Thus, while the encounters *en route* in *Jacques* are fleeting, the meeting at the inn forged between Jacques and his master and the Marquis and his secretary produces yet another sustained narration. This antithesis reflects the inherent sociability of the inn, which provides a respite from the purely functional status of the road.

Jacques le Fataliste *ou* son maître: Whose Storyline is it Anyway?

Earlier we saw how a failure to recognize the artificial order of the *Roman comique* was likely to produce a reading in which the actors' retrospective narrations were perceived as digressions analogous to the Spanish *nouvelles*, rather than as integral and fundamental components of the structuring narrative of the novel. Although *ordo artificialis* fails with few exceptions to find a home in the dominant forms of novelistic discourse in the eighteenth century, from the *memoirs* to picaresque and epistolary fiction, it does not entirely disappear.[32] *Jacques* provides a

224 JACQUES LE FATALISTE

further example of undiagnosed artificial order; if this is less obvious than the case of the *Roman comique*, it is paradoxically because it is all the more extreme: the reader is in a position to discover what Diderot's novel has truly been about only in its final pages, and even these may leave him none the wiser. A synopsis of the essential storyline of *Jacques* may therefore be appropriate at this point:

Two friends, Jacques's master and the Chevalier de St Ouin, make the acquaintance of a young lady, Agathe. The master is attracted to Agathe, but unaware that she has been sleeping with the Chevalier, with whose child she is in fact pregnant. Agathe conspires with the Chevalier and her own family to entrap the master, who is invited into her bed one night only so that he may be caught *en flagrant délit* and so coerced into marrying her. Although he succeeds in avoiding a marriage, he is condemned to pay maintenance for the illegitimate child of his treacherous former friend. Ten years later, the master and his servant, Jacques, undertake a journey during which, to pass the time, the latter tells the story of his first true love, who nursed him back to health following his wounding in a battle. The journey ends when the master stops to look in on the Chevalier's child, who is now with his *nourrice*. To his surprise, he finally comes face to face with the Chevalier himself once more, and exacts his revenge with a sword before fleeing the scene, leaving Jacques behind to be captured. After some time apart, the master and Jacques are happily reunited in the comfort of a nobleman's castle, which by good fortune is also the home of Jacques's long-lost beloved, whom Jacques marries.[33]

Ernest Simon pertinently reminds the reader that '*Jacques le fataliste* contains two autobiographical narratives', and that 'critical tradition about the novel has usually emphasized Jacques'.[34] The way in which the novel is constructed, however, suggests that the emphasis on Jacques may be misplaced: just as the master proves to be the true fatalist of *Jacques*, so he proves to be its true hero: it is his story of betrayal and revenge, not *les amours de Jacques*, which surreptitiously provides the narrative with a teleological structure.[35] The journey and the travellers' tales, both of which the reader may have assumed to be aimless and errant, are eventually revealed to have been heading towards the predetermined and precise destination its obscured *telos* had silently demanded all along.

From the very beginning of *Jacques*, Diderot's narrator invites and provokes misreadings of the kind of story he is telling:

Comment s'étaient-ils rencontrés? Par hazard, comme tout le monde. Comment s'appellaient-ils? Que vous importe? D'où venaient-ils? Du lieu le plus prochain. Où allaient-ils? Est-ce que l'on sait où l'on va? Que disaient-ils? Le maitre ne disait rien; et Jacques disait que son capitaine disait que tout ce qui nous arrive de bien et de mal ici-bas était écrit là-haut. (p. 3)

This opening paragraph, in which 'the reader and narrator vie with each other for control of the narrative discourse',[36] may also be seen to represent the conflict between potential embedding and embedded narratives. While the fictive reader invokes the common *topoi* of travel, from those of encounter to those of departure and arrival, the narrator immediately eliminates these to reduce the sense of journey to that of movement in a spatial void—or to one of Tristram's lines on a page.[37] Diderot blindfolds his reader, so that he, like Jacques and his master, may say 'Nous marchons dans la nuit au-dessous de ce qui est écrit là-haut' (p. 109) and embark on a journey without knowing the destination. He therefore goes considerably further than Cervantes, who opens the *Quijote* with his own, less radical suppression of geo-graphical detail: 'En un lugar de la Mancha, *de cuyo nombre no quiero acordarme*' [In a village of la Mancha, the name of which *I choose not to recall*] (*DQ* I. 1; my translation and italics). Diderot's reader loses a sense of time as well as place; as Merle Perkins notes, 'what is at first striking in examining the references to time in the novel is the different duration that various writers assign to *Jacques*, ranging from eight days to four months'.[38]

It initially appears that the journey itself is insignificant: the only question in the opening paragraph that the narrator answers properly is 'Que disaient-ils?', implying that this dialogue is the priority of the narrative; as Caldwell remarks, 'with the "correct" question the game of riddles ends, and the story, at last, begins'.[39] As Caldwell's suggestion that Jacques's story is *the* story reflects, most readers tend to accept the subordinate role to which the journey is assigned in this opening. The view of Naigeon, Diderot's first editor, demonstrates that there is nothing new about this perception of the travels of Jacques and his master, although his assertion that *Jacques* was 'trop long de moitié'[40] indicates that he regarded the narration of Jacques's *amours* to be as expendable as the account of this journey:

Si j'apprenais un jour qu'un homme très attaché à la mémoire de Diderot [...] a jeté au feu la dernière copie de *Jacques le Fataliste*, mais qu'il a conservé religieusement l'épisode de Mme de la Pommeraye, peut-être en regretteraisje quelques autres pages pour lesquelles j'aurais demandé grâce, mais je me consolerais bientôt de cette perte, en faisant réflexion que la partie qui reste de cet ouvrage, est au fond la seule qui soit véritablement digne d'être lue et qui méritât d'être écrite.[41]

While Caldwell and Naigeon appear to diverge in their priorities as readers of *Jacques*, the views of both are founded upon an acceptance of the narrator's directions to the reader in the opening paragraph of the novel. Naigeon's insistence that only the interpolated story of Mme de la Pommeraye is worth retaining from Diderot's manuscript moreover implies a reading of *Jacques* not as a novel but as a collection of *contes*—as a *Decamerone* or a *Canterbury Tales*—in which the framing situation exists only in order to accommodate a series of internal narrations. The view that the destination of the journey in *Jacques* is of no more significance than, for example, that of Canterbury to the composition of *The Canterbury Tales* remains popular, when the resolution of the novel in fact entirely depends upon Jacques and his master reaching a precise location at a precise moment.

Even before the end of the opening paragraph there are signs that the narrative hierarchy is less stable than the narrator would have us believe. Having initially refused to name his two travellers—'Comment s'appellaient-ils? Que vous importe?'—the narrator is almost immediately obliged to concede this information to his reader.[42] Despite their suggested irrelevance in this preliminary exchange, the travels of master and servant soon appear to resist the subordinate position imposed upon them. The original impression of aimlessness generated at the beginning of the novel does not endure, for the reader discovers two pages later that there is a specific purpose for the journey even if he is not privy to it: when the fictive reader asks for the second time where Jacques and his master are going, the narrator responds, 'si j'entame le sujet de leur voyage, adieu les amours de Jacques' (p. 5). The mention of a 'sujet' constitutes the first narratorial indication that the travels of Jacques and his master are neither as random nor as errant as is commonly supposed, although the account of Jacques's *amours* is once more presented here as the narrative priority. As any reader of *Jacques* knows, however, the journey increasingly encroaches upon the narration it was ostensibly intended to frame, leading Walter Rex to remark that 'the "frame" situation in its formless, directionless, irregular, meandering *disponibilité* might almost seem like an ambling invitation to disruption'.[43] Rex is unquestionably justified in his claim that the framing narrative fails to insulate the internal narrations of Jacques and his master from interruption and disruption as a conventional frame should; this is precisely, however, because it is not the conventional frame he, like Naigeon, assumes it to be: his description of the journey frame as 'formless' and 'directionless' reveals too restrictive a view of the part played by the journey in *Jacques*.

In these early stages of *Jacques*, the narrator ostensibly labours to minimize the potential of the journey to disrupt Jacques's story. When, as we saw earlier, Jacques is interrupted by night falling the moment he begins his narration, the circumstances of this intrusion by the frame is narrated with telegrammatic brevity. Given his own highly intrusive approach, there is a curious reluctance on the part of the author-narrator to allow the journey to interfere with the internal narrations of his characters: on this occasion, before returning to Jacques's *récit*, he ironically digresses at length in order to demonstrate his restraint at not prolonging this brief interruption. As pauses in the physical progress of Jacques and his master produce pauses in the former's narration, the end of each day is generally marked by a shift from the hypodiegetic narrative to its diegetic frame. This mixture of restraint and licence may also be discerned in Diderot's account of the second night of his travellers' journey, as a potentially romanesque enounter with the 'brigands' at the unnamed inn is narrated with calm understatement but followed by another extensive narratorial intrusion. Rather than suppressing in advance the romanesque possibilities his narrative throws up, Diderot takes care to elaborate these possibilities before rejecting them. At such moments, he forcefully reasserts his authority over the reader, often prefaced with the threatening formulation, 'il ne tiendrait qu'à moi [...]'.[44] So insistent is he on this point that his narrative becomes as much a record of what does not happen to Jacques and his master as of what does, as he aims to distance his narrative from that of the common *romancier*. When, for example, the fellow-travellers leave the sinister *auberge louche*, the narrator relates a non-event as the *brigands* Jacques had earlier confronted in the same inn do not give chase:

Comme ils en étaient là, ils entendirent à quelque distance derriere eux du bruit et des cris, ils retournerent la tête et virent une troupe d'hommes armés de gaules et de fourches qui s'avançaient vers eux à toutes jambes. Vous allez croire que c'étaient les gens de l'auberge, les valets et les brigands dont nous avons parlé [...] Vous allez croire que cette petite armée tombera sur Jacques

> et son maitre, qu'il y aura une action sanglante, des coups de bâton donnés, des coups de pistolets tirés, et il ne tiendrait qu'à moi que tout cela n'arrivât, mais adieu la vérité de l'histoire, adieu le récit des amours de Jacques. Nos deux voyageurs n'étaient point suivis. (pp. 17–18)

This is the type of moment that has led Thomas Kavanagh to argue that Diderot's novel anticipates Valéry's famous call for 'the ultimate novel, the novel finally purifying that form of the deterministic illusion so apparently inseparable from the genre':[45] 'Peut-être serait-il intéressant de faire *une* fois une œuvre qui montrerait à chacun de ses nœuds la diversité qui s'y peut présenter à l'esprit, et parmi laquelle il *choisit* la suite unique qui sera donnée dans le texte. Ce serait là substituer à l'illusion d'une détermination unique et imitatrice du réel, celle du *possible-à-chaque-instant*.'[46] It is easy to see how *Jacques* might correspond to this model, providing one takes the narrator's assertions of his freedom of choice at face value—particularly if one identifies the narrator closely with Diderot himself at such moments. The narrator is not, however, as free as his highly vocal defiance of romanesque norms suggests, for there is a 'but', which asserts its own presence during the course of the novel: as he remarks himself in the passage cited above, 'il ne tiendrait qu'à moi que tout cela n'arrivât, *mais* adieu la vérité de l'histoire, adieu le récit des amours de Jacques' (italics added). He is constrained both explicitly by his desire to avoid romanesque excesses and stay within the boundaries of the *vrai*[47] and implicitly by his adoption of an artificially ordered, teleological structure, hinted at here by his stated intention to pursue Jacques's *récit* to its conclusion.

Despite the cool brevity with which Jacques's prior confrontation with the bandits at the inn is described, the second night of *Jacques* provides a clear indication of the encroachment of the journey upon its interpolation; Jacques and his master no longer travel through a blank space but a bleak, sinister landscape: 'Ils traversaient une contrée peu sûre en tout temps, et qui l'était bien moins encore alors que la mauvaise administration et la misere avaient multiplié sans fin le nombre des malfaiteurs. Ils s'arrêterent dans la plus misérable des auberges [...] L'hôte, l'hôtesse, les enfans, les valets, tout avait l'air sinistre' (p. 11). As the journey increasingly intrudes upon Jacques's story, the narrator conveys the impression that this is despite his best efforts. Thus, as if exasperated by the disruptions effected by the first two nights, he refuses to state where they spend the third night of their journey and accuses the reader of 'une curiosité bien incommode' (p. 29). As we saw earlier, however, he is ultimately obliged to disclose this information when Jacques—for the only time in the course of his journey—is obliged to go backwards on his journey. It therefore seems that the narrator's attempts to edit his travellers' progress are doomed to fail, and consequently so are his apparent efforts to prioritize Jacques's narration. In his inability to suppress potential deviations from his ostensible subject, the narrator of *Jacques* resembles Tristram. Although *Tristram Shandy* is ostensibly an account of an actual life while *Jacques* is explicitly fictional, Diderot's narrator repeatedly avers a commitment to the truth that brings him closer than one might have expected to Sterne's fictional autobiographer.[48] Diderot may indeed be said to parody the literary use of the journey as a structural principle of narrative by subjecting it to a level of 'vérité' that it cannot sustain as a frame; *Jacques* thus becomes the narrative of a frame that cannot hold.

The narratorial interference in the progress of Jacques's story arguably menaces the postponement of narrative resolution in such a way as to suggest the importance of this *récit* to the reader. Diderot's implied reader resembles that of La Place's *Tom Jones* in that he is totally immersed in the narrative he is engaged in reading, rejecting anything that defers such a resolution; he is, in other words, the same impatient reader whom Du Plaisir and Valincour describe.[49] Javitch argues that Ariosto's interruptive method in the *Furioso* stretches suspense or anticipation beyond its breaking point, that the self-conscious interruptions and intrusions turn an initially frustrated reader into a detached reader who no longer immerses himself in the fiction but observes and enjoys it from outside.[50] According to this view, Ariosto thereby teaches the reader a stoic detachment from life's own trials and tribulations. This lesson in stoicism could be seen to have its counterpart in *Jacques* if we see the constant interruptions and intrusions in the latter as a lesson in fatalism. Neither Ariosto nor Diderot, however, would wish a reader to become so detached as to lose interest in the action; if the narratorial interference did not generate at least some local frustration in the reader there would be little point in it. When the fictive reader of *Jacques* declares his interest in hearing more about the 'livres précieux' stolen by Gousse, the narrator responds, '—Mais Jacques et son maitre? mais les amours de Jacques? Ah! Lecteur, la patience avec laquelle vous m'écoutez me prouve le peu d'intérêt que vous prenez à mes deux personnages, et je suis tenté de les laisser où ils sont' (p. 86). Diderot's lesson in fatalism would paradoxically fail if it were entirely to succeed: he clearly does not want his reader to be an 'automate' like the master: 'Il ne dort pas, il ne veille pas non plus; il se laisse exister: c'est sa fonction habituelle' (p. 33).

An apparent shift in narrative priorities during the course of an anecdote regarding a 'Poëte de Pondichéry' hints at a larger role for the journey than the reader had previously been led to believe. The narrator responds to his fictive reader, 'Mais, Lecteur, quel rapport cela a-t-il avec le *voyage* de Jacques le Fataliste et de son Maitre' (p. 48; italics added), and thereby implies that the journey has supplanted Jacques's story as the prioritized narrative. The reader may well be forgiven for no longer knowing at this point in the novel whether he should be more interested in the journey or Jacques's *récit*: the apparent conflict here, however, masks the underlying fact that these apparently separate narratives constitute two different segments of another, larger narrative, the true beginning of which is deferred for almost 300 pages of the Droz edition (and just eighty pages before the end). As my earlier synopsis indicates, it is the story of the Maître's betrayal by St Ouin rather than Jacques's *amours* that provides *Jacques* with its well-hidden structure. The use of *ordo artificialis* requires the novel to open not at the beginning of the master's story but just before its end—long after the act of betrayal, but only just before the act of revenge, with the two travellers unwittingly heading to the scene of a dramatic denouement. Their mysterious journey is finally shown to belong to this larger narrative when it precipitates the climactic final confrontation with St Ouin:

A l'instant la porte du nourricier s'ouvre, un homme se montre, le maitre de Jacques pousse un cri et porte la main à son épée, l'homme en question en fait autant. Les chevaux s'effrayent du cliquetis des armes, celui de Jacques casse sa bride et s'échappe, et dans le même instant le cavalier contre lequel son maitre se bat est étendu mort sur la place [...] L'homme tué était le Chevalier de St Ouin que le hazard avait conduit précisément ce jour-là avec Agathe chez le nourrice de leur enfant. (p. 373)

As Ernest Simon observes, 'The master ultimately provides the answer to the reader's insistent question, "Où allaient-ils?"'[51] Rarely has *le hazard* been invoked more ironically or seemed more preordained, as the part played by the master's travels is revealed to extend beyond that of a simple *récit cadre*—the prior instability of which may now be seen to reflect the tension between the double function of the journey as a framing device and as a structuring narrative. Recognition of the *ordo artificialis* of *Jacques* moreover sheds new light on the opening paragraph, for it is clear in retrospect that the narrator was obliged to suppress the details of the journey in order to conceal its structural role: the reader was not told where Jacques and his master were going, as this would have pre-empted the master's story and ruined the structural integrity of the narrative. The structural similarities with Scarron's work are in fact revealing: the personal histories told by master and servant, like those told by Le Destin and his fellow-actors in the *Roman comique*, derive from the author's employment of *ordo artificialis*. Just as the arrival of Saldagne in the vicinity of Le Mans marks the point at which the (romanesque) past arrives in the present, the comparatively late reappearance of St Ouin signals the merging of diegetic frame and hypodiegetic interpolation in *Jacques*. Despite appearances, therefore, *Jacques* is in fact a classically ordered narrative; what is more, in contrast to the *Roman comique*, it is complete.

Just as the journey of Jacques and his master exceeds its ostensible role as a narrative frame, so the story of Jacques's *amours* transcends the boundaries of an autonomous *récit encadré*. At the opening of *Jacques*, there are two narrative threads waiting for resolution: while the master's revenge plot requires an act of revenge to be complete, so Jacques's story, a *conte d'amour*, requires the traditional reunion and marriage of the separated lovers. Diderot is in this respect far more conventional than his *antiromanesque* rhetoric suggests, as the observations of an earlier *antiromancier*, Charles Sorel, confirms: 'Vous sçavez tous que dans les Romans, les histoires amoureuses qui se racontent, ne sont jamais finies; elles ne trouvent leur accomplissement qu'au bout du livre.'[52] The elegance of Diderot's structure is such that the climax of the master's revenge story provides the cause that effects the resolution of the servant's love story, bringing about the reunion of Jacques and Denise (as well as Jacques and his master) at Desglands's chateau. It is only in the final pages that this hitherto concealed shaping teleology is revealed and that one may see clearly the first time that Jacques's *récit* is not autonomous but dependent upon the unfolding of the Maître's story. Amyot's observation in the preface to his *Aethiopica*, 'tousjours l'entendement demeure suspendu, jusques à ce que l'on vienne à la conclusion',[53] is ultimately even more appropriate to *Jacques*. The reader may in fact not realize until the penultimate paragraph of the novel that one narrative thread had

been left untied. Only at this late point does it transpire that the
resolution of Jacques's story entails not the sexual act his narration has
been approaching but the reunion and marriage with Denise that his
journey has finally brought him:

> Une nuit le château de Desglands est attaqué par les Mandrins. Jacques
> reconnait la demeure de son bienfaiteur et de sa maitresse, il intercede et
> garantit le château du pillage. On lit ensuite le détail pathétique de l'entrevue
> inopinée de Jacques, de son maitre, de Desglands, de Denise et de Jeanne.—
> C'est toi, mon ami?—C'est vous, mon cher Maitre?—Comment t'es-tu
> trouvé parmi ses gens-là?—Et vous, comme[nt] se fait-il que je vous
> rencontre ici ... C'est vous, Denise?—C'est vous, Monsieur Jacques?
> Combien vous m'avez fait pleurer! ...—Cependant Desglands criait : Qu'on
> apporte des verres et du vin! vîte, vîte. C'est lui qui nous a sauvé la vie à tous
> ...—Quelques jours après le vieux Concierge du château décéda. Jacques
> obtient sa place et épousa Denise ... (p. 378)

The constant interruptions to Jacques's narration ultimately prove to
have a revealing affinity with the restless narrative shifts of the *Furioso*.
The reader of *Jacques*, waiting for a sexual resolution that never arrives,
is placed in a position that recalls that of the reader of Ruggiero's
attempted rape of Angelica. In both cases, the reader's experience echoes
that of the characters: Ruggiero's comic failure to get his armour off
in time to rape Angelica, and Jacques's sustained attempt to seduce
Denise, become textually as well as sexually frustrating as the narration
of the resolution of each is postponed by the respective authors.[54]
Javitch's remark that 'we constantly witness individuals [...] whose
pleasurable goals are either denied by unpredictable changes or granted
too briefly or too late to be gratifying'[55] may thus be applied as accurately
to certain readers of *Jacques* as to the characters of the *Furioso*.

Although the master executes the revenge that resolves his enmity
with St Ouin and Jacques's story concludes in marriage, the general
consensus among critics remains that *Jacques* does not end, or that the
ending is so undermined or subverted as to constitute an anti-ending:
Rex describes the wedding of Jacques and Denise as a '(non-)
conclusion',[56] while Brewer speaks for many when he states,
'Diderot's novel parodies the teleological narrative by supplying [...]
three paragraphs containing three possible endings'.[57] Although there
is clearly a subversive or parodic component to the conclusion of
Jacques, the widely held view that Diderot supplies three alternative
endings is in fact a severe distortion, because it implies that each of
these could be substituted for the others—that each ending ends the

same narrative strand. The truth is that the first two endings pertain to the conclusion of Jacques's narration of his past affair with Denise—and are hair-splitting at that. Only the last ending constitutes *The End*, the conclusion to the larger narrative in which it is embedded and, therefore, the novel as a whole. The union of Jacques and Denise, and, just as significantly, the reunion of Jacques and his master, thus find a textual echo in the union of their two stories.

While the reader of *Jacques* may have considerable difficulty predicting the circumstances in which the novel might end, there are signs that Diderot at least has no doubt in which direction his narrative is always heading. The pivotal role of the master's story is indicated, for example, by the deferral of its introduction long after the point at which it is first mentioned:

LE MAITRE. — Je fus une fois en ma vie plus malheureux que toi.
JACQUES. — Vous payâtes après avoir avoir couché?
LE MAITRE. — Tu l'as dit.
JACQUES. — Est-ce que vous ne me raconterez pas cela?
LE MAITRE. — Avant que d'entrer dans l'histoire de mes amours il faut être sorti de l'histoire des tiennes. (p. 42)

While Diderot here suggests some sort of order to the sequence of narrations, there are clearer indications that the journey of Jacques and his master may arrive at the conventional ending a *conte d'amour* demands:

L'HÔTESSE.— Ces Messieurs vont-ils loin?
JACQUES. — Nous n'en savons rien.
L'HÔTESSE. — Ces Messieurs suivent quelqu'un.
JACQUES. — Nous ne suivons personne.
L'HÔTESSE. — Ils vont, ou ils s'arrêtent, suivant les affaires qu'ils ont sur la route.
JACQUES. — Nous n'en avons aucune.
L'HÔTESSE. — Ces Messieurs voyagent pour leur plaisir.
JACQUES. — Ou pour leur peine.
L'HÔTESSE. — Je souhaite que ce soit le premier.
JACQUES. — Votre souhait n'y fera pas un zeste, ce sera selon qu'il est écrit là-haut.
L'HÔTESSE. — Oh! C'est un mariage.
JACQUES. — Peutêtre qu'oui peutêtre que non. (pp. 127–8)

Jacques and his master are on their way to a wedding, even if they do not—and could not—know it yet.

Given that *Jacques* ends with the conclusion of Jacques's *conte d'amour*, it could be argued that the story of the servant rather than that of the master provides the narrative with its teleological structure, and that Jacques's journey to his own marriage with Denise is a *récit cadre* that frames and then fuses his own and his master's narrations. The decisively progressive moment in the narrative as a whole, however, and the only event during the course of the journey that actually pertains to the resolution of either story, is the killing of St Ouin. This indicates the privileging of the master's story over that of his servant, as Jacques himself suggests when he complains that his master's story has made much easier progress than his own: 'Monsieur, deux choses: l'une, c'est que je n'ai jamais pu suivre mon histoire sans qu'un diable ou un autre ne m'interrompît, et que la vôtre va tout de suite. Voilà le train de la vie' (p. 322). Jacques's story is, moreover, rooted in the Maître's story in a way that the master's story is clearly not rooted in Jacques's: whereas the master affects—and even effects— the resolution of the Jacques–Denise love plot, Jacques's narration of his *amours* has no impact on the master's revenge plot—it is merely a verbal event, a *passe-temps* filling in the space between discrete events. As Ernest Simon reflects, 'the skeleton of a conventional plot that Diderot left in the novel connects with the master's story, and not at all with that of the valet'.[58]

The recognition of the privileged position of the master's story provides an enlightening perspective on two of the most substantial interpolations in *Jacques*: the stories of Mme de la Pommeraye and of Père Hudson. While both of these evidently resonate in general terms with the issues of determinism explored in the rest of the narrative, a more precise connection with the main storyline becomes apparent: like the story of the Maître and the Chevalier, these are tales of betrayal and revenge. The master's revenge moreover provides the context within which the apparently conflicting messages of these two *contes* may be understood, for, while Mme de la Pommeraye fails in her attempt to determine the lives of others (let alone her own), Père Hudson succeeds brilliantly in his parallel attempt to do the same. The master's execution of his revenge, which might easily have seemed to illustrate an act of defiant self-determination, ultimately confirms the description of him as an *automate*. The fixed teleology of his story is such that betrayal entails revenge as surely as cause entails effect. When the master exacts his revenge he is therefore simply enacting what has already been *écrit là-haut*. The master['s] narrative implies therefore what is made more explicit in his servant's story: an unbreakable chain of cause and effect leading Jacques from the battleground to Desglands's castle, and from separation to inevitable reunion with Denise. Whether the reader is surprised by the *ordo artificialis* of Diderot's narrative, or whether he remains oblivious to it, it is there nevertheless; a rule of narrative thus unmistakeably if unexpectedly reflects the universal law of cause and effect.

The difficulty of a position that chooses to accept the apparent arbitrariness of *Jacques* (rather than seek any hidden order that might explain it) is that it necessitates reading Diderot's narrative as a critique of determinism, despite the obvious problems this entails:

> On the one hand, the novel's main character, Jacques, repeatedly insists that all the stories we read [...] confirm his conviction that all actions are bound together by strict relations of cause and effect corresponding to the irresistable dictates of the Great Scroll. On the other hand, everything about the way we as readers come to experience these stories [...] consolidates an opposite impression of total indetermination, of a chaos absolutely alien to the operation of any deterministic principle.[59]

Kavanagh, an exponent of this view, recognizes this apparently irreconcilable contradiction and seeks to resolve it by arguing that *Jacques* is really an anti-deterministic tract; this in turn allows him to restate the common view of *Jacques* as an anarchic *antiroman*: '*Jacques le fataliste*'s demolition of traditional narrative discourse parallels and confirms the *Encyclopédie*'s subversion of the teleological principles of order and purposefulness usually presiding over that genre's didacticism.'[60] Interpretations of the 'message' of *Jacques* evidently rest upon one's impression of it as a reading experience. While the commonly perceived absence of teleology and order in the structure of the narrative will tend to suggest an indeterminate and disordered universe, the reading outlined here of a teleologically ordered structure by contrast suggests a deterministic universe. In this respect, the latter has one clear advantage over its alternative as it erases the apparent contradiction of an anti-deterministic text written by a determinist thinker.

Unless the reader recognizes the *ordo artificialis* of *Jacques* and the teleology it entails, it may well be true that 'what the reader finally takes away from this novel is an unfettered vision of chaos and indetermination, of a world which is fundamentally recalcitrant to man's attempts to impose upon it his various systems of reason, law, and predictability'.[61] The reader who does recognize the structure of Diderot's narrative will find order, however, beneath the surface of chaos. This is not to suggest that the implementation of a classical model of narrative makes *Jacques* a classically unified work of art: the deferral of the true beginning for three-quarters of the novel provides a frame for a multitude of disconnected anecdotes and stories as well as Jacques's connective love story. Nevertheless, an awareness of the structural role played by *ordo artificialis* crucially enables us to distinguish more confidently between digression and progression in *Jacques*—between the central storyline around which the narrative is constructed and the deviations from that storyline.

While Kavanagh may reasonably assert that 'Life, in other words, be it Jacques's, the Master's, or anyone else's, can never be lived as a "story", as an organized, coherent narrative guided by a single, all-encompassing telos',[62] it is worth emphasizing that *Jacques* should not be regarded as ateleological simply because its structuring *telos* does not create a perfectly unified whole out of all the incidents and accidents that interrupt Jacques and his master on their journey. In this respect Scarron's digressive yet artificially ordered *Roman comique* furnishes Diderot with an important precedent. Despite all the narratorial interference that plagues Jacques in the act of narration, Diderot's novel moreover demonstrates time after time that, if life cannot be lived as a story (despite the efforts of Don Quijote to do just that), it can at least be written, read, and, just as pertinently, spoken as one. *Jacques* is indeed both structured around and inhabited by *hommes-récits*, walking, talking stories. It is, moreover, striking that both Jacques and his master do attempt to 'read' each other's lives (and those of others[63]) as stories, albeit with varying success: while Jacques is able to read correctly his master's history as a story or *conte*, repeat-edly pre-empting and anticipating the narration of his misfortunes, the master's parallel attempts to anticipate the direction of Jacques's story repeatedly fail.[64]

For all its *antiromanesque* rhetoric, *Jacques* is not the free, indeterminate novel it purports to be, and throughout the course of the narrative there are subtle indications to the attentive reader—or re-reader—of the teleological approach confirmed by its preordained order. Diderot's undermining of romanesque expectations is only the first stage in a two-stage process: first he subverts the reader's expectations, then he subverts his consequent lack of expectations. This double subversion is discernible throughout the course of the narrative, and, as we have seen, in the very order of the narrative, but may be illustrated most simply in Diderot's handling of the theft of the master's horse, an event that finds the narrator anticipating the reader anticipating the significance of a horse's appearance in the road ahead: 'Vous allez croire, Lecteur, que ce cheval est celui qu'on a volé au maître de Jacques: et vous vous tromperez. C'est ainsi que cela arriverait dans un roman, un peu plutôt ou un peu plus tard, de cette manière ou autrement; mais ceci n'est point un roman, je vous l'ai déjà dit [...]' (p. 50). Like the non-appearance of the brigands from the *auberge louche*, the non-appearance of the master's horse at this point is inserted to reassert the antagonistic relationship between *Jacques* and its romanesque target. This second non-event, however, ultimately proves to constitute a postponement rather than a rejection of roman-esque procedures, for the master is subsequently happily reunited with his horse towards the end of his journey with Jacques (pp. 351–2). Diderot's narrator thus ties up this loose narrative thread only once his reader has ceased to expect such a romanesque resolution. He does so without commentary, and while his initial subversion of the reader's expectations is highly vocal, the subsequent reaffirmation of these values is thus silently allowed to slip by the reader unnoticed. The separation of master and horse moreover provides a further example of Diderot's playful engagement with romanesque practice, as he employs the *romancier*'s stock device for the protracting of his narrative: separation and reunion. While the conventional author of such works separates and reunites lovers, as Diderot does with Jacques and Denise, the author of *Jacques* here separates and reunites a man and his horse.

Although even the most attentive reader could not be expected to anticipate the artificial order of the narrative and its role in the resolution of the novel, the narratorial rhetoric of capricious spontaneity may not deter all readers from giving up on the possibility of a satisfying conclusion. Despite first impressions, it transpires that Diderot's narrator likes to finish what he started: with only two arguable exceptions,[65] he never embarks on a story without seeing it, albeit not always immediately, to a conclusion. As his battle with the fictive reader over the narration of the 'poëte de Pondichéry' anecdote illustrates (pp. 48–9), he is aware that 'tout auditeur qui me permet de commencer un récit s'engage d'en entendre la fin' (p. 87). The reader's hopes of resolution may be further raised when another of the narrator's threats ends reassuringly with a promise that the stories of both the hostess and Jacques will eventually be told in their entirety:

Eh bien, Lecteur, à quoi tient-il que je n'éleve une violente querelle entre ces trois personnages? que l'hôtesse ne soit prise par les épaules, et jettée hors de la chambre par Jacques; que Jacques ne soit pris par les épaules et chassé par son Maitre; que l'un ne s'en aille d'un côté, l'autre d'un autre; et que vous n'entendiez ni l'histoire de l'hôtesse,[66] ni la suite des amours de Jacques? Rassurez-vous, je n'en ferai rien. (p. 135)

The narrator enunciates such threats repeatedly, but it becomes increasingly clear that he has no intention of executing them. His commitment to finishing what he starts is curiously reminiscent of the 'enfant de la Lingère', who refused to say 'A' on the grounds that 'je n'aurais pas sitôt dit A, qu'ils voudront me faire dire B' (p. 288)—even though it is Jacques who is alleged to resemble this child 'comme deux gouttes d'eau, avec cette différence que, depuis son mal de gorge on avait de la peine à lui faire dire A, mais une fois en train, il allait de lui-même jusqu'à la fin de l'alphabet' (p. 289). As the opening paragraph of *Jacques* confirms, Diderot's narrator combines the child's initial resistance to submit himself to a teleological sequence with Jacques's clear enthusiasm for the narrative process. As storytelling 'machines', both Jacques and his narrator are compelled to finish what they have begun: 'la machine était montée, et il fallait qu'elle allât jusqu'à la fin' (p. 343).

While the criticism of the 1960s sought to maintain the idea of *Jacques* as an *antiroman* at the same time as it insisted upon the order and unity of its underlying structure, and more recent criticism has alternatively argued that Diderot's text rejects these classical principles in order to reflect the arbitrariness of novelistic discourse, recognition of the teleological order at work on this narrative allows the reader to avoid some of the contradictions endemic to each of these approaches. Although the extreme manner in which *ordo artificialis* is introduced might arguably be taken to represent a parodic assault on this roman-esque convention, the fact that it seems designed to pass unnoticed suggests instead that the target here is not the romanesque but the reader's failure to recognize it when he sees it. The implementation of this classical technique fits into the pattern of vocal subversion followed by quiet reaffirmation, which is at the core of Diderot's approach to his novel. If he flouts the conventions of *roman* and *conte* in *Jacques* ultimately to reassert rather than abandon them, this should not come entirely as a surprise to the reader of his other fiction. The same process is at work in *Ceci n'est pas un conte*, where the narrator undermines the reader's expectations with the apparently subversive title, but then exceeds these expectations by supplying him with not one but two *contes*.[67] Diderot's purpose is plainly not to prevent his reader from reading *romans* and *contes*, but to make him a self-conscious reader of these forms of fiction and of the conventions upon which they depend. *Jacques* is, above all, a celebration of storytelling, as the initial exasperation of its narrator towards his reader's insatiable thirst for *contes*—an all-embracing term—ultimately confirms:

Et puis, Lecteur, toujours des contes d'amours [...] Toutes vos nouvelles en vers ou en prose sont des contes d'amour; presque tous vos poëmes, élégies, églogues, idylles, chansons, épitres, comédies, tragédies, opéra, sont des contes d'amour; presque toutes vos peintures et sculptures ne sont que des contes d'amour. Vous êtes aux contes d'amour pout toute nourriture depuis que vous existez, et vous ne vous en lassez point. L'on vous tient à ce régime et l'on vous y tiendra longtemps encore, hommes et femmes, grands et petits enfans, sans que vous en lassiez. En vérité cela est merveilleux. (p. 238)

The narrator of *Jacques* takes digressiveness to such an extreme that many readers may lose any sense of a teleological approach to its construction. The manner in which Diderot defers the true beginning of the novel to a point where it may barely be identified as such may reasonably lead one to question how meaningfully the master's story may be described as the *main* narrative of *Jacques*. In a work that embraces so many stories, however, the master's unhappy tale stands out as the one with the strongest claim: it is the one narrative upon which all others depend, the crucial structuring component that ironically allows Diderot to create the appearance of a structureless text—and thus begs the question of whether the standard practice of shortening the title from *Jacques le Fataliste et son maître* to *Jacques le Fataliste* is not doing the master, and his author, a considerable injustice.

From Inn to Castle

Although the featureless space in which Jacques and his master begin their travels does not remain so for long, the topography of *Jacques* never fully emerges from the initial void into which Diderot plunges his reader. Despite its repeated intrusions upon the internal storytelling of the two travellers, the journey does not entirely discard the invisibility its ostensible role as a frame would demand. The narrator apparently seeks to counteract the journey's transgressions by erasing any geographical markers that might dispel the reader's sense of disorientation. As Francis

Pruner notes, only one town along the route taken by Jacques and his master is named, and even here there is a certain amount of confusion as to exactly where this is (there is more than one town called Conches in France).[68] Of the more substantial stories told in *Jacques*, only that of Mme de la Pommeraye is assigned a specific geographical location. Diderot's 'histoire d'un mariage saugrenu' (p. 210) is a quintessentially Parisian *conte*, which leads the reader from the *tripot* run by the d'Aisnons on the 'rue Traversiere, à l'Hôtel de Hambourg' (p. 202) to the more elevated society that congregates in the 'Jardin du Roi' (pp. 172–3),[69] where they meet the Marquis des Arcis for the first time. It is striking, however, to note the degree of geographical suppression that features even in this inserted *conte*, as the d'Aisnons keep their address from the Marquis (p. 175)—ostensibly in order to protect their reputation as 'dévotes'.

The narrator's opening challenge to his fictive reader is the first of many occasions in *Jacques* when geographical information is withheld. Roger Kempf reveals other instances of this procedure:

> Prestige de la géographie, des noms, des coordonnées utiles? Dans *Jacques*, il ne fait le point que pour nous désorienter: «à quelque distance derrière eux ... à plus d'une lieue à la ronde ... au lieu le moins éloigné ... à une égale distance des deux villages ...» «Il n'y avait donc pas loin de la commune au village?» demande le maître. «Pas plus loin que du village à la commune», répond Jacques.[70]

The last of these examples reveals that Jacques is as reluctant as his author to provide any geographical detail, as if location were an irrelevance only a *romancier* would make the mistake of supplying. While this reticence may seem wilful at times, there are moments when it serves a philosophical or a narrative purpose: when asked by the hostess, 'Ces messieurs vont-ils loin?', Jacques thus responds 'Nous n'en savons rien' (p. 127) in keeping with his fatalistic beliefs; when asked by his master the name of the village in which he spent his convalescence, he replies, 'Si je vous le nommais, vous sauriez tout' (p. 105), as it would allow his companion to make the connection with Desglands's castle. Jacques is not the only character to echo the narrator's opening sallies in the course of his narration: Gousse, for example, when asked 'D'où venez-vous?', answers simply 'D'où j'étais allé' (p. 84).

Because of this geographical evasiveness, the reader of *Jacques* cannot measure the progress of the two travellers as he may, for example, that of Don Quijote or Tom Jones. While he always knows where the journeys of Cervantes's or Fielding's heroes must end (and thus how far from their destinations they are at any given point), he can only tell how close he is to the conclusion of Jacques's travels by counting the number of pages left to read. As suggested earlier, one has the impression of movement rather than progress in *Jacques*, and the concealed *telos* leaves the reader with little sense of the journey as a dynamic principle. This is essentially because, while the *gîtes* in which Jacques and his master rest from their journey are invested with certain particularities, the road between them remains blank despite the various incidents that occur *en route*. The country through which master and servant pass is rarely described except in abstract terms: one is told, for example, that it is 'une contrée peu sûre' (p. 11) yet no topographical detail is supplied. The absence of a realized landscape distinguishes *Jacques* from the other works examined above, and moreover creates the impression that the inns and houses where Jacques and his master pause in their travels are disconnected from each other: these places seem insular and isolated from the world outside, rather than attached to it by the road. This impression is reinforced by the manner in which these wayside locations appear physically to divorce themselves from the road that leads travellers there. The *Grand Cerf* follows in the Cervantine tradition of magnetic inns, attracting guests and preventing them from departing; however, while Palomeque's guests stay willingly in his inn and are in no hurry to leave, those at the *Grand Cerf* are given no choice in the matter—one *impasse* brings Jacques and his master to an inn, another prevents them from leaving:

Jacques, son maitre et les autres voyageurs qui s'étaient arrêtés au même gîte crurent que le ciel s'éclaircirait sur le midi; il n'en fut rien, et la pluie de l'orage ayant gonflé le ruisseau qui séparait le faubourg de la ville au point qu'il eût été dangereux de le passer, tous ceux dont la route conduisait de ce côté prirent le parti de perdre une journée et d'attendre. Les uns se mirent à causer; d'autres à aller et venir, à mettre le nez à la porte, à regarder le ciel et à rentrer en jurant et frappant du pied; plusieurs à politiquer et à boire, beaucoup à jouer, le reste à fumer, à dormir et à ne rien faire. Le maitre dit à Jacques: J'espere que Jacques va reprendre le récit de ses amours, et que le ciel qui veut que j'aie la satisfaction d'en entendre la fin, nous retient ici par le mauvais temps. (pp. 124–5)

This first delay, which occurs the morning after the arrival of Jacques and his master, is followed by another the following day, as the local flooding continues to bar the road ahead (p. 215). Unlike that of a castle, the temporary (half-)moat of the *Grand Cerf* is designed to prevent egress rather than ingress, thus allowing the hostess time to tell her *conte* to her guests.

The hostess of the *Grand Cerf* is as magnetic a presence as the inn that she keeps; while her physical appearance attracted attention in her youth—'On se détournait de quatre lieues pour séjourner ici' (p. 159)— now her gift for storytelling draws Jacques and his master to her. She in turn is drawn to them, as they share her love of the *conte*; her husband indeed notes the special relationship that forms between his wife and 'ces Messieurs avec lesquels il me semble que tu te trouves bien' (p. 132); when Jacques and his master are delayed, they therefore choose to eat with the hostess, enjoying the same privilege that Tom Jones briefly enjoys with Mrs Whitefield, the hostess of *The Bell*.[71] The character of the hostess constitutes a simultaneous invocation and rejection of a romanesque formula. Although Jacques and his master criticize her narrative technique, they are intrigued by her evident talent for storytelling: the master remarks, 'cette femme raconte beaucoup mieux qu'il ne convient à une femme d'auberge' (p. 148) and suspects that her own history may be as entertaining as that of Mme de la Pommeraye. The hostess acknowledges this to be the case, revealing that she was brought to the *Grand Cerf* by 'des circonstances extraordinaires' (p. 170) but refusing to say much more: 'Je raconte volontiers les aventures des autres, mais non pas les miènes. Sachez seulement que j'ai été élevée à St Cyr, où j'ai peu lu l'Evangile et beaucoup de romans. De l'Abbaye royale à l'auberge que je tiens il y a loin' (p. 170).

Like Palomeque in the *Quijote*, Diderot's hostess is another innkeeper with a voracious appetite for romances; in contrast to Palomeque, however, she not only reads romances but appears to have acted her part in a romanesque *intrigue* of her own. Her reference to St Cyr implies her nobility as well as the absence of an estate,[72] and this in turn provides a clue both to her hapless relationship with her husband and to her particular interest in the story of Mme de la Pommeraye. Just as the various pairings of the troupe in the *Roman comique* imply that equal social status is a prerequisite for a happy marriage,[73] there is a suggestion here that the hostess's unhappiness is rooted in the difference in birth between herself and her husband. She is, moreover, a peculiarly appropriate narrator for the story she tells: like the d'Aisnons, she is reduced to the lowly position of 'hôtesse'— although not in the kind of *tripot* managed by the d'Aisnons—and, as they have, has shared her bed with someone she does not love: when

Jacques ironically ponders upon Mlle d'Aisnon and 'la triste nécessité d'accepter un nouvel amant tous les soirs', the hostess responds, 'Ne riez pas; c'est la plus cruelle chose. Si vous saviez le supplice quand on n'aime pas!' (p. 165).

While the road in *Jacques* remains featureless, the overnight *gîtes* that punctuate it illustrate Diderot's adoption of some rudimentary topographical formulae. He appears, we have already seen, to play with the conventional identification of open country with the romanesque on the first night of the journey, when the possibility of adventure is raised at an inn only to be rejected.[74] The *Grand Cerf* moreoever appears to have been situated with some care by Diderot neither in open country nor within city walls, but in the 'faubourg' of an unnamed town. Its proximity to the town precludes the kind of incident threatened at the previous inn without excluding the potential introduction of the romanesque by interpolation; in this respect, the *Grand Cerf* may be seen to belong to the same category of inn as the *Biche*, as indeed the striking correspondence between these two names suggests. Located between town and country, the *Grand Cerf* is able to accommodate the different forms of discourse with which each is allied. Kempf observes accurately, 'Foyer de la parole, l'auberge est aussi le lieu de rencontre du romanesque (les malheurs du marquis) et de la vérité (le malheur du compère endetté)';[75] even if the terms of his opposition—the 'romanesque' and the 'vrai'—may seem simplistic, they are nonetheless those upon which Diderot's narrator himself insists throughout the narrative.[76]

The inns in *Jacques* inherit many of the features observed above in those of earlier journey-based fiction; as soon as the *Grand Cerf* is mentioned, it is clear that it has the same tendency to erupt in noise and confusion as its antecedents in Cervantes, Scarron and Fielding:

Jacques et son Maître avaient atteint le gîte où ils avaient la nuit à passer. Il était tard, la porte de la ville était fermée et ils avaient été obligés de s'arrêter dans le faubourg. Là, j'entends un vacarme ...—Vous entendez! Vous n'y étiez pas, il ne s'agit pas de vous.—Il est vrai. Eh bien, Jacques, son maitre ... On entend un vacarme effroyable. Je vois deux hommes ...—Vous ne voyez rien, il ne s'agit pas de vous, vous n'y étiez pas.—Il est vrai. Il y avait deux hommes à table causant assez tranquillement à la porte de la chambre qu'ils occupaient; une femme, les deux poings sur les côtés, leur vomissait un torrent d'injures [...] (pp. 113–14)

This tableau introduces the three characters—the Marquis, his secretary and the hostess—who dominate the course of the narrative for the next hundred pages. The source of the uproar, the hostess's dog, causes disruption at the inn a second time just as her mistress is about to begin her narration, and puts 'toute l'hôtellerie en tumulte' (p. 136). Although the disruptive domestic life of the inn is a familiar motif by the time of *Jacques*, Diderot differs from his precedents in allowing everyday events rather than dramatic incident[77] to divert the reader's attention from the guests to the staff. The majority of the interruptions to the hostess's narration are characterized by their mundanity, with various requests and enquiries being bellowed by other servants of the inn; the irrelevance of these, from the reader's point of view, is epitomized by one that appears particularly redundant, if no less plausible: 'Ma femme?—Qu'est-ce?—Rien' (p. 145). Diderot's narrator once again gives the impression of refusing to edit his narrative as if this would compromise its 'vérité'. Whereas the interruptions to internal narrations in the *Quijote* or *Joseph Andrews*, for example, are strategically situated to provide brief interludes, and consequently demonstrate authorial regulation rather than lack of control, Diderot subjects the inn, and the road that leads there, to a degree of chaotic realism that initially seems to threaten the possibility of any narrative progression.

The manner in which the hostess's *conte* is incorporated in *Jacques* reflects this impression of unedited, unprioritized dialogue; the narrator makes no typographical distinction between the conversation of the Marquis des Arcis and Mme de la Pommeraye and that of the hostess, Jacques and his master. Jacques's interjections in particular are presented as if they formed part of the internally narrated dialogue:

MADe DE LA POMMERAYE. — Marquis, l'affaire est grave et demande de la réflexion.
LE MARQUIS. — Je n'en ai fait qu'une, mais elle est solide, c'est que je ne puis jamais être plus malheureux que je le suis.
MADe DE LA POMMERAYE. — Vous pourriez vous trompez.
JACQUES. — La traîtresse!
LE MARQUIS. — Voici donc enfin, mon amie, une négociation dont je puis, ce me semble, vous charger honnêtement. (p. 198)

During the hostess's regularly interrupted narration, the only emphatic typographical attempt to separate the diegetic and hypo-diegetic levels of narrative is by the use of parenthesis. In contrast to the dialogue unfolding within the room occupied by Jacques and his master, when one of the staff in another part of the inn calls to the hostess, the dialogue between the two is recorded parenthetically—as if the parentheses formally represented the walls of the room.[78] At such points the hostess's narration typographically frames and subordinates the domestic life of the inn. In spatial terms, the bedroom is privileged over the rest of the inn in a manner that recalls the practice of Scarron in the *Roman comique*. The *Grand Cerf*, like the *Biche*, presents the upstairs as a progressive narrative space and the downstairs as a disruptive, digressive space; the intrusions by the staff below thus constitute spatial as well as diegetic changes of level that reflect the etymological origins of *digression*, which, as Kavanagh notes, comprises 'the key notion of the level, the grade (*gradus*) designating that from which the deviation is made'.[79] Thus, when the hostess, 'fatiguée de ces interruptions, descendit' (p. 142) and hence literally changes level, her narration is interrupted.

Diderot's exploitation of the upstairs/downstairs opposition moreover recalls that of Fielding in *Tom Jones* in drawing the reader's attention to the spatial manifestation of social status. The hierarchy of master and servant in *Tom Jones*, as we saw above, is reflected in the different parts of the inn to which each confines himself: Partridge, although he adamantly denies being Tom's servant, always settles in the kitchen, where stories and gossip are exchanged, while Tom heads upstairs. In both *Joseph Andrews* and *Tom Jones*, while the guests privately exchange confidential personal histories upstairs, far more than they would wish is publicly revealed about them downstairs by their characteristically chattering servants. The same principle is demonstrated in *Jacques* when the hostess of the *Grand Cerf* reveals her source for the story of Mme de la Pommeraye: 'si vous n'étiez pas plus pressé de vous coucher que moi, je vous la raconterais tout comme leur domestique l'a dite à ma servante qui s'est trouvée par hazard être sa payse, qui l'a redite à mon mari qui me l'a redite' (p. 119). Like the interpolated *novelas* of the *Quijote* and the *Roman comique*, the story of Mme de la Pommeraye has become public property.

Jacques, in contrast to Partridge, follows his master upstairs; his presence there reflects their special relationship, as it implies a rejection of the conventional dominance of master over servant. The unorthodox nature of their association is revealed at another inn when Jacques's fall from the hangman's horse leads to a reversal of roles, the master telling him, 'Tu es mon serviteur quand je suis malade ou bien portant, mais je suis le tien quand tu te portes mal' (p. 91). At the *Grand Cerf*, however, when the master seeks to remind Jacques that his admission upstairs is a privilege and not a right—'souvenez-vous que vous n'êtes et ne serez jamais qu'un Jacques' (p. 223)—his servant's insolence leads them to an angry confrontation. The master's attempts to reclaim his authority over Jacques by ordering him downstairs do not succeed:

LE MAITRE. — Jacques, vous êtes un insolent, vous abusez de ma bonté. Si j'ai fait la sottise de vous tirer de votre place, je saurai bien vous y remettre. Jacques, prenez votre bouteille et votre coquemard, et descendez là-bas.
JACQUES. — Cela vous plaît à dire, Monsieur; je me trouve bien ici, et je ne descendrai pas là-bas.
LE MAITRE. — Je te dis que tu descendras.
JACQUES. — Je suis sûr que vous ne dites pas vrai. Comment, Monsieur, après m'avoir accoutumé pendant dix ans à vivre de pair à compagnon [...] (p. 223)

An argument ensues as the master insists, 'Tu descendras', and Jacques stubbornly responds 'Je ne descendrai pas' (p. 225). The *impasse* is resolved by the hostess, who determines, 'Jacques descendra, et quand il aura descendu il remontera, il rentrera dans toutes les prérogatives dont il a joui jusqu'à ce jour' (p. 226).

While Jacques and his master invert the usual master–servant hierarchy in their dealings with each other, in their intercourse with the outside world their relationship maintains a degree of convention. Although the master corrects the Marquis des Arcis when he refers to Jacques as his servant,[80] when they spend the night in an unnamed chateau a communal spirit is demonstrated, but also demonstrated to have its limits: 'Tout en causant on arriva à la couchée, et l'on fit chambrée commune. Le maitre de Jacques et le Marquis des Arcis souperent ensemble, Jacques et le jeune homme furent servis à part. Le maitre ébaucha en quatre mots au Marquis l'histoire de Jacques et son tour de tête fataliste. Le Marquis parla du jeune homme qui le suivait' (p. 234). As the two masters share a meal and a *conte*, the two servants are sent to eat and talk elsewhere; the temporary separation of Jacques and his master proves surprisingly productive, as it allows the Marquis to give a history of his secretary while, in another room, the secretary tells a story of his own to Jacques (which Jacques in turn relates to his master). The tradition of servants providing accounts of their employers is thus inverted here, as Jacques and Richard are dismissed so that their histories may entertain their masters in their absence.

As I suggested in opening this chapter, *Jacques* provides a compendium of the various *gîtes* available to the traveller of eighteenth-century roads. The progress of the two protagonists, however, arguably marks a retreat from both the contemporary realities and the fictionalities of travel. The narrations of Jacques and his master, and the narrator's account of their journey together, all visit humble if not disreputable surroundings at an early stage, from the peasant's cottage that accommodates Jacques to the seedy tavern frequented by St Ouin,[81] and the aforementioned 'plus miserable des auberges' of the second night of their journey. In each of these settings Diderot paints a resolutely contemporary picture: the master's narration thus evokes an urban decadence reminiscent of Wilson's story in *Joseph Andrews* (and thus of the old man's story in *Tom Jones*), while the 'chaumière' and the inhospitable inn reflect in different ways the poverty of a rural community.

Although Diderot's exploitation of the metaphorical associations of inn and castle suggests contrasting literary genres, the representation of actual *gîtes* in *Jacques* offers less sharply defined distinctions between locations. Kempf's general remark that 'l'auberge s'offre alors comme une réplique de la maison, un refuge contre le voyage'[82] may as easily be reversed; as in Fielding's fiction in particular,[83] the private and public households in *Jacques* resemble and duplicate each other. Jacques's desperate situation as an injured soldier thus forces him to use the peasants' home as if it were a public inn (or hospital), while he is subsequently obliged to pay the surgeon for food and lodging as if the latter were an innkeeper. When he and his master travel with the Marquis des Arcis and Richard, they find accommodation in a chateau that seems more like an inn than a castle or mansion: 'Nos quatre personnages se rejoignirent au château. On dina bien, on dina gaiement, et sur le soir on se sépara avec promesse de se revoir' (p. 254).

Certain fundamental differences between private homes and public houses nevertheless persist. The peasant cottage, like the inn in which Jacques and his master encounter the 'brigands', is notable for the lack of privacy it affords; ironically, this innlike characteristic may be attributed to the fact that it is ill-suited to the hospitable role that Jacques requires it to perform. The 'chaumière' offers an intimate view of domestic life, and Jacques's enforced immobility there allows him an ideal position from which to observe and eavesdrop upon his hosts: 'Leur chambre n'était séparée de la mienne que par des planches à claire voie sur lesquelles on avait collé du papier gris et sur ce papier quelques images enluminées. Je ne dormais pas, et j'entendis la femme qui disait à son mari [...]' (p. 24); an account of the conversation and subsequent lovemaking that takes place between husband and wife follows. As Jane Rush notes, 'la chambre à coucher jouit d'un statut particulier dans les historiettes dideroiennes: les barrières entre spectateurs et participants s'évanouissent pour produire un espace non-hiérarchisé, propre à la création d'un univers et d'un langage comiques'.[84]

The reader does not, however, spend the rest of *Jacques* in such modest surroundings. The time spent at the 'chaumière' has a natural counterpoint in Jacques's stay at Desglands's castle, where Jacques gains an insight into a very different domestic setting. Although Diderot subtly deromancifies the castle, it retains enough of its romanesque genealogy to provide Jacques and his master with a haven from the outside world:

> Lorsque tant de ses contemporains chantent le 'bonheur sous le chaume', Diderot se refuse au mythe de la campagne comme refuge. Je ne vois d'asile supportable, dans le paysage de *Jacques*, que le château, et parfois le presbytère, encore qu'il faille compter avec les curés à portion congrue. Le château apparait comme un abri où l'on participe de la rusticité d'alentour, sans devoir renoncer à la sociabilité ni au confort.[85]

The concurrent travelling and storytelling of Jacques and his master thus lead the reader from impoverished beginnings to the comparatively rarified environment of Desglands's castle.

Francis Pruner claims that 'le dernier aspect capital de l'homme primitif—avant l'institution des lois sociales—nous est présenté dans l'épisode pseudo-picaresque de l'auberge louche'.[86] This allegorical interpretation is certainly plausible, given Jacques's remark that 'Tous dans cette maison nous avons peur les uns des autres, ce qui prouve que nous sommes tous des sots' (p. 13). It is also possible, however, that, rather than representing the 'homme primitif', the inn represents the 'homme moderne'; this would indeed be supported by the subsequent allegory in which 'un château immense' is said to have been taken over by 'une vingtaine de vauriens qui s'étaient emparés des plus somptueux appartemens' (p. 30). Pruner perhaps under-estimates the literariness of the allegory here and in particular the literary connotations of the inn and castle *topoi*. Diderot's allegory of inn and castle implies a process of social breakdown or deterioration rather than evolution, and represents the invasion of a chivalric past by a present inflected with picaresque brutality. In this respect *Jacques* has an affinity with Cervantes's *Quijote* that goes far deeper than the pairing of master and servant or occasional allusion. One senses in Diderot's text the same nostalgia for the age of chivalry that many have discerned in Cervantes's parodying narrative; following Jacques's account of the captain's duels with his friend, the narrator remarks of their 'coin de folie',

> Celui de nos deux Officiers fut pendant plusieurs siecles celui de toute l'Europe, on l'appellait l'esprit de la Chevalerie. Toute cette multitude brillante, armée de pied en cap, décorée de diverses livrées d'amour, caracolant sur des palefrois, la lance au poing, la visiere haute ou baissée, se regardant fierement, se mesurant de l'œil, se menaçant, se renversant sur la poussiere, jonchant l'espace d'un vaste tournois des éclats d'armes brisées, n'étaient que des amis jaloux du mérite en vogue [...] nos deux Officiers n'étaient que deux paladins, nés de nos jours avec les mœurs des anciens. (p. 88)

As Nicholas Cronk observes, 'Nous reconnaissons facilement cette condition quichottesque, et ce couple d'amis obsédés par les valeurs des romans de chevalerie est un clin d'œil indiquant au lecteur quichotisé qu'il s'agit chez *Jacques* d'une «continuation» du monde romanesque de *Don Quichotte*.'[87] Diderot's romantic defence of the chivalric, if not the Quixotic, reflects the regressive dynamic of *Jacques* that leads the reader on a journey from inn and 'chaumière' to castle, and thus from the harsh reality of the present to a romanesque sanctuary of the past. This process is not dissimilar to that of the *Quijote*, where the savage anti-romance of the first part subsides in the second—a shift in tone topographically reflected in the transition from inn to castle.

Jacques, like each of the texts examined above, is demonstrably the work of an enthusiastic reader as well as author; Diderot's allusions to the works he admires and those he holds in contempt and his engagement with the romanesque reveal a reader writing about his experience of reading. The poignant sense of wonder he expresses in his paean to 'l'esprit de la Chevalerie' suggests that behind all the *antiromanesque* parody of *Jacques* there is an author with a pronounced Quixotic streak of his own. As avid a reader of *contes* as his implied reader, Diderot—and not merely in his incarnation as narrator—appears, like Parson Adams, to prefer textual to physical travel: he remarks in a letter, 'le voyage me fait bien; c'est cependant une sotte chose que de voyager. J'aimerais autant un homme qui, pouvant avoir une compagnie charmante dans un coin de sa maison, passerait toute sa journée à descendre du grenier à la cave et à remonter de la cave au grenier.'[88] In direct opposition to Fielding,[89] Diderot recommends the book over the world; a reluctant traveller, he prefers to journey in narrative, where his digressions provide the textual equivalent of an inn: as he comments in the *Salon* of 1763, 'cette contention me fatigue, et la digression me repose'.[90]

Notes to Chapter 7

1. Quotations are from Denis Diderot, *Jaques le Fataliste et son maitre*, ed. Simone Lecointre and Jean Le Galliot (Paris: Droz, 1976). References are to page only. 'Jaques' has been modernized to 'Jacques' throughout.

2. Diderot, *Correspondance inédite*, ed. André Babelon, 2 vols. (Paris: Gallimard, 1931), ii. 71 (28 July 1781).

3. One might also note Tristram's medicinal view of his work as being written 'against the spleen; in order, by a more frequent and a more convulsive elevation and depression of the diaphragm, and the succussations of the intercostal and abdominal muscles in laughter, to drive the *gall* and other *bitter juices* from the gall bladder, liver and sweet-bread of his majesty's subjects, with all the inimicitious passions which belong to them, down into their duodenums' (*TS* IV. 22).

4. Kempf, *Diderot et le roman*, 186.

5. Diderot, 'Réflexions sur l'ode', in *Œuvres complètes*, ed. Jules Assézat and Maurice Tourneux, 20 vols. (Paris: Garnier, 1875–7), vi. 413. The *Réflexions* date from 1770, and are thus contemporaneous with the writing of *Jacques*.

6. Diderot, *Lettre sur les sourds et les muets*, ed. Paul Hugo Meyer, *Diderot Studies*, 7 (1965), 45.

7. Published, no doubt coincidentally, only two years after the publication of *Tom Jones* in England (and one year after the La Place translation, which omitted Fielding's introductory chapters and thus his travel metaphors).

8. Diderot, *Lettre*, 86.

9. Published in *Lettres inédites de Mme de Staël à Meister*, ed. L. Usteri and E. Ritter (Paris: Hachette, 1903), 12 September 1771. See also Jean Garagnon, 'Diderot et la genèse de *Jacques le Fataliste*: sur une lettre de Meister père', *Studi Francesi*, 27 (1983), 81–2.

10. Cf. the use of *camino* in the *Quijote* (see above, Ch. 5).

11. Diderot also uses the related *déroute* in its literal sense when Jacques and his regiment are said to be 'à la déroute de l'armée ennemie' (p. 6).

12. See above, Ch. 5, 'The Reader as Travelling Companion'.

13. See above, Ch. 5, 'The Reader as Travelling Companion', and Ch. 6, 'The Miniaturization of the Digressive Landscape'.

14. When they set off on the fourth day of their journey, the master expects Jacques's story to begin as soon as they are on the road: 'ils n'eurent pas fait vingt pas, que le maitre dit à Jacques, après avoir toutefois selon son usage pris sa prise de tabac: Eh bien, Jacques, et l'histoire de tes amours' (p. 32).

15. See, for example, the fleeting episode of a doctor and the travelling companion he deliberately injures, following which the narrator remarks: 'Que cette

aventure ne deviendrait-elle pas entre mes mains, s'il me prenait en fantaisie de vous désespérer! Je donnerais de l'importance à cette femme; j'en ferais la nièce d'un Curé du village voisin; j'ameuterais les paysans de ce village. Je me préparerais des combats et des amours, car enfin cette paysanne était belle sous le linge, Jacques et son maître s'en étaient apperçus' (p. 7).

16. Less than five of the ninety pages that Jacques and his master spend at the *Grand Cerf* are devoted to the servant's story, with the vast majority being taken up by the hostess's interpolation.

17. See below, pp. 227–8.

18. Cf. Don Quijote's identical gesture (see above, Ch. 2).

19. See also, for another view of the horse metaphor, Leon Schwartz, '*Jacques le Fataliste* and Diderot's Equine Symbolism', *Diderot Studies*, 16 (1973), 241–51.

20. The narrator remarks, Jacques 'nous laissa dormir son maitre et moi tant qu'il nous plut' (p. 124).

21. For a further exploration of the typographical approaches of both Sterne and Diderot, see Michael Vande Berg, '"Pictures of Pronunciation": Typographical Travels through *Tristram Shandy* and *Jacques le fataliste*', *Eighteenth-Century Studies*, 21 (1987–8), 21–47.

22. Cf. the moment when Jacques's horse interrupts the master in mid-sentence: 'Le cheval de Jacques ne permit pas à son maitre d'achever; il part comme un éclair, ne s'écartant ni à droite ni à gauche, suivant la grande route' (p. 82).

23. See above, Ch. 4, '*Joseph Andrews*: Progress Barred'.

24. The manner in which a change of horse is accompanied by a transition from one story to another recalls the metaphor employed by Apuleius in the preface to *The Golden Ass*: 'Iam haec equidem ipsa vocis immutatio desultoriae scientiae stilo quem accessimus respondet' [Now in fact this very changing of language corresponds to the type of writing we have undertaken, which is like the skill of a rider jumping from one horse to another] (*GA* I. 1).

25. As quoted above: 'Nous croyons conduire le destin; mais c'est toujours lui qui nous mene' (p. 40).

26. Cf. *Tristram Shandy*, in which Tristram is a 'writer-galloper' (*TS* VII. 4).

27. Donal O'Gorman, 'Hypotheses for a New Reading of *Jacques le Fataliste*', *Diderot Studies*, 19 (1978), 129–43 (143).

28. For mounting as restarting a story, the following is a typical example: 'Ils remonterent sur leurs chevaux, et Jacques dit à son maitre: Vous en étiez de vos amours au moment où après avoir été heureux deux fois, vous vous disposiez peutêtre à l'être une troisième' (p. 356).

29. Cf. above, Ch. 6, 'The Miniaturization of the Digressive Landscape'.

30. O'Gorman, 'Hypotheses for a New Reading of *Jacques le Fataliste*', 42.

31. Kempf, *Diderot et le roman*, 187.

32. *Manon Lescaut* provides another striking example of *ordo artificialis*, as Prévost opens the narrative with Des Grieux and Manon about to embark for Louisiana, then retraces the preceding events through Des Grieux's lengthy retrospective narration.

33. Cf. the fuller précis of Jean Terrasse, which provides the consensual view of *Jacques* (Jean Terrasse, 'Le Temps et l'espace dans les romans de Diderot', *SVEC* 379 (1999), 109–11).

34. Ernest Simon, 'Fatalism, the Hobby-Horse and the Esthetics of the Novel', *Diderot Studies*, 16 (1973), 253–74 (266).

35. A hint of this surreptitious approach to narrative is revealed during the course of *Jacques* by the narrator's suggested improvements to Goldoni's *Bourru bienfaisant*: 'Je vous entends, Lecteur, voilà, dites-vous, le vrai dénoûment du *Bourru Bienfaisant*. Je le pense. J'aurais introduit dans cette piece, si j'en avais été l'auteur, un personnage qu'on aurait pris pour épisodique et qui ne l'aurait point été [...]' (p. 133).

36. Roy Chandler Caldwell, Jr., 'Backtalk: Agonistic Dialogue in *Jacques le Fataliste*', *Diderot Studies*, 26 (1995), 29–45 (30).

37. See above, Ch. 6, p. 183.

38. Merle Perkins, 'Diderot and the Time–Space Continuum: His Philosophy, Aesthetics and Politics', *SVEC* 211 (1982), 80.

39. Caldwell, 'Backtalk: Agonistic Dialogue in *Jacques le Fataliste*', 32.

40. J. A. Naigeon, *Mémoires historiques et philosophiques sur la vie et les ouvrages de D. Diderot* (Paris: Brière, 1821), 312.

41. Ibid. 315–16.

42. One could also argue that Diderot's narrator protests too much the insignificance of the journey, and that, by denying the reader any details, only excites his curiosity further; my feeling is, however, that Diderot's opening immediately destroys rather than encourages the reader's confidence in the relevance of the journey.

43. Walter Rex, 'Diderot's Counterpoints: The Dynamics of Contrariety in his Major Works', *SVEC* 363 (1998), 225.

44. For example, 'il ne tiendrait qu'à moi de vous faire attendre un an, deux ans, trois ans, le récit des amours de Jacques, en le séparant de son maitre et en le faisant courir à chacun tous les hazards qu'il me plairait' (p. 5), or, 'Il ne tiendrait qu'à moi d'arrêter ce cabriolet, et d'en faire sortir avec le Prieur et sa compagne de voyage une suite d'événements en conséquence desquels vous ne sauriez ni les amours de Jacques, ni celles de son maitre; mais je dédaigne toutes ces ressources-là' (p. 315).

45. Thomas M. Kavanagh, '*Jacques le Fataliste*: An Encyclopedia of the Novel', in Jack Undank and Herbert Josephs (eds.), *Diderot: Digression and Dispersion, a Bicentennial Tribute*, French Forum Monographs, 58 (Lexington, KY: French Forum, 1984), 150–65 (164).

46. 'Fragments des mémoires d'un poème', in *Œuvres de Paul Valéry*, ed. Jean Hytier (Paris: Gallimard, 1957), i. 1467, quoted in Kavanagh, '*Jacques le Fataliste*: An Encyclopedia of the Novel', 164.

47. Diderot's narrator emphasizes on more than one occasion that the truth distinguishes his narrative from those of the common *romancier*: 'rien de plus aiser que de filer un roman. Demeurons dans le vrai' (p. 315). In a letter to Sophie Volland that contains Diderot's only reference to Fielding, *vérité* is also held to be the distinguishing hallmark of the fiction of Fielding and Richardson: 'Je ne serai content ni de vous ni de moi que je ne vous aie amené à goûter la vérité de *Pamela*, de *Tom Jones*, de *Clarice* et de *Grandison*', in Diderot, *Correspondance*, ed. Georges Roth and Jean Varloot, in 16 vols. (Paris: Éditions de Minuit, 1955–70), 20 Oct. 1760, iii. 174.

48. For example, the previously quoted 'il ne tiendrait qu'à moi que tout cela n'arrivât, mais adieu la vérité de l'histoire, adieu le récit des amours de Jacques' (p. 18), or, 'Mon projet est d'être vrai, je l'ai rempli [...] Demeurons dans le vrai' (p. 315).

49. See above, Ch. 3, 'The Reader and the *Roman comique*'.

50. Javitch, '*Cantus interruptus* in the *Orlando furioso*'. Cf. Parish's view of the *Roman comique* (see above, Ch. 3, 'The Reader and the *Roman comique*').

51. Simon, 'Fatalism, the Hobby-Horse and the Esthetics of the Novel', 266.

52. Sorel, *Le Berger extravagant*, vii. 77.

53. Jacques Amyot, *L'Histoire aethiopique de Heliodorus* [...] *Nouvellement traduite du grec en françoys* (Paris: Estienne Grouleau, 1547), 'Proësme du translateur', fo. A iiir.

54. *OF* X. 113 ff. (see above, Ch. 4 n. 23).

55. Javitch, '*Cantus interruptus* in the *Orlando furioso*', 78.

56. Rex, *Diderot's Counterpoints*, 219. While Gilles Loüys diverges from other critics by ranking *Jacques* alongside such 'récits incomplets' as *Les Égarements du cœur et de l'esprit* on the inexplicable grounds that 'la fin du récit ne met pas fin à l'histoire (qui pourrait être continuée)', he reaffirms the view that *Jacques* does not satisfactorily conclude ('Typologie des romans inachevés', in *L'Œuvre inachevée*, ed. Annie Rivara and Guy Lavorel, Actes du colloque international (11–12 Dec. 1998) (Lyon: Aprime, 1999), 281–9 (286).

57. Daniel Brewer, *The Discourse of Enlightenment in Eighteenth-Century France: Diderot and the Art of Philosophizing* (Cambridge: Cambridge University Press, 1993), 224–5.

58. Simon, 'Fatalism, the Hobby-Horse and the Esthetics of the Novel', 266.

59. Kavanagh, '*Jacques le Fataliste*: An Encyclopedia of the Novel', 153. Rex has recently expressed the contradiction thus: 'From a materialist, who saw the universe as working through laws of cause and effect, one might logically expect that his fictional universe do the same [...] It is equally clear, however, that in this work, this particular materialist took special pleasure in openly breaking the rules he himself created, and that the target is not merely the novel as conventionally conceived but the 'fatalism' his own philosophy would seem to imply' (Rex, *Diderot's Counterpoints*, 244).

60. Thomas M. Kavanagh, *Enlightenment and the Shadows of Chance: The Novel and the Culture of Gambling in Eighteenth-Century France* (Baltimore: Johns Hopkins Press, 1993), 245.

61. Kavanagh, '*Jacques le Fataliste*: An Encyclopedia of the Novel', 161.

62. Ibid. 162.

63. Most notably the story of Mme de la Pommeraye, which produces a characteristically literary response from both Jacques and his master as they discuss its artistic merits and weaknesses (pp. 208–9).

64. When, for example, the master exclaims, 'Ah! malheureux! ah! coquin infame! Je te vois arriver', Jacques correctly responds, 'Mon maître je crois que vous ne voyez rien' (p. 9). The master also complains that Jacques's contrastingly accurate anticipation of his own story is spoiling his pleasure in telling: 'Tu vas anticipant sur le raconteur, et tu lui ôtes le plaisir qu'il s'est promis de ta surprise' (p. 322).

65. The first exception, which has dubiously been claimed by those convinced of the perfect order of *Jacques* to be a 'deliberate error', pertains to the master's unfulfilled promise of the story of his own experience of monks: 'Une autre fois je te dirais cela' (p. 60). The second exception concerns the hostess of the *Grand*

Cerf, whose romanesque history is hinted at but never delivered (see below, pp. 242–3).

66. A reference to the story of Mme de la Pommeraye, rather than the hostess's own life story.

67. It is tempting to suggest that the title should be read with the emphasis on the 'un' rather than the 'conte': as *Ceci n'est pas <u>un</u> conte*, rather than *Ceci n'est pas un <u>conte</u>*.

68. See Francis Pruner, *L'Unité secrète de 'Jacques le Fataliste'* (Paris: Minard, 1970), 21–2.

69. Now known as the *Jardin des Plantes*.

70. Kempf, *Diderot et le roman*, 185–6.

71. See above, Ch. 4, 'Leaving the Road: The House as Storytelling *Locus*'.

72. Bénac notes that there was at St Cyr the 'Fondation de Mme de Maintenon pour l'éducation des jeunes filles nobles sans fortune, ce qui définit l'origine de l'hôtesse' (Denis Diderot, *Œuvres romanesques*, ed. Henri Bénac (Paris: Garnier, 1981), 912).

73. See above, Ch. 3, 'The Journey of the Troupe as Narrative Frame'.

74. This inn, open to romanesque incident, follows the example of the wayside inn in the *Roman comique* from which Le Destin rescues L'Étoile rather than the urban *Biche*, the site of storytelling rather than adventures.

75. Kempf, *Diderot et le roman*, 187.

76. For example, 'Il est bien évident que je ne fais point un roman, puisque que je néglige ce qu'un romancier ne manquerait pas d'employer. Celui qui prendrait ce que j'écris pour la vérité serait peutêtre moins dans l'erreur que celui qui le prendrait pour une fable' (p. 18).

77. Such as when the host and a chambermaid are found *in flagrante* in *Joseph Andrews* (see above, Ch. 4, '*Joseph Andrews* and *Tom Jones*: The Topography of the Inn').

78. There are many instances of this, such as 'mais cette femme avait été si malheureuse avec un premier mari qu'elle ... (—Madame?—Qu'est-ce?—La clef du coffre à l'avoine.—Voyez au clou, et si elle n'y est pas, voyez au coffre.)— qu'elle aurait mieux aimé s'exposer à toutes sortes de malheurs qu'au danger d'un second mariage' (p. 140).

79. Kavanagh, '*Jacques le Fataliste*: An Encyclopedia of the Novel', 150.

80. When the Marquis remarks 'Vous avez là un serviteur qui n'est pas ordinaire', the Master responds, 'Un serviteur! Vous avez bien de la bonté, c'est moi qui suis le sien' (p. 234).

81. 'Au dessert, deux Marmottes s'approcherent de notre table avec leurs vielles, le Brun les fit asseoir. On les fit boire, on les fit jaser, on les fit jouer. Tandis que mes trois convives s'amusaient à en chiffonner une, sa compagne qui était à côté de moi me dit tout bas: Monsieur, vous êtes là en bien mauvaise compagnie, il n'y a pas un de ces gens-là qui n'ait son nom sur le Livre Rouge' (p. 306). The 'Livre Rouge' was a police register. It is furthermore pertinent to note that Jacques traces the start of his misfortunes back to a 'cabaret': 'Que le Diable emporte le Cabaretier et son cabaret!' (p. 3).

82. Kempf, *Diderot et le roman*, 187.

83. See above, Ch. 4, 'Domesticity and the Road'.

84. Jane Rush, 'La Tradition comique et son renouveau dans les historiettes de

Jacques le Fataliste et son maître', *Recherches sur Diderot et sur l'Encyclopédie*, 15 (Oct. 1993), 41–53 (44).

85. Kempf, *Diderot et le roman*, 140.

86. Pruner, *L'Unité secrète de 'Jacques le Fataliste'*, 30.

87. Nicholas Cronk, '"*Jacques le Fataliste et son Maître*": un roman quichotisé', *Recherches sur Diderot et sur l'Encyclopédie*, 23 (Oct. 1997), 63–78 (68).

88. Diderot, *Correspondance*, ii. 226 (17 Aug. 1759). Diderot employs the same analogy of a man going from cellar to attic elsewhere; see, for example, his letter of 12 Oct. 1760—in which he also remarks, 'je n'approuve qu'on s'éloigne de son pays que depuis dix-huit ans jusqu'à vingt-deux' (ibid. iii. 131). His apparent disapproval of physical rather than intellectual wandering is also displayed in the *Supplément au voyage de Bougainville*, when he remarks of a mathematician: 'voilà qu'il passe subitement d'une condition méditative et retirée au metier actif, pénible, errant et dissipé de voyageur' (*Œuvres philosophiques*, ed. Paul Vernière (Paris: Bordas, 1990), 456–7).

89. See above, Ch. 5, 'The Reader as Travelling Companion'.

90. See also the following page, where Diderot adds: 'Je me sens encore las. Suivons donc encore un moment cette digression' (*Essais sur la Peinture et Salons de 1759, 1761, 1763* (Paris: Hermann, 1984), 212, 213).

CONCLUSION

If, as Bakhtin suggests, the chronotope of the road dominates early adventure novels of everyday life, the digressive comic fiction of the early modern era finds the inn and the road battling for any monopoly the road may previously have enjoyed. This battle simultaneously reflects the tension in prose fiction between (to borrow Tristram's terms) the digressive and progressive modes of narrative discourse. Don Quijote regards the inn as an irrelevance, a distraction from the chivalric adventures he seeks, and he proves to be correct in this regard as he is consigned to the background for much of his time there. Similarly, the *Biche* in the *Roman comique* constitutes an anti-progressive space, in which burlesque misadventures and communal entertainments divert the narrative from the pursuit of its romanesque course. The Odyssean theme of impeded *nostos* looms over many of the fictions discussed above, and the inn has an important part to play in luring travellers away from the road home. Joseph's homeward journey is characterized by the manner in which he is repeatedly 'bounced' from the road to the inn. The ostensible protagonists of these works, from Don Quijote to Joseph to Jacques and his master, find the attention shifting from their stories to those rooted in the domestic life of the inn—to the chambermaids and shrewish innkeeper's wives who often run these inns with little help from the innkeeper himself, and, of course, to the other guests. In *Jacques*, the inn thus provides an oasis from the world outside by turning the world outside into a story.

In the fiction of the early modern period, the inn plays an instrumental role in the introduction of digressive material, and in so doing liberates narrative from the confines of a single register or a single storyline. Crucial to this diversifying function of the inn is its ability to accommodate plausibly characters from a wide range of social classes. From the *albergo* of the *Furioso* to the *Grand Cerf* in *Jacques*, the inn is represented, like death, as a great leveller.[1] As one may see most strikingly in the curious melting pot of Palomeque's establishment, this cross-section of society also constitutes a cross-section of literary forms and styles. Because of this hospitable approach towards the traveller and his tale, the inns of early modern fiction stand as monuments to digression, and their widespread presence—particularly in French and English eighteenth-century fiction—reflects the persistence of a model of reading generally presumed to have disappeared with the rise of neoclassicism. The inn, and the temporary abandonment of the hitherto prioritized storyline that its appearance in a narrative generally implies, is inherently anti-classical. As the guests in Palomeque's inn or the *Biche*—or, indeed, in the taverns of *Candide* or *Manon Lescaut*—congregate to tell stories, the model of communal oral consumption one associates with Chaucer or Boccaccio is clearly still alive in some form. The tension between the classical model of reception and this alternative model is reflected in the friction between progression and digression evident in so much European fiction of the seventeenth and eighteenth centuries. The hostility of some criticism to such perceived 'excrescences'[2] as the Man of the Hill's story in *Tom Jones* reflects the enduring importance of the principle of formal unity to the reader even in the age of postmodernism, and of the tensions that arise when our own reading habits clash with those of an earlier period.

The tension between models of reading is spatially expressed in many novels of the early modern period as the conflict between the anticipated destination of the traveller and the inn that delays his arrival there. In these and other works, this may alternatively be expressed narratologically as the conflict between a disconnective interpolation and the teleological plot in which it is embedded. In a work such as *La Princesse de Clèves*, where the intercalated stories have a formative impact on the heroine's final decision, the classical model of reading may be perceived to be in the ascendancy. By contrast, Marivaux's *La Vie de Marianne*, in which another character's internal narration endlessly displaces the resolution of the heroine's story, sees the non-classical model of reading prevail. Terence Cave has indeed remarked that 'one particularly striking symptom of the persistence of such earlier habits of reading is the publication of so many unfinished narratives', and goes on to note that 'even fictions that exploit the technique of *ordo artificialis* according to the model of Greek romance often remain unfinished'.[3] One could tentatively impute to such (literally) irresolute authors, from Scarron to a host of eighteenth-century *romanciers*, a Cide Hamete-like reluctance on the part of the author to embrace wholly the rigours of a classical approach.[4]

Although the fate of the inn is inextricably intertwined with the fortunes of digressive and interpolating fiction in the seventeenth and eighteenth centuries, it is not confined to the realm of novelistic discourse. Indeed, through the popularity of one work in particular, Fielding's *Tom Jones* (via La Place's translation), the inn notably moves from the novelist's page to the dramatist's stage. Cronk notes the success of Philidor's opéra-comique version of *Tom Jones*,[5] although the case of the playwright Pierre-Jean-Baptiste Choudard Desforges is even more striking. Desforges wrote two comedies based on *Tom Jones*: *Tom Jones à Londres* (1782) and *Tom Jones et Fellamar* (1787), both of which are notably set in London, the setting with which La Place, as we have already seen, was most comfortable. The continuing influence of Fielding on Desforges may also be discerned in the *Le Sourd, ou l'Auberge pleine* (1790). As if compensating for his suppression of the inn in his previous plays, the playwright now makes one the exclusive location for his comedy—and one, moreover, that retains many of the characteristics one would associate with Fielding's fictionalized version. Mlle Legras, the 'maîtresse de l'auberge', is a forceful innkeeper who apparently has no husband,[6] and who enjoys gossiping about her guests with her chambermaid, Petrouille. Her inn furthermore resonates not simply with Fielding's fiction but with the whole Cervantine tradition of inns, as she complains, 'Ma maison est si pleine, que je serais peut-être obligée de veiller cette nuit pour céder ma chambre à quelqu'un.'[7]

Although the physical world of travel is strikingly invaded by, and subsumed in, the narratorial rhetoric and intellectual errancy of Fielding, Sterne and Diderot, it manages, even in *Tristram Shandy*, to survive in its own right. The relationship between *Tristram Shandy* and *Jacques* serves as evidence that literary history is no teleological narrative, in which each work simply continues the work of its most recent precursor. The *Quijote* is as alive to Diderot as *Tristram Shandy*, and the world of travel that the former represents is as significant an influence upon *Jacques* as the mental wanderings of the latter. One may nevertheless sense in Diderot's work the last throw of the die, as the physical errancy of master and servant is dominated by the imaginative errancy of the narrator. As the reader becomes aware that Jacques and his master are physical manifestations of an author's internal dialogue of free will and determinism, one senses that matter has indeed irretrievably become metaphor and that the journey is undertaken not outside, on the road and in the inn, but in the mind of the author.

Even here, in this shift from the physical to the mental universe, the *Quijote* asserts its paradigmatic presence. Martínez-Bonati remarks of Cervantes's knight errant, 'Whereas in the First Part he suffers primarily physical battering, in the Second his torment is mental. Also we find a growing predominance of conversations over adventures, of the urban environment over the rural, of the residences of hidalgos and nobles over inns along the road.'[8] Words and the intellect from which they stem thus finally displace actions. The master's violent revenge on his rival at the end of *Jacques*, after a journey in which dialogue has replaced the duel, seems oddly anachronistic, as if, like Jacques's captain and his friend, the master was 'né [...] de nos jours, avec les mœurs des anciens' (*JF* 585).

With the movement towards greater psychological sophistication and realism in the nineteenth century, Bakhtin observes a chronotopic shift from the public to the private sphere,[9] or, as Sue Vice puts it, 'the withdrawal from fields and roads to boudoirs and parlours'.[10] Although the inn is an essentially public space, it nevertheless represents an intermediary phase in the transition of chronotopes. It occupies the middle ground between the domestic sphere and the road of adventures while remaining open to each, accommodating both private conversations and public confrontations. As the appetite for digressive fiction apparently wanes, the inn loses its prominence in the fictional landscape of the novel. While it continues to appear on occasion as a *locus* in the nineteenth century, these are strikingly often the most eighteenth-century-like of nineteenth-century novels.[11] By the time of the modernist and postmodernist experiments in form of the twentieth century, it is too late for the inn to make a comeback—it is no longer pre-eminent as the place of encounter and exchange. When Calvino's *Se una notte di inverno un viaggiatore* turns from the bookshop to the realm of travel in its parodic tour of narrative conventions, the bar of a railway station has now succeeded the coaching inn.

Notes to the Conclusion

1. In this respect the inn has something in common with death, the other great leveller; it may, therefore, be pertinent to note Spenser's connection of the two in *The Faerie Queene* when Guyon warns Palmer, 'death is an equal doome | To good and bad, the common Inne of rest' (II. 1. 59, ll. 1–2). As we saw in Chapter 6 above, both Montaigne and Tristram intriguingly identify the inn as the setting in which they would choose to die (see above, Ch. 6 n. 43).
2. Watt, *The Rise of the Novel*, 268.

3. Cave cites Aneau's *Alector*, Béroalde de Verville's *Voyage des Princes Fortunez* and the *Astrée*; I would add the *Roman comique* to this list.

4. Unfinished novels in the eighteenth century in France, from Marivaux's *La Vie de Marianne* and *Le Paysan parvenu* to Crébillon's *Les Égarements du cœur et de l'esprit*, are too common to be regarded simply as exceptions to the rule.

5. Nicholas Cronk, '*Tom Jones* in Eighteenth-Century France', *Drottningholms Slottstheater* (1995), 94–6 (96).

6. Although there is a stage direction, referring to the 'Chambre de M. de Legras', which suggests that she is possibly a widow.

7. Pierre-Jean-Baptiste Choudard Desforges, *Le Sourd, ou l'Auberge pleine*, 2nd edn. (Paris: Toubon, 1795), I. iv. 6.

8. Martínez-Bonati, '*Don Quixote*' *and the Poetics of the Novel*, 93.

9. Bakhtin, *The Dialogic Imagination*, 122 ff.

10. Sue Vice notes that Bakhtin's history of the chronotope charts 'a progressive decline, a regrettable move away from open space to the parlour' (*Introducing Bakhtin* (Manchester: Manchester University Press, 1997), 206, 205).

11. See, to give just two examples, Constant's *Adolphe*, in which the narrative is generated by a chance encounter at an inn (as it is in *Manon Lescaut*, to which *Adolphe* owes a great deal), and Dickens's *Pickwick Papers*, a work in which many critics have discerned Fielding's influence.

BIBLIOGRAPHY

Primary Sources and Editions

ALEMÁN, MATEO, *The Rogue or the Life of Guzman de Alfarache*, trans. James Mabbe, ed. Charles Whibley, 4 vols. (London: Constable & Co., 1924).
—— *Aventuras y vida de Guzmán de Alfarache*, ed. Benito Brancaforte, 2 vols. (Madrid: Cátedra, 1979).
ANON., *An essay on the new species of writing founded by Mr. Fielding, 1751* (London: W. Owen, 1751); reprinted by the Augustan Reprint Society, ed. Alan D. McKillop (Los Angeles: William Andrews Clark Memorial Library, University of California), 95 (1962).
ANON., *Lazarillo de Tormes*, in *Two Spanish Picaresque Novels*, trans. Michael Alpert (London: Penguin, 1969).
—— *La vida de Lazarillo de Tormes y de sus fortunas y adversidades*, ed. Germán Bleiberg (Madrid: Alianza, 1980).
APULEIUS, *Metamorphoses*, ed. and trans. J. Arthur Hanson, 2 vols., Loeb Classical Library (Cambridge, MA: Harvard University Press, 1989).
ARIOSTO, LODOVICO, *Orlando furioso*, trans. Guido Waldman (Oxford: Oxford University Press, 1974).
—— *Orlando furioso*, ed. Lanfranco Caretti, 2 vols. (Turin: Einaudi, 1992).
ARISTOTLE, *Poetics*, trans. Stephen Halliwell, Loeb Classical Library (Cambridge, MA: Harvard University Press, 1995).
BOSWELL, JAMES, *Boswell's Life of Johnson*, ed. G. Birkbeck Hill, rev. L. F. Powell, 6 vols. (Oxford: Clarendon Press, 1934–64).
BOUGEANT, GUILLAUME-HYACINTHE, *Le Voyage merveilleux du Prince Fan-Férédin dans la Romancie, Contenant plusieurs observations historiques, géographiques, physiques, critiques et morales,* ed. Jean Sgard and Geraldine Sheridan (Saint-Étienne: Université de Saint-Étienne, 1992).
BURTON, ROBERT, *The Anatomy of Melancholy*, ed. Thomas C. Faulkner, Nicolas K. Kiessling and Rhonda L. Blair, 3 vols. (Oxford: Clarendon Press, 1989–94).
CALVINO, ITALO, *Se una notte d'inverno un viaggiatore* (Turin: Einaudi, 1979).
CERVANTES, MIGUEL DE, *El ingenioso hidalgo don Quijote de la Mancha*, ed. Luis Andrés Murillo, 2 vols. (Madrid: Castalia, 1978).
—— *Don Quixote*, trans. Charles Jarvis, ed. E. C. Riley (Oxford: Oxford University Press, 1992).

CHAUCER, GEOFFREY, *The Riverside Chaucer*, 3rd edn. (Oxford: Oxford University Press, 1987).

COLERIDGE, SAMUEL TAYLOR, *Table Talk*, 2 vols., ed. Carl Woodring, in *The Collected Works of Samuel T. Coleridge*, Bollingen Series, LXXV (London: Routledge, 1990).

CONSTANT, BENJAMIN, *Adolphe* (Paris: Garnier-Flammarion, 1989).

DAMPIER, WILLIAM, *A New Voyage Round the World*, 1729 edn. reprint, ed. Sir Albert Gray (London: Argonaut, 1927).

DESFORGES, PIERRE-JEAN-BAPTISTE CHOUDARD, *Le Sourd, ou l'Auberge pleine*, 2nd edn. (Paris: Toubon, 1795).

DICKENS, CHARLES, *The Pickwick Papers* (Oxford: Oxford University Press, 1986).

DIDEROT, DENIS, *Œuvres complètes*, ed. Jules Assézat and Maurice Tourneux, 20 vols. (Paris: Garnier, 1875–7).

—— *Correspondance inédite*, ed. André Babelon, 2 vols. (Paris: Gallimard, 1931).

—— *Correspondance*, ed. George Roth and Jean Varloot, 16 vols. (Paris: Éditions de Minuit, 1955–70).

—— *Lettre sur les sourds et les muets*, ed. Paul Hugo Meyer, *Diderot Studies*, 7 (1965).

—— *Jaques le Fataliste et son maître*, ed. Simone Lecointre and Jean Le Galliot (Paris: Droz, 1976).

—— *Œuvres romanesques*, ed. Henri Bénac (Paris: Garnier, 1981).

—— *Essais sur la peinture et Salons de 1759, 1761, 1763* (Paris: Hermann, 1984).

—— *Supplément au voyage de Bougainville*, in *Œuvres philosophiques*, ed. Paul Vernière (Paris: Bordas, 1990), 455–516.

DU PLAISIR, L'ABBÉ, *Sentiments sur les lettres et l'histoire*, ed. Philippe Hourcade (Geneva: Droz, 1975).

FIELDING, HENRY, *Histoire de Tom Jones, ou l'enfant trouvé*, trans. Pierre-Antoine de La Place, 4 vols. (London: Nourse, 1750).

—— *Joseph Andrews*, ed. Martin C. Battestin (Middletown, CT: Wesleyan University Press, 1967).

—— *Tom Jones*, ed. Martin C. Battestin and Fredson Bowers, 2 vols. (Oxford: Wesleyan University Press, 1975).

—— *Joseph Andrews*, ed. Homer Goldberg (New York: Norton, 1987).

—— *The Covent-Garden Journal and A Plan of the Universal Register-Office*, ed. B. A. Goldgar (Oxford: Clarendon Press, 1988).

—— *Joseph Andrews*, trans. abbé Desfontaines, ed. Serge Soupel (Paris: Flammarion, 1990).

—— *A Journey from this World to the Next*, in *Miscellanies*, vol. ii, ed. Hugh Amory and Bertrand A. Goldgar (Oxford: Wesleyan University Press, 1993).

—— *The Journal of a Voyage to Lisbon* (Oxford: Oxford University Press, 1997).

FURETIÈRE, ANTOINE, *Le Roman bourgeois* in *Romanciers du XVIIe siècle*, ed. Antoine Adam (Paris: Gallimard, 1958).

GOLDSMITH, OLIVER, *She Stoops to Conquer: or the Mistakes of a Night*, in *Collected Works*, ed. Arthur Friedman, 5 vols. (Oxford: Clarendon Press, 1966), v. 101–217.

GOODALL, WILLIAM, *The Adventures of Captain Greenland, Written in Imitation of all those Wise, Learned, Witty, and Humorous Authors, who either already have, or hereafter may Write in the same Stile and Manner* (London: R. Baldwin, 1752).

HOMER, *The Odyssey*, Budé edn., ed. and trans. Victor Bérand, 2 vols., 4th edn. (Paris: Les Belles Lettres, 1947).

—— *The Odyssey*, trans. A. T. Murray, rev. George Dimock, 2 vols., Loeb Classical Library (Cambridge, MA: Harvard University Press, 1998).

HORACE, *Satires, Epistles, Ars Poetica*, trans. H. Rushton Fairclough, Loeb Classical Library (Cambridge, MA: Harvard University Press, 1929).

JOHNSON, SAMUEL, *Johnsonian Miscellanies*, ed. G. Birkbeck Hill, 2 vols. (Oxford: Clarendon Press, 1897).

—— *Johnson's Dictionary: A Modern Selection*, ed. E. L. McAdam Jr. and George Milne (London: Victor Gollancz, 1963).

MARIVAUX, PIERRE CARLET DE CHAMBLAIN DE, *La Vie de Marianne* (Paris: Garnier, 1957).

—— *Pharsamon ou les Nouvelles Folies romanesques*, in *Marivaux: Œuvres de Jeunesse*, ed. Frédéric Deloffre (Paris: Gallimard, 1972).

MONTAIGNE, MICHEL DE, *Essais*, ed. Maurice Rat, 2 vols. (Paris: Garnier, 1962).

MONTALVO, GARCI RODRÍGUEZ DE, *Amadís de Gaula*, ed. Juan Manuel Cacho Blecua, 2 vols. (Madrid: Cátedra, 1987).

—— *Amadís of Gaul*, trans. E. B. Place and H. C. Behm, 2 vols. (Lexington, KY: University of Kentucky Press, 1974–5).

'Orbilius', 'An Examen of *The History of Tom Jones, a Foundling*' (London: W. Owen, 1750), Letter I.

PHILIDOR, *Tom Jones: Comédie lyrique en trois actes, imitée du roman anglois de M. Fielding* (Paris: Duchesne, 1770).

PRÉVOST, L'ABBÉ, *Histoire du Chevalier des Grieux et Manon Lescaut* in *Romanciers du XVIIIe siècle*, ed. Étiemble (Paris: Gallimard, 1960).

RABELAIS, FRANÇOIS, *Gargantua*, in *Œuvres complètes*, ed. Pierre Jourda, 2 vols. (Paris: Garnier, 1962).

REARDON, B. P. (ed.), *Collected Ancient Greek Novels* (London: University of California Press, 1989).

SCARRON, PAUL, *Le Roman comique*, ed. Henri Bénac, 2 vols. (Paris: Les Belles Lettres, 1951).

—— *Le Romant comique*, in *Romanciers du XVIIe siècle*, ed. Antoine Adam (Paris: Gallimard, 1958), 531–797.

—— *Le Roman comique*, ed. Émile Magne (Paris: Garnier, 1973),

SHAKESPEARE, WILLIAM, *The Complete Works*, ed. Peter Alexander (London: Collins, 1951).
—— *The Winter's Tale*, ed. J. H. P. Pafford (London: Routledge, 1963).
SOREL, CHARLES, *Le Berger extravagant*, 3 vols. (Rouen, 1640).
—— *Bibliothèque françoise*, 2nd edn. (Paris: Compagnie des librairies du Palais, 1667).
—— *De la connoissance des bons livres* (Paris: André Pralard, 1671).
—— *Histoire comique de Francion*, in *Romanciers du XVIIe siècle*, ed. Antoine Adam (Paris: Gallimard, 1958).
SPENSER, EDMUND, *The Faerie Queene*, ed. A. C. Hamilton (London: Longman, 1977).
STAËL, MME DE, *Lettres inédites de Mme de Staël à Meister*, ed. L. Usteri and E. Ritter (Paris: Hachette, 1903).
STERNE, LAURENCE, *Letters of Laurence Sterne*, ed. Lewis P. Curtis (Oxford: Clarendon Press, 1935).
—— *The Life and Opinions of Tristram Shandy, Gentleman*, ed. Melvyn and Joan New, 3 vols. (Gainesville, FL: University of Florida Press, 1978–84).
—— *A Sentimental Journey through France and Italy*, ed. Tom Keymer (The Everyman Library; London: J. M. Dent, 1994).
TALLEMANT DES RÉAUX, GÉDÉON, *Historiettes*, ed. Antoine Adam, 2 vols. (Paris: Gallimard, 1970).
TROYES, CHRÉTIEN DE, *Erec et Enide* (Paris: Flammarion, 1994).
VALÉRY, PAUL, 'Fragments des mémoires d'un poème', in *Œuvres de Paul Valéry*, ed. Jean Hytier (Paris: Gallimard, 1957), i. 1467
VALINCOUR, JEAN HENRI DU TROUSSET, SIEUR DE, *Lettres à Madame la Marquise *** sur le sujet de la Princesse de Clèves*, facsimile of the 1678 edn. (Tours: Université de Tours, 1972).
VIRGIL, *Aeneid*, Budé edn., ed. and trans. Jacques Perret, 3 vols. (Paris: Les Belles Lettres, 1981).
Le Voyage en France: Anthologie des voyageurs européens en France, du Moyen Âge à la fin de l'Empire, ed. Jean M. Goulemot, Paul Lidsky and Didier Masseau (Paris: Robert Laffont, 1995).

Secondary Sources

ADAMS, D. J., *Diderot, Dialogue and Debate* (Liverpool: F. Cairns, 1986).
ADAMS, PERCY G., *Travel Literature and the Evolution of the Novel* (Lexington, KY: University of Kentucky Press, 1983).
ALLEN, WALTER, *The English Novel* (London: Penguin, 1991).
ALTER, ROBERT, *Partial Magic: The Novel as a Self-Conscious Genre* (Berkeley and Los Angeles: University of California Press, 1975).
ARMAS, FREDERICK DE, *Paul Scarron* (New York: Twayne, 1972).
ARMSTRONG, NANCY, *Desire and Domestic Fiction: A Political History of the Novel* (Oxford: Oxford University Press, 1987).

BAKHTIN, MIKHAIL, *The Dialogic Imagination: Four Essays*, trans. Caryl Emerson and Michael Holquist, ed. Michael Holquist (Austin, TX: University of Texas Press, 1981).

BAL, MIEKE, *Narratologie: Essais sur la signification narrative dans quatre romans modernes* (Paris: Klincksieck, 1977).

BANHAM, R. BRACHT, 'Inventing the Novel', in Amy Mandelker (ed.), *Bakhtin in Contexts: Across the Disciplines* (Evanston, IL: Northwestern University Press, 1995), 79–87.

BARDON, MAURICE, *'Don Quichotte' en France au XVIIe et au XVIIIe siècle, 1605–1815* (Paris: Honoré Champion, 1931).

BARTHES, ROLAND, 'L'effet de réel', in *Communications*, 11 (1968); repr. in *Le Bruissement de la langue* (Paris: Seuil, 1984), 167–74.

BAYNE-POWELL, ROSAMOND, *Travellers in Eighteenth-Century England* (London: John Murray, 1951).

BENNINGTON, GEOFFREY, *Sententiousness and the Novel: Laying down the Law in Eighteenth-Century French Fiction* (Cambridge: Cambridge University Press, 1985).

BERG, MICHAEL VANDE, ' "Pictures of Pronunciation": Typographical Travels through *Tristram Shandy* and *Jacques le fataliste*', *Eighteenth-Century Studies* 21 (1987–8), 21–47.

BERTHELOT, ANNE, 'The Romance as *Conjoincture* of Brief Narratives', *L'Esprit créateur*, 33 (1993), 51–60.

BOOTH, WAYNE C., 'The Self-Conscious Narrator in Comic Fiction before *Tristram Shandy*', *PMLA* 67 (1952), 163–85.

—— *The Rhetoric of Fiction* (Chicago: University of Chicago Press, 1983).

BRADY, FRANK, '*Tristram Shandy*: Sexuality, Morality, and Sensibility', *Eighteenth-Century Studies*, 4 (1970), 41–56.

BRAND, C. P., *Ariosto: A Preface to the 'Orlando furioso'* (Edinburgh: Edinburgh University Press, 1974).

BREMNER, GEOFFREY, *Order and Chance: The Pattern of Diderot's Thought* (Cambridge: Cambridge University Press, 1983).

BREWER, DANIEL, *The Discourse of Enlightenment in Eighteenth-Century France: Diderot and the Art of Philosophizing* (Cambridge: Cambridge University Press, 1993).

BROWN, HOMER OBED, 'Of the Title to Things Real: Conflicting Stories', *ELH* 55 (1988), 917–54.

—— 'Why the Story of the Origin of the (English) Novel Is an American Romance (If Not the Great American Novel)', in Deirdre Lynch and William B. Warner (eds.), *Cultural Institutions of the Novel* (London: Duke University Press, 1996), 11–43.

—— *Institutions of the English Novel: From Defoe to Scott* (Philadelphia: University of Pennsylvania Press, 1997).

BROWNLEE, KEVIN, and BROWNLEE, MARINA, *Romance: Generic Transformations from Chrétien de Troyes to Cervantes* (Hanover, NH: University Press of New England, 1985).

BRÜCKNER, MATILDA TOMARYN, *Narrative Invention in Twelfth-Century French Romance: The Convention of Hospitality (1160–1200)* (Lexington, KY: French Forum, 1980).

BURCKHARDT, SIGURD, 'Tristram Shandy's Law of Gravity', *ELH* 28 (1961), 70–88.

CALDWELL, ROY CHANDLER, JR., 'Backtalk: Agonistic Dialogue in *Jacques le Fataliste*', *Diderot Studies*, 26 (1995), 29–45.

CALVINO, ITALO, 'The Structure of *Orlando furioso*', in *The Uses of Literature*, trans. Patrick Creagh (London: Harvest, 1986).

CARVER, ROBERT, 'The Protean Ass: The "Metamorphoses" of Apuleius from Antiquity to the English Renaissance', unpublished doctoral thesis (Oxford University, 1991).

CASH, ARTHUR, *Laurence Sterne: The Early and Middle Years* (London: Methuen, 1975).

—— *Laurence Sterne: The Later Years* (London: Methuen, 1986).

CAVE, TERENCE, 'Suspense and the Pre-History of the Novel', *Revue de littérature comparée*, 70 (1996), 507–16.

CAWS, MARY ANN, *Reading Frames in Modern Fiction* (Princeton: Princeton University Press, 1985).

CHAMBERS, DOUGLAS, *The Reinvention of the World: English Writing 1650–1750* (London: Arnold, 1996).

CHARDON, HENRI, *Scarron inconnu et les types des personnages du 'Roman comique'* (Paris: Champion, 1903).

CHARLES, SHELLY, 'Le *Tom Jones* de La Place ou la fabrique d'un roman français', *Revue d'histoire littéraire*, 6 (1994), 931–58.

CHÊNERIE, MARIE-LUCE, *Le Chevalier errant dans les romans arthuriens en vers des XIIᵉ et XIIIᵉ siècles* (Geneva: Droz, 1986).

CHIBKA, ROBERT L., 'Taking "The Serious" Seriously: The Introductory Chapters of *Tom Jones*', *The Eighteenth Century: Theory and Interpretation*, 31 (1990), 23–45.

CIORANESCU, ALEXANDRE, *L'Arioste en France: Des origines à la fin du XVIIIᵉ siècle*, 2 vols., *Publications de l'École roumaine en France III* (Paris: Éditions des Presses Modernes, 1939).

CLOSE, ANTHONY J., *Don Quixote* (Cambridge: Cambridge University Press, 1990).

CONRAD, PETER, *Shandyism: The Character of Romantic Irony* (Oxford: Blackwell, 1978).

COULET, HENRI, *Le Roman jusqu'à la Révolution* (Paris: Armand Colin, 1967).

CROCE, BENEDETTO, *Estetica come scienza dell'espressione e linguistica generale* (Bari: Gius. Laterza & Figli, 1912).

—— *Aesthetic as Science of Expresssion and General Linguistic*, trans. Douglas Ainslie (London: Vision Press, 1967).

CRONK, NICHOLAS, '*Tom Jones* in Eighteenth-Century France', *Drottning-holms Slottstheater* (1995), 94–6.

—— ' "Jacques le Fataliste et son Maître": un roman quichotisé', *Recherches sur Diderot et sur l'Encyclopédie*, 23 (Oct. 1997), 63–78.

CURTIUS, ERNST ROBERT, *European Literature and the Latin Middle Ages*, trans. Willard E. Trask (Princeton: Princeton University Press, 1990).

DAVIS, KATHLEEN M., 'The Sacred Condition of Equality—How Original were Puritan Doctrines of Marriage?', *Social History*, 5 (1977), 563–80.

DAVIS, LENNARD, *Factual Fictions: The Origins of the English Novel* (New York: Columbia University Press, 1983).

—— *Resisting Novels: Ideology and Fiction* (New York: Methuen, 1987).

—— 'Dialectics on the Loose: The History of the Novel in Infinite Regress', *The Eighteenth Century: Theory and Interpretation*, 30 (1989), 43–50.

DEJEAN, JOAN, *Scarron's 'Roman comique': A Comedy of the Novel, a Novel of Comedy* (Bern: Peter Lang, 1977).

DERRIDA, JACQUES, 'La loi du genre', *Colloque international sur le genre* (Strasbourg: Université de Strasbourg, 1980), 183–211.

DIDIER, BÉATRICE, ' "Je" et subversion du texte: Le narrateur dans *Jacques le Fataliste*', *Littérature*, 48 (1982), 92–105.

DOD, JOHN, and CLEAVER, ROBERT, *A Godly Forme of Householde Gouernment: For the Ordering of Private Families according to the Direction of God's Word* (London: Thomas Man, 1614).

DOODY, MARGARET ANNE, *The True Story of the Novel* (New Brunswick, NJ: Rutgers University Press, 1996).

DOROSZLAÏ, ALEXANDRE, GUIDI, JOSÉ, VIÉJUS, MARIE-FRANÇOISE and RICHON, ANDRÉ (eds.), *Éspaces réels et éspaces imaginaires dans le 'Roland furieux'* (Paris: Nouvelle Sorbonne, 1991).

DUDLEY, EDWARD, 'Don Quijote as Magus: The Rhetoric of Interpolation', *Bulletin of Hispanic Studies*, 49 (1972), 355–68.

DUNN, PETER N., 'Framing the Story, Framing the Reader: Two Spanish Masters', *Modern Language Review*, 91 (1996), 94–106.

EL SAFFAR, RUTH, *Distance and Control in 'Don Quixote': A Study in Narrative Technique* (North Carolina Studies in the Romance Languages and Literatures; Chapel Hill, NC: University of North Carolina Press, 1975).

FABRE, JEAN, *Idées sur le roman: De Madame de Lafayette au Marquis de Sade* (Paris: Klincksieck, 1979).

FEIL, J. P., 'Fielding's Character of Mrs Whitefield', *Philological Quarterly*, 39 (1960), 508–10.

FERRARI, GIOVANNI, 'Diderot: *Jacques le Fataliste*', *Les Lettres romanes*, 36 (1982), 213–34, 295–316.

FERRIAR, JOHN, *Illustrations of Sterne: With Other Essays and Verses* (London: Cadell & Davies, 1798).

FISH, STANLEY, *Is there a Text in this Class?* (Cambridge, MA: Harvard University Press, 1980).

FISHELOW, DAVID, *Metaphors of Genre: The Role of Analogies in Genre Theory* (University Park, PA: Pennsylvania State University Press, 1993).

FLUCHÈRE, HENRI, *Laurence Sterne, de l'homme à l'œuvre* (Paris: Gallimard, 1961).

FOLKENFLIK, ROBERT, 'The Heirs of Ian Watt', *Eighteenth-Century Studies*, 25 (1991–2), 203–17.

FOWLER, ALASTAIR, *Kinds of Literature: An Introduction to the Theory of Genres and Modes* (Oxford: Clarendon Press, 1982).

FRAZIER, HARRIET C., *A Babble of Ancestral Voices: Shakespeare, Cervantes and Theobald* (The Hague: Mouton, 1974).

FRYE, NORTHROP, *Anatomy of Criticism* (Princeton: Princeton University Press, 1957).

—— *The Secular Scripture: A Study of the Structure of Romance* (Cambridge, MA: Harvard University Press, 1976).

GARAGNON, JEAN, 'Diderot et la genèse de *Jacques le Fataliste*: Sur une lettre de Meister père', *Studi Francesi*, 27 (1983), 81–2.

GARAPON, ROBERT, 'Les Préparations dans *Le Roman comique* de Scarron', *Actes du colloque Renaissance-classicisme du Maine, Le Mans 1971* (Paris: A.-G. Nizet, 1975), 11–18.

GENETTE, GÉRARD, *Figures III* (Paris: Seuil, 1972).

GILMAN, STEPHEN, *The Novel According to Cervantes* (Berkeley and Los Angeles: University of California Press, 1989).

GOLDBERG, HOMER, 'Comic Prose Epic or Comic Romance: The Argument of the Preface to *Joseph Andrews*', *Philological Quarterly*, 43 (1964), 193–215.

—— 'The Interpolated Tales in *Joseph Andrews* or "The History of the World in General" Satirically Revised', *Modern Philology*, 63 (1966), 295–310.

GOLDKNOPF, DAVID, 'The Failure of Plot in *Tom Jones*', *Criticism*, 11 (1969), 262–74.

HARRIES, ELIZABETH W., 'Sterne's Novels: Gathering up the Fragments', *ELH* 49 (1982), 35–49.

HART, THOMAS, *Cervantes and Ariosto: Renewing Fiction* (Princeton: Princeton University Press, 1989).

HERRERO, JAVIER, 'Sierra Morena as Labyrinth: From Wildness to Christian Knighthood', *Forum for Modern Language Studies*, 17 (1981), 55–67.

HODGSON, RICHARD H., 'The Parody of Traditional Narrative Structures in the French Anti-Novel from Charles Sorel to Diderot', *Neophilologus*, 66 (1982), 340–8.

HOLQUIST, MICHAEL with REED, WALTER L., 'Six Theses on the Novel—and Some Metaphors', *New Literary History*, 11 (1979–80), 413–23.

HUNTER, J. PAUL, *Occasional Form: Henry Fielding and the Chains of Circumstance* (Baltimore: Johns Hopkins University Press, 1975).

—— *Before Novels: The Cultural Contexts of Eighteenth-Century English Fiction* (New York: Norton, 1990).

—— 'The Novel and the Contexts of Discourse', in Richard B. Schwartz (ed.), *Theory and Tradition in Eighteenth-Century Studies* (Carbondale, IL: Southern Illinois University Press, 1990), 118–40.

—— 'Novels and History and Northrop Frye', *Eighteenth-Century Studies*, 24 (1990–1), 225–41.

—— 'The Novel and Social/Cultural History', in John Richetti (ed.), *The Cambridge Companion to the Eighteenth-Century Novel* (Cambridge: Cambridge University Press, 1996), 9–40.

HUTCHINSON, STEVEN, *Cervantine Journeys* (Madison: University of Wisconsin Press, 1992).

HUTSON, LORNA, 'Fortunate Travellers: Reading for the Plot in Sixteenth-Century England', *Representations*, 41 (1993), 83–103.

JAVITCH, DANIEL, '*Cantus interruptus* in the *Orlando furioso*', *MLN* 95 (1980), 66–80.

—— *Proclaiming a Classsic: The Canonization of 'Orlando furioso'* (Princeton: Princeton University Press, 1991).

JOLY, MONIQUE, *Études sur 'Don Quichotte'* (Paris: Sorbonne, 1996).

KAVANAGH, THOMAS M., 'The Vacant Mirror: A Study of Mimesis through Diderot's "Jacques le fataliste"', *SVEC* 104 (1973).

—— '*Jacques le Fataliste*: An Encyclopedia of the Novel', in Jack Undank and Herbert Josephs (eds.), *Diderot: Digression and Dispersion, a Bicentennial Tribute*, French Forum Monographs, 58 (Lexington, KY: French Forum, 1984), 150–65.

—— *Enlightenment and the Shadows of Chance: The Novel and the Culture of Gambling in Eighteenth-Century France* (Baltimore: Johns Hopkins Press, 1993).

KEMPF, ROGER, *Diderot et le roman, ou le démon de la présence* (Paris: Seuil, 1964).

LANHAM, RICHARD, *A Handlist of Rhetorical Terms*, 2nd edn. (Berkeley and Los Angeles: University of California Press, 1991).

LEVER, MAURICE, *Le Roman français au XVIIe siècle* (Paris: Presses Universitaires de France, 1981).

LEWIS, C. S., 'Spenser', in G. B. Harrison (ed.), *Major British Writers*, 2 vols. (London: Harcourt, Brace, 1954), 91–104.

LOÜYS, GILLES, 'Typologie des romans inachevés', in *L'Œuvre inachevée*, ed. Annie Rivara and Guy Lavorel, Actes du colloque international (11–12 Dec. 1998) (Lyon: Aprime, 1999), 281–9.

LOY, J. ROBERT, *Diderot's Determined Fatalist: A Critical Appreciation of 'Jacques le fataliste'* (New York: King's Crown Press, 1950).

—— '*Jacques* Reconsidered: Digression as Form and Theme', in Jack Undank and Herbert Josephs (eds.), *Diderot: Digression and Dispersion, a Bicentennial Tribute*, French Forum Monographs, 58 (Lexington, KY: French Forum, 1984), 166–79.

LYNCH, JAMES J., *Henry Fielding and the Heliodoran Novel: Romance, Epic, and Fielding's New Province of Writing* (London: Associated University Presses, 1986).

MACE, NANCY A., *Henry Fielding's Novels and the Classical Tradition* (Newark, DE: University of Delaware Press, 1996).

MCKEON, MICHAEL, *The Origins of the English Novel 1600–1740* (Baltimore: Johns Hopkins University Press, 1987).

—— 'The Origins of the English Novel', *Modern Philology*, 82 (1984), 76–86.

MCNAMARA, SUSAN P., 'Mirrors of Fiction within *Tom Jones*: The Paradox of Self-Reference', *Eighteenth-Century Studies*, 12 (1979), 372–90.

MAGNE, ÉMILE, *Scarron et son milieu* (Paris: Émile-Paul, 1924).

MANCING, HOWARD, *The Chivalric World of 'Don Quijote': Style, Structure, and Narrative Technique* (Columbia, MO: University of Missouri Press, 1982).

MARTÍNEZ-BONATI, FÉLIX, *'Don Quixote' and the Poetics of the Novel,* trans. Dian Fox (Ithaca, NY: Cornell University Press, 1992).

MAY, GEORGES, *Le Dilemme du roman au XVIIIe siècle* (Paris: Presses Universitaires de France, 1963).

—— 'The Influence of English Fiction on the French Mid-Eighteenth-Century Novel', in Earl R. Wasserman (ed.), *Aspects of the Eighteenth Century* (Baltimore: Johns Hopkins University Press, 1965), 265–81.

MERRY, BARBARA, *Menippean Elements in Paul Scarron's 'Roman comique'* (New York: Peter Lang, 1991).

MILLER, HENRY K., *Henry Fielding's 'Tom Jones' and the Romance Tradition*, English Literary Studies Monograph Series, 6 (Victoria, BC: University of Victoria, 1976).

MOREL, JACQUES, 'La Composition du *Roman comique*', *L'Information littéraire*, 5 (1970), 212–17.

MORTIER, ROLAND, 'La Fonction des Nouvelles dans le *Roman comique*', *CAIEF* 18 (1966), 41–51.

MURATORE, MARY-JO, *Mimesis and Metatextuality in the French Neo-Classical Text* (Geneva: Droz, 1994).

MURILLO, LUIS ANDRÉS, *A Critical Introduction to 'Don Quixote'* (New York: Peter Lang, 1988).

NABOKOV, VLADIMIR, *Lectures on 'Don Quixote'*, ed. Fredson Bowers (London: Weidenfeld & Nicolson, 1983).

NAIGEON, J. A., *Mémoires historiques et philosophiques sur la vie et les ouvrages de D. Diderot* (Paris: Brière, 1821).

NAVARRO GONZÁLEZ, ALBERTO, *Las dos partes del 'Quijote'* (Salamanca: University of Salamanca, 1979).

NEW, MELVYN, *Laurence Sterne as Satirist: A Reading of 'Tristram Shandy'* (Gainesville, FL: University of Florida Press, 1969).

NOVAK, MAXIMILIAN, 'Some Notes toward a History of Fictional Forms', *Novel*, 6 (1973), 120–33.

NUTTALL, A. D., *A Common Sky: Philosophy and the Literary Imagination* (London: Sussex University Press, 1974).

—— *Openings: Narrative Beginnings from the Epic to the Novel* (Oxford: Clarendon Press, 1992).

O'GORMAN, DONAL, 'Hypotheses for a New Reading of *Jacques le Fataliste*', *Diderot Studies*, 19 (1978), 129–43.

ORR, LEONARD, *Problems and Poetics of the Nonaristotelian Novel* (Lewisburg, PA: Bucknell University Press, 1991).

ORTEGA Y GASSET, JOSÉ, *Meditaciones del 'Quijote'* (Madrid: Revista de Occidente, 1914).

OSTOVICH, HELEN, 'Reader as Hobby-Horse in *Tristram Shandy*', *Philological Quarterly*, 68 (1989), 325–42.

PALMA, GIUSEPPE DALLA, *Le strutture narrative dell 'Orlando furioso'* (Florence: Olschki, 1984).

PARISH, RICHARD, 'Scarron's *Roman comique*: Contradictions and Terms', *Seventeenth-Century Studies*, 16 (1994), 105–18.

—— *Scarron: 'Le Roman comique'* (London: Grant & Cutler, 1998).

PARKES, JOAN, *Travel in England in the Seventeenth Century* (Oxford: Oxford University Press, 1925).

PAULSON, RONALD, *Satire and the Novel in Eighteenth-Century England* (New Haven: Yale University Press, 1967).

—— *Don Quixote in England: The Aesthetics of Laughter* (Baltimore: Johns Hopkins University Press, 1998).

PERKINS, MERLE, 'Diderot and the Time–Space Continuum: His Philosophy, Aesthetics and Politics', *SVEC* 211 (1982).

PERONA VILLAREAL, DIEGO, *Geografía Cervantina* (Madrid: Albia, 1988).

PIERCE, FRANK, *Amadís de Gaula* (Boston: Twayne, 1976).

PORTER, ROY, *English Society in the Eighteenth Century*, 2nd edn. (London: Penguin, 1990).

POWERS, LYALL H., 'Tom Jones and Jacob de la Vallée', *Papers of the Michigan Academy of Science, Arts, and Letters*, 47 (1962), 659–67.

PROPP, VLADIMIR, *Le radici storiche dei racconti di fate* (Turin: Einaudi, 1949).

PROUST, JACQUES, *Lectures de Diderot* (Paris: Armand Colin, 1974).

PRUNER, FRANCIS, *L'Unité secrète de 'Jacques le Fataliste'* (Paris: Minard, 1970).

REECE, STEVE, *The Stranger's Welcome: Oral Theory and the Aesthetics of the Homeric Hospitality Scene* (Ann Arbor: University of Michigan Press, 1993).

REED, WALTER L., *An Exemplary History of the Novel: The Quixotic versus the Picaresque* (Chicago: University of Chicago Press, 1981).

REX, WALTER, 'Diderot's Counterpoints: The Dynamics of Contrariety in his Major Works', *SVEC* 363 (1998).

RICHETTI, JOHN (ed.), *The Cambridge Companion to the Eighteenth-Century Novel* (Cambridge: Cambridge University Press, 1996).

RILEY, E. C., *Cervantes's Theory of the Novel* (Oxford: Oxford University Press, 1962).

RIMMON-KENAN, SHLOMITH, *Narrative Fiction: Contemporary Poetics* (London: Methuen, 1983).

ROBERT, MARTHE, *Roman des origines et origines du roman* (Paris: Gallimard, 1972).

ROSE, MARGARET A., *Parody: Ancient, Modern, and Post-Modern* (Cambridge: Cambridge University Press, 1993).

ROSS, CHARLES, *The Custom of the Castle: From Malory to 'Macbeth'* (Berkeley and Los Angeles: University of California Press, 1997).

ROUSSET, JEAN, 'Insertions et interventions dans le *Roman comique*', *L'Esprit créateur*, 11/2 (1971), 141–53.

RUSH, JANE, 'La Tradition comique et son renouveau dans les historiettes de *Jacques le Fataliste et son maître*', *Recherches sur Diderot et sur l'Encyclopédie*, 15 (Oct. 1993), 41–53.

RUSSELL, P. E., *Cervantes* (Oxford: Oxford University Press, 1985).

SALAZAR RINCÓN, JAVIER, *El mundo social del 'Quijote'* (Madrid: Gredos, 1986).

SCHWARTZ, LEON, '*Jacques le Fataliste* and Diderot's Equine Symbolism', *Diderot Studies*, 16 (1973), 241–51.

SELIG, KARL-LUDWIG, '*Don Quixote* and the Exploration of (Literary) Geography', *Revista canadiense de estudios hispanicos*, 6 (1982), 341–57.

SERROY, JEAN, *Roman et réalité: Les Histoires comiques au XVIIe siècle* (Grenoble: Presses Universitaires de Grenoble, 1980).

SHKLOVSKY, VICTOR, 'La Construction de la nouvelle et du roman', in *Théorie de la littérature*, trans. and ed. Tzvetan Todorov (Paris: Seuil, 1965), 170–96.

—— *Theory of Prose*, trans. Benjamin Sher (Elmwood Park, IL: Dalkey Archive Press, 1990).

SHOWALTER, ENGLISH, *The Evolution of the French Novel, 1641–1782* (Princeton: Princeton University Press, 1972).

SIMON, ERNEST, 'The Function of the Spanish Stories in Scarron's *Roman comique*', *L'Esprit créateur*, 3/3 (1963), 130–6.

—— 'Fatalism, the Hobby-Horse and the Esthetics of the Novel', *Diderot Studies*, 16 (1973), 253–74.

SIMPSON, R. G. (ed.), *Henry Fielding: Justice Observed* (London: Vision and Barnes & Noble, 1985).

TERRASSE, JEAN, 'Le Temps et l'espace dans les romans de Diderot', *SVEC* 379 (1999).

THOMAS, HENRY, *The Romance of 'Amadís of Gaul'* (Oxford: Bibliographical Society, 1912).

TODOROV, TZVETAN, *Introduction à la littérature fantastique* (Paris: Seuil, 1970).

—— *Poétique de la prose* (Paris: Seuil, 1971).

VICE, SUE, *Introducing Bakhtin* (Manchester: Manchester University Press, 1997).

VINAVER, EUGÈNE, *The Rise of Romance* (Oxford: Clarendon Press, 1971).

VOS, WIM DE, 'Le Cheval comme métaphore de la narration dans *Jacques le Fataliste*', *Diderot Studies*, 25 (1993), 41–8.

WARNER, WILLIAM B., 'The Elevation of the Novel in England: Hegemony and Literary History', *ELH* 59 (1992), 577–96.

—— *Licensing Entertainment: The Elevation of Novel Reading in Britain, 1684–1750* (Berkeley and Los Angeles: University of California Press, 1998).

WATT, IAN, *The Rise of the Novel: Studies in Defoe, Richardson and Fielding* (London: Chatto & Windus, 1957).

—— 'Serious Reflections on *The Rise of the Novel*', *Novel*, 1 (1968), 205–18.

WICKS, ULRICH, *Picaresque Narrative, Picaresque Fictions: A Theory and Research Guide* (Westport, CT: Greenwood Press, 1989).

WILLIAMSON, EDWIN, *The Half-way House of Fiction: 'Don Quixote' and Arthurian Romance* (Oxford: Clarendon Press, 1984).

INDEX

Page numbers in bold type indicate the principal discussion of the work in question